MODERN LITURGY
Planning Guide

 Resource Publications, Inc.
160 E. Virginia St. # 290
San Jose, CA 95112

I

Editorial Director: Kenneth Guentert
Editor: Jim Holland
Contributing Writers: Robert Zappulla,
Paul Dellio, Katie Nosbisch, Thomas
Welbers, Kenneth Guentert
Design and Typesetting: Ben Lizardi

ISBN 0-89390-088-5
Library of Congress Catalog No.:
86-62618
Printed in the United States of
America 5 4 3 2 1

TABLE OF CONTENTS

Table of Contents

SEASON OF THE YEAR

YEAR B

ADVENT-CHRISTMAS SEASON AND RELATED FEASTS

LENT-EASTER SEASON

SOLEMNITIES OF THE LORD FOLLOWING EASTER SEASON

SEASON OF THE YEAR

Table of Contents

YEAR C

ADVENT-CHRISTMAS SEASON AND RELATED FEASTS

LENT-EASTER SEASON

SOLEMNITIES OF THE LORD FOLLOWING EASTER SEASON

SEASON OF THE YEAR

ALL YEARS

OTHER SOLEMNITIES AND FEASTS OF THE LORD

PREFACE

Modern Liturgy magazine has been doing its Planning Guide since the October issue of 1982.

We thought it would be easy — and handy — to gather three complete cycles from the magazine into one universal Planning Guide.

The result is handy, we trust, but it was not as easy to put together as we thought initially.

First, we had to update the material. Many creative ideas had to be eliminated simply because they do not apply in every or even most years. For example, the fourteenth Sunday in Ordinary Time does not always coincide with Fourth of July weekend and the second Sunday of Easter does not always coincide with Yom HaShoa.

Second, we had to add material for Sundays and feast days that were not addressed in the magazine. Some Sundays, such as the Second Sunday after Christmas, do not come up every year. Other Sundays were pre-empted by solemnities. And since the magazine's Planning Guide focused on *Sunday* planning, it usually did not address feasts and solemnities unless they fell on Sunday. Finally, some feasts include more than one set of readings, sometimes for a vigil. We tried to cover all the possible Sundays and major solemnities, even though a few (eg. Sacred Heart of Jesus) never come up on Sunday and are unlikely to be a major planning item for most parish liturgists.

However, we did not do complete commentaries on all alternate readings and occasionally refer you back to Cycle A when readings repeat themselves. In cases where we already had two or three sets of commentaries on a three-cycle feast (eg. Holy Family), we decided to include what we had so that you could benefit from the additional commentary and ideas.

Some suggestions for using this volume:

1) "Readings." For further Scripture commentary, see *The Jerome Biblical Commentary,* your favorite lectionary commentary and especially *Banquet of the Word* by Thomas Welbers (Resource Publications, Inc.). For ease of use, *The Modern Liturgy Planning Guide* follows the same order as *Banquet of the Word.*

2) "Idea Starters." They are just that — idea starters. Use them to get your own creative juices flowing. Be sure to check out the "Idea Starters" for the corresponding feasts in the other two cycles — even when the readings are different.

3) "Music." Two resources of further help are *The Music Locator,* especially its thematic index, and *The Psalm Locator,* which indexes songs to Psalms. Both are available from Resource Publications, Inc.

4) For more on all of the above, see the Planning Guide as it appears in *Modern Liturgy* magazine.

If you find any errors or ommissions, please write to Editor, Modern Liturgy Planning Guide, 160 E. Virginia St. #290, San Jose, CA 95112. We'll correct subsequent editions. Also, if you have planning suggestions, you would like to share, please write to the editor at the above address. *Modern Liturgy* magazine is interested.

Special thanks to: Bob Zappulla, who wrote most of the "Idea Starters", compiled most of the music suggestions, and developed the Planning Form; Katie Nosbisch, who wrote the Scripture commentary for most of Cycle C; Paul Dellio, who wrote Scripture commentary for Cycles A and B; Thomas Welbers, who wrote commentary for several Sundays and whose book, *Banquet of the Word,* we used as a reference for writing commentaries for the missing feasts; Jim Holland, who compiled this mammoth project into one place and added some missing pieces; Lisa Kaufman, who proofread the works; and Ben Lizardi, who did the typesetting and design.

Kenneth Guentert
Editorial Director

FIRST SUNDAY OF ADVENT

YEAR A

READINGS

Isaiah (2:1-5)
The difficulties and unfaithfulness of the Israel of Isaiah are transcended in this reading, giving way to a vision of the ideal Kingdom of the future. The prophet heralds a messianic state where Israel serves as a beacon to all the world, drawing people to God through itself so they can experience his peace and justice.

Romans (13:11-14)
Paul details how the "people of the Kingdom" live. Their actions are the signs of the new order built on peace and justice. Deeds which demonstrate loving care for one another, moderation and trust are the hallmarks of women who "put on the Lord Jesus."

Matthew (24:37-44)
The Matthean reading is culled from an exegesis on Hebrew Scripture background, not only the Noah story, but also much apocalyptic literature. The stress here is on preparedness to receive God's Kingdom which comes when we least expect it. Hence the need to live in a way which energizes the gift of divine life in a believer's life!

FOCUS

If we live our lives in such a way that we are always ready to receive the Lord Jesus when he comes, then we will help to make the Kingdom a reality in our lives now. The peace and justice of which Isaiah and Paul speak can only happen on a general scale when they are realities in the lives of all people.

Jesus exhorts his followers to "be prepared," though not out of an unhealthy fear. Rather he wishes them to use their preparedness as an instrument to bring their wills and lives into proximity with the life of the Father. *Fiat voluntatis,* "Thy will be done," is a resolve which requires dedication and effort each day. Such a posture enables the believer to receive the Lord when he comes regardless of circumstance.

IDEA STARTERS

- *CCT Lectionary:* Is 2:1-5; Ps 122; Rm 13:11-14; Mt 24:36-94.
- Advent begins on Saturday evening with Evening Prayer. Sponsor a pot-luck Thanksgiving/New Church Year party after a celebration of Vespers.
- At Saturday celebrations of Evening Prayer, light the Advent Wreath candles from the Paschal Candle. Wreaths may be blessed during the Light Service, after the Hymn and before the Thanksgiving.
- Explore books containing Advent customs and symbols. Integrate these into worship and organizational meetings. At liturgy, a revived custom becoming popular is the use of blue vestments and paraments throughout Advent. The Gospel Canticle of Zechariah (Luke 1:68-79) is a fine hymn for use throughout the season, especially in place of the *Gloria* or after Communion.
- Omit the Introductory Rites at today's Eucharist, using as a processional "The Great Litany" found in *Lutheran Book of Worship.*

- Ecumenical Evening Prayer, Advent lessons and carols, and Liturgy of the word may suitably be celebrated each week at different parishes.
- For your consideration: Penitential Rite C-ii; omit Gloria; Opening Prayer; Intercessions for world peace, Jerusalem, moral living, the Kingdom of God in our midst and yet to come; Reconciliation Eucharistic Prayer II; Memorial Acclamation A; Advent Solemn Blessing.

MUSIC

- Psalm 122
- *Creator of the Stars of Night* (ICEL)
- *The Dawn of the Day* (Deiss/NALR)
- *Glory and Praise* (Tucciarone/Resource)
- *God is Light* (Page/Resource)
- *Hark! A Herald Voice Is Calling* (ICEL)
- *I Long for You* (Dameans/NALR)
- *In Your Love Remember Me* (Kendzia/NALR)
- *Let Heaven Rejoice* (Jesuits/NALR)
- *Let Us Walk In the Light of the Lord* (Haugen/Quiet Breeze)
- *Like a Shepherd* (Dameans/NALR)
- *Praise Canticle* (Haas/Cooperative Ministries)
- *Rise Up Jerusalem* (Schoenbachler/NALR)
- *Song of Isaiah* (Gilsdorf/Resource)
- *The Sun is Rising* (Weston Priory)
- *Watchman, How Goes the Night?* (Deiss/NALR)
- *Your Love is Finer Than Life* (Haugen/GIA)

ADVENT PLANNING SHEET   Date _____

Parish focus _____

Environment & art _____

Ritual notes _____

Faith development (eg., bulletin item) _____

Children's faith experience _____

Prelude _____

Hymn of gathering _____

Sprinkling baptismal water acclamation _____

Penitential rite_____Opening Prayer _____

Responsory _____Gospel acclamation _____

General intercessions _____

At the preparation & presentation _____

Preface dialog _____Preface _____

Preface acclamation _____

Eucharistic prayer _____Memorial acclamation _____

Eucharistic amen _____

The Lord's prayer _____

Breaking of bread _____

The communion hymn _____

The post-communion hymn _____

Blessing _____At the dismissal _____

Memoranda:

SECOND SUNDAY
OF ADVENT

YEAR A

READINGS
Isaiah (11:1-10)
We continue in the Book of Isaiah to hear further description of the coming messianic age. The prophet endows the Messiah with all of the charisma of Israel's great men. The "gifts of the Spirit" are characteristic of the new age. The Messiah will re-establish a paradise state once lost. All of dissonant nature will be returned to harmony as in the creation moment.

Romans (15:4-9)
Paul indicates that all Scripture should be used as a source of encouragement and support for the Christian community as it struggles to live a life of perfection in the Lord Christ. Paul also addresses the concept of Christ, gift to both Jews and Gentiles, as sign of God's faithfulness and mercy.

Matthew (3:1-12)
John the Baptist is introduced into the liturgy. John is a figure who in announcing the Lord's coming confronts the hypocrisy and complacency of his society. His radical lifestyle serves as an image of the lives of those who follow the Messiah.

FOCUS
Those who live "in the Kingdom" are endowed with the "gifts of the Spirit" (according to Isaiah). Armed with this charisma they are able to cooperate in the work of redeeming all of creation. With the power of these gifts nothing is impossible. Even the most unlikely to live in peace are brought to a state of harmony. First, however, we must be challenged and crossed by images of how God *should* act, and helped to see that God will be God in spite of our attempts to circumscribe his free gift of salvation.

When we make ourselves vulnerable to "crossings," as the Baptist did, we become effective witnesses of the incredible vitality of a life lived in God.

IDEA STARTERS
- *CCT Lectionary:* Is 11:1-10; Ps 72:1-8; Rm 15:4-13; Mt 3:1-12.
- Advent is a season for a confirmed, serious Christian. Today the readings give us the opportunity to reflect on the Holy Spirit, who came to us in Baptism and Confirmation, and to recall the gifts of the Spirit and our use of them in the world.
- Display a Jesse Tree today. Explain who Jesse is and what the tree signifies in the bulletin.
- The text from Isaiah may be acted out at a children's Liturgy of the Word.
- Today's readings lend themselves to the celebration of Confirmation.
- The lessons provide a call to conversion. A reflection written in the bulletin may lead to advertisement of your Advent penance liturgy.
- We are in our second week of the new church year: have we kept our eyes steadfast on the Master?
- For your consideration: Sprinkling Baptismal Water A; Opening Prayer;

Intercessions for peace with justice, non–believers, national leaders, the poor, harmony, prophets, conversion; Advent Preface II (P 2); Eucharistic Prayer III; Memorial Acclamation C; Advent Solemn Blessing.

MUSIC

- Psalm 72
- *Abba, Father* (Gilsdorf/Resource)
- *Alleluia* (Page/Resource)
- *All the Ends of the Earth* (Jesuits/NALR)
- *Be Glad, O People* (Weston Priory)
- *Choose Life* (Weston Priory)
- *Go Up to the Mountain* (Weston Priory)
- *I Have Loved You* (Joncas/NALR)
- *In the Day of the Lord* (Gutfreund/NALR)
- *I Will Sing, I Will Sing* (Dyer/Celebration Services)
- *Jesus In Our Hands* (Wise/GIA)
- *John the Baptist* (Gilsdorf/Resource)
- *The Kingdom of God* (Deiss/NALR)
- *Locusts and Wild Honey* (Weston Priory)
- *Mighty Lord* (Jesuits/NALR)
- *On Jordan's Bank* (ICEL)
- *Only In God* (Jesuits/NALR)
- *Prepare Ye* (Prezio/K&R)
- *Redeemer Lord* (Jesuits/NALR)
- *Rise Up, Jerusalem* (Schoenbachler/NALR)
- *Sing Alleluia Sing* (Dameans&NALR)
- *Spirit of God* (Weston Priory)
- *Turn to Me* (Jesuits/NALR)
- *We Are Called* (Patterson/Resource)

ADVENT PLANNING SHEET   Date _____

Parish focus _____

Environment & art _____

Ritual notes _____

Faith development (eg., bulletin item) _____

Children's faith experience _____

Prelude _____

Hymn of gathering _____

Sprinkling baptismal water acclamation _____

Penitential rite_____Opening Prayer _____

Responsory _____Gospel acclamation _____

General intercessions _____

At the preparation & presentation _____

Preface dialog _____Preface _____

Preface acclamation _____

Eucharistic prayer _____Memorial acclamation _____

Eucharistic amen _____

The Lord's prayer _____

Breaking of bread _____

The communion hymn _____

The post-communion hymn _____

Blessing _____At the dismissal _____

Memoranda:

THIRD SUNDAY
OF ADVENT

YEAR A

READINGS

Isaiah (35:1-6,10)

This, the third advent reading from Isaiah, continues to present the Kingdom in an ideal form. In addressing Jews of the post-exilic period, Isaiah attributes the best of each country to the New Israel. Here, all that is good in creation is transformed by the loving power of Yahweh. The Jewish people are reminded that the power of God strengthens their weakness and renews their courage.

James (5:7-10)

James, using the analogy of the farmer working the soil, counsels patience to the early Christian community. They will be able to withstand persecution and hardship if they practice patience and charity with one another. In their sufferings, James advocates the prophets "who spoke in the name of the Lord" as models.

Matthew (11:2-11)

Jesus associates recognition of the Kingdom with the "gifts" of the messianic age: the sick are healed, the poor receive the Good News, the dead are raised to life. He then salutes John the Baptist as the greatest of the prophets, while indicating that all who place their faith in Jesus are held in high esteem in the Kingdom.

FOCUS

Renewed and redeemed creation is a powerful theme of Advent. Patience, fidelity and love are the tools through which this is accomplished. Both Isaiah and James were speaking of the splendor of a community fully alive in the Lord, who is Emmanuel, "God with us."

Each reading addresses the problem of suffering. The paradox is revealed that suffering is the fertilizer that enables those ransomed by the Lord to share in his life. Through suffering creation is renewed and redeemed, bringing forth all its potential, even beyond its wildest imaginings and deepest longings. Jesus uses the Baptist as the example of one who, giving little thought to his own welfare, gives himself fully to the process of redemption. By "crossing" the natures of his contemporaries, and, more important, first allowing himself to be "crossed," he emerges as the greatest of the prophets. James, echoing Jesus, indicates to the Christian community that by taking "the prophets who spoke in the name of the Lord" as models they may be great in the Kingdom of Heaven.

IDEA STARTERS

- *CCT Lectionary:* Is 35:1-10; Ps 146:5-10; Jm 5:7-10; Mt 11:2-11
- Advent is now half over. The readings give us a glimpse of the rejoicing to be fully realized when the Lord returns. In fact, Jesus announces the Kingdom of God in our midst. In James we hear again the call to patient preparedness, to living each day in fraternal charity. This is the peace of

the Kingdom; this is the peace revealed at Christmas.
- Today's first reading and Gospel provide suitable texts for a communal celebration of Anointing the Sick.
- The readings paint a picture of what most would call the perfect world. Let children illustrate what the perfect world is to them and post their illustrations for all to see.
- An adult forum may discuss "Prophets and Prophecy: Past and Present" based, perhaps, on the Advent Lectionary.
- For your consideration: Alternative Opening Prayer; Intercessions for the blind, deaf, lame, fearful, weak, oppressed, widow(er)s, farmers, imprisoned, hope, joy; Eucharistic Prayer IV; Memorial Acclamation B; Advent Solemn Blessings.

MUSIC

- Psalm 146
- *And the Father Will Dance* (Landry/NALR)
- *Beatitudes* (Dameans/NALR)
- *Come to the Water* (Andersen/Resource)
- *The Dawn of the Day* (Deiss/NALR)
- *Eye Has Not Seen* (Haugen/GIA)
- *Hark, the Glad Sound* (ICEL)
- *He Has Anointed Me* (Dameans/NALR)
- *How Beautiful* (Wise/GIA)
- *How Beautiful on the Mountains* (Deiss/NALR)
- *How Can I Keep From Singing?* (Traditional)
- *Jesus, Remember Me* (Taize/GIA)
- *John the Baptist* (Gilsdorf/Resource)
- *Lay Your Hands* (Landry/NALR)
- *Let the Valleys Be Raised* (Jesuits/NALR)
- *Lord of Glory* (Jesuits/NALR)
- *Patience, People* (Jesuits/NALR)
- *Renewal Song* (Andersen/Resource)
- *Seek the Lord* (Jesuits/NALR)
- *Sing to God a Brand New Canticle* (Quinlan/NALR)
- *Song of the Prophet* (Weston Priory)
- *A Time Will Come for Singing* (Jesuits/NALR)
- *To Be Your Bread Now* (Haas/Cooperative Ministries)

ADVENT PLANNING SHEET   Date _____

Parish focus _____
Environment & art _____
Ritual notes _____
Faith development (eg., bulletin item) _____
Children's faith experience _____
Prelude _____
Hymn of gathering _____
Sprinkling baptismal water acclamation _____
Penitential rite_____Opening Prayer _____
Responsory _____Gospel acclamation _____
General intercessions _____
At the preparation & presentation _____
Preface dialog _____Preface _____
Preface acclamation _____
Eucharistic prayer _____Memorial acclamation _____
Eucharistic amen _____
The Lord's prayer _____
Breaking of bread _____
The communion hymn _____
The post-communion hymn _____
Blessing _____At the dismissal _____
Memoranda:

FOURTH SUNDAY OF ADVENT

YEAR A

READINGS
Isaiah (7:10-14)
The sign of Emmanuel is assurance to frightened Ahaz that though his enemies are strong, God, dwelling with him and Israel, is stronger than all his enemies.
Romans (1:1-7)
Paul proclaims Jesus Son of Man and Son of God through the power of the Holy Spirit. The sign of his sonship is the Resurrection. This sign is responsible for making Paul an apostle and calling into existence the community of faith.
Matthew (1:18-24)
Matthew tells the story of how the pregnancy of Mary, a virgin, while a scandal to those without vision, serves as a sign of hope and promise when seen through the eyes of faith (Joseph) listening in obedience.

FOCUS
The readings for today seem to stress the importance of the sign. For Ahaz, weak and timorous in faith, the sign of the fertile virgin giving birth is presented as a means of support and encouragement. The Gospel of Matthew repeats this theme and brings it to completion in the pregnancy of Mary the Virgin, open and vulnerable to God's creative work. Joseph also serves as a model for Christian people. He cooperates with the work of the Spirit by "listening with the ear of his heart." Rather than staying caught in his own ego development and conflict, he freely gives it to the Spirit, who transforms it and brings it to a new and sublime place (which is far beyond Joseph's ability to understand when he decides to sacrifice his own ego-conflict in submissive, trusting obedience to the Father). Finally, Paul points to the ultimate sign: that of Jonah referred to by Jesus himself in his ministry. Paul underscores the fact that in the Resurrection, made possible by the Incarnation, the church is called into being.

Thus, at the completion of Advent, Paul demonstrates the inextricable union and integrity of God's plan of salvation. Incarnation, redemption and resurrection are all one mystery, simply varying facets of the same diamond.

IDEA STARTERS
- *CCT Lectionary:* Is 7:10-16; Ps 24; Rm 1:1-7; Mt 1:18-25.
- Note that the second reading is the introduction to the "Gospel of Paul." The passage provides the source for a perfect homily, summing up the past three weeks of Advent as well as looking forward to the celebration of Christmas.
- The Gospel account talks about the name of Jesus and Joseph's acceptance of God's will. Salvation is given to those who have faith in God's Word.
- Mary, one of the major Advent characters, may be the center of a meditation in preparation for Christmas.
- Church decor and bulletin art may appropriately incorporate symbols of

the "O Antiphons." Design an ecumenical service based upon the singing of each late Advent weekday verse.
- Have a pre-Christmas decoration party on December 17th (or any day thereafter) as we begin looking toward the commemoration of the Lord's nativity.
- For your consideration: Opening Prayer; Intercessions for civil leaders, creation's proper use, ministers of the Word, future parents; Advent Preface II (P 2); Memorial Acclamation D; Advent Solemn Blessing.

MUSIC

- Psalm 24
- *Amazing Grace* (traditional)
- *Arise! Come Sing in the Morning* (Zsigray/NALR)
- *Canticle of the Sun* (Haugen/GIA)
- *Come, Thou Long Expected Jesus* (ICEL)
- *Creation of the Stars of Night* (ICEL)
- *Earthen Vessels* (Jesuits/NALR)
- *Emmanuel Among Us* (Culbreth/Resource)
- *Exult You Just Ones* (Jesuits/NALR)
- *Glorious In Majesty* (Cothran/GIA)
- *He Is the Lord* (Haas/Cooperative Ministries)
- *Hymn of the Lord's Supper* (Ivanic/GIA)
- *I Will Sing, I Will Sing* (Dyer/Celebration Services)
- *Let the King of Glory Come* (Joncas/NALR)
- *Mary's Prayer* (Petrucelli/Resource)
- *O Antiphons* (Gilsdorf/Resource)
- *Praise the Lord, My Soul* (Parker/GIA)
- *Praise We the Lord this Day* (ICEL)
- *Rise Up, Jerusalem* (Schoenbachler/NALR)
- *This Alone* (Jesuits/NALR)
- *We Were Strangers* (Deiss/NALR)
- *Yahweh, the Faithful One* (Jesuits/NALR)

ADVENT PLANNING SHEET

Date _____

Parish focus _____

Environment & art _____

Ritual notes _____

Faith development (eg., bulletin item) _____

Children's faith experience _____

Prelude _____

Hymn of gathering _____

Sprinkling baptismal water acclamation _____

Penitential rite _____ Opening Prayer _____

Responsory _____ Gospel acclamation _____

General intercessions _____

At the preparation & presentation _____

Preface dialog _____ Preface _____

Preface acclamation _____

Eucharistic prayer _____ Memorial acclamation _____

Eucharistic amen _____

The Lord's prayer _____

Breaking of bread _____

The communion hymn _____

The post-communion hymn _____

Blessing _____ At the dismissal _____

Memoranda:

SOLEMNITY OF CHRISTMAS
Christmas Vigil Mass A

READINGS
Isaiah (62:1-5)
The marriage image of God and Israel in this reading foreshadows both the perfect union of divinity and humanity in Christ himself and the relationship of Christ to the church as his bride.
Acts of the Apostles (13:16-17,22-25)
Paul delivers the Good News to a crowd of Jews in Antioch by recalling God's election of their ancestors to be his chosen people.
Matthew (1:1-25)
Matthew asserts that Jesus is the Christ, the Messiah, the Anointed One. It is in Jesus that the messianic hopes of the Jews are fulfilled. He does so by use of a geneology, thus placing Jesus in the royal line of King David.

(See *Christmas Mass During the Day* for further notes.)

CHRISTMASTIME PLANNING SHEET Date _____

Parish focus _____

Environment & art _____

Ritual notes _____

Faith development (eg., audit ed.) _____

Children's faith experience _____

Prelude _____

Hymn of gathering _____

Sprinkling baptismal water _____

Gloria in excelsis _____

Opening Prayer _____

Responsory _____

First reading _____ Responsory _____

Second reading _____ Gospel acclamation _____

Gospel _____ Profession of faith _____

General intercessions _____

At the preparation & presentation _____

Preface dialogue _____ Preface _____

Preface acclamation _____

Eucharistic prayer _____ Memorial acclamation _____

Eucharistic amen _____

The Lord's prayer _____

Breaking of bread _____

The communion hymn _____

The post-communion hymn _____

Blessing _____ At the dismissal _____

Memoranda:

SOLEMNITY OF CHRISTMAS
Christmas Midnight Mass   A

READINGS
Isaiah (9:1-6)
For ancient peoples "light" represented new life and liberation. Darkness was
associated with slavery. For Isaiah the Messiah would be, above all, the
Liberator. This Liberator–Messiah is given royal titles: "God–hero," "Father-
Forever," "Wonder–Counselor," and "Prince of Peace."
Titus (2:11-14)
Since the birth of Christ, living a moral life becomes more than good
citizenship. It becomes a witness to the presence of God.
Luke (2:1-14)
Luke is not so much concerned with recording the historical facts surrounding
the birth of Jesus as he is with imparting the significance of the coming of
the Christ into the world. This reading is filled with contrasts; human poverty
and divine glory, darkness and light.

(See *Christmas Mass During the Day* for further notes.)

CHRISTMASTIME PLANNING SHEET Date _____

Parish focus _____

Environment & art _____

Ritual notes _____

Faith development (eg., audit ed.) _____

Children's faith experience _____

Prelude _____

Hymn of gathering _____

Sprinkling baptismal water _____

Gloria in excelsis _____

Opening Prayer _____

Responsory _____

First reading _____ Responsory _____

Second reading _____ Gospel acclamation _____

Gospel _____ Profession of faith ____

General intercessions _____

At the preparation & presentation _____

Preface dialogue _____ Preface _____

Preface acclamation _____

Eucharistic prayer _____ Memorial acclamation ___

Eucharistic amen _____

The Lord's prayer _____

Breaking of bread _____

The communion hymn _____

The post-communion hymn _____

Blessing _____ At the dismissal _____

Memoranda:

SOLEMNITY OF CHRISTMAS
Christmas Mass at Dawn
A

READINGS
Isaiah (62:11-12)
The arrival of the Savior transforms the people. They are no longer "abandoned" but "cherished."
Titus (3:4-7)
Morality in Christ takes on a positive attitude. The point is not to avoid wrong doing, but to live fully human lives. This can happen only as members of Christ's Body.
Luke (2:15-20)
Luke makes a significant point that the shepherds were the first to know the Christ Child. It is established right from the beginning that Christ has come to call the poor and lowly.

(See *Christmas Mass During the Day* for further notes.)

CHRISTMASTIME PLANNING SHEET Date _____

Parish focus _____

Environment & art _____

Ritual notes _____

Faith development (eg., audit ed.) _____

Children's faith experience _____

Prelude _____

Hymn of gathering _____

Sprinkling baptismal water _____

Gloria in excelsis _____

Opening Prayer _____

Responsory _____

First reading _____Responsory _____

Second reading _____Gospel acclamation _____

Gospel _____Profession of faith _____

General intercessions _____

At the preparation & presentation _____

Preface dialogue _____Preface _____

Preface acclamation _____

Eucharistic prayer _____Memorial acclamation _____

Eucharistic amen _____

The Lord's prayer _____

Breaking of bread _____

The communion hymn _____

The post-communion hymn _____

Blessing _____At the dismissal _____

Memoranda:

SOLEMNITY OF CHRISTMAS
Christmas Mass During the Day   A

READINGS
Isaiah (52:7-10)
This reading is a fragment of a victory hymn sung by pilgrims returning with
the Lord to the Holy City. The song recounts the joy felt by the people at
their return to their home in and through the Lord. Just as the protection of
Yahweh, given to the returning exiles, was a sign of God's mighty fidelity,
so now, this new and final sign, the birth of the Messiah, displays God's loving
commitment to his people.

Hebrews (1:1-6)
The basis and content of hope is the gift of God's Son — Jesus the Christ.
Through Jesus' obedience to the Father's will we can discern the image of
God's glory. Through his obedience we have been cleansed of sin and Jesus
is installed as supreme authority. The allusion to Psalm 110, verse 1 is quoted
to establish this fact.

John (1:1-18)
John acknowledges Jesus as pre-existent, co-equal Logos, in whose Incarnation
all are saved and brought into the love of the Father. John (the Evangelist)
points to the figure of the Baptist, who, in testifying to Jesus's messiahship,
makes credible the writings of the Evangelist. Those who live in the light are
brought to life, not by the flesh, but by the envigorating Spirit of God. Through
the light we are able to share in the love that is God's life. While the Law was
God's gift through Moses, the author signifies that God's enduring love is
given to us through Jesus Christ.

FOCUS
As the ancient exiles returning to Jerusalem were protected by Yahweh, the
birth of the Lord is our sign and shield. We are reminded of his great love
for us through his nativity, the fulfillment of an age old promise. The reading
from Hebrews reminds us that the basis of our hope and joy is Jesus, the gift
of the Father. In his obedience and through his sufferings, we see the glory
of God and are able to share the very life of the Trinity. The Prologue of John's
Gospel, a masterpiece of exalted christology, sets Jesus before us as God in
human form coming from the Father and returning to him. Our ability to
love and grow in his life is determined by our willingness to acknowledge
him as Lord and submit to his will.

IDEA STARTERS
- *CCT Lectionary:* Is 9:2-7; Ps 9; Titas 2:11-14; Lk 2:1-20 (I); Is 62:6-70, 10-12;
  Ps 97; Titus 3:4-7; Lk 2:8-20 (II); Is 52:7-10; Ps 98; Hb 1:1-12; Jn 1:1-14.
- Choose one set of readings from the four Old Testament, New Testament,
  and Gospel lessons available in the Roman Lectionary. Note that, although
  organized into four Masses, the readings are interchangeable. Examine which
  of the readings have not been used and will not be read in the near future.
- Have children carry in figures of the Holy Family and place them in the
  manger during the processions.
- At evening services, contrasting the use of candles at other liturgies, have

the people light their candles after Communion, and dim the lights during a peaceful final hymn (e.g. "Silent Night") until only candlelight illumines the church.

- Sing Gloria; light the four white candles on the Advent Wreath; sing different Christmas carols on the various feast days.
- Encourage home customs and cultural experiences for the days of Christmas with family or friends.
- For your consideration: Penitential Rite C–iii; Intercessions for peace, rulers of nations, the married, the newborn; Christmas Preface; Memorial Acclamation D; Christmas Solemn Blessing.

MUSIC

- Psalm 89, 96, 97, 98
- *A Child Is Born* (Keyes/Resource)
- *Children, Run Joyfully* (Jesuits/NALR)
- *Gloria* (Taize/GIA)
- *A Great and Mighty Wonder* (ICEL)
- *A Light Has Shone* (Weston Priory)
- *Lord, Today* (Dameans/NALR)
- *Morning Softly Awakens* (Weston Priory)
- *Nothing Is Greater* (Toolan/Resource)
- *Shout for Joy, O You Earth* (Smith/WLP)
- *Sing! Rejoice* (Marchionda/WLP)
- *Song of the Lord's Appearance* (Joncas/Coop Ministries)
- *Today is Born our Savior* (Hilliard/Resource)
- *Wake From Your Sleep* (Jesuits/NALR)

CHRISTMASTIME PLANNING SHEET Date _____

Parish focus _____

Environment & art _____

Ritual notes _____

Faith development (eg., audit ed.) _____

Children's faith experience _____

Prelude _____

Hymn of gathering _____

Sprinkling baptismal water _____

Gloria in excelsis _____

Opening Prayer _____

Responsory _____

First reading _____ Responsory _____

Second reading _____ Gospel acclamation _____

Gospel _____ Profession of faith _____

General intercessions _____

At the preparation & presentation _____

Preface dialogue _____ Preface _____

Preface acclamation _____

Eucharistic prayer _____ Memorial acclamation _____

Eucharistic amen _____

The Lord's prayer _____

Breaking of bread _____

The communion hymn _____

The post-communion hymn _____

Blessing _____ At the dismissal _____

Memoranda:

FEAST OF THE HOLY FAMILY

YEAR A

READINGS

Sirach (3:2–6,12–14)
The Hebrew Scriptures present a view of the family as the context in which one experiences immortality. One lives on in one's children. Children are a great blessing because they assure the continuation of one's name and one's legacy and because they add to the resources of the family unit.

Colossians (3:12–21)
Paul presents us with a morality based on the fact of our belonging to God. It is love, not a set of moral precepts, that should inform our morality and direct our actions. It is up to us to make room in our hearts for God's love. This is the core of Christ's message.

Matthew (2:13–15,19–23)
We are presented here with a stark and unromanticized picture of the Holy Family. Displaced, alienated, poor and alone, Joseph, Mary and Jesus face a hostile world and provide a model of perseverance. We are left with a picture of a family of faith, motivated by trust in God.

FOCUS

The Scriptures provide a multi-faceted picture of family. By belonging to a family we are connected to history and to the future. Our life goes back as far as our earliest ancestors and as far forward as our most distant descendants.

Family assures us a place in history and, according to Hebrew Scripture, a place in eternity. Belonging to God's family gives us a foundation for living a satisfying, moral life.

IDEA STARTERS

- *CCT Lectionary:* Is 63:7–9; Ps 111; Hb 2:10–18; Mt 2:13–15, 19–23.
- The structure and make-up of the family is changing at a rapid pace. Today a minority of Americans live in traditional families. How can we expand our notion of family to include singles, single parents, and non-related communities?
- How can our parish community show appreciation for its children? Be sure to incorporate children into today's liturgy.
- Family is where we learn hospitality, compassion, openness and tolerance. How is our church family a place of learning such values?
- For your consideration: Intercessions for families, singles, the married, children, homosexuals.

MUSIC

- Psalm 128
- *Come Weal, Come Woe* (Jesuits/NALR)
- *Come You Shepherds* (Meltz/WLP)
- *A Child Is Born* (Keyes/Resource)
- *Children, Run Joyfully* (Jesuits/NALR)
- *Gloria* (Taize/GIA)
- *A Great and Mighty Wonder* (ICEL)
- *A Light Has Shone* (Weston Priory)
- *Lord, Today* (Dameans/NALR)
- *Morning Softly Awakens* (Weston Priory)
- *Nothing Is Greater* (Toolan/Resource)
- *Shout for Joy, O You Earth* (Smith/WLP)
- *Sing! Rejoice* (Marchionda/WLP)
- *Song of the Lord's Appearance* (Joncas/Coop Ministries)
- *O Thou Joyful Day* (Christmas Carol)

CHRISTMASTIME PLANNING SHEET Date _____

Parish focus _____

Environment & art _____

Ritual notes _____

Faith development (eg., midweek program) _____

Children's faith experience _____

Prelude _____

Hymn of gathering _____

Penitential rite _____

Opening Prayer _____

Reading cycle _____ First reading _____

Responsory _____ Second reading _____

Lenten gospel acclamation _____ Gospel _____

RCIA rites & acclamations _____

General intercessions _____

At the preparation & presentation _____

Preface dialog _____ Preface _____

Preface acclamation _____

Eucharistic prayer _____ Memorial acclamation _____

Eucharistic amen _____

The Lord's prayer _____

Breaking of bread _____

The communion hymn _____

The post-communion hymn _____

Blessing _____ At the dismissal _____

Memoranda:

SOLEMNITY OF MARY, MOTHER OF GOD, JANUARY 1

YEARS A, B AND C

READINGS
Numbers (6:22–27)
This short passage is most likely a fragment from the Liturgy of the Temple and marks the special filial relationship between God and Israel.
Galatians (4:4–7)
Paul states that the law, delivered by angels, was man's temporary guardian, until the moment when "The Deliverer" should appear, who will free them from the Law and make them the adopted sons of God.
Luke (2:16–21)
Jesus, in submitting to the Law, frees all from it, leading them to the position of heirs of God. Thus the shepherds glorify God, spreading news which they hardly perceive, while Mary contemplates the glory she has helped to usher into human history, in her role as *Theotokos,* Mother of God.

FOCUS
Law, sonship, freedom, all are strains woven through this Solemnity of Mary, Mother of God and Octave Day of Christmas. The Law was a temporary guide and guardian until that day should come when the Lord "will let his face shine on us and bless us." This day, Paul tells us, comes with the appearance of the Messiah in human form. This birth delivers us into sonship and frees us from a now irrelevant Law. We share the joy of the shepherds, while realizing on a deep level the cause of that joy. We honor Mary, Mother of God, who invites us to contemplate with her the grace of so great a gift.

IDEA STARTERS
- *CCT Lectionary:* Nom 6:22–27; Ps 67; Gl 4:4–7 or Ph 2:9–13; Lk 2:15–21; or Dt 8:1–10; Ps 117; Rw 21:1–6A; Mt 25:31–46 (New Year).
- This day is observed as the World Day of Prayer for Peace or Mary, Mother of God (RC); The Name of Jesus (Episcopalian/Lutheran).
- The Roman Lectionary provides ample material for a homily about peace, Mary, the Name of the Lord, or New Year's Day. Focus in upon one of the three lessons and develop your ideas.
- Sponsor an ecumenical observance of lessons and carols for Christmas this week. Be sure Christmas is still being observed by your community.
- A bulletin article about names can provide a basis for individual research about the significance of biblical names, as well as the meaning of each person's name.
- For your consideration: Alternative Opening Prayer; Intercessions for the new year, motherhood and fatherhood, right use of God's name, peace; Christmas Preface II (P4); Ordinary Solemn Blessing I.

MUSIC

- Psalm 67
- *Ave Maria* (Zsigray/NALR)
- *Ave Maria* (Wise/GIA)
- *The Beautiful Mother* (Jesuits/NALR)
- *The Christmas Alleluia* (Blunt/WLP)
- *Christians, Awake* (ICEL)
- *Emanuel* (Jesuits/NALR)
- *Emmanuel Born this Night* (Johnston/WLP)
- *From Heaven Above* (ICEL)
- *Gentle Night* (Jesuits/NALR)
- *The God Whom Earth and Sea and Sky* (ICEL)
- *Hail Mary: Gentle Woman* (Landry/NALR)
- *He Has Come* (Wise/GIA)
- *Lullabye* (Joncas/Coop Ministries)
- *The Lord Has Come* (Adrias/WLP)
- *Mary's Prayer* (Petrucelli/Resource)
- *Peace* (Olivier/Resource)
- *Peace Song* (Stenson/Resource)
- *A Song of Blessings* (Wise/GIA)
- *Today is Born a Savior* (Hilliard/Resource)

CHRISTMASTIME PLANNING SHEET Date _____

Parish focus _____

Environment & art _____

Ritual notes _____

Faith development (eg., midweek program) _____

Children's faith experience _____

Prelude _____

Hymn of gathering _____

Penitential rite _____

Opening Prayer _____

Reading cycle _____ First reading _____

Responsory _____ Second reading _____

Lenten gospel acclamation _____ Gospel _____

RCIA rites & acclamations _____

General intercessions _____

At the preparation & presentation _____

Preface dialog _____ Preface _____

Preface acclamation _____

Eucharistic prayer _____ Memorial acclamation _____

Eucharistic amen _____

The Lord's prayer _____

Breaking of bread _____

The communion hymn _____

The post-communion hymn _____

Blessing _____ At the dismissal _____

Memoranda:

SOLEMNITY OF
THE EPIPHANY

YEARS
A, B, & C

READINGS
Isaiah (60:1-6)
Once more the words of Isaiah ring out. Here, the Lord addresses Jerusalem, promising a return of past glory and even greater glory than what has been. In her restoration all peoples and nations will come to her bringing treasures and homage. Renewed Jerusalem will not use her position to boast, but rather will invite all to share in the salvation God displays in and through her. One great hymn of praise from all people will ascend to the Lord from the heart of Zion, daughter of the Holy One of Israel.

Ephesians (3:2-3,5-6)
Paul emphasizes the fact that in Christ Jesus all are made into a new, single human body (family) with Christ as head. This has been accomplished through the Incarnation and the preaching of the Good News.

Matthew (2:1-12)
The story of the Magi who came from afar to worship the Christ points to the epiphanic dimension of the Christmas Season. Israel receives the promise and openly and with love receives it. Then transformed, she spreads the word to the world, awaiting its response. Herod and his court are representative of those who, caught in fear and suspicion, reject the word of love. Try though they may, the salvation of God will not be impeded by their wiles.

FOCUS
Christ is the one who calls all people, Jew and Gentile, into the New Jerusalem, a holy city, beloved of God. This city serves as a beacon of his love and light, summoning all to share in his life. Paul states clearly that it is the spirit, revealing the Good News to people through prophets and apostles, who is responsible for one's ability to respond to the call of Christ, to be "all in all." Only our fears, idols and stubbornness will keep us from this free invitation.

IDEA STARTERS
- *CCT Lectionary:* Is 60:1-6; Ps 72:1-14; Eph 3:1-12; Mt 2:1-12
- Use of gold vestments and incense will help illustrate the solemnity of this day.
- Close the Christmas season on the evening of the Baptism of the Lord celebrating Epiphany lessons and carols (ecumenically).
- During the procession have children carry in figures of the Three Kings and place them in the manger.
- Traditionally, the day of Epiphany recalled three manifestations of Jesus: to the Magi, at his baptism, and at the wedding at Cana. How might you incorporate these themes?
- Have members of your community bring a friend today, sharing the light of faith.
- The custom of proclaiming this year's special holy days may be sung today.
- For your consideration: Alternative Opening Prayer; Intercessions for foreign nations, Jews and Gentiles, living God's Word daily; Epiphany Preface (P6); Memorial Acclamation D; Epiphany Solemn Blessing.

MUSIC

- Psalm 72
- *Arise, Shine Out* (Bennet/Resource)
- *Come Weal, Come Woe* (Jesuits/NALR)
- *Every Stone Shall Cry* (Joncas/Coop Ministries)
- *Of the Father's Love Begotten* (ICEL)
- *The People that Walk in Darkness* (Jesuits/NALR)
- *Prepare the Way* (Bodrique/WLP)
- *Rise Up, Zion* (Miffleton/WLP)
- *Shepherds and Kings* (Weston Priory)
- *Songs of Thankfulness and Praise* (traditional)
- *Star-light* (Ellis&Lynch/NALR)
- *We Have Seen His Star* (Miffleton/WLP)
- *Worship and Praise* (Keyes/Resource)

CHRISTMASTIME PLANNING SHEET Date _____

Parish focus _____

Environment & art _____

Ritual notes _____

Faith development (eg., midweek program) _____

Children's faith experience _____

Prelude _____

Hymn of gathering _____

Penitential rite _____

Opening Prayer _____

Reading cycle _____First reading _____

Responsory _____Second reading _____

Lenten gospel acclamation _____Gospel _____

RCIA rites & acclamations _____

General intercessions _____

At the preparation & presentation _____

Preface dialog _____Preface _____

Preface acclamation _____

Eucharistic prayer _____Memorial acclamation _____

Eucharistic amen _____

The Lord's prayer _____

Breaking of bread _____

The communion hymn _____

The post-communion hymn _____

Blessing _____At the dismissal _____

Memoranda:

SECOND SUNDAY
AFTER CHRISTMAS

YEARS
A, B AND C

READINGS

Sirach (24:1-4,8-12)
In today's first reading Sirach praises wisdom as the manifestation of God among the people. God's wisdom comes in a word that is creative, healing and redeeming.

Ephesians (1:3-6,15-18)
In this introduction to the letter to the Ephesians, the early church is told that God has chosen them, as he had chosen the people of Israel, to share in his wisdom, a wisdom that has its fullness in Christ.

With belief in Jesus comes the inheritance of God's wisdom and the assurance that we are his children.

John (1:1-18)
(See Commentary for Christmas Mass During the Day)

FOCUS

We encounter wisdom through words, the Word of Scripture, the words of children, or a word from a friend. But how numerous are words in our lives and how rare true wisdom.

We are a people of words. Our society is based on information and our religion on a book. Today's readings give us pause to consider the power of words in our lives. But as a people of words do we sometimes ignore the wisdom to be found in other sources; in the beauty of nature, for instance? Today also provides an opportunity to examine our lives with a view towards non-word sources of wisdom.

IDEA STARTERS

- *CCT Lectionary:* Jer 31:7-14 or Fcc 24:1-4, 12-16; Ps 147:12-20; Eph 1:3-6, 15-18.
- How is wisdom different from knowledge, understanding and information? What is the relationship of wisdom to words?
- Be sure to incorporate a period of extended silence into today's liturgy (e.g after the Gospel).
- Are we attentive to the wisdom of those in our lives? Our children? Friends? Spouses? What opportunities does our parish community provide for its members to hear the thoughts, dreams, ideas and hopes of one another? Perhaps today would be a good time to launch a parish discussion group.
- For your consideration: Intercessions for teachers, preachers, writers, theologians.

MUSIC

- Psalm 147
- *Dwelling Place* (Jesuits/NALR)
- *Eye Has Not Seen* (Haugen/GIA)
- *Let Every Voice Sing* (Johnson/PMB)
- *Messenger Song* (Gilsdorf/Resource)
- *Taste and See* (Haugen/GIA)
- *Teach Me Your Ways* (Foster/Resource)
- *Teach Me Your Ways, O Lord* (Culbreth/Resource)
- *You Are Near* (Jesuits/NALR)

CHRISTMASTIME PLANNING SHEET Date _____

Parish focus _____

Environment & art _____

Ritual notes _____

Faith development (eg., midweek program) _____

Children's faith experience _____

Prelude _____

Hymn of gathering _____

Penitential rite _____

Opening Prayer _____

Reading cycle _____First reading _____

Responsory _____Second reading _____

Lenten gospel acclamation _____Gospel _____

RCIA rites & acclamations _____

General intercessions _____

At the preparation & presentation _____

Preface dialog _____Preface _____

Preface acclamation _____

Eucharistic prayer _____Memorial acclamation _____

Eucharistic amen _____

The Lord's prayer _____

Breaking of bread _____

The communion hymn _____

The post-communion hymn _____

Blessing _____At the dismissal _____

Memoranda:

FEAST OF THE BAPTISM OF THE LORD YEAR A

READINGS
Isaiah (42:1-4,6-7)
Isaiah's Spirit-filled servant is an image of the role of the people of Israel. For Christians this image has traditionally been attached to Christ and his church.
Acts of the Apostles (10:34-38)
Paul makes two significant points to Cornelius and his family; first is the progress from knowledge of Jesus to faith in him as the Christ and the second is the Resurrection as the model and promise of the resurrection of all believers.
Matthew (3:13-17)
The account of Jesus' baptism in the Gospel of Matthew, as compared to those in the other Gospels, reveals a concern for the establishment of Jesus' roots in the Jewish tradition and his ministry as a continuation and the capstone of the line of the prophets.

FOCUS
Baptism is, perhaps more than anything else, an initiation into the Body of Christ and into the church. It welcomes us into participation of a believing community with a rich tradition and history. The baptism of Jesus was a sign of his participation and an initiation into the tradition of the prophets. Hence, it is the most appropriate beginning for his prophetic ministry.

IDEA STARTERS
- *CCT Lectionary:* Is 42:1-9; Ps 29; Ads 10:34-43; Mt 3:13-17.
- Today's liturgy provides an appropriate context for infant baptism or the confirmation of adults.
- Baptism was the beginning of Jesus' public ministry. How do we view baptism or confirmation as our initiation into a life of prophetic witness?
- Today's bulletin might contain an article dealing with the question: Why did Jesus need to be baptized?
- For your consideration: Opening Prayer; Intercessions for the newly baptized, newborns, all believers.

MUSIC
- Psalm 29
- *All Those Who Love Me* (Weston Priory)
- *Banks of the Jordan* (Duesing/Resource)
- *Dedication Song* (Raffa/Resource)
- *Dwelling Place* (Jesuits/NALR)
- *Hymn of Praise* (Dicie/Resource)
- *The Goodness of God* (Weston Priory)
- *We Were Strangers* (Deiss/NALR)

CHRISTMASTIME PLANNING SHEET Date _____

Parish focus _____

Environment & art _____

Ritual notes _____

Faith development (eg., midweek program) _____

Children's faith experience _____

Prelude _____

Hymn of gathering _____

Penitential rite _____

Opening Prayer _____

Reading cycle _____First reading _____

Responsory _____Second reading _____

Lenten gospel acclamation _____Gospel _____

RCIA rites & acclamations _____

General intercessions _____

At the preparation & presentation _____

Preface dialog _____Preface _____

Preface acclamation _____

Eucharistic prayer _____Memorial acclamation _____

Eucharistic amen _____

The Lord's prayer _____

Breaking of bread _____

The communion hymn _____

The post-communion hymn _____

Blessing _____At the dismissal _____

Memoranda:

READINGS
Joel (2:12–18)
Our relationship with God is mediated through the community. We know God as a *people* of faith.
Second Corinthians (5:20–6:2)
It is up to the initiated, those already baptized, to guide and welcome and accompany the catechumens preparing for baptism at Easter.
Matthew (6:1–6,16–18)
The Lenten call is to inner conversion. As we enter the lenten season we enter into a period of meditation on the call of Jesus to transform our lives, to become more fully alive and more fully loving.

FOCUS
The call to interior conversion.

IDEA STARTERS
- Simplicity is the order of the day. The gathering rites consist of hymn, sign of the cross, greeting, and collect.
- Be sure ashes are not given outside of a liturgical service.
- Consider allowing people to mark each other with ashes.
- Use Evening Prayer for distribution of ashes.
- Invite families or ministers of the sick to take ashes to shut-ins.
- Should catechumens be signed with ashes and be called to be "reconciled" to the Lord? Should young children be signed with a penitential symbol?

MUSIC
- Psalm 51
- *All Flesh Is Grass* (Haugen/GIA)
- *Ashes* (Conry/NALR)
- *Come Home Child* (Farrel/PMB)
- *Draw Near, O Lord* (Douglas/Resource)
- *Hosea* (Weston Priory)
- *Lord, We Are Sorry* (Raffa/Resource)
- *O Lord, You Are My Refuge* (Dicie/Resource)
- *Praise the Lord, O My Soul* (Jesuits/NALR)
- *Return All Things* (Dicie/Resource)
- *This Is Our Acceptable Time* (Gannon/PMB)

LENTEN PLANNING SHEET

Date _____

Parish focus _____

Environment & art _____

Ritual notes _____

Faith development (eg., midweek program) _____

Children's faith experience _____

Prelude _____

Hymn of gathering _____

Penitential rite _____

Opening Prayer _____

Reading cycle _____First reading _____

Responsory _____Second reading _____

Lenten gospel acclamation _____Gospel _____

RCIA rites & acclamations _____

General intercessions _____

At the preparation & presentation _____

Preface dialog _____Preface _____

Preface acclamation _____

Eucharistic prayer _____Memorial acclamation _____

Eucharistic amen _____

The Lord's prayer _____

Breaking of bread _____

The communion hymn _____

The post-communion hymn _____

Blessing _____At the dismissal _____

Memoranda:

FIRST SUNDAY OF LENT   YEAR A

READINGS
Genesis (2:7-9,3:1-7)
Humanity, the crown of God's creative activity, is raised up from the dust and formed in God's image to do naught but love the Creator. From the intimacy of this spousal call, humanity achieves a greater knowledge of good and evil, this knowledge is purchased at the price of our inheritance as daughters and sons of God.

Romans (5:12-19)
Paul presents us with the "Divine Foil" of Adam. Christ, the New Adam, is the gift of God that reconciles fallen humanity to God. He is the proof of God's gracious love, for he, in his obedience to God's will, eradicates many offenses and acquits us of all guilt.

Matthew (4:1-11)
Unlike the first Adam, Jesus, the "first fruits of the new creation," submits lovingly to God's will. In so doing, he inaugurates a new age, where God serves as the focus and center of all things. Through loving obedience we are freed to a deeper and fuller realization of our self-hood, in and through God's will.

FOCUS
On this Sunday we are called to review the initial rupture, and its cause, between God and humanity. Humanity chooses to separate itself from God and to become a god itself. In so doing, it rejects the Lord's spousal call and elects to live in isolation. Paul reminds us that Jesus, the perfect man and the new Adam, is the one who, through his obedience, repairs the break between creature and creator. The Gospel gives us a living example of this in Jesus, who rejects the Satan who tempted the first human being successfully. Men and women choose isolation while still in the midst of the garden, God's gift to humanity. Jesus, for all, chooses union and fruitfulness in the midst of the desert experience.

IDEA STARTERS
- *CCT Lectionary:* Gn 2:4b-9, 15-17, 25-3:7; Ps 130; Rom 5:12-19; Mt 4:1-11.
- The Lenten season is rich with traditions, and is a special time for the Christian community. Investigate Lenten customs held in high esteem by your parish members and incorporate them into your Lenten schedule.
- Lent is the time to intensify preparation of new members. See the *Rite of Christian Initiation of Adults* (RCIA) for more information. Celebrate the "Rite of Election" at today's Eucharist.
- The Lenten focus to turn away from sin may be highlighted by elaborating on the Penitential Rite throughout the season.
- Recall that the word "Alleluia" disappears from the Lenten liturgies.
- How will you mark the Lenten Sundays as in the season, yet not of the season?
- For your consideration: Opening Prayer; Penitential Rite; Intercessions for sinners, criminals, the victims of crime, those we have wronged.

MUSIC

- Psalm 51
- *On Eagles' Wings* (Joncas/NALR)
- *Turn to Me* (Jesuits/NALR)
- *Forty Days and Forty Nights* (ICEL)
- *Blest Be the Lord* (Jesuits/NALR)
- *Abba, Father* (Gilsdorf/Resource)
- *Don't Be Afraid* (Schmitz/Resource)
- *For You Are My God* (Jesuits/NALR)
- *Glory and Praise* (Jesuits/NALR)
- *Only in God* (Jesuits/NALR)
- *In Your Love Remember Me* (Kendzia/NALR)
- *Praise the Name of the Lord* (Patterson/Resource)

LENTEN PLANNING SHEET   Date _____

Parish focus _____

Environment & art _____

Ritual notes _____

Faith development (eg., midweek program) _____

Children's faith experience _____

Prelude _____

Hymn of gathering _____

Penitential rite _____

Opening Prayer _____

Reading cycle _____First reading _____

Responsory _____Second reading _____

Lenten gospel acclamation _____Gospel _____

RCIA rites & acclamations _____

General intercessions _____

At the preparation & presentation _____

Preface dialog _____Preface _____

Preface acclamation _____

Eucharistic prayer _____Memorial acclamation _____

Eucharistic amen _____

The Lord's prayer _____

Breaking of bread _____

The communion hymn _____

The post-communion hymn _____

Blessing _____At the dismissal _____

Memoranda:

SECOND SUNDAY OF LENT   YEAR A

READINGS
Genesis (12:1-4)
Abraham serves as a type for Christ, the New Man. Without question or argument, Abraham quietly and obediently follows God's invitation to start again, to seek a new home. In so doing he will enter into a new covenant with God and become the father of a great nation. This nation will serve as the light through which all people will be led to the saving power of God.
Second Timothy (1:8-10)
We have been refined and made holy by God through God's gracious gift, Jesus Christ. He, Christ, is the promise of all ages who defeats death, robbing it of its sway over life, through the power of the Gospel.
Matthew (17:1-9)
In the transfiguration, Jesus Christ is revealed as the transcendent Glory of God, incarnated in the flesh. The Old Covenant witnesses the glory of this action in the persons of Moses and Elijah. The pillars of the New Covenant are also present to witness the greatness of this event.

FOCUS
The Transfiguration event is the pivotal mystery presented to us in this set of readings. Abraham, as an obedient, listening servant, submits to the authority of God, and therefore transcends his own limitations through the power of God's saving grace. Paul indicates the primary position of Jesus in the plan of salvation by hailing him as a life-giver through his saving death. Jesus' transfiguration as God-man provides us with the hope that we too may be transformed if we listen to God's voice in our life.

IDEA STARTERS
- *CCT Lectionary:* Gn 12:1-8; Ps 33:18-22; Rom 4:1-17; Jm 3:1-17.
- The *Roman Lectionary* focuses upon the Transfiguration of the Lord. It serves as a glimpse of the resurrection to come.
- The use of the mountain as God's dwelling place may be a source for meditations in the parish bulletin. Sponsor a parish retreat or day of recollection. During Lent, we are challenged to approach the throne of God face-to-face and we pray for our renewal and reconciliation.
- At a children's liturgy, dramatize the Gospel passage (using boys and girls in the skit).
- At evening prayer, be sure to use the *Lucenarium* in place of the Introductory Rites.
- For your consideration: Opening Prayer; Intercessions for the Jewish people, family, international peace, those suffering hardship, the grace of God; Second Lenten Sunday Preface (P13); Eucharistic Prayer II; Memorial Acclamation C; Lenten Solemn Blessing.

MUSIC
- Psalm 33
- *Remember Your Love* (Dameans)
- *For Us To Live* (Weston Priory)
- *Hymn of the Lord's Supper* (Ivancic/GIA)
- *We Are Many Parts* (Haugen/GIA)
- *Transfiguration* (Landry/NALR)
- *Song Of Covenant* (Toolan/Resource)
- *Our God Has Saved Us* (Bennet/Resource)
- *Praise the Lord* (Keyes/Resource)

LENTEN PLANNING SHEET

Date _____

Parish focus _____

Environment & art _____

Ritual notes _____

Faith development (eg., midweek program) _____

Children's faith experience _____

Prelude _____

Hymn of gathering _____

Penitential rite _____

Opening Prayer _____

Reading cycle _____ First reading _____

Responsory _____ Second reading _____

Lenten gospel acclamation _____ Gospel _____

RCIA rites & acclamations _____

General intercessions _____

At the preparation & presentation _____

Preface dialog _____ Preface _____

Preface acclamation _____

Eucharistic prayer _____ Memorial acclamation _____

Eucharistic amen _____

The Lord's prayer _____

Breaking of bread _____

The communion hymn _____

The post-communion hymn _____

Blessing _____ At the dismissal _____

Memoranda:

THIRD SUNDAY OF LENT   YEAR A

READINGS

Exodus (17:3-7)
Though they are the recipients of God's gift of freedom and the witnesses of God's mighty saving deeds on their behalf, the Israelites still refuse to trust, and grumble against the Lord. Their fear that they will die of thirst betrays their profound lack of faith in the Lord, their champion and deliverer.

Romans (5:1-2,5-8)
God cares for the grumbling Hebrews, though they show their infidelity in their querulousness. In spite of their ingratitude, God rescues them and delivers them from thirst. Jesus, God's act of grace, delivers us from the bondage of our sins and sets us alive in God's love, while we are enemies of God. Such an extravagance in generosity could only come from the heart of God.

John (4:5-42)
In the Gospel reading, Jesus models what Paul has just referred to, indicating that the Lord is the saving gift of God to humanity. Jesus speaks with the Samaritan woman. He not only speaks with her, but also asks her for a drink. Finally, he offers her water of eternal life and shares this gift with all her neighbors. The stunned apostles learn a profound lesson in the gracious generosity of God.

FOCUS

The water theme, a primary one of the paschal season, is central to today's liturgy. The Hebrews are quenched of their burning thirst, despite their rebellion against the loving God, who supplies their every need. Paul reminds us that Jesus saved us even though we were still in the darkness of sin and therefore enemies of God. In the Gospel, Jesus lives this theological lesson for us. He breaks out of the religious restrictions of his people. He speaks with a woman, a person of little consequence in the eyes of the Law, and a Samaritan, one of those hated by the Jews as half-breed schismatics. In so doing, he offers to this woman the opportunity to drink deeply from a source from which they would expect to receive little.

IDEA STARTERS

- *CCT Lectionary:* Ex 17:3-7; Ps 95; Rom 5:1-11; Jn 4:5-42.
- Use the first scrutiny found in the *Sacramentary* and RCIA based upon today's *Lectionary.* Be sure to provide an explanation of this ritual in the bulletin.
- Place desert symbols near empty holy water fonts.
- For your consideration: Opening Prayer; Gospel (full form); Intercessions for trust, environmental protection, patience, an end to prejudice, hospitality; Third Lenten Sunday Preface (P14); Memorial Acclamation D; Lenten Solemn Blessing.

MUSIC

- Psalm 95
- *Believe* (McGrath/Resource)
- *Eagle's Wings* (Andersen/Resource)
- *I Long for You O Lord* (Dameans/NALR)
- *You Will Draw Water* (Conry/NALR)
- *We Thank You, Father* (Weston Priory)
- *O Healing River* (Joncas/traditional)
- *Song of Gathering* (Wise/GIA)
- *Our Peace and Integrity* (Weston Priory)
- *Though the Mountains May Fall* (Jesuits/NALR)
- *Come, Let Us to the Lord* (ICEL)

LENTEN PLANNING SHEET

Date _____

Parish focus _____

Environment & art _____

Ritual notes _____

Faith development (eg., midweek program) _____

Children's faith experience _____

Prelude _____

Hymn of gathering _____

Penitential rite _____

Opening Prayer _____

Reading cycle _____ First reading _____

Responsory _____ Second reading _____

Lenten gospel acclamation _____ Gospel _____

RCIA rites & acclamations _____

General intercessions _____

At the preparation & presentation _____

Preface dialog _____ Preface _____

Preface acclamation _____

Eucharistic prayer _____ Memorial acclamation ____

Eucharistic amen _____

The Lord's prayer _____

Breaking of bread _____

The communion hymn _____

The post–communion hymn _____

Blessing _____ At the dismissal _____

Memoranda:

FOURTH SUNDAY OF LENT YEAR A

READINGS
First Samuel (16:6-7,10-13)
Samuel, indeed the whole house of Jesse, learned a lesson in today's reading: "Not as man sees does God see...The Lord looks into the heart." Out of all Jesse's sons, the Lord chose David, the youngest, the least likely. God's instruments are chosen to give glory to God through the very fact of their weakness.
Ephesians (5:8-14)
Paul reminds us that Jesus, the Light, has delivered us out of darkness into his light. Our actions and behavior should reflect the light we share in and through him. Through this light we are raised from the death of sin to new life in Christ.
John (9:1-41)
This Gospel serves as a dramatic setting for the light theme which the two previous readings establish. The man born blind is delivered from physical darkness, and is given light to see spiritually as well. He discovers and responds to the light given in the life of Jesus. The pharisees, those who should recognize the light, continue to walk in darkness and are therefore blinded to the saving power of Jesus. They chose to stay in the death of sin and cannot share in new life.

FOCUS
David is filled with the Spirit of God: "The Spirit rushed upon David from the day." He is infused with the Spirit and brilliance of God's life-giving glory. Jesus incarnates the message that Paul relates. He shows himself to be the bringer of light. The man born blind is delivered from darkness and immediately begins to live a new life committed to Jesus, while the pharisees, intent on destroying the light, condemn themselves and appear before people as those without light walking without the truth.

IDEA STARTERS
- *CCT Lectionary:* Sm 16:1-13; Ps 23; Eph 5:8-14; Jn 9:1-41.
- Today the second scrutiny is celebrated according to the texts in the *Sacramentary, Lectionary,* and RCIA.
- Display the candles and the "fire holder" to be used at the Great Easter Vigil. (The symbolism of light in today's Gospel points toward the great *Lucenarium* at the Vigil.) Continue using the desert symbols.
- The Gospel lends itself to a fine one-act play. At a youth or children's liturgy, act out the Bible story. Have everyone, except the blind man, hold a lit candle. As each person completes his or her lines, he or she blows out his or her candles, except Jesus, who at the end gives his candle to the blind man.
- For your consideration: Opening Prayer; Gospel (full form); Intercessions for peace in the Middle East, present day descendents of Jesse and David, response to God's call, farmers, healing; Fourth Lenten Sunday Preface (p15); Eucharistic Prayer III; Memorial Acclamation D; Lenten Solemn Blessing.

MUSIC

- Psalm 23
- *Awake O Sleeper* (Dameans/NALR)
- *The Fullness of God* (Andersen/Resource)
- *Let Us Walk In the Light* (Haugen/GIA)
- *I Am the Light* (Repp/K&R)
- *Light Our Way* (Hummer/Resource)
- *The Lord Is My Light* (Jesuits/NALR)
- *Father, We Came Here* (Schoenbachler/NALR)
- *The Moon Shines Bright* (ICEL)
- *Praise! Praise the Lord* (Sessions/Resource)

LENTEN PLANNING SHEET   Date _____

Parish focus _____

Environment & art _____

Ritual notes _____

Faith development (eg., midweek program) _____

Children's faith experience _____

Prelude _____

Hymn of gathering _____

Penitential rite _____

Opening Prayer _____

Reading cycle _____First reading _____

Responsory _____Second reading _____

Lenten gospel acclamation _____Gospel _____

RCIA rites & acclamations _____

General intercessions _____

At the preparation & presentation _____

Preface dialog _____Preface _____

Preface acclamation _____

Eucharistic prayer _____Memorial acclamation _____

Eucharistic amen _____

The Lord's prayer _____

Breaking of bread _____

The communion hymn _____

The post-communion hymn _____

Blessing _____At the dismissal _____

Memoranda:

FIFTH SUNDAY OF LENT   YEAR A

READINGS
Ezekiel (37:12-14)
Ezekiel points to the future life of those committed to God. They should be returned to life through the power of the Spirit and returned to the kingdom, the land that is their own.
Romans (8:8-11)
Paul indicates how this infusion of new life is to take place. Jesus, the New Man, the Life of God, who lives eternally with God, will bring all those alive in the Spirit to the fullness of God's life. In this passage we have one of Paul's typical contrasts. The Spirit is the model for those filled with divine life. The flesh, on the other hand, is associated with those separated from God and committed to life without God.
John (11:1-45)
In the account of the raising of Lazarus we have the completion of both the first and second readings. Lazarus, committed to the Lord and filled with God's Spirit, is called out of his tomb. He owes this gift to Jesus, hailed by Martha as, "the Way, the Truth, and the Life." The pharisees, those committed to the flesh, to life without God's Spirit, cannot receive life and are condemned by their own stubborness to death and sin, to an existence devoid of God, the very core of life. The way is prepared for the conflict between light (life) and darkness (death). From the results of this conflict the victory will be given to the King of the Ages, who "once was dead but now lives in God."

FOCUS
The three readings today are a steady progression in the development of the same theme. That theme can be simply stated as, "How do we go about obtaining and securing life?" Ezekiel tells us that a convenanted relationship with God, and fidelity to it (the Covenant), will restore those who have died to the fullness of God's life. They need only trust in God and they will find a secure foundation on which to build. Paul points to the instrument or channel through which the just will be restored to God. Jesus embodies the fullness of God's message and power. Those who proclaim him as Lord and serve him are committed to the truth and will live forever.

IDEA STARTERS
- *CCT Lectionary:* Ez 37:1-14; Ps 116:1-9; Rom 8:6-11; Jn 11:1-45.
- Today's rubric as the final day of scrutiny for the elect.
- Especially among youth, there is an interest in people who have claimed to have seen a glimpse of the next life. What was Lazarus's claim?
- Today's liturgy calls us to reflect on our belief in the resurrection of the body and the life everlasting. It may be appropriate to place newly budding pussywillows and the sweet chrisms used at sacraments of initiation and healing with the other lenten symbols.
- Sponsor an ecumenical forum to discuss life after death, or the stages those approaching death face.
- For your consideration: Opening Prayer; Intercessions for healers, therapists, newborns.

MUSIC

- Psalm 130
- *I Am The Resurrection* (Dameans/NALR)
- *May We Praise You* (Jesuits/NALR)
- *Eye Has Not Seen* (Haugen/GIA)
- *I Am The Bread Of Life* (Toolan/GIA)
- *My Refuge* (Vessels/GIA)
- *New Life* (Malone/Resource)
- *Resurrection Song* (Sexton/Resource)
- *O Father We Have Wandered* (ICEL)
- *The Truth Will Make You Free* (Gilsdorf/Resource)

LENTEN PLANNING SHEET   Date _____

Parish focus _____

Environment & art _____

Ritual notes _____

Faith development (eg., midweek program) _____

Children's faith experience _____

Prelude _____

Hymn of gathering _____

Penitential rite _____

Opening Prayer _____

Reading cycle _____First reading _____

Responsory _____Second reading _____

Lenten gospel acclamation _____Gospel _____

RCIA rites & acclamations _____

General intercessions _____

At the preparation & presentation _____

Preface dialog _____Preface _____

Preface acclamation _____

Eucharistic prayer _____Memorial acclamation _____

Eucharistic amen _____

The Lord's prayer _____

Breaking of bread _____

The communion hymn _____

The post-communion hymn _____

Blessing _____At the dismissal _____

Memoranda:

PASSION/PALM SUNDAY   YEAR A

READINGS

Isaiah (50:4-7)
The Third Song of the Servant of Yahweh is the first lesson for today. It portrays the servant of God as one whose love and fidelity to God enable him to go to any length, to make any sacrifice to show his love for Yahweh. This unshakeable loyalty is built on the knowledge and firm hope that God will be the support of those who love and are loved by God.

Philippians (2:6-11)
By using the ancient Christian hymn to Christ, the apostle indicates to the Gentiles how Christ fulfills the description set out in the Isaian reading today. Jesus, in loving obedience, offers himself to God and so is raised to glory, through the vehicle of his suffering.

The Passion Narrative of Matthew
In the drama of the Passion we see the incarnation of the preceding two readings. Jesus silently, humbly, and obediently goes to his death. He freely enters into suffering so that his victory will result in the reconciliation of mankind with God.

FOCUS
The essence of the paschal mystery is in the paradox that victory comes through defeat, that life is born out of death, and that power, that is, true power, can be found only in complete vulnerability. The tomb, like the womb, while apparently barren and sterile, is the incubator of new life. *Per crucem ad lucem.*

IDEA STARTERS
- *CCT Lectionary:* Mat 21:1-11; Is 50:4-9a; Ps 31:9-16; Phil 2:5-11; Mat 26:14-27;66.
- If there are many churches in your area, consider meeting at a central location for the Liturgy of the Palms. Many Christians observe the palm celebration followed by the meditation on our Lord's passion. Have an ordained minister preside using the prayers and responses of his or her denomination.
- If your parish uses the Solemn Entrance, involve children in this simple procession. As the observance of the Passion begins, young children may celebrate their own Liturgy of the Word, perhaps by using a filmstrip of the last days of Christ's life.
- The symbols of the day vary from the palm of triumph to the thorns of death. Adorn the processional cross with palm and red paraments. The presider may wear a red cope at the liturgy of the palms, and then vest into a chasuble for the remainder of the liturgy (of the passion).
- Avoid play acting the passion account. Investigate the possibility of using a speech choir for some kind of choral reading.
- For your consideration: Liturgy of the Palms w/Procession; Alternative Opening Prayer; Passion (full form); Intercessions for Jerusalem, humility, witness, the tortured and oppressed, equality, the suffering, the betrayed, innocent victims, and an end to capital punishment; Passion Sunday Preface (P17); Eucharistic Prayer II; Lenten Solemn Blessing.

MUSIC

- Psalm 22
- *Jesus Is Lord* (Toolan/Resource)
- *Jesus The Lord* (Jesuits/NALR)
- *Only This I Want* (Jesuits/NALR)
- *Redeemer Lord* (Jesuits/NALR)

- *Song of Abandonment* (Landry/NALR)
- *Let Heaven Rejoice* (Jesuits/NALR)
- *Hosanna* (Medling/Resource)
- *Blessings on the King* (Jesuits/NALR)
- Jesus, the Lord (Keyes/Resource)

LENTEN PLANNING SHEET   Date _____

Parish focus _____

Environment & art _____

Ritual notes _____

Faith development (eg., midweek program) _____

Children's faith experience _____

Prelude _____

Hymn of gathering _____

Penitential rite _____

Opening Prayer _____

Reading cycle _____First reading _____

Responsory _____Second reading _____

Lenten gospel acclamation _____Gospel _____

RCIA rites & acclamations _____

General intercessions _____

At the preparation & presentation _____

Preface dialog _____Preface _____

Preface acclamation _____

Eucharistic prayer _____Memorial acclamation _____

Eucharistic amen _____

The Lord's prayer _____

Breaking of bread _____

The communion hymn _____

The post-communion hymn _____

Blessing _____At the dismissal _____

Memoranda:

HOLY THURSDAY: MASS OF THE LORD'S SUPPER

YEARS A, B AND C

READINGS

Exodus (12:1-8,11-14)
The lamb, whose sacrifice is a sign of salvation, is a foreshadowing of the sacrifice of Christ.

First Corinthians (11:23-36)
By recalling the words of Jesus, Paul emphasizes that by participating in the Eucharist we are participating in the death of Christ.

John (13:1-15)
John's Gospel does not describe the institution of the Eucharist. However, in his description of the washing of the disciples' feet by Jesus, he gets to its essence; "As I have done for you, you must do for others."

IDEA STARTERS

- *CCT Lectionary:* Ex 12:1-14, 1 Cor 11:23-26; Jn 13:1-15.
- Viewing each day's liturgy as one "station" on the road toward Easter morn may provide guidelines fostering the flow of each day's principal liturgy into the next. To miss one of the triduum liturgies is to miss a part of the central mystery of our lives as Christians. Thus, the three days must be planned as one liturgy.
- Tonight the assembly once again reflects on its daily mission to "love one another" even in the advent of pain. The pastor symbolically demonstrates the Lord's command by washing the feet of a representative group of people from your community. Be sure to include those preparing for entrance into full communion and confirmation. This "washing" is a foreshadowing of the commitment called forth upon one's rising up from the baptismal bath.
- The liturgy of the Eucharist is celebrated simply (in order to contrast the festivity of the Great Vigil).
- The procession with the reserved sacrament marks our reverence for the real presence of Jesus Risen in our midst and is worshipped and adored as we begin our paschal fast.
- All crosses/crucifixes are removed from the church or covered with red linen.
- The elect hear a story of death and life in ancient Egypt. They hear Paul "hand on" a traditional meal of sharing in the death and resurrection of the Lord. They see their pastor imitate Jesus in stripping himself of a place of authority in order to serve humbly in love (washing feet).

MUSIC

- Psalm 116:12-13, 15-18
- *Bread, blessed and broken* (Evans/ML 10:7)
- *Glorius in majesty* (Cothran/GIA)
- *I am a rock* (Fisherfolk/ML 10:4)
- *Jesus in our hands* (Wise/GIA)
- *Love divine* (Light/ML 12:3)
- *Love consecrates the humblest* (McManus/PMB)
- *Only this I want* (Jesuits/NALR)
- *Our blessing cup* (Joncas/NALR)
- *Said Judas to Mary* (Galliard/Carter)
- *The bread of our days* (Goglia/ML 12:4)
- *To be your bread now* (Haas/Cooperative music)
- *Ubi caritas* (Taize/GIA)
- *When we eat this bread* (Joncas/Cooperative music)
- *Where charity and love prevail* (Westendorf/PMB)
- *We remember* (Haugen/GIA)

CYCLE A

TRIDUUM PLANNING SHEET

Date _____

Parish focus _____

Environment & art _____

Ritual notes _____

Faith development (eg., midweek program) _____

Children's faith experience _____

Prelude _____

Hymn of gathering _____

Sprinkling baptismal water acclamation _____

Opening Prayer _____

Reading cycle _____ First reading _____

Responsory _____ Second reading _____

Lenten gospel acclamation _____ Gospel _____

RCIA rites & acclamations _____

General intercessions _____

At the preparation & presentation _____

Preface dialog _____ Preface _____

Preface acclamation _____

Eucharistic prayer _____ Memorial acclamation _____

Eucharistic amen _____

The Lord's prayer _____

Breaking of bread _____

The communion hymn _____

The post-communion hymn _____

Blessing _____ At the dismissal _____

Memoranda:

GOOD FRIDAY: CELEBRATION OF THE LORD'S PASSION

YEARS A, B AND C

READINGS
Isaiah (52:13-53:12)
The fourth of the servant songs brings to light the paradox of salvation: life comes out of death.
Hebrews (4:14-16,5:7-9)
Jesus is the perfect mediator between the human and the divine, because he shares fully in both.
John (18:1-19:42)
In his narrative of the passion and death of Jesus, John is less concerned with the details of Jesus' suffering than with the manifestation of Jesus' divinity throughout.

IDEA STARTERS
- *CCT Lectionary:* Is 52:13-53:12; Heb 4:14-16; Jn 18:1-19:42.
- Celebrating the *Liturgy of the Hours* at various times of the day provides an opportunity for prayer during the paschal fast.
- The general intercessions of the day extend the bendiction won by Christ upon all humanity. They may have a common sung response between the deacon's invitation and the presider's prayer.
- The passion narrative may be divided into scenes, each proclaimed by a different reader. The assembly may then sing an antiphon, hymn verse, or other acclamation appropriate to the section read.
- The veneration of the cross (at three stations similar to tomorrow's Vigil) is the symbolic climax of this day. The cross "lifted up" and the venerating of the wood (Does your cross have a corpus on it, making a "crucifix"?) marks the value of this sign from time immemorial.
- Silence, the predominant atmosphere of our three-day fast and vigil, continues.
- How would the elect compare the passion account proclaimed from the synoptic gospel on Sunday with today's proclamation from St. John?

MUSIC
- Psalm 31:2, 6, 12-13, 15-17, 25.
- *Be at peace* (Evans/ML 10:4)
- *For our sake* (Farney/ML 12:6)
- *Grain of wheat* (Farney/ML 12:6)
- *Holy cross* (Douglas/ML 9:8)
- *I Corinthians I* (Mullins/ML 10:8)
- *Lift high the cross* (Kitchin/PMB)
- *Love is stronger than death* (Dicie/ML 11:9)
- *Tree of life* (Haugen/GIA)
- *With You* (Sexton/ML 8:8)
- *We acclaim the cross of Jesus* (Siwek/PMB)
- *When I behold the wondrous cross* (Watts/PMB)
- *When we think how Jesus suffered* (Jabusch/PMB)

TRIDUUM PLANNING SHEET

Date _____

Parish focus _____

Environment & art _____

Ritual notes _____

Faith development (eg., midweek program) _____

Children's faith experience _____

Prelude _____

Hymn of gathering _____

Sprinkling baptismal water acclamation _____

Opening Prayer _____

Reading cycle _____ First reading _____

Responsory _____ Second reading _____

Lenten gospel acclamation _____ Gospel _____

RCIA rites & acclamations _____

General intercessions _____

At the preparation & presentation _____

Preface dialog _____ Preface _____

Preface acclamation _____

Eucharistic prayer _____ Memorial acclamation _____

Eucharistic amen _____

The Lord's prayer _____

Breaking of bread _____

The communion hymn _____

The post-communion hymn _____

Blessing _____ At the dismissal _____

Memoranda:

THE EASTER VIGIL   YEAR A

READINGS
Genesis (1:1-2:2)
Genesis (22:1-18)
Exodus (14:15-15:1)
Isaiah (54:5-14)
Isaiah (55:1-11)
Baruch (3:9-15,32-4:4)
Ezekiel (36:16-28)
Romans (6:3-11)
Matthew (28:1-10)

IDEA STARTERS

- The quietness of the community continues throughout this day. Only the Liturgy of the Hours is celebrated (with the only Saturday evening prayer in the year). "The Church waits at the Lord's tomb, meditating on his suffering and death." The paschal fast continues until after the Great Vigil.
- During the day, RCIA rites of the ephiphetha, recitation of the creed, and prebaptismal anointing may be celebrated.
- After nightfall, the faithful gather in the darkness to celebrate the "passover of the Lord." The suggested ritual in the *Sacramentary* needs to be digested and pastorally applied.
- Having the elect gather around the easter water during the singing of the litany of saints may visually illustrate that fellowship into which they will be baptized (and also guarantees them a good view of the water during the blessing).
- If the elect face the assembly during their public renunciation of evil and profession of faith, the assembly will probably see the faith alive in their faces!
- After each baptism, have the assembly sing an acclamation of joy.
- When the sponsors dress the neophytes in white robes and present the "pillar style" baptismal candles to them, the baptismal party becomes a blaze of light before the assembly.
- Call attention to the fact that the neophytes pray "the Lord's Prayer" for the first time at the family table of the Paschal Lamb.
- Be sure the neophytes go to coffee hour "white clad" so all will most assuredly greet them!

MUSIC
- Psalm 118:1-2, 16-17, 22-23
- *Alleluia, Risen Lord* (Farney/ML 12:7)
- *Breaking of the bread* (Feiten/ML 8:3)
- *Canticle of the sun* (Haugen/GIA)
- *Christ the Lord is risen today* (Leeson/PMB)
- *Easter hymn* (Duesing/ML 11:2)
- *Hail thee festival day* (Fortunatus/PMB)
- *Jesus is life* (Landry/NALR)
- *Let all the earth* (Landry/NALR)
- *Praise to be God* (Patterson/ML 9:6)
- *Resurrection song* (Sexton/ML 8:8)
- *Sing to the mountains* (Jesuits/NALR)
- *The goodness of God* (Weston Priory)
- *This is the day* (Goglia/ML 10:7)
- *This is the day* (Haugen/GIA)
- *This is the day* (Joncas/Cooperative music)
- *You are my witness* (Fisherfolk/ML 10:4)

TRIDUUM PLANNING SHEET.

Date _____

Parish focus _____

Environment & art _____

Ritual notes _____

Faith development (eg., midweek program) _____

Children's faith experience _____

Prelude _____

Hymn of gathering _____

Sprinkling baptismal water acclamation _____

Opening Prayer _____

Reading cycle _____First reading _____

Responsory _____Second reading _____

Lenten gospel acclamation _____Gospel _____

RCIA rites & acclamations _____

General intercessions _____

At the preparation & presentation _____

Preface dialog _____Preface _____

Preface acclamation _____

Eucharistic prayer _____Memorial acclamation _____

Eucharistic amen _____

The Lord's prayer _____

Breaking of bread _____

The communion hymn _____

The post-communion hymn _____

Blessing _____At the dismissal _____

Memoranda:

EASTER SUNDAY YEARS A, B AND C

READINGS

Acts of the Apostles (10:34,37-43)
Peter proclaims in the midst of the people the Good News of Jesus, the Messiah, preaching, suffering, dead, buried, and raised to glory. As witnesses to the great Christ-event, Peter and the Eleven testify to Jesus. All who place their faith in him will share in his Resurrection and be raised to life in God's love.

Colossians (3:1-4) or First Corinthians (5:6-8)
In the two choices presented for today's feast, Paul sets before us the impact of the Resurrection on our lives. In Colossians he directs our vision to Christ, dwelling in glory in God. Christ is the one who delivers us into glory.

In the fragment from First Corinthians, Paul uses the analogy of yeast to point to the effects those living in the light of Christ's Resurrection have on the world. They discard the corrupt, the immoral, and the wicked, and in the power of Christ help the world to rise to a rejuvenated state.

John (20:1-9)
In the Johannine reading we hear the familiar story of the discovery of the Resurrection by Peter and John. Mary Magdalen, the Apostle of the Resurrection, brings the news to the Apostles. Peter and John set off for the tomb. When they discover the situation they believe, though they are struck with wonder.

FOCUS

Not by coincidence does the church present us with the preaching of Peter on Pentecost for the first reading of Easter Sunday. Both feasts are inextricably united. Christ's resurrection brings to life the church, his bride. Paul in both readings defines the Christian community as that body which is leaven, enrichment to the world. As we listen to John's account of the resurrection event, we celebrate our own gift of faith, as those who have not seen but believe.

IDEA STARTERS

- *CCT Lectionary:* Acts 10:34-43 or Jer 31:1-6; Ps 118:14-24; Col 3:1-4 or Acts 10:34-43; Jn 1-18 or Mat 28:1-10.
- The church, especially the font and Easter Candle, the altar and ambo, and the tabernacle and cross, should be adorned with beautiful flowers.
- Use the Paschal Candle in the gathering procession.
- Gold vestments mark the solemnity of Easter.
- Let the "alleluias" abound.
- Replace the customary greeting ("The grace of our Lord...") with the traditional Easter welcome: (minister) "Alleluia! Christ is risen!" (assembly) "The Lord is risen indeed! Alleluia!"
- On Easter, omit the Penitential Rite since a renunciation of sin takes place during the Reaffirmation of Baptismal Vows.
- Sing the canticle from Revelation, "This is the Feast," as the Hymn of Praise during the gathering rites as found in *Lutheran Book of Worship.*
- At the Breaking of the Bread, sing the verse, "Alleluia! Christ, our Passover..." Musical arrangements are available in many newly published hymnals for the Episcopal Church (USA).

- Add the Double Alleluia following the dismissal throughout the season.
- At the Intercessions, pray for the transformation of the world, the neophytes, our re-commitment to living out Jesus Risen in our lives, hope for all the world.

MUSIC
- Psalm 118
- *Alleluia* (Page/Resource)
- *Christ the Lord Is Risen Today* (ICEL)
- *Sing to the Mountains* (Jesuits/NALR)
- *Oh Yes, Lord Jesus Lives* (Landry/NALR)
- *This Is the Day* (Haugen/GIA)
- *This Is the Day* (Schoenbachler/PAA)
- *Jesus Is Life* (Landry/NALR)
- *Resurrection Sons* (Sexton/Resource)
- *Happy Are They* (Miffelton/Resource)

EASTER PLANNING SHEET   Date _____

Parish focus _____

Environment & art _____

Ritual notes _____

Faith development (eg., midweek program) _____

Children's faith experience _____

Prelude _____

Hymn of gathering _____

Sprinkling baptismal water acclamation _____

Opening Prayer _____

Reading cycle _____First reading _____

Responsory _____Second reading _____

Lenten gospel acclamation _____Gospel _____

RCIA rites & acclamations _____

General intercessions _____

At the preparation & presentation _____

Preface dialog _____Preface _____

Preface acclamation _____

Eucharistic prayer _____Memorial acclamation _____

Eucharistic amen _____

The Lord's prayer _____

Breaking of bread _____

The communion hymn _____

The post-communion hymn _____

Blessing _____At the dismissal _____

Memoranda:

SECOND SUNDAY OF EASTER

YEAR A

READINGS

Acts of the Apostles (2:42–47)
In this reading we are presented with the idyllic Christian community. All are united in Christ through the instruction of the apostles. All things are shared corporately. Prayer and Eucharist are the cement which binds this New Israel, and love (Christ's Life) is the product of such cohesiveness.

First Peter (1:3–9)
Peter articulates the source of the new life. It is created in and through the paschal mystery. Since it has been tried through the "fire of Christ's saving act," it can never come to an end. It will ever shine and grow from glory to glory. Nothing can diminish its splendor. The sufferings of life pale in the splendor of its glory. Without seeing the source of this greatness, we the Christian community believe, for we have responded to the testimony of his witnesses and are fed by his loving care through his pastors.

John (20:19–31)
The familiar story of Thomas, struggling to accept the testimony of the apostles, seems to be the counter-point to the Petrine reading. Thomas depicts the death of the old dispensation, with its reliance on the material world, as it is confronted by the resplendent light of the new creation. This resurrected and recreated life frees all those who seek freedom from the chains of sin. This liberating office is passed on through the "New Priesthood" until the fulfillment of the kingdom.

FOCUS
The readings for today construct the theme that Christ's Body is built up through his resurrection and the loving acceptance of that fact by his followers. All who profess him are enabled to share in his community of believers and are daily strengthened through prayer and the Eucharist. They are freed from a reliance on the material world and given a vision which pierces the veil of creation. With the eyes of faith, they see the resplendent glory of God in the person of Jesus. With this picture they mirror this splendor in their corporate lives.

IDEA STARTERS
- *CCT Lectionary:* Acts 2:14a, 22-32; Ps 16:5-11; I Pt 1:3-9; Jn 20:19-31.
- Throughout the season, celebrate the rite of Sprinkling Baptismal Water during the Gathering Rites. Use water blessed at the Easter Vigil and redesign the Easter Blessing Prayer found in the *Sacramentary* for this rite.
- *Rite of Christian Initiation of Adults*(RCIA): The ritual directs that during the Easter season the neophytes should remain in their special places with their sponsors. The second readings from First Peter are especially addressed to them.
- For your consideration: Alternative Opening Prayer; Profession of Faith (Nicene Creed) should be highlighted; Intercessions for parish communal life, those who teach theology and religious ed., and for those they teach, those in spiritual or material need, for exultant hearts in worship, and for the neophytes; Easter Preface I (P 21); Eucharistic Prayer I w/Easter propers; Memorial Acclamation D; Easter Solemn Blessing.

MUSIC

- Psalm 118
- *Praised Be the Father* (Dameans/NALR)
- *He Is the Lord* (Haas/Cooperative Ministries)
- *I Believe in the Sun* (Landry/NALR)
- *I Believe in You* (Wise/GIA)
- *I Will Sing, I Will Sing* (Dyer/Celebration)
- *Let All the Earth* (Dameans/NALR)
- *Praise and Honor* (Tucciarone/Resource)
- *Lift Up Your Hearts* (Jesuits/NALR)
- *Happy Are They* (Miffleton/Resource)
- *That Easter Day With Joy* (ICEL)
- *We Are Called* (Patterson/Resource)
- *Wherever Two Or More* (The Fisherfolk/Resource)

EASTER PLANNING SHEET   Date _____

Parish focus _____

Environment & art _____

Ritual notes _____

Faith development (eg., midweek program) _____

Children's faith experience _____

Prelude _____

Hymn of gathering _____

Sprinkling baptismal water acclamation _____

Opening Prayer _____

Reading cycle _____First reading _____

Responsory _____Second reading _____

Lenten gospel acclamation _____Gospel _____

RCIA rites & acclamations _____

General intercessions _____

At the preparation & presentation _____

Preface dialog _____Preface _____

Preface acclamation _____

Eucharistic prayer _____Memorial acclamation _____

Eucharistic amen _____

The Lord's prayer _____

Breaking of bread _____

The communion hymn _____

The post-communion hymn _____

Blessing _____At the dismissal _____

Memoranda:

THIRD SUNDAY OF EASTER   YEAR A

READINGS
Acts of the Apostles (2:14,22-28)
Peter's Pentecost homily is once again set before our eyes. Peter proclaims Jesus as the Messiah, the one who could not be defeated or destroyed, in spite of the worst of peoples' plans. In a final crescendo of praise, Peter quotes David in one of his psalms and indicates that this psalm was David's praise of Jesus.
First Peter (1:17-21)
Christ's blood has ransomed us from a way of life bent on destruction and death. This purchase has rendered us strangers in a land which does not accept the Lord. Yet his sacrifice strengthens us and aids us in our time here in this foreign place. The paschal mystery is our bulwark against works of darkness by centering our faith and hope in God alone.
Luke (24:13-35)
The disciples on the road to Emmaus are confronted by a Jesus whom they do not recognize due to his new resurrected state. He demolishes their preconceptions about the Messiah and life in him and, in the process, re-vivifies their hope. In the Eucharist, the enduring sign of his presence, he discloses himself to them, as he will to all ages.

FOCUS
The new creation, Jesus, Lord and Messiah, is the key to life lived in God. He (Jesus) establishes us as God's children and re-orients our perspective, redirecting it from ego-centered to theo-centered, and so divests us of our old patterns of approaching him, and sets us on a new path and direction. The Eucharist, his sign and manifestation of presence among us, helps us to experience his life in our midst.

IDEA STARTERS
- *CCT Lectionary:* Acts 2:14a, 36-41; Ps 116:12-19; I Pt 1:17-23, Lk 24:13-35.
- Today's Gospel gives us an account of an informal liturgy. Jesus greets the disciples, talks with them, interprets the scriptures for them, and hears their prayers of anguish over the events in their world. The gathering comes to a climactic conclusion in the breaking of bread. Then, the disciples run out to tell others the Good News. "Lord, be known to us in the breaking of the bread!"
- Evaluate your liturgical space. Is the table of God's Word (ambo) equal in dignity, honor, and respect as given to the table of the Blessed Sacrament (altar)?
- Evaluate your ritual celebration. Is the homily a time when God's Word is "broken and given" to the listeners? Is the Fraction Rite of the Mass always seen as an important action, to be *noticed* by the assembly?
- It would be appropriate to schedule celebrations of the First Eucharist to coincide with today's Lectionary and this season of full initiation into the Church.
- For your further consideration: Alternative Opening Prayer; Intercessions for proper use of charismatic gifts, good action, an end to injustice, counselors, prophets, soujourners, and neophytes; Easter Preface V (P 25); Memorial Acclamation C; Easter Solemn Blessing.

MUSIC

- Psalm 16
- *Breaking of the Bread* (Feiten/Resource)
- *Gather Us In* (Haugen/GIA)
- *Here Is My Life* (Wise/GIA)
- *I the Living Bread* (Mullins/Resource)
- *In Those Days* (Deiss/NALR)

- *In Him We Live* (Landry/NALR)
- *The Seed That Falls* (Lisicky/Resource)
- *Our Blessing Cup* (Joncas/NALR)
- *Praise the Lord, My Soul* (Parker/GIA)
- *This Bread* (Conry/NALR)
- *God and Man at Table* (Stamps/Dawn Teacher)

EASTER PLANNING SHEET

Date _____

Parish focus _____

Environment & art _____

Ritual notes _____

Faith development (eg., midweek program) _____

Children's faith experience _____

Prelude _____

Hymn of gathering _____

Sprinkling baptismal water acclamation _____

Opening Prayer _____

Reading cycle _____First reading _____

Responsory _____Second reading _____

Lenten gospel acclamation _____Gospel _____

RCIA rites & acclamations _____

General intercessions _____

At the preparation & presentation _____

Preface dialog _____Preface _____

Preface acclamation _____

Eucharistic prayer _____Memorial acclamation _____

Eucharistic amen _____

The Lord's prayer _____

Breaking of bread _____

The communion hymn _____

The post-communion hymn _____

Blessing _____At the dismissal _____

Memoranda:

FOURTH SUNDAY OF EASTER

YEAR A

READINGS

Acts of the Apostles (2:14,36–41)
In this reading we see the community response to Peter's proclamation of Jesus as Messiah and Lord. "What are we to do?" Baptism is the response. Entrance into Jesus' death through the regenerative waters of Baptism unites us to Christ and enables us to receive his Spirit.

First Peter (2:20–25)
Christ is the model for Christian behavior. Loving quiet obedience is his sign of self-sacrifice. His alacrity to do God's will has turned us from straying sheep to the flock held in the embrace of the Good Shepherd.

John (10:1–10)
Jesus points to himself as sheepgate and shepherd, the pastor of the flock and the only way to God. In the intimacy of his love, where we are known by name (i.e., for who and what we are), he lovingly cares for and directs us. There is no other path of salvation outside of the Christ!

FOCUS

Through the ages, Jesus, the Shepherd of Souls and Sheepgate or pathway to salvation, is the only response to the question, "How are we to be saved?" By his loving obedience to God's will he has rejuvenated creation. He gives us his solemn word that if we will live his law of love, we will dwell with God through eternity and beyond.

IDEA STARTERS

- *CCT Lectionary:* Acts 2:42-47; Ps 23; I Pt 2:19-25; Jn 10:1-10.
- Today's readings provide a source for a homily or bulletin article about our role in the church. Church vocations, ordained, religious, and lay workers, all have a share in leading their fellow Christians to the shepherd at the gate.
- At a children's Liturgy of the Word, dramatize today's Gospel passage.
- It would be appropriate for the bishop to gather the neophytes for a celebration of a Cathedral Eucharist using today's lectionary.
- In the bulletin discuss the meaning of the word "pastor" and a pastor's work in the church of God.
- For your further consideration: Alternative Opening Prayer; Intercessions for perseverance in the faith, for mothers, neophytes, the suffering and oppressed, forgiveness, and living in eternal life; Easter Preface II (P 22); Eucharistic Prayer III; Memorial Acclamation B; Easter Solemn Blessing.

MUSIC

- Psalm 23
- *At The Lamb's High Feast* (ICEL)
- *Be Glad, O People* (Weston Priory)
- *Be Not Afraid* (Jesuits/NALR)
- *Come to the Waters* (Gildorf/Resource)
- *Come to Me* (Hummer/Resource)
- *I Saw the Living Water* (Deiss/NALR)
- *Like A Shepherd* (Jesuits/NALR)
- *The Lord Is My Shepherd* (Wise/GIA)
- *Shepherd's Alleluia* (Landry/NALR)
- *You Are My Witnesses* (Fisherfolk/Resource)

EASTER PLANNING SHEET

Date _____

Parish focus _____

Environment & art _____

Ritual notes _____

Faith development (eg., midweek program) _____

Children's faith experience _____

Prelude _____

Hymn of gathering _____

Sprinkling baptismal water acclamation _____

Opening Prayer _____

Reading cycle _____ First reading _____

Responsory _____ Second reading _____

Lenten gospel acclamation _____ Gospel _____

RCIA rites & acclamations _____

General intercessions _____

At the preparation & presentation _____

Preface dialog _____ Preface _____

Preface acclamation _____

Eucharistic prayer _____ Memorial acclamation _____

Eucharistic amen _____

The Lord's prayer _____

Breaking of bread _____

The communion hymn _____

The post-communion hymn _____

Blessing _____ At the dismissal _____

Memoranda:

FIFTH SUNDAY OF EASTER YEAR A

READINGS
Acts of the Apostles (6:1-7)
Any conflict can be resolved if the Spirit of Love is included in the process of discernment. The institution of the deaconate is the result of the early community responding to the movement of the Spirit, even in the midst of its anger and argument over the distribution of food. The community's openness to the Spirit enabled the Spirit to move through the corporate body and to grow in love as a result.
First Peter (2:4-9)
By Christ, the New Israel is the chosen, consecrated priest to the world. Its apostolate is the proclamation of Jesus, the one rejected, persecuted, and murdered as God's own son and the glory of the new creation.
John (14:1-12)
Jesus is the image of God. The reflected glory of God shines in the human face of the God-man. All who respond to his Word, follow his law of love, and imitate his example of self-sacrificing love see God and live in his life of love.

FOCUS
Jesus, the way, the truth, and the life, is the only path to God. All those who acknowledge this become consecrated to his service and bear the mark of his love to the world. The Spirit of God dwells in them and they live in his love. They become both signs and instruments of his love in the world, and they are forever growing into his body through the work of the Spirit in their lives.

IDEA STARTERS
- *CCT Lectionary:* Acts 7:55-60; Ps 31:1-8; I Pt 2:2-10; Jn 14:1-14.
- We celebrated Easter Day four weeks ago. Have we remained faithful to our Lenten resolutions? Are we still exuberant singing "alleluias from head to toe"?
- A homily or bulletin article about the priesthood of all believers may clear up questions in parishioners' minds.
- Religious education forums and classes may investigate, "Who (or what) is my way, my truth and my life?" Use values clarification exercises.
- The Acts 6 passage provides a kick-off for a study of deacons:permanent and transitional. Honor your deacons with a special coffee hour after today's liturgy.
- For your consideration: Opening Prayer; Intercessions for widow(er)s, the hungry, the ordained and religious, waiters and waitresses, neophytes, and the life of the world to come; Easter Preface III (P 23); Eucharistic Prayer I; Memorial Acclamation A; Easter Solemn Blessing.

MUSIC
- Psalm 33
- *As the Father Has Sent Me* (O'Brien/Resource)
- *Eye Has Not Seen* (Haugen/GIA)
- *Go Out To the Whole World* (Gilsdorf/Resource)
- *In Those Days* (Deiss/NALR)
- *Jesus, Remember Me* (Taize/GIA)
- *Let the Earth Resound* (Deiss/NALR)

- *Lord of the Dance* (Carter/Galliard)
- *May We Praise* (Jesuits/NALR)
- *Litany of Praise* (Antioch/K&R)
- *Our Life and Our Song* (Conry/NALR)

- *Praise Canticle* (Haas/Cooperative Ministries)
- *Sing of Christ, Proclaim* (ICEL)
- The Truth Will Make You Free (Gilsdorf/Resource)

EASTER PLANNING SHEET   Date _____

Parish focus _____

Environment & art _____

Ritual notes _____

Faith development (eg., midweek program) _____

Children's faith experience _____

Prelude _____

Hymn of gathering _____

Sprinkling baptismal water acclamation _____

Opening Prayer _____

Reading cycle _____ First reading _____

Responsory _____ Second reading _____

Lenten gospel acclamation _____ Gospel _____

RCIA rites & acclamations _____

General intercessions _____

At the preparation & presentation _____

Preface dialog _____ Preface _____

Preface acclamation _____

Eucharistic prayer _____ Memorial acclamation _____

Eucharistic amen _____

The Lord's prayer _____

Breaking of bread _____

The communion hymn _____

The post-communion hymn _____

Blessing _____ At the dismissal _____

Memoranda:

SIXTH SUNDAY OF EASTER   YEAR A

READINGS
Acts of the Apostles (8:5–8,14–17)
In the reading from Acts we see individual apostles serving the people of Samaria. First, Philip brings them the Good News of the Lord Jesus. That accomplished, Peter and John, through the imposition of hands, confirm the community, baptizing them in the Spirit.

First Peter (3:15–18)
The Lord Jesus suffered death so we might be led to God. Our lives as Christians must be patterned on his. No person should find us acting in ways which do not reflect his life. Living as Jesus did will determine that even our sufferings become sacred, for through him they will be offered to God.

John (14:15–21)
Jesus, the promised one, pledges to send the Paraclete, the Holy Spirit. The Holy Spirit will be a constant presence for us, our advocate with God and our support in the world. Jesus concludes by reminding us that we can know those who love him by their actions. Those who follow his Law are loved by God and enjoy the revelation of the Lord himself.

FOCUS
Today's readings point to the fullness of life for the Christian. Jesus can only come fully alive for us if we are open to and subsequently filled with his Spirit. First we proclaim him as Lord, then his Spirit is poured out on us.

IDEA STARTERS
- *CCT Lectionary:* Acts 17:22–31; Ps 66:8–20; I Pt 3:13–22; Jn 14:15–21.
- Jesus speaks of unity in today's Gospel. Have a parish picnic this holiday weekend. Let the rejoicing in fellowship rise "to a fever pitch."
- Today's readings lend themselves to a parish sacramental celebration of Confirmation.
- An adult forum on conscience and authority may clear up the false notion viewing conscience as license.
- Gather last year's neophytes for an anniversary of baptism celebration. Have them plan the parish celebration honoring this year's neophytes. (See *Rite of Christian Initiation of Adults* (RCIA), nos. 237–238.)
- For your consideration: Opening Prayer; Intercessions for charismatic healers, preachers, priests, bishops, those preparing for confirmation, the neophytes, the suffering, stewardship of God's creation, openness to the Spirit's power; Easter Preface IV (P 24); Eucharistic Prayer II; Memorial Acclamation B; Easter Solemn Blessing.

MUSIC
- Psalm 66
- *All Those Who Love Me* (Weston Priory)
- *Come Holy Spirit* (Culbreth/Resource)
- *Jubilate, Servite* (Taize/GIA)
- *Heart of a Servant* (Mullins/Resource)
- *Yahweh* (Weston Priory)
- *Let All the Earth* (Haugen/GIA)
- *And the Father Will Dance* (Landry/NALR)
- *Blest Be the Lord* (Jesuits/NALR)
- *Dwelling Place* (Jesuits/NALR)
- *Only A Shadow* (Landry/NALR)
- *We're Going On a Picnic* (White/Resources)

EASTER PLANNING SHEET

Date _____

Parish focus _____

Environment & art _____

Ritual notes _____

Faith development (eg., midweek program) _____

Children's faith experience _____

Prelude _____

Hymn of gathering _____

Sprinkling baptismal water acclamation _____

Opening Prayer _____

Reading cycle _____ First reading _____

Responsory _____ Second reading _____

Lenten gospel acclamation _____ Gospel _____

RCIA rites & acclamations _____

General intercessions _____

At the preparation & presentation _____

Preface dialog _____ Preface _____

Preface acclamation _____

Eucharistic prayer _____ Memorial acclamation _____

Eucharistic amen _____

The Lord's prayer _____

Breaking of bread _____

The communion hymn _____

The post-communion hymn _____

Blessing _____ At the dismissal _____

Memoranda:

SOLEMNITY OF THE ASCENSION

YEAR A

READINGS
Acts of the Apostles (1:1-11)
The Ascension is the transition from Christ's activity as Savior on earth to the continuation of his ministry by the church as the "saving community."
Ephesians (1:17-23)
The celebration of the Ascension is not a celebration of his departure, but of his exultation to God's right hand.
Matthew (28:16-20)
Through his death and resurrection, Jesus has been given lordship over heaven and earth by the Father. His return to the right hand of the Father in his Ascension is a necessary part of his saving act.

The Ascension is not a departure from his people. Rather, through the Ascension, the disciples are assured of Christ's continuing presence.

FOCUS
The Ascension of Jesus, his return to the Father's right hand, is an integral part of his death, resurrection and continuing presence with the church. If he does not go, the Spirit cannot come.

IDEA STARTERS
- *CCT Lectionary:* Acts 1:1-11; Eph 1:15-23; Lk 24:46-53 or Mk 16:9-16, 19-20.
- How are departures in our lives, the coming and goings of friends and family, the death of loved one's, salvific? Perhaps this could serve as the topic of a bulletin article.
- Highlight the message in today's liturgy that by his departure Jesus passes on his ministry to we who are his Church.
- Today is a celebration of Christ's glory. Let today's liturgy reflect this theme through the use of music, signs, symbols and rituals that express Christ's magnificence.
- For your consideration: Intercessions for absent friends, the church, missionaries, the neophytes, orphans.

MUSIC
- Psalm 47
- *All The Ends of the Earth* (Foster/Resource)
- *As the Father Has Sent Me* (O'Brien/Resource)
- *Jubilate, Servite* (Taize/GIA)
- *Heart of a Servant* (Mullins/Resource)
- *Let All the Earth* (Haugen/GIA)
- *The Radiance of His Glory* (Toolan/Resource)
- *They Knew Him* (Gilsdorf/Resource)
- *Only A Shadow* (Landry/NALR)
- *We're Going On a Picnic* (White/Resources)

EASTER PLANNING SHEET

Date _____

Parish focus _____

Environment & art _____

Ritual notes _____

Faith development (eg., midweek program) _____

Children's faith experience _____

Prelude _____

Hymn of gathering _____

Sprinkling baptismal water acclamation _____

Opening Prayer _____

Reading cycle _____First reading _____

Responsory _____Second reading _____

Lenten gospel acclamation _____Gospel _____

RCIA rites & acclamations _____

General intercessions _____

At the preparation & presentation _____

Preface dialog _____Preface _____

Preface acclamation _____

Eucharistic prayer _____Memorial acclamation _____

Eucharistic amen _____

The Lord's prayer _____

Breaking of bread _____

The communion hymn _____

The post-communion hymn _____

Blessing _____At the dismissal _____

Memoranda:

SEVENTH SUNDAY OF EASTER

YEAR A

READINGS
Acts of the Apostles (1:12-14)
After the Lord's Ascension the apostles gather together with Mary, his mother, and await the outpouring of his Spirit.
First Peter (4:13-16)
Christ is the source of all joy and all consolation. Even if we suffer humiliation we know that he is with us, guiding us, giving us the ability to unite our suffering with his and therefore to see it as redemptive. Suffering for Christ is heroic and a source for glory.
John (17:1-11)
The hour of glorification for Jesus is the paschal mystery. Jesus asks God to glorify him not for his own good but for the good of those who believe in him, that their faith might be rewarded and they will be enabled to experience the fullness of life.

FOCUS
From suffering to glory, from sorrow to joy, from anticipation to fulfillment, all these seem to be keys to today's celebration. There is an adventine quality to the liturgy, appropriate since we await the descent of the Spirit. In any anticipatory moment there is a sense of pain and suffering, if only the desire to have the fullness of what (or whom) is hoped for. The Paschal Mystery is the ultimate form of this kind of experience. Through agony and pain, victory and glory are revealed. Paul points out that as the master does so also must the disciples. We should expect our glory to be the product of suffering. We can be courageous in this, since Jesus has walked this path before us and is present to us as we walk it now.

IDEA STARTERS
- *CCT Lectionary:* Acts 1:6-14; Ps 68:1-10; I Pt 4:12-15, 5:6-11; Jn 17:1-11.
- The days between Ascension and Pentecost are customarily marked by a novena of prayers for preparation for the commemoration of Pentecost. Look forward to the re-creation of God's earth.
- These days are the second time during the year the universal church prays for the unity of the churches by the power of Christ's Spirit. Announce ecumenical observances in the bulletin.
- It may be appropriate to have a minister from a neighboring parish share a homily at today's liturgy.
- Involve children from a local Christian orphanage in today's worship. Take an offering for the home. We must never forget them.
- For your consideration: Opening Prayer; Intercessions for travellers, religious and laity devoted to prayer, security in the Lord, just law and authority, orphans, neophytes, unity, eternal life; Reconciliation Eucharistic Prayer II; Memorial Acclamation C; Ascension Solemn Blessing (adapted).

MUSIC

- Psalm 27
- *Your Love Is Forever* (Dameans/NALR)
- *One Thing I Ask* (Jesuits/NALR)
- *Alleluia, My Word* (Wise/GIA)
- *All I Ask of You* (Weston Priory)
- *Eye Has Not Seen* (Haugen /GIA)
- *Let Us Walk in the Light* (Haugen/GIA)
- *We Are Called* (Patterson/Resource)
- *Sing A New Song* (Jesuits/NALR)
- *You Are My Witnesses* (Fisherfolk/Resource)
- *The Dawn of Day* (Deiss/NALR)
- *Sing Alleluia Sing* (Dameans/NALR)
- *Alleluia the Lord of Love* (Repp/K&R)
- *Hail the Day that Sees Him Rise* (ICEL)
- *Come Holy Spirit* (Culbreth/Resource)

EASTER PLANNING SHEET

Date _____

Parish focus _____

Environment & art _____

Ritual notes _____

Faith development (eg., midweek program) _____

Children's faith experience _____

Prelude _____

Hymn of gathering _____

Sprinkling baptismal water acclamation _____

Opening Prayer _____

Reading cycle _____ First reading _____

Responsory _____ Second reading _____

Lenten gospel acclamation _____ Gospel _____

RCIA rites & acclamations _____

General intercessions _____

At the preparation & presentation _____

Preface dialog _____ Preface _____

Preface acclamation _____

Eucharistic prayer _____ Memorial acclamation _____

Eucharistic amen _____

The Lord's prayer _____

Breaking of bread _____

The communion hymn _____

The post-communion hymn _____

Blessing _____ At the dismissal _____

Memoranda:

SOLEMNITY
OF PENTECOST

YEARS
A, B AND C

READINGS
Acts of the Apostles (2:1-11)
The familiar story of the Pentecost event is placed before us. The driving wind, reminiscent of Ezekiel, the tongues of fire, the inversion of the Babel story, the firing of the hearts of the timorous, and the illumination of thousands to the fact of God's love for humanity, all are signs of the outpouring of the Spirit on the world.

First Corinthians (12:3-7,12-13)
No one can proclaim Jesus as Lord except under the direct inspiration of the Spirit. This is the same Spirit which binds the members of the Body, from many into one. The many gifts given to persons are bestowed on their bearers for the good of the Body. In the Spirit both the gift and the person are enabled to develop to their fullest.

John (20:19-23)
The Spirit calms the troubled hearts of the apostles and encourages their timid hearts. It enables them to become liberators of the hearts of persons, through the sacramental healing Jesus bestows on them. The Spirit is indeed a balm for humanity.

FOCUS
Veni Lumen Corida seems to be the theme of today's Eucharist. The Spirit heals division and brings light to all hearts. It enables us to experience the fullness of living as vital members in the body of Christ. In this body we are freed from the shackles of alienation and death and caught up in a pilgrimage to God. Healed of our own offenses we become healers for humanity, firing the earth with the invigorating love of God.

IDEA STARTERS
- *CCT Lectionary:* Acts 2:1-21 or Is 44:1-8; Ps 104:24-34;I Cor 12:3b-13 or Acts 2:1-21; Jn 20:19-23 or Jn 7:37-39.
- Today is the Eighth Sunday of Easter, the Fiftieth Day, Whitsunday, the Commemoration of the Descent of the Holy Spirit, a festival of the church. How do these different titles focus our attention on this day?
- Celebrate a Vigil of Pentecost with all the Vigil readings from the *Lectionary for Mass* incorporated into the "Office of Readings" (from the *Liturgy of the Hours*). Honor the neophytes baptized at Easter at this celebration; also have a pot-luck supper. See *RCIA*, no. 237.
- Even without neophytes, a celebration for the entire parish is appropriate. This is the day we celebrate *ourselves:* those infused by the power of the Spirit called to make the Kingdom of God a visible reality.
- Have a special festival Eucharist. Carry large banners with bells. Use incense. How can you involve members of the assembly in a special way? (What Epiphany has traditionally been to Christmas, Pentecost is to Easter.)
- For your further consideration: Opening Prayer; Sequence (sung); Intercessions for enthusiasm, those unable to speak, different ministries, unity, forgiveness, the neophytes; Pentecost Preface (P 28); Eucharistic Prayer I (w/propers); Memorial Acclamation D; Holy Spirit Solemn Blessing.

CYCLE A

MUSIC

- Psalm 104
- *Come Holy Spirit* (Culbreth/Resource)
- *Sequence: "Veni, Sancte Spiritus"* (ICEL)
- *Canticle of the Sun* (Haugen/GIA)
- *Gather Us In* (Haugen/GIA)
- *Morning Has Broken* (Farjeon)
- *Song of Gathering* (Wise/GIA)
- *Spirit of God* (Weston Priory)
- *Nothing Is Greater* (Toolan/Resource)
- *Send Us Your Spirit* (Haas/Cooperative Ministries)
- *New Life* (Malone/Resource)
- *In Praise of His Name* (Jesuits/NALR)
- *The Spirit is a-Movin'* (Landry/NALR)
- *The Love of God* (Deiss/NALR)
- *Send Us Your Spirit* (Kendzia/NALR)
- *There Is One Lord* (Dameans/NALR)
- *We Thank You, Father* (Weston Priory)

EASTER PLANNING SHEET   Date _____

Parish focus _____

Environment & art _____

Ritual notes _____

Faith development (eg., in newsletter/classes) _____

Children's faith experience _____

Prelude _____

Hymn of gathering _____

Sprinkling/Penitential rite _____

Hymn of praise _____

Opening Prayer _____

First reading _____ Responsory _____

Second reading _____ Gospel acclamation _____

Gospel _____ Profession of faith _____

General intercessions _____

At the preparation & presentation _____

Preface dialog _____ Preface _____

Preface acclamation _____

Eucharistic prayer _____ Memorial acclamation _____

Eucharistic amen _____

The Lord's prayer _____

Breaking of bread _____

The communion hymn _____

The post-communion hymn _____

Blessing _____ At the dismissal _____

Memoranda:

SOLEMNITY OF THE HOLY TRINITY
Sunday after Pentecost

YEAR A

READINGS
Exodus (34:4-6,8-9)
Throughout history God has attempted to reveal himself to people. The Sinai event was a tremendous advance in this process. Moses, Servant of God, hears God pronounce his name, and amidst great splendor is made aware that this great and magnificent God wishes to engage in an intimate relationship with the People of Israel. The transcendent reaches out to the finite.
Second Corinthians (13:11-13)
The incarnation has joined humanity and divinity. In the light of so great an act of love, we are enabled to live in gentle peace and loving harmony with one another. Without the gift of trinitarian love, this would never be possible.
John (3:16-18)
Jesus is the God of Sinai dwelling among humanity, Emmanuel. The act of the incarnation has changed human history and its approach to God. The search for intimacy between God and humanity is completed in Jesus. For those who accept him and struggle to live as he lived, the possibility of love is established.

FOCUS
Trinitarian love simply demonstrates the endless possibility and expression of and for love in the Godhead. Indeed God loves because love and God are one. Not content to stay trapped in "majesty and cloud," the transcendent becomes immanent. As our flesh, God enables us to share in divine life and by so doing demonstrates his profound capacity for love. Those who follow God can participate in the same kind of loving and life-giving experience.

IDEA STARTERS
- *CCT Lectionary:* Deut 4:32-40; Ps33:1-12; II Cor 13:5-14; Mat 28:16-20.
- The presider may appropriately chant the opening invocation, greeting, and Opening Prayer today.
- The assembly may appropriately sing the Hymn of Praise, "Glory to God."
- Have children design posters or banners of traditional symbols of the Holy Trinity (e.g., circles and shamrocks) and display them in the narthex.
- Celebrate Ecumenical Evening Prayer to end the feast day.
- The second lesson provides directives for sharing the peace of the Lord.
- Infant baptism may appropriately be celebrated at today's Eucharist.
- For your further consideration: Gathering Rites sung; Sprinkling Baptismal Water A; Opening Prayer; "Athanasian" Creed (in *Lutheran Book of Worship*); Intercessions for kindness, fidelity, openness, encouragement, forgiveness, the life everlasting; Trinity Preface (P 43) or Eucharistic Prayer IV; Ordinary Solemn Blessing II.

MUSIC

- Daniel 3:52-56
- *Dwelling Place* (Jesuits/NALR)
- *Glory and Praise* (Jesuits/NALR)
- *I Thank My God* (Andersen/Resource)
- *Praise the Lord, My Soul* (Jesuits/NALR)
- *The Fullness of God* (Andersen/Resource)
- *I Have Loved You* (Joncas/NALR)
- *God Is Love* (Hutson/Resource)
- *Remember Your Love* (Dameans/NALR)
- *Shalom* (Reagan/NALR)
- *Sing to God a Brand New Canticle* (Quinlan/NALR)
- *The Dawn of the Day* (Deiss/NALR)
- *Lift Up Your Hearts* (Jesuits/NALR)
- *You Will Draw Water* (Conry/NALR)
- *Be Glad, O People* (Weston Priory)
- *Happy Those Who Hear the Word of God* (Weston Priory)
- *We Thank You, Father* (Weston Priory)
- *I Will Sing* (Dyer/Celebration)
- *A Song of Blessing* (Wise/GIA)
- *One Lord* (Haas/Cooperative Ministries)
- *We Believe in One True God* (ICEL)
- *Our God Is Love* (Repp/K&R)

SUNDAY PLANNING SHEET   Date _____

Parish focus _____

Environment & art _____

Ritual notes _____

Faith development (eg., in newsletter/classes) _____

Children's faith experience _____

Prelude _____

Hymn of gathering _____

Sprinkling/Penitential rite _____

Hymn of praise _____

Opening Prayer _____

First reading _____ Responsory _____

Second reading _____ Gospel acclamation _____

Gospel _____ Profession of faith _____

General intercessions _____

At the preparation & presentation _____

Preface dialog _____ Preface _____

Preface acclamation _____

Eucharistic prayer _____ Memorial acclamation _____

Eucharistic amen _____

The Lord's prayer _____

Breaking of bread _____

The communion hymn _____

The post-communion hymn _____

Blessing _____ At the dismissal _____

Memoranda:

SOLEMNITY OF CORPUS CHRISTI
Sunday after Trinity

YEAR A

READINGS
Deuteronomy (8:2–3,14–16)
Moses reminds the people that God has provided for them from the beginning of the Exodus. Their hunger and thirst have been repeatedly assuaged, and this bounty is the sign and symbol of God's love and fidelity.
First Corinthians (10:16–17)
In the sacred bread and holy wine, the body, blood, soul, and divinity of Christ, we are united as one body and are knit together into the flesh and blood of the Risen Lord.
John (6:51–58)
Jesus is the "new manna" provided by God for God's people's sustenance. All those who eat the flesh and drink the blood of the Lord are infused with the life of the Trinity and freed to share in the love of the Godhead.

FOCUS
God approaches us on the level of our needs. God recognizes that people need to eat, to drink, and continually to be nourished, and fills our longings. Instead of stopping at our physical fulfillment, God assumes our human needs into a dimension beyond our dreams, and provides the opportunity to share his life and to love as he loves. The Eucharist is the embodiment of the paschal mystery celebrated through time.

IDEA STARTERS
- *CCT Lectionary* (Proper 7): Gn 28:10–17; Ps 91:1–10; Rom 5:12–19; Mat 10:24–33.
- A number of themes and readings are being used throughout the U.S. today. While Roman Catholics are celebrating the role of the Eucharist in Christian life, some Lutherans and Episcopalians are commemorating the Nativity of John the Baptist; still others are celebrating the Second Sunday after Pentecost. Where is the primacy of Sunday as Day of the Lord?
- Celebrate First Eucharist today at all parish Masses.
- Celebrate a eucharistic procession with a neighboring parish. See *Worship of the Eucharist and Holy Communion Outside of Mass.*
- It would be appropriate to re-commission eucharistic ministers on this day.
- If your parish seeks to implement the sharing of the Eucharist under the forms of bread and wine, today would be a good day to start.
- For your consideration: Choose the Opening Prayer based upon the focus of the homily; omit the Sequence; Intercessions for the hungry, nomads, street people, Christian community, sharing of our wealth, sustenance for life through faith; Holy Eucharist Preface II (P 48); Memorial Acclamation C; highlight the Breaking of the Bread; Ordinary Solemn Blessing V.

MUSIC

- Psalm 147
- *Look Beyond* (Dameans/NALR)
- *Our Blessing Cup* (Joncas/NALR)
- *Gift of Finest Wheat* (Kreutz/Westendorf)
- *I Am the Bread of Life* (Toolan/GIA)
- *Breaking of the Bread* (Feiten/Resource)
- *Share a Little Bit of Your Love* (Repp/K&R)
- *The Bread of Life* (Dicie/Resource)
- *The Bread of Our Days* (Goglia/Resource)
- *Praise to Our Victorious King* (Lindh/Augsburg)
- *Draw Near and Take the Body* (ICEL)
- *I Am the Living Bread* (Mullins/Resource)
- *O Living Bread from Heaven* (ICEL)
- *Gather Us In* (Haugen/GIA)
- *Here Is My Life* (Wise/GIA)
- *Hymn of the Lord's Supper* (Ivancic/GIA)
- *Jesus, in Our Hands* (Wise/GIA)
- *To Be Your Bread Now* (Haas/Cooperative Ministries)
- *Earthen Vessels* (Jesuits/NALR)
- *All That We Have* (Dameans/NALR)
- *A Banquet Is Prepared* (Jesuits/NALR)
- *God and Man at Table* (Stamps)
- *Jesus, the Bread of Life* (Brown/NALR)
- *One Bread, One Body* (Jesuits/NALR)
- *In Your Love Remember Me* (Kendzia/NALR)
- *The Bread of Rejoicing* (Deiss/NALR)

SUNDAY PLANNING SHEET   Date _____

Parish focus _____

Environment & art _____

Ritual notes _____

Faith development (eg., in newsletter/classes) _____

Children's faith experience _____

Prelude _____

Hymn of gathering _____

Sprinkling/Penitential rite _____

Hymn of praise _____

Opening Prayer _____

First reading _____ Responsory _____

Second reading _____ Gospel acclamation ____

Gospel _____ Profession of faith ____

General intercessions _____

At the preparation & presentation _____

Preface dialog _____ Preface _____

Preface acclamation _____

Eucharistic prayer _____ Memorial acclamation ___

Eucharistic amen _____

The Lord's prayer _____

Breaking of bread _____

The communion hymn _____

The post-communion hymn _____

Blessing _____ At the dismissal _____

Memoranda:

SOLEMNITY OF THE SACRED HEART
YEAR A
(Friday After The Second Sunday After Pentecost)

READINGS
Deuteronomy (7:6–11)
The description of the covenant in Deuteronomy was written about six hundred years after the event took place and reflects the situation in Israel shortly before the Babylonian exile. At this point the people had weakened and lost faith. The recalling of the gift of the Law to Moses emphasizes God's love in making them his chosen people.

First John (4:7–16)
It is only, ultimately, our love for one another that assures God's presence with us. This love is the only thing that will convince others that what we say is more than empty words.

Matthew (11:25–30)
Jesus' poverty of spirit calls us to a simplicity of outlook and life. He presents it as the only ultimate cure for the burdensomeness of lives filled with preoccupation with doing the right thing under the Law.

FOCUS
The compassion of God.

IDEA STARTERS
- For entrance procession, use Litany of the Sacred Heart of Jesus.
- Honor those who "labor in the vineyard," the social service ministers, with a low-key Evening Prayer and a wine and cheese reception afterwards.

MUSIC
- Psalm 103
- *The Lord Is Kind and Merciful* (Haugen/GIA)
- *Renewal Song* (Andersen/Resource)
- *How Good Is the Lord* (Landry/NALR)
- *Come to Me* (Hummer/Resource)
- *O Lord, Be Not Mindful* (Deiss/WLP)
- *Come to Me* (Johnson/Resource)
- *Our Help* (Oosterhuis/Huijbers/NALR)
- *New Life* (Lawrence/Resource)

PLANNING SHEET

Date _____

Parish focus _____

Environment & art _____

Ritual notes _____

Faith development (eg., in newsletter/classes) _____

Children's faith experience _____

Prelude _____

Hymn of gathering _____

Sprinkling/Penitential rite _____

Hymn of praise _____

Opening Prayer _____

First reading _____Responsory _____

Second reading _____Gospel acclamation _____

Gospel _____Profession of faith _____

General intercessions _____

At the preparation & presentation _____

Preface dialog _____Preface _____

Preface acclamation _____

Eucharistic prayer _____Memorial acclamation _____

Eucharistic amen _____

The Lord's prayer _____

Breaking of bread _____

The communion hymn _____

The post-communion hymn _____

Blessing _____At the dismissal _____

Memoranda:

SECOND SUNDAY OF THE YEAR

READINGS

Isaiah (49:3,5-6)
As we proceed in the liturgical year, moving into Ordinary Time, the church presents us with a continuation of Isaiah's servant songs, using the "Second Servant Song." The servant, Israel, speaks as an individual, describing his relationship to God and his mission. In verses 5 and 6, however, the servant tells us that he will "restore the survivors of Israel." We can see that the servant has become the ideal of faithful Israel.

First Corinthians (1:1-3)
In the salutation of his first letter to the Corinthians, Paul reiterates what we have been focusing on for the last few weeks. He (Paul) has been called to serve the church of Christ, composed of all people, consecrated in Christ Jesus, and called to be holy.

John (1:29-34)
John the Baptist uses an Isaian title, Lamb of God, to identify Jesus. For the writer of the fourth Gospel there is a touch of irony in the fact that, though John the Baptist preceded Jesus in his ministry, Jesus, in reality, existed before John and everything, sharing the same nature as the Father and Spirit: God!

FOCUS

Jesus is the Servant of Yahweh, Lamb of God. He calls all people to enter the church, his body, by accepting the call to holiness offered them by the Father through himself. John the Baptist testifies to the exaltation of the Son that "this is God's chosen one."

IDEA STARTERS

- *CCT Lectionary:* Is 49:1-7; Ps 40:1-11; 1 Cor 1:1-19; Jn 1:29-34.
- Using today's lessons, celebrate the Baptism of the Lord as a parish. Use white vestments. Baptize a child at today's liturgies.
- Newsletter possibilities: Paul's Letter to the Corinthians; John's Gospel doesn't mention the action of Jesus' baptism; "Lamb of God" — What does it mean and why is it used during the Mass?
- The liturgical calendar appoints the color green to be used throughout much of the year. Green, however, has different shades. Perhaps evergreen paramounts would fit in well with the winter season.
- Have your liturgy team discuss the use of the ICET version of the Agnus Dei. See *Prayers We Have in Common* (Revised), (Philadelphia: Fortress Press). Sing the litany "Lamb of God" during the breaking of bread and pouring of the cup.
- Observe Martin Luther King, Jr.'s birthday with an interfaith or ecumenical service.
- For your consideration: Rite of Baptism; Sprinkling Baptismal Water C (adapted); Alternate Opening Prayer (from Feast of the Lord's Baptism); Intercessions for contemporary prophets (Martin Luther King, Jr.), personal response to God's choosing us, the newly baptized and catechumens; Preface of Lord's Baptism (P7); Eucharistic Prayer I (w/Epiphany proper); Memorial Acclamation D; Ordinary solemn Blessing II.

MUSIC

- Psalm 40
- *Abba, Father* (Landry/NALR)
- *Anthem* (Conry/NALR)
- *Before the Sun Burned Bright* (Jesuits/NALR)
- *City of God* (Jesuits/NALR)
- *Come Let Us Join Our Cheerful Songs* (ICEL)
- *Earthen Vessels* (Jesuits/NALR)
- *Exult You Just Ones* (Jesuits/NALR)
- *Eye Has Not Seen* (Haugen/GIA)
- *Happy Are They* (Landry/NALR)
- *He Is the Lord* (Haas/Cooperative Ministries)
- *Here I Am, Lord* (Jesuits/NALR)
- *Here Is My Life* (Wise/GIA)
- *I Am the Living Bread* (Mullins/Resource)
- *I in Them* (Gilsdorf/Resource)
- *Jubilate Servite* (Taize/GIA)
- *Mighty Lord* (Jesuits/NALR)
- *1 Corinthians 1* (Mullins/Resource)
- *On Jordan's Bank* (ICEL)
- *Make Your Home in Me* (Gilsdorf/Resource)
- *Spirit of God* (Weston Priory)
- *Take My Life and Let It Be* (ICEL)
- *Though the Mountains May Fall* (Jesuits/NALR)
- *The Word Who Is Life* (Landry/NALR)

SUNDAY PLANNING SHEET   Date _____

Parish focus _____

Environment & art _____

Ritual notes _____

Faith development (eg., in newsletter/classes) _____

Children's faith experience _____

Prelude _____

Hymn of gathering _____

Sprinkling/Penitential rite _____

Hymn of praise _____

Opening Prayer _____

First reading _____ Responsory _____

Second reading _____ Gospel acclamation _____

Gospel _____ Profession of faith _____

General intercessions _____

At the preparation & presentation _____

Preface dialog _____ Preface _____

Preface acclamation _____

Eucharistic prayer _____ Memorial acclamation _____

Eucharistic amen _____

The Lord's prayer _____

Breaking of bread _____

The communion hymn _____

The post-communion hymn _____

Blessing _____ At the dismissal _____

Memoranda:

THIRD SUNDAY
OF THE YEAR

YEAR A

READINGS
Isaiah (8:23-9:3)
Isaiah states that the birth of a new prince, who will continue the Davidic line, is indeed a gift of God and cause for rejoicing. References to Zebulun, Naphtali and Galilee more than likely refer to territories taken by the Assyrians after 734 B.C.E., obviously dwelling in the darkness and awaiting deliverance.
First Corinthians (1:10-13,17)
The cross of Christ, the ultimate act of service and love, is the center of the Gospel. Splitting into factions and party loyalties are not only unimportant, but destructive. They distract attention from what is of most import: the living of the Gospel of Christ.
Matthew (4:12-23)
Following the arrest of the Precursor, Jesus begins his ministry. First he goes to Galilee, looked down upon by cosmopolitan Judea, and calls his first apostles. These men will be instrumental in establishing the church founded by Christ.

FOCUS
Jesus is the light which those in darkness see. He brings to all the Good News of salvation and there is nothing of greater import than this. Each individual, from the great Baptist, to the apostles, to their disciples, are only members working to build up the Lord's body: his bride the church, founded by him.

IDEA STARTERS
* *CCT Lectionary:* Is 9:1-4; Ps 27:1-6; 1 Cor 1:10-17; Mt 4:12-23.
* Today formally begins the series of pericopes from Matthew. Give biblical commentary through the bulletin or an adult forum.
* You may wish to (re)commission readers to "proclaim the good news of the Kingdom" after today's homily.
* The illustration of metanoia given in the Gospel should reawaken God's call to each one of us: "Repent and follow!"
* For your consideration: Penitential Rite C-v;Alternative Opening Prayer; Gospel (long form); Intercessions for peace and joy among all peoples, trust and comfort in the Lord, hope for the future, conversion, Christian mission; Ordinary Sundays Preface I (P29); Eucharistic Prayer III; Memorial Acclamation D; epiphany Solemn Blessing (adapted).

MUSIC

- Psalm 27
- People of God (Deiss/NALR)
- *The Apostles' Song* (Shade/K&R)
- *Church of God* (ICEL)
- *Come To Me* (Johnson/Resource)
- *Come Unto Me, All Who Are Weary* (Jesuits/NALR)
- *Come With Me Into the Fields* (Jesuits/NALR)
- *The Eternal Gifts of Love* (Prezio/K&R)
- *The Goodness of God* (Weston Priory)
- *How Beautiful on the Mountains* (Deiss/NALR)
- *I Am the Light* (Repp/K&R)
- *The Kingdom of God* (Deiss/NALR)
- *Let All the World With Songs Rejoice* (ICEL)
- *Let Us Walk In the Light of the Lord* (Haugen/Quiet Breeze)
- *Light of the World* (Kendzia/NALR)
- *Like a Sunflower* (Landry/NALR)
- *Nothing Is Greater* (Toolan/Resource)
- *The People That in Darkness Walked* (ICEL)
- *Rise Up, Jerusalem* (Jesuits/NALR)
- *Seek the Lord* (Jesuits/NALR)
- *Service* (Dameans/NALR)
- *Sing Out His Goodness* (Dameans/NALR)
- *Sing Out in Thanksgiving* (Jabusch/NALR)
- *We Are Called* (Patterson/Resource)

SUNDAY PLANNING SHEET   Date _____

Parish focus _____

Environment & art _____

Ritual notes _____

Faith development (eg., in newsletter/classes) _____

Children's faith experience _____

Prelude _____

Hymn of gathering _____

Sprinkling/Penitential rite _____

Hymn of praise _____

Opening Prayer _____

First reading _____ Responsory _____

Second reading _____ Gospel acclamation _____

Gospel _____ Profession of faith _____

General intercessions _____

At the preparation & presentation _____

Preface dialog _____ Preface _____

Preface acclamation _____

Eucharistic prayer _____ Memorial acclamation _____

Eucharistic amen _____

The Lord's prayer _____

Breaking of bread _____

The communion hymn _____

The post-communion hymn _____

Blessing _____ At the dismissal _____

Memoranda:

FOURTH SUNDAY
OF THE YEAR

YEAR A

READINGS
Zephania (2:3,3:12-13)
For Zephania, the "Day of the Lord" was a day of judgment of the nations and of the People of God themselves for their unfaithfulness. The humiliation of God's people will serve a double purpose: it will traumatically force Israel to reassess her infidelity and return to the Lord and, in making the Lord her sole protection, will serve as a sign to the nations of Yahweh's might and love for those who place their trust in him.

First Corinthians (1:26-31)
Centuries later Paul reiterates the message of Zephania to the troubled and scandal-ridden Corinthian Church. By raising up the lowly, the humbled and those despised among the Corinthians, God glorifies himself.

Matthew (5:1-12)
In Matthew's account of the Sermon on the Mount, Jesus presents us with the "New Law" under which the humbled and despised ones live. Each Beatitude is a renunciation of what the world holds as wisdom.

FOCUS
Perhaps an appropriate title or motto for this Sunday would be the old spiritual maxim *Per Crucem ad Lucem.* All three readings, in a most beautiful and concise way, blend the concept that acknowledging that God is the One who is the source of everything, that only through sacrificing our will to his can we ever become that which we truly are. Such a perspective insures life and an infusion of divine love.

IDEA STARTERS
- *CCT Lectionary:* Mic 6:1-8; Ps 37:1-11; 1 Cor 1:18-31; Mt 5:1-12.
- Beginning today, until Lent, the Gospel passages will be from the Sermon on the Mount. A bulletin article or series about the Church's application of Jesus' ethical teachings may prove worthwhile.
- A suggestion for a bulletin article: "Jesus: Matthew's New Moses." Explain the traditional biblical symbols employed by Matthew in chapters 5-7.
- The Beatitudes are usually an important part of catechetical instruction. How might you involve students studying the Beatitudes in today's liturgy?
- Use the processional cross and decorated lectionary as a reminder of our boast in the Lord.
- For your consideration: Alternative Opening Prayer; Intercessions for humility, justice, the hungry, oppressed, captives, the blind, the just and wicked, for wisdom, the poor, consolation, peacemakers; Eucharistic Prayer IV; Ordinary Solemn Blessing IV.

MUSIC

- Psalm 146
- *All That We Have* (Dameans/NALR)
- *Amazing Grace* (ICEL)
- *Beatitudes* (any setting)
- *Be Not Afraid* (Jesuits/NALR)
- *Bless, O Lord, Your People* (Pinson/NALR)
- *Breathe On Me, O Breath of God* (ICEL)
- *Come to the Water* (Jesuits/NALR)
- *Eagle's Wings* (Andersen/Resource)
- *Gather Us In* (Haugen/GIA)
- *Glory and Praise* (Jesuits/NALR)
- *If God Is For Us* (Jesuits/NALR)
- *In Those Days* (Deiss/NALR)
- *Like a Shepherd* (Jesuits/NALR)
- *Lord, To Whom Shall We Go?* (Joncas/NALR)
- *Magnificat* (any setting)
- *My Peace, My Love, My Joy* (Page/Resource)
- *0 Christ Our Hope* (ICEL)
- *Peace Is Flowing Like A River* (Landry/NALR)
- *Praise the Lord, My Soul* (Parker/GIA)
- *Sing to God a Brand New Canticle* (Quinlan/NALR)
- *Taste and See* (Haugen/GIA)
- *That There May Be Bread* (Weston Priory)
- *You Are Near* (Jesuits/NALR)
- *Zephania's Song* (Andersen/Resource)

SUNDAY PLANNING SHEET

Date _____

Parish focus _____

Environment & art _____

Ritual notes _____

Faith development (eg., in newsletter/classes) _____

Children's faith experience _____

Prelude _____

Hymn of gathering _____

Sprinkling/Penitential rite _____

Hymn of praise _____

Opening Prayer _____

First reading _____ Responsory _____

Second reading _____ Gospel acclamation _____

Gospel _____ Profession of faith _____

General intercessions _____

At the preparation & presentation _____

Preface dialog _____ Preface _____

Preface acclamation _____

Eucharistic prayer _____ Memorial acclamation _____

Eucharistic amen _____

The Lord's prayer _____

Breaking of bread _____

The communion hymn _____

The post-communion hymn _____

Blessing _____ At the dismissal _____

Memoranda:

FIFTH SUNDAY
OF THE YEAR

YEAR A

READINGS
Isaiah (58:7-10)
The desire for and establishment of justice is the way to ensure the life of the Lord in the individual's life. Concern for the hungry, oppressed, all who are disenfranchised, is the only way to allow the Lord's light to shine through you. Once this happens, you become the reflection of the light who brightens the dark.
First Corinthians (2:1-5)
Paul states that for the Christian, the only wisdom is that of the cross. From a sign of repudiation and failure, God reconciled humanity to himself: failure is victory. Christian faith rests on this great incongruity and, in consequence, rejects the supposed wisdom of the world.
Matthew (5:13-16)
Christians are the light which brightens the world and the salt which seasons it! They function in such a way so that all might be brought to a greater knowledge of and love for God.

FOCUS
Light from wisdom seems to be a major concept of today's scripture readings. This wisdom is in direct contrast to the wisdom of the world and so makes those who follow it enemies of the world, the very world which needs their light and seasoning to keep from the darkness and insipidity of life lived without God, in sin.

IDEA STARTERS
- *CCT Lectionary:* Is 58:3-9a; Ps 112:4-9;I Cor 2:1-11; Mat 5:13-16.
- Today's readings suitably call your parishioners to respond to the needs of others. Promote contributions to food and clothing drives, St. Vincent de Paul Societies, etc.
- The readings for the day stress the Epiphany theme of light: we are called to be manifestations of our Risen Lord.
- Could celebrating the ritual for blessing candles found in the *Sacramentary* for February 2 be adapted for use today?
- At a children's liturgy, stress the salt and light themes from the Gospel. How might you visually illustrate the light? Would a no-salt/some-salt/too-much-salt "taste test" further incarnate God's Word to the children?
- Do a historical study of the rites at the Preparation of the Altar and the Presentation of the Gifts (formerly called the Offertory). Have members of the assembly bring up some gifts for the needy.
- For your consideration: Opening Prayer; Intercessions for the hungry, oppressed and homeless, for openness to the Lord and those around us, spiritual wisdom, faithful witness to the glory of God; Ordinary Sundays Preface I (P29) or Eucharistic Prayer IV; Ordinary Solemn Blessing III.

MUSIC

- Psalm 112
- *Awake O Sleeper* (Dameans/NALR)
- *Be Glad, Be Happy* (Gilsdorf/Resource)
- *City of God* (Jesuits/NALR)
- *Father, Hear the Prayer We Offer* (ICEL)
- *Glory and Praise* (Jesuits/NALR)
- *I Am the Light* (Repp/K&R)
- *Jubilate Deo* (Taize/GIA)
- *The Lord is My Light* (Rousseau/Resource)
- *One Lord* (Haas/Cooperative Ministries)
- *Processional Song* (Toolan/Resource)
- *Sing Out His Goodness* (Dameans/NALR)
- *What You Hear in the Dark* (Jesuits/NALR)

SUNDAY PLANNING SHEET   Date _____

Parish focus _____

Environment & art _____

Ritual notes _____

Faith development (eg., in newsletter/classes) _____

Children's faith experience _____

Prelude _____

Hymn of gathering _____

Sprinkling/Penitential rite _____

Hymn of praise _____

Opening Prayer _____

First reading _____Responsory _____

Second reading _____Gospel acclamation _____

Gospel _____Profession of faith _____

General intercessions _____

At the preparation & presentation _____

Preface dialog _____Preface _____

Preface acclamation _____

Eucharistic prayer _____Memorial acclamation _____

Eucharistic amen _____

The Lord's prayer _____

Breaking of bread _____

The communion hymn _____

The post-communion hymn _____

Blessing _____At the dismissal _____

Memoranda:

SIXTH SUNDAY OF THE YEAR

YEAR A

READINGS

Sirach (15:15-20)
The passage from Sirach presents us with a picture of God as the Mighty One, who is all-wise, all-knowing and all-good. God sets before us the decision of choosing him (life) or death. The reading makes it clear that God wishes us to choose life, but will not force us; the decision is our own.

First Corinthians (2:6-10)
Paul tells the Corinthians that the wisdom which Christians possess is not a wisdom of the age, limited in its vision to the perspective of humanity. Rather it is a wisdom which emanates from the very body of the crucified one and is the manifestation of God's glory. This wisdom prepares those who receive it to enter the fullness of life.

Matthew (5:17-37)
In this exegesis on the Beatitudes, Jesus challenges those who would follow him to go beyond the mere prescriptions of the Law, which bind people to a sin-condition and to fulfill the Law by surpassing it. Thus, we must not simply refrain from physical murder, but must also not kill with our tongue. We cannot engage in the actions of ritual and ceremony if our worship of God is not displayed in our relationships with brothers and sisters. If we live like this we will have no need for ostentation in our speech (e.g., unnecessary oaths). Rather, we will be able to say yes or no, because our words will gain credibility from our actions.

FOCUS
The author of wisdom has sent his wisdom into the world. Though he was rejected and crucified, he turned apparent defeat into victory and now lives forever. Those who accept the invitation to share in this life bear this wisdom in their very bodies. Their actions display the effects of this wisdom. They transcend legal proscriptions by inculcating values which are Jesus' own. These values stress ultimate trust in God, loving care for people, and a vision which looks to the Eschaton as its omega point.

IDEA STARTERS
- *CCT Lectionary:* Deut 30:15-20 or Eccl 15:15-20; Ps 119:1-8; I Cor 3:1-9; Mat 5:17-26.
- Continuing the study of the Preparation of the Gifts, following the litany of Intercessions, conclude with the collect from the Rite of Peace, and share the peace "before bringing your gifts to the altar."
- An adult forum may study the role of the Law in contemporary Judaism. Invite a rabbi from the neighborhood synagogue.
- The long form of the Gospel illustrates the "heart of the law" which is Jesus' call to perfection.
- What is the mystery, the hidden wisdom which God has revealed to us?
- For your consideration: Alternative Opening Prayer; Gospel (long form); Intercessions for loyalty and faithfulness, personal spiritual growth, peace among nations, the kingdom of God in our midst, reconciliation, truth; Ordinary Sundays Preface VIII IV.

MUSIC

- Psalm 119
- *Alleluia, Your Word* (Deiss/NALR)
- *As the Father Has Sent Me* (O'Brien/Resource)
- *Come to Me, All Who Are Weary* (Jesuits/NALR)
- *Earthen Vessels* (Jesuits/NALR)
- *Eye Has Not Seen* (Haugen/GIA)
- *Lord, To Whom Shall We Go?* (Conry/NALR)
- *Lord, To Whom Shall We Go?* (Joncas/NALR)
- *On the Road* (Wood/Resource)
- *Song of the Exile* (Haugen/GIA)
- *Speak, Lord* (Dameans/NALR)
- *That There May be Bread* (Weston Priory)
- *To Be Your Bread* (Haas/Cooperative Ministries)
- *We Are Called* (Pattersen/Resource)

SUNDAY PLANNING SHEET   Date _____

Parish focus _____

Environment & art _____

Ritual notes _____

Faith development (eg., in newsletter/classes) _____

Children's faith experience _____

Prelude _____

Hymn of gathering _____

Sprinkling/Penitential rite _____

Hymn of praise _____

Opening Prayer _____

First reading _____Responsory _____

Second reading _____Gospel acclamation _____

Gospel _____Profession of faith _____

General intercessions _____

At the preparation & presentation _____

Preface dialog _____Preface _____

Preface acclamation _____

Eucharistic prayer _____Memorial acclamation _____

Eucharistic amen _____

The Lord's prayer _____

Breaking of bread _____

The communion hymn _____

The post-communion hymn _____

Blessing _____At the dismissal _____

Memoranda:

SEVENTH SUNDAY OF THE YEAR

YEAR A

READINGS

Leviticus (19:1-2,17-18)
Even in the Old Dispensation, the Lord's intent is clear: love is the factor which must determine and infuse all of his people's actions. Love for the Lord is seen through love for his people.

First Corinthians (3:16-23)
We belong to Christ and Christ is God's, so we belong to God. This is the end of the Christian's journey as Paul sees it. We are the temples of God and are therefore precious to God. God will defend us and keep us close, as long as we recall that all that we have is God's. No wisdom, no learning, no person can interpose himself between us and God.

Matthew (5:38-48)
Jesus broadens the Levitical concept of neighbor to include all people. As he has loved all so must we. This love is the hallmark of those who are children. God places little value in treating those who are our own in a loving way, while excluding others. In God's love all are brothers and sisters.

FOCUS

Love seems to be the overriding message of today's service of readings. Leviticus states that the instinctual center of love for family and love for country men, and Paul states that our acceptance of God as our sole support, places us in a singular relationship with God. God dwells in us, we become God's temples, and God protects and sustains us. Jesus expands the notion of neighbor to include all people. He presents us with the idea that if we give everything over to God, nothing can be taken from us. We can give our coat as well as our shirt, since all comes from God and therefore is meant to be shared with everyone.

IDEA STARTERS

- *CCT Lectionary:* Is 49:8-13; Ps 62:5-12; I Cor 3:10-11, 16-23; Mt 5:27-37.
- To be baptized is to be holy. To develop one's self intellectually, physically, emotionally, and spiritually is to be whole. To be Christian is to be both.
- The call to perfection lies in one's ability to have faith, hope and love. Have children make collages for the church bulletin board of people being whole-holy human beings.
- A parish fair of Christian lifestyles would be appropriate today. How are all, laity, ordained and religious, called to be a holy-whole?
- Evaluate your use of assistant ministers: greeters, musicians, readers, eucharistic ministers, acolytes, etc.
- Does your parish provide both educational and recreational occasions for all the people of your community?
- For your consideration: Alternative Opening Prayer; Intercessions for forgiveness, divisions among people, going the extra mile; Ordinary Sundays Preface III (P31); Eucharistic Prayer III; Ordinary Solemn Blessing V.

MUSIC

- Psalm 103
- *Praise the Lord, My Soul* (Jesuits/NALR)
- *Almighty God, Your Word is Cast* (ICEL/GIA)
- *Dwelling Place* (Jesuits/NALR)
- *Grace and Peace* (Gilsdorf/Resource)
- *Keeping Festival* (Toolan/Resource)
- *Teach Me Your Ways* (Foster/Resource)
- *Peace Song* (Stenson/Resource)
- *Remember Your Love* (Dameans/NALR)
- *Service* (Dameans/NALR)
- *We Remember* (Haugen/GIA)
- *We Sinned* (ICEL/GIA)
- *Yahweh* (Weston Priory)

SUNDAY PLANNING SHEET

Date _____

Parish focus _____

Environment & art _____

Ritual notes _____

Faith development (eg., in newsletter/classes) _____

Children's faith experience _____

Prelude _____

Hymn of gathering _____

Sprinkling/Penitential rite _____

Hymn of praise _____

Opening Prayer _____

First reading _____ Responsory _____

Second reading _____ Gospel acclamation _____

Gospel _____ Profession of faith _____

General intercessions _____

At the preparation & presentation _____

Preface dialog _____ Preface _____

Preface acclamation _____

Eucharistic prayer _____ Memorial acclamation _____

Eucharistic amen _____

The Lord's prayer _____

Breaking of bread _____

The communion hymn _____

The post-communion hymn _____

Blessing _____ At the dismissal _____

Memoranda:

EIGHTH SUNDAY OF THE YEAR

READINGS

Isaiah (49:14-15)
The Lord's love is abiding. Even when we feel forsaken, God is present to us like a mother, tenderly caring for us, the children of God's heart.

First Corinthians (4:1-5)
Christ is the judge. No person, no court, not even one's own conscience can indict. Only the Lord passes judgment, by bringing into his light all that is hidden in darkness. If we are trustworthy he will reward us with the gift of God's love.

Matthew (6:24-34)
Our faith, if it is strong, can conquer our fears. These fears are based on a reluctance to hand over to God the care for us that is God's. We must simply open ourselves to God's love, and everything else will be provided for us.

FOCUS

God's care for us is as profound as that of a mother for her infant. God loves and knows us completely. God judges us on that knowledge and our willingness to place our lives in God's care. When we do this, we bloom in beauty like the lily and soar serenely like the humble sparrow, always aware that God is the One who holds all things in God's gentle loving plan.

IDEA STARTERS

- *CCT Lectionary:* Lev 19:1-2,9-18; Ps 119:33-40; 1 Cor 4:1-5;Mt 5:38-48.
- Today's readings from Isaiah and Matthew may provide the parish artist with some food for thought.
- A bulletin article on the Motherhood of God could draw from the feminine images given in the lessons.
- Have children act out a contemporary parable illustrating the common focus of the first and third lections.
- The Corinthians passage calls us to live the mysteries of God revealed in Christ with purity of intention. Is our parish a welcoming place to all people who come and share worship with us?
- Evaluate your community's status quo. What masters (idols) are leading them away from a faithful single-heartedness set on God?
- For your consideration: Sprinkling Baptismal Water B; Intercessions for the lonely, for mothers, the ordained, steadfastness in God, stewardship of creation, for an end to abuse of human beings, prejudice and useless anxiety; Children's Eucharistic Prayer I; Memorial Acclamation C; Lord's Prayer sung; Ordinary Solemn Blessing II.

MUSIC

- Psalm 62
- *As a Little Child* (Gilsdorf/Resource)
- *Alleluia... My Word* (Wise/GIA)
- *All That We Have* (Dameans/NALR)
- *Be Glad, O My People* (Weston Priory)
- *Canticle of the Sun* (Haugen/GIA)
- *God Who Made the Earth* (ICEL/GIA)
- *Hymn of the Lord's Supper* (Ivancic/GIA)
- *If God is for Us* (Jesuits/NALR)
- *In Those Days* (Deiss/NALR)
- *Isaiah 49* (Landry/NALR)
- *Now Thank We All Our God* (ICEL/GIA)
- *Only A Shadow* (Landry/NALR)
- *Our Father, Our Mother* (Wise/GIA)
- *Psalm of Love* (Raffa/Resource)
- *Song of Wonder* (Jabusch/NALR)
- *Taste and See* (Haugen/GIA)
- *Though the Mountains May Fall* (Jesuits/NALR)
- *Till You* (Repp/K&R)
- *So Does the Lord Provide* (Page/Resource)
- *Yahweh, the Faithful One* (Jesuits/NALR)
- *You Are Near* (Jesuits/NALR)

SUNDAY PLANNING SHEET

Date _____

Parish focus _____

Environment & art _____

Ritual notes _____

Faith development (eg., in newsletter/classes) _____

Children's faith experience _____

Prelude _____

Hymn of gathering _____

Sprinkling/Penitential rite _____

Hymn of praise _____

Opening Prayer _____

First reading _____Responsory _____

Second reading _____Gospel acclamation _____

Gospel _____Profession of faith _____

General intercessions _____

At the preparation & presentation _____

Preface dialog _____Preface _____

Preface acclamation _____

Eucharistic prayer _____Memorial acclamation _____

Eucharistic amen _____

The Lord's prayer _____

Breaking of bread _____

The communion hymn _____

The post-communion hymn _____

Blessing _____At the dismissal _____

Memoranda:

NINTH SUNDAY OF THE YEAR

YEAR A

READINGS

Deuteronomy (11:18,26–28)
The Law should always be set before Israel's eyes, like a jewel worn on the forehead. The Lord offers his people the Law as an invitation to life. Honoring it will assure an abundance of grace. Breaking the Law welcomes death and its resultant terrors.

Romans (3:21–25,28)
Those who place their faith in Jesus are justified. He frees them from the Law, a reminder of their sin-condition, and delivers them into the fullness of life, which his blood has purchased. God has established Jesus as the ransom for all who believe in him. Only faith in him brings life.

Matthew (7:21–27)
To respond to Jesus, hear his word, accepting it and integrating it into one's life, is the key to true peace. Once this is done and the believer converts from sin, life is a possibility.

FOCUS

Under the "old order," the Law gave an opportunity to approach God. At the same time it reminded us of our sinfulness. With Christ we have the ability to reconcile ourselves to God and to live fully in the spirit. God is the expiation of our sin.

IDEA STARTERS

- *CCT Lectionary:* Ex 24:12-18; Ps 2:6-11; II Pt 1:16-21; Mt 17:1-9.
- The *CCT Lectionary* marks this Sunday before Lent as "The Transfiguration of Our Lord." The Sundays after Epiphany are thus sandwiched between two great epiphanies: our Lord's Baptism and today's feast. At both, Jesus is revealed as God's Son. Today Jesus talks with two great heroes of the Jews as he prepares to go to Jerusalem. What could they have been talking about?
- Publicize your parish Lenten program. Let us prepare to go to Jerusalem as our Lord did.
- Mark this final Sunday of using the word "Alleluia" creatively: through song, banners, and procession. "Enclose and seal up the word...until the appointed time."
- For your consideration (Ordinary): Opening Prayer; Intercessions for a life centered upon God, and for a faith which calls us to action; Ordinary Sundays Preface VII (P 35); Eucharistic Prayer II; Memorial Acclamation D; Ordinary Solemn Blessing III.
- For your consideration: white vestments, Eucharistic Prayer I; Memorial Acclamation D; Ordinary Solemn Blessing III.

MUSIC

- Psalm 31
- *My Refuge* (Vessels/GIA)
- *Anthem* (Conry/NALR)
- *Christ Is Made the Sure Foundation* (ICEL/GIA)
- *For You Are My God* (Jesuits/NALR)
- *Glorious In Majesty* (Cothran/GIA)
- *Go Out To the Whole World* (Gilsdorf/Resource)
- *How Can I Keep From Singing?* (traditional)
- *How Firm a Foundation* (ICEL/GIA)
- *I Lift Up My Soul* (Jesuits/NALR)
- *I Will Sing, I Will Sing* (Dyer/Celebration)
- *Jesus, Remember Me* (Taize/GIA)
- *Let Your Face Shine Upon Us* (Haugen/GIA)
- *Like a Sunflower* (Landry/NALR)
- *Mighty Lord* (Jesuits/NALR)
- *Spread Your Love* (Page/Resource)
- *The House Built on the Rock* (Deiss/NALR)
- *The Wind Song* (Wise/GIA)
- *We Are Called* (Pattersen)
- *You Will Draw Water* (Conry/NALR)

SUNDAY PLANNING SHEET   Date _____

Parish focus _____

Environment & art _____

Ritual notes _____

Faith development (eg., in newsletter/classes) _____

Children's faith experience _____

Prelude _____

Hymn of gathering _____

Sprinkling/Penitential rite _____

Hymn of praise _____

Opening Prayer _____

First reading _____Responsory _____

Second reading _____Gospel acclamation _____

Gospel _____Profession of faith _____

General intercessions _____

At the preparation & presentation _____

Preface dialog _____Preface _____

Preface acclamation _____

Eucharistic prayer _____Memorial acclamation _____

Eucharistic amen _____

The Lord's prayer _____

Breaking of bread _____

The communion hymn _____

The post-communion hymn _____

Blessing _____At the dismissal _____

Memoranda:

TENTH SUNDAY OF THE YEAR

YEAR A

READINGS

Hosea (6:3-6)
Hosea's love for his harlot-wife was unconditional. He loved her through and in spite of her unfaithfulness. So God's love for his people is not conditional on their faithfulness. However, as the wife of the prophet could know his love only when she returned to it, so God's people can only experience his love when they are faithful and attentive to him. The reading from Hosea speaks of the certainty of God's love.

Romans (4:18-25)
Abraham is the great model of faith and faithfulness for Paul. It is Abraham's faith that makes his relationship with God possible, and through this relationship God is able to work mightily. This is Paul's call to the Romans, to not be stuck in a life of mere adherence to rules, but to know God's power and love through Abraham-like faith.

Matthew (9:9-13)
The love and forgiveness of Jesus are not offered as a reward for right action. Rather they are offered as a way out of a life of emptiness and sin. Conversion is not a prior condition for encountering Jesus; rather, encountering Jesus results in a conversion of heart. This message is put in the context of Jesus' call of Matthew to be his disciple. Jesus calls not the virtuous but the sinner.

FOCUS

The power of faith to change lives lies at the very heart of the Good News. We are changed as soon as we begin to believe — changed by the experience of believing. Faith is a letting go of our perception that we are in control of our lives. It is only by such letting go that God is able to enter and transform us. Those who know this transforming love are the ones who will best be able to take it to others.

IDEA STARTERS

- *CCT Lectionary:* GN 23:1-18; Rm 4:13-18; Mt 9:9-13.
- Focus the Pentitential Rite on the healing power of God's forgiveness. How is our spiritual health, physical health and emotional health connected?
- Abraham offers a model of faith and hope. He is the spiritual father of all who believe in God: Jews, Muslims and Christians alike. How can we highlight our connection with this great Jewish saint? Perhaps today's liturgy can include Jewish songs, symbols or rituals.
- For your consideration: Opening Prayer; Intercession for all believers, Muslims, Jews, non-believers, healers, preachers.

MUSIC

- Psalm 50
- *Abba Father* (Landry/NALR)
- *Abba, Father* (Gilsdorf/Resource)
- *Be Not Afraid* (Jesuits/NALR)
- *Believe* (McGrath/Resource)
- *Blest By the Hand of the Lord* (Page/Resource)
- *Exult You Just Ones* (Jesuits/NALR)
- *I Believe In You* (Wise/GIA)
- *O Lord of Life* (Lisicky/Resource)
- *Praise Be the Father* (Dameans/NALR)
- *You Are Near* (Jesuits/Nalr)

CYCLE A

SUNDAY PLANNING SHEET

Date _____

Parish focus _____

Environment & art _____

Ritual notes _____

Faith development (eg., in newsletter/classes) _____

Children's faith experience _____

Prelude _____

Hymn of gathering _____

Sprinkling/Penitential rite _____

Hymn of praise _____

Opening Prayer _____

First reading _____ Responsory _____

Second reading _____ Gospel acclamation _____

Gospel _____ Profession of faith _____

General intercessions _____

At the preparation & presentation _____

Preface dialog _____ Preface _____

Preface acclamation _____

Eucharistic prayer _____ Memorial acclamation _____

Eucharistic amen _____

The Lord's prayer _____

Breaking of bread _____

The communion hymn _____

The post-communion hymn _____

Blessing _____ At the dismissal _____

Memoranda:

ELEVENTH SUNDAY OF THE YEAR

YEAR A

READINGS
Exodus (19:2-6)
The destiny of Israel as the chosen people is not to simply enjoy a relationship of favor with God. The promise of God to deliver and save Israel is to have the effect of manifesting God's glory to all people.

As the priest's function is to mediate between God and people, Israel's role as God's elect is to mediate between God and all the nations of earth.
Romans (5:6-11)
Through his death Christ has empowered us to experience the ultimate reality which is God. But we can do so only by entering into Christ's death ourselves. This is the way in which Paul defines salvation in today's reading. Through Christ's death we are reconciled with God. By sharing in his death we are assured a share in his eternal life.
Matthew (9:36-10:8)
Being called by God inevitably results in being sent. Jesus chooses his apostles to be the means by which all people will hear the Good News. The apostles are gathered not simply to enjoy the kingdom, but to bring it to the world.

FOCUS
Today's readings speak to the scriptural notion of being called or chosen by God. The message that comes through loud and clear is that those chosen by God are to be witnesses of his love to the world. Salvation is not simply deliverance from a life of emptiness and sin, it is an initiation into service of the Gospel. Israel's deliverance was to be a light to the nations. The apostles were chosen to preach the Kingdom of God to all the nations. We are a people with a mission. Being called and being sent are two sides of the same coin, and are the essence of our faith.

IDEA STARTERS
- *CCT Lectionary:* Gn 25:19-34; Ps 46; Rm 5:6-11; Mt 9:35, 10:8.
- After today's liturgy have a special reception for those who bring communion to the sick of the parish.
- How do we live out our Christian call to witness to God's healing love?
- A bulletin article might address the question: What about the Jews? What does it mean for contemporary Judaism that God has chosen them?
- For your consideration: Opening Prayer; Intercessions for Christian unity, preachers, ministers, rabbis, religious ed teachers.

MUSIC
- Psalm 100
- *As the Father Has Sent Me* (O'Brien/Resource)
- *All the Ends of the Earth* (Jesuits/NALR)
- *Blessed Are Those Who Love the Lord* (Downey/Resource)
- *Earthen Vessels* (Jesuits/NALR)
- *He Has Anointed Me* (Dameans/NALR)
- *In Him We Live* (Landry/NALR)
- *Messenger Song* (Gilsdorf/Resource)
- *Priestly People* (Deiss/PMB)

SUNDAY PLANNING SHEET

Date _____

Parish focus _____

Environment & art _____

Ritual notes _____

Faith development (eg., in newsletter/classes) _____

Children's faith experience _____

Prelude _____

Hymn of gathering _____

Sprinkling/Penitential rite _____

Hymn of praise _____

Opening Prayer _____

First reading _____ Responsory _____

Second reading _____ Gospel acclamation _____

Gospel _____ Profession of faith _____

General intercessions _____

At the preparation & presentation _____

Preface dialog _____ Preface _____

Preface acclamation _____

Eucharistic prayer _____ Memorial acclamation ____

Eucharistic amen _____

The Lord's prayer _____

Breaking of bread _____

The communion hymn _____

The post-communion hymn _____

Blessing _____ At the dismissal _____

Memoranda:

TWELFTH SUNDAY OF THE YEAR

YEAR A

READINGS

Jeremiah (20:10–13)

Jeremiah feels within his heart the stern yet loving call of God. At the same time he experiences the rejection of his people. God's call is relentless. It requires no less than the total giving of self. Jeremiah's response is to acknowledge and praise God's greatness and saving power.

Romans (5:12–15)

Paul's references to Adam as the first to sin and reject God and Christ as the redeemer of humanity serve to help us understand the universality of sin and of salvation. Both apply to all people, not just a chosen few. Adam is significant here as a sign of our common vulnerability to, and participation in, evil. Just so the liberation from sin offered by Christ is not exclusive but is available to all.

Matthew (10:26–33)

Matthew records Jesus' instructions to those he is sending out to spread the Good News. They must be prepared to face opposition, and so must understand the power of the Gospel. As God's chosen they will be taken care of. Their faith in this truth is sufficient to drive out all fear.

FOCUS

With God's call comes disruption of life and, sometimes, alienation from others. Today's readings emphasize the difficult side of being called to preach the Good News. It is not news that others are always ready to hear and understand and appreciate. For those unwilling to give up the comfort of feeling that they alone are in control of their lives, the Gospel can come as a rude shock. In such cases the only criteria for judging our effectiveness is our faithfulness to the Gospel itself.

IDEA STARTERS

- *CCT Lectionary:* Gn 28:10–17; Ps 91:1–10; Rm 5:12–19; Mt 10:24–33.
- Acknowledge and appreciate those in the community who read the Scriptures at liturgy. Do so with a special coffee after Mass.
- Emphasize the proclamation of the readings at the liturgy today.
- Does our faith ever affect our relationships with non-believers? Should it? A bulletin article on this theme might be appropriate for today.
- For your consideration: Opening Prayer; Intercessions for contemporary prophets and martyrs, political leaders, ethicists, non-believers.

MUSIC

- Psalm 89
- *Be Not Afraid* (Jesuits/NALR)
- *Earthen Vessels* (Jesuits/NALR)
- *I Have Loved You* (Joncas/NALR)
- *If God Is for Us* (Jesuits/NALR)
- *Let the Earth Resound* (Deiss/NALR)
- *Messenger Song* (Gilsdorf/Resource)
- *Sing and Shout* (Raffa/Resource)
- *Sing of Christ, Proclaim* (ICEL)

SUNDAY PLANNING SHEET

Date _____

Parish focus _____

Environment & art _____

Ritual notes _____

Faith development (eg., in newsletter/classes) _____

Children's faith experience _____

Prelude _____

Hymn of gathering _____

Sprinkling/Penitential rite _____

Hymn of praise _____

Opening Prayer _____

First reading _____ Responsory _____

Second reading _____ Gospel acclamation _____

Gospel _____ Profession of faith _____

General intercessions _____

At the preparation & presentation _____

Preface dialog _____ Preface _____

Preface acclamation _____

Eucharistic prayer _____ Memorial acclamation _____

Eucharistic amen _____

The Lord's prayer _____

Breaking of bread _____

The communion hymn _____

The post-communion hymn _____

Blessing _____ At the dismissal _____

Memoranda:

THIRTEENTH SUNDAY OF THE YEAR

YEAR A

READINGS
Second Kings (4:8-11,14-16)
In this reading the reward for extending hospitality to God's prophet, Elisha, is the miracle of a barren womb conceiving and giving birth. Hospitality always results in life. Being open to others and opening our hearts always gives birth to something new.

Romans (6:3-4,8-11)
Union with Christ means union in his death as well as his Resurrection. Death to self is death to what is false in us so that our true selves can be born. Entering into death is letting go of our need to control, liberating us to be the best we can possibly be. The death of our ego is required if we are to be truly open to others.

Matthew (10:37-42)
Discipleship brings both reward and great cost. Both are part of the mission to bring the Good News to others. The Resurrection comes at the end of the difficult road of emptying the self. In this Gospel the promise that we will find our life by giving it up is coupled with the promise that hospitality will result in a prophet's reward. Letting go of our life and opening our life to others go hand in hand.

FOCUS
The Liturgy of the Word for today highlights the connection between the scriptural theme of dying to self and the call to hospitality. Traditionally dying to self has been interpreted as having to do with discipline and self-sacrifice. What light does the connection between dying to self and hospitality bring to this discussion?

Hospitality requires two things: space and the willingness to share that space. Space in our life for others can only be created when we let go of all the clutter that goes with believing we are in control. Ego and false pretenses fill our lives to the exclusion of other people. When we stop being caught up in ourselves we have room for others, including God.

IDEA STARTERS
- *CCT Lectionary:* Gn 52:22-32; Ps 17:17,15; Rm 6:3-11; Mt 10:34-42.
- How does our parish community show hospitality to others? Recognize greeters today.
- What organizations in our community offer hospitality to the homeless? Perhaps a bulletin article can desribe some of these.
- How do we die to ourselves? This is an important scriptural theme. What does it have to say to us today?
- For your consideration: Opening Prayer; Intercession for the sick, the homeless, orphans, the mentally ill, the poor, those who work with the homeless.

MUSIC

- Psalm 89
- *A Banquet is Prepared* (Jesuits/NALR)
- *As a Family* (Page/Resource)
- *Come to the Water* (Gilsdorf/Resource)
- *Come to the Lord* (Meyette/Resource)

- *Dwelling Place* (Jesuits/NALR)
- *In Him We Live* (Landry/NALR)
- *Prepare the Way* (Bodrique/WLP)
- *Only in God* (Jesuits/NALR)
- *Song of Gathering* (Wise/GIA)

SUNDAY PLANNING SHEET   Date _____

Parish focus _____

Environment & art _____

Ritual notes _____

Faith development (eg., in newsletter/classes) _____

Children's faith experience _____

Prelude _____

Hymn of gathering _____

Sprinkling/Penitential rite _____

Hymn of praise _____

Opening Prayer _____

First reading _____Responsory _____

Second reading _____Gospel acclamation _____

Gospel _____Profession of faith _____

General intercessions _____

At the preparation & presentation _____

Preface dialog _____Preface _____

Preface acclamation _____

Eucharistic prayer _____Memorial acclamation _____

Eucharistic amen _____

The Lord's prayer _____

Breaking of bread _____

The communion hymn _____

The post-communion hymn _____

Blessing _____At the dismissal _____

Memoranda:

SOLEMNITY OF PETER AND PAUL

READINGS
Acts (12:1-11)
In this section of Acts we are told of the first persecution of the church under Herod. James is beheaded and Peter is arrested. While in prison awaiting trial, Peter is delivered from his persecutors by the intervention of an angel of the Lord. The writer emphasizes that this occurs during Passover. The allusions to the Exodus event and the paschal mystery are vivid.

Second Timothy (4:6-8,17-18)
Paul points to his suffering for the church of Christ. He attributes it all to the Lord, who "will bring me safe to his heavenly kingdom." Paul indicates that his final award awaits him on the "Day of the Lord." This additional allusion to the Passover, the Exodus, and the paschal mystery firmly plants Paul's suffering in the soil of the sufferings of Jesus, where they receive meaning and are delivered to victory.

Matthew (16:13-19)
Peter's confession is prompted by the Spirit. His openness to "the movement of the Divine" in his life enables Christ to make him a servant and to make him responsible to the church. Emanating from the Spirit of God, Peter's word will be effective and liberating.

FOCUS
Passover in both the old and new dispensations is a thread which is woven through today's feast. Suffering born in faith and patience, even received as gift, can result not only in the deliverance but the triumph of the faithful servant. Peter and Paul were able to serve Christ's church so effectively because they were open to the Spirit in their lives. This provided them with a vision which enabled them to see suffering as joined to the work of Christ on the cross. In so sharing their sufferings with Christ they secure a sharing in his glory.

IDEA STARTERS
- *CCT Lectionary* (Proper 8): Gn 32:22-32; Ps 17:1-7, 15; Rom 6:3-11; Mt 10:34-42.
- The Roman Calendar observes the day of Peter and Paul today. Their day was transferred from Friday, June 29, when that date was reserved for a special feast in honor of our Lord. Other calendars mark this day as "Pentecost 3."
- At a children's liturgy, celebrate apostleship and discipleship. "We are called, we are chosen: we are Christ for one another."
- A bulletin article may speak about the marvelous paradox of God using human beings to bring others into a closer relationship with the Trinity. "Take my hands and make them as your own."
- There is only one ministry (service, the mission of the church), yet there are many ministers. At Baptism we accepted the ministry of our Lord as a part of our lives.
- Images (icons, sculpture, tapestries, among others) of Peter and Paul may be given special prominence today. Consult *Environment and Art in Catholic Worship,* nos. 98-99, for guidelines concerning their use.

- For your consideration: Sprinkling Baptismal Water B; Opening Prayer (Day); Intercessions for healing, rejoicing in God, missionaries, forgiveness, Church unity, faithfulness, contemporary martyrs, persecuted Christians, justice and judges, sport competitors, the Magisterium; Peter and Paul Preface (P63); Eucharistic Prayer III; Memorial Acclamation D; Solemn Blessing of Peter and Paul.

MUSIC

- Psalm 19
- Psalm 34
- *All the Ends of the Earth* (Jesuits/NALR)
- *Anthem* (Conry/NALR)
- *The Cry of the Poor* (Jesuits/NALR)
- *Do You Really Love Me* (Landry/NALR)
- *Eye Has Not Seen* (Haugen/GIA)
- *For All Your Saints in Warfare* (LBW)
- *Glorious in Majesty* (Cothran/GIA)
- *Go Up to the Mountain* (Weston Priory)
- *How Beautiful on the Mountains* (Deiss/NALR)
- *Let All the World With Songs* (ICEL)
- *One Lord* (Haas/Coop Ministries)
- *Only This I Want* (Jesuits/NALR)
- *Silver and Gold Have I None* (Traditional)
- *Something Which Is Known* (Weston Priory)
- *Song of the Prophet* (Weston Priory)
- *Take My Hands* (Temple/FCC)
- *There Is One Lord* (Dameans/NALR)
- *Witnesses* (Weston Priory)

SUNDAY PLANNING SHEET   Date _____

Parish focus _____

Environment & art _____

Ritual notes _____

Faith development (eg., in newsletter/classes) _____

Children's faith experience _____

Prelude _____

Hymn of gathering _____

Sprinkling/Penitential rite _____

Hymn of praise _____

Opening Prayer _____

First reading _____Responsory _____

Second reading _____Gospel acclamation _____

Gospel _____Profession of faith _____

General intercessions _____

At the preparation & presentation _____

Preface dialog _____Preface _____

Preface acclamation _____

Eucharistic prayer _____Memorial acclamation _____

Eucharistic amen _____

The Lord's prayer _____

Breaking of bread _____

The communion hymn _____

The post-communion hymn _____

Blessing _____At the dismissal _____

Memoranda:

FOURTEENTH SUNDAY OF THE YEAR

YEAR A

READINGS
Zechariah (9:9-10)
As surprising and unexpected as the Messiah is, so too shall be his reign of peace. His peace shall be established not through the instruments of worldly rulers, but through gentleness and the unassuming simplicity of God.
Romans (8:9,11-13)
The Spirit of God living in us brings us to life. This Spirit which raised Jesus from death to life brings us to life in the church. We are indebted to Christ for our life lived in grace.
Matthew (11:25-30)
The wisdom of God is not dependent on the forms from which humans seek and derive wisdom. God's wisdom comes through the simple and childlike. Chief among these examples is Jesus, himself the very image of God. Through his gentleness he refreshes and renews all who seek their rest in him.

FOCUS
Surprise seems to be the central point contained in the Liturgy today. The Messiah and his kingdom will not be bound by the conventions and constructs of people. Those who accept this fact, while they seem insignificant, bear the life of Jesus to the world.

IDEA STARTERS
- *CCT Lectionary* (Proper 9): Ex 1:6-14, 22-2:10; Ps 124; Rom 7:14-25a; Mt 11:25-30.
- Conduct a summer forum on the Bishops' pastoral, *The Challenge of Peace: God's Call and Our Response,* in the light of the Kingdom parables presented via these summer Sundays.
- You may wish to paraphrase the words of Jesus (Mt. 11:25b-27)into a collect to be used at some point in worship today.
- The vestments used throughout Ordinary Time may appropriately shift in green nuance. Summer Sunday paraments may be of a lighter and brighter tone than those used in autumn.
- For your consideration: Intercessions for rulers of nations, end to war and disunity, for the oppressed, thankfulness, acting in the Spirit, acceptance of God's Word, refreshment; Eucharistic Prayer IV; Memorial Acclamation D; Ordinary Solemn Blessing II.

MUSIC
- Psalm 145
- *Abba, Father* (Landry/NALR)
- *Blessings on the King* (Jesuits/NALR)
- *By the Love* (Weston Priory)
- *Come to Me* (Weston Priory)
- *Come Unto Me* (Jesuits/NALR)
- *Every Day I Will Praise You* (Gilsdorf/Resource)
- *Good Morning, Zachary* (Gutfreund/NALR)
- *He Has Anointed Me* (Dameans/NALR)
- *A Hymn to God's Love* (Mondoy/Resource)
- *I Heard the Voice of Jesus Say* (ICEL)
- *In Him We Live* (Landry/NALR)
- *In Those Days* (Deiss/NALR)
- *Let Heaven Rejoice* (Jesuits/NALR)
- *Like A Shepherd* (Jesuits/NALR)
- *Renewal Song* (Andersen/Resource)
- *Song of Wonder* (Jabusch/NALR)
- *Spirit of God* (Weston Priory)
- *We Were Strangers* (Deiss/NALR)

SUNDAY PLANNING SHEET

Date _____

Parish focus _____

Environment & art _____

Ritual notes _____

Faith development (eg., in newsletter/classes) _____

Children's faith experience _____

Prelude _____

Hymn of gathering _____

Sprinkling/Penitential rite _____

Hymn of praise _____

Opening Prayer _____

First reading _____ Responsory _____

Second reading _____ Gospel acclamation ___

Gospel _____ Profession of faith ___

General intercessions _____

At the preparation & presentation _____

Preface dialog _____ Preface _____

Preface acclamation _____

Eucharistic prayer _____ Memorial acclamation ___

Eucharistic amen _____

The Lord's prayer _____

Breaking of bread _____

The communion hymn _____

The post-communion hymn _____

Blessing _____ At the dismissal _____

Memoranda:

FIFTEENTH SUNDAY OF THE YEAR

YEAR A

READINGS

Isaiah (55:10-11)
The Word of God is alive and vital. It produces growth and new life as do the winter snows and spring rains. God's plan can never be abolished.

Romans (8:18-23)
All creation waits with the pain of expectation to be delivered into the glory to which it has been predestined. Even the Children of Light await the completion of the redemptive process in their corporate and individual lives.

Matthew (13:1-23)
Parables are not so much didactic stories as morality tales. Their power lies in their ability to captivate the attention of the listeners and to surprise them with an unexpected conclusion. This familiar form used by rabbis for centuries was also used by Jesus. The well-known parable for today describes the various ways God's word is received and how it fails or takes root in the hearts of the hearers. Jesus explains to the apostles that they, with their knowledge of God's mystery, do not need to learn from parables. Many of his listeners, who are slow to believe, may be aided by this device.

FOCUS

God's Word is effective. It brings forth life and faith in the hearts of the hearers. Those who misplace their priorities and allow other concerns to blind them will lose their ability to see the true meaning of life.

IDEA STARTERS

- *CCT Lectionary* (Proper 10): Ex 2:11-22; Ps 69:6-15; Rom 8:9-17; Mt 13:1-9, 18-23.
- The Gospel lesson today focuses upon hearing and living Christ's Good News. Carry the Book of the Gospels proudly in today's gathering procession. Possibly include candles and incense in a Gospel pocession.
- Encourage every family to pray daily lections as part of their morning and evening prayers. Remind your community of the importance of owning a Bible and using it!
- You may invite families to bring fresh plants from their gardens to be placed before the ambo today. At the Sprinkling of Baptismal Water, also sprinkle the plants. "Jesus, God's Word, has visited the land and watered it."
- A parish celebration of Anointing the Sick may incorporate today's readings.
- For your consideration: Sprinkling Baptismal Water A; Opening Prayer; Gospel (full form); Intercessions for favorable weather, an abundance of fruits from the earth, hearts open to God's Word, farmers, the suffering and sorrowful, hopefulness; Ordinary Sundays Preface VIII (P36); Eucharistic Prayer I; Ordinary Solemn Blessing V.

MUSIC

- Psalm 65
- *Alleluia, Your Word* (Deiss/NALR)
- *All Those Who Love Me* (Weston Priory)
- *Arise, Shine Out* (Bennett/Resource)
- *Blessed Jesus, at Your Word* (ICEL)
- *Glory and Praise* (Jesuits/NALR)
- *Happy Those Who Hear* (Weston Priory)
- *The House Built On a Rock* (Deiss/NALR)
- *In the Day of the Lord* (Gutfreund/NALR)
- *The Kingdom of God* (Deiss/NALR)
- *Like Cedars They Shall Stand* (Jesuits/NALR)
- *Lord, To Whom Shall We Go* (Joncas/NALR)
- *May We Praise You* (Jesuits/NALR)
- *The Seed That Falls* (Lisicky/Resource)
- *Sing Out His Goodness* (Dameans/NALR)
- *Speak, Lord* (Dameans/NALR)
- *The Truth Will Make You Free* (Gilsdorf/Resource)

SUNDAY PLANNING SHEET   Date _____

Parish focus _____

Environment & art _____

Ritual notes _____

Faith development (eg., in newsletter/classes) _____

Children's faith experience _____

Prelude _____

Hymn of gathering _____

Sprinkling/Penitential rite _____

Hymn of praise _____

Opening Prayer _____

First reading _____Responsory _____

Second reading _____Gospel acclamation _____

Gospel _____Profession of faith _____

General intercessions _____

At the preparation & presentation _____

Preface dialog _____Preface _____

Preface acclamation _____

Eucharistic prayer _____Memorial acclamation _____

Eucharistic amen _____

The Lord's prayer _____

Breaking of bread _____

The communion hymn _____

The post-communion hymn _____

Blessing _____At the dismissal _____

Memoranda:

SIXTEENTH SUNDAY OF THE YEAR

YEAR A

READINGS
Wisdom (12:13,16-19)
Once again in this reading from Wisdom God's greatness is clearly shown to be different from that which people expect. God's omnipotence leads to greater gentility. God's justice is the source of compassion; God's perfection rises out of disbelief. Those who wish to be followers of God are expected to behave and act in the same fashion.

Romans (8:26-27)
Our weakness is the background against which the spirit operates and manifests God's greatness. Even our prayer is the uttering of the Spirit in us.

Matthew (13:24-43)
The Judean/Cannanite farming culture serves as the background for three parables today. Within the Body of Christ there will always be both faithful and unfaithful members, much like fields yielding wheat and weeds. God, in time, will sort them out and deliver them to their reward.

The mustard seed: who would expect from so tiny a seed so great a tree? God's Word can produce even more surprising results. The Word of the Lord is like yeast: it enlarges the whole loaf of bread (the church) and makes it full and rich.

FOCUS
God's Spirit continually acts in its own manner, producing greatness from the most unlikely sources, underpinning the prayer of the church, changing the definitions of justice, power, love, and greatness, and reordering the whole to fit the perspective of the Divine.

IDEA STARTERS
- *CCT Lectionary:* (Proper 11): Ex 3:1-12; Ps 103:1-13; Rom 8:18-25; Mt 13:24-30, 36-43
- Jesus again offers a picture of the kingdom of heaven. He explains what will happen when the reign of God comes into full form.
- "Does hell really exist?" This question deserves an answer! What is the connection between the kingdom in our midst and the life of the world to come?
- What role does each of us play in the kingdom? How do we call forth the gifts and talents of all those we meet?
- Sponsor a pot-luck brunch after the Sunday liturgy, either in the shade of a tree or in an air-conditioned room. This may provide a possibility for a group to study Christian belief. Today's topic may be based on the second reading.
- If the Romans selection serves as a basis for the homily, it may be appropriate to sing the prayers: collects, litanies, and Lord's Prayer.
- At a children's liturgy, the focus may be why Jesus used parables. Children from vacation bible school may act out the stories. Older children may be used to explain similarities between parables and Aesop's fables.
- For your consideration: Opening Prayer; Gospel (full form); Intercessions for unbelievers, doubters, for concern, justice, kindness, fidelity, for those in cloistered or monastic lifestyles, farmers, bakers; Ordinary Sundays Preface IV (P32); Eucharistic Prayer II; Memorial Acclamation C; Ordinary Solemn Blessing IV.

CYCLE A

MUSIC

- Psalm 86
- *Awaken My Heart* (Deiss/NALR)
- *Be Still, My Friends* (Andersen/Resource)
- *Beatitudes* (Dameans/NALR)
- *Behold the Mountain of the Lord* (ICEL)
- *Choose Life* (Weston Priory)
- *Come, You Thankful People, Come* (ICEL)
- *The Dawn of the Day* (Deiss/NALR)
- *Heart of a Servant* (Mullins/Resource)
- *Hosea* (Weston Priory)
- *I Have Loved You* (Joncas/NALR)
- *I Lift Up My Soul* (Jesuits/NALR)
- *I Rejoiced* (Jesuits/NALR)
- *Jesus, Remember Me* (Taize/GIA)
- *Let Us Walk in the Light* (Haugen/Quiet Breeze)
- *Remember Your Love* (Dameans/NALR)
- *The Seed That Falls* (Lisicky/Resource)
- *Though the Mountains May Fall* (Jesuits/NALR)
- *Turn to Me* (Jesuits/NALR)
- *Watchman, How Goes the Night?* (Deiss/NALR)

SUNDAY PLANNING SHEET   Date _____

Parish focus _____

Environment & art _____

Ritual notes _____

Faith development (eg., in newsletter/classes) _____

Children's faith experience _____

Prelude _____

Hymn of gathering _____

Sprinkling/Penitential rite _____

Hymn of praise _____

Opening Prayer _____

First reading _____Responsory _____

Second reading _____Gospel acclamation _____

Gospel _____Profession of faith _____

General intercessions _____

At the preparation & presentation _____

Preface dialog _____Preface _____

Preface acclamation _____

Eucharistic prayer _____Memorial acclamation ___

Eucharistic amen _____

The Lord's prayer _____

Breaking of bread _____

The communion hymn _____

The post-communion hymn _____

Blessing _____At the dismissal _____

Memoranda:

SEVENTEENTH SUNDAY OF THE YEAR

YEAR A

READINGS

First Kings (3:5,7-12)
In accepting his own limitations and weaknesses and placing himself solely on God's support, Solomon pleases God and enriches himself. He receives the fullness of divine grace and becomes a vessel of divine justice and wisdom.

Romans (8:28-30)
In the context of God's experience of time, the ever-present now, we are chosen to live as God's children and to image God's Glory to others. As we do this we become more closely united to God, who in turn glorifies us.

Matthew (13:44-52)
The three parables used today (the Buried Treasure, the Pearl of Great Price, and the Fisher's Net) contain the essential elements of the meaning of most parables. They point to the great value of the Kingdom and to the idea that this value makes the coat, while great, a joy to pay. "The Fisher's Net" accents the idea that the heralding of the Good News attracts both good and bad; only God can separate them at the Eschaton .

FOCUS

The ability to discern that which is truly valuable or important from that which is of less import seems to be an overriding concern today. Knowing and accepting ourselves as God does is the challenge we are asked to take up. This can only be done if we recognize the centrality of God to our lives and the importance of God's grace in revitalizing our weak condition.

IDEA STARTERS

- *CCT Lectionary* (Proper 12): Ex 3:13-20; Ps 105:1-11; Rom 8:26-30; Mt 13:44-52.
- Where our heart is, there your treasure will be. Design a listing of treasures for your Sunday bulletin. End with the question: "Are our hearts set on the greater gifts?"
- Involve children in Sunday worship by having them role play a contemporary scene based upon the parables of Jesus proclaimed today.
- Evaluate your liturgical space: Do those furnishings we revere truly *appear* to be important? What can your worship team adapt or remove to make your building an appropriately focused house for the church?
- For your consideration: Opening Prayer; Gospel (full form); Intercessions for wisdom, faithfulness, households, youth, realtors, merchants, national leaders, those who go fishing (for sport or occupation); Ordinary Sundays Preface V (P33); Eucharistic Prayer I; Memorial Acclamation B; Solemn Blessing III.

MUSIC

- Psalm 119
- *All That We Have* (Dameans/NALR)
- *Beatitudes* (Dameans/NALR)
- *Believe* (McGrath/Resource)
- *Dwelling Place* (Jesuits/NALR)
- *Earthen Vessels* (Jesuits/NALR)
- *Eye Has Not Seen* (Haugen/GIA)
- *The Father's Care* (Keyes/Resource)
- *Here I Am, Lord* (Jesuits/NALR)
- *In Your Love, Remember Me* (Kendzia/NALR)
- *Like A Sunflower* (Landry/NALR)
- *Mountains and Hills* (Jesuits/NALR)
- *My Refuge* (Vessels/GIA)
- *Only In God* (Jesuits/NALR)
- *Seek First His Kingdom Over You* (Mullins/Resource)
- *Take, Lord, Receive* (Jesuits/NALR)
- *Take My Life and Let It Be* (ICEL)
- *They Knew Him* (Gilsdorf/Resource)
- *We Praise You* (Dameans/NALR)

SUNDAY PLANNING SHEET   Date _____

Parish focus _____

Environment & art _____

Ritual notes _____

Faith development (eg., in newsletter/classes) _____

Children's faith experience _____

Prelude _____

Hymn of gathering _____

Sprinkling/Penitential rite _____

Hymn of praise _____

Opening Prayer _____

First reading _____Responsory _____

Second reading _____Gospel acclamation _____

Gospel _____Profession of faith _____

General intercessions _____

At the preparation & presentation _____

Preface dialog _____Preface _____

Preface acclamation _____

Eucharistic prayer _____Memorial acclamation _____

Eucharistic amen _____

The Lord's prayer _____

Breaking of bread _____

The communion hymn _____

The post-communion hymn _____

Blessing _____At the dismissal _____

Memoranda:

EIGHTEENTH SUNDAY OF THE YEAR

YEAR A

READINGS
Isaiah (55:1-3)
Isaiah points to God as the source of all that is good and as necessary for life.
The basics of nourishment are attributed to God: bread, water, wine, and milk.
These gifts are given freely; indeed nothing we can do gains them. God in
compassion offers them as a sign of loving fidelity to the covenant.
Romans (8:35,37-39)
Paul underscores the notion that nothing can take us away from the all-
embracing love of Christ, the tangible manifestation of God's Love in the
world.
Matthew (14:13-21)
Matthew relates the miracle of the loaves and fishes. Here Jesus satiates the
hunger of thousands out of what seems to be very little indeed.

FOCUS
This set of readings seems to focus on a eucharistic motif. Isaiah indicates that
God is the ultimate source of nourishment. God provides for the people's
deepest needs and desires. In the Gospel, with the retelling of the feeding of
the five thousand, Jesus, the Bread of Life, uses the physical hunger of people
with his ability to fill that need as an analogy to his ability to be bread and
wine for all people, bread and wine that will satisfy forever. Paul demonstrates
the unshakeable and unending character of Jesus' love for us by linking it
directly to God's love and by indicating its eternal and invincible character.

IDEA STARTERS
- *CCT Lectionary* (Proper 13): Ex 12:1-14; Ps 143:1-10; Rom 8:31-39; Mt
  14:13-21.
- Today's readings give you an opportunity to explain "The Kingdom Game."
  Jesus gives us a foretaste of the feast to come. In the Eucharist we imagine
  ourselves in the fullness of the Kingdom.
- The water and bread symbols used in this day's lessons provide an
  opportunity to discuss the sacraments of initiation and the response they
  evoke from us.
- An interpretation given to the Gospel miracle is centered around the hearers
  of God's Word: the people shared what they had with their neighbors. How
  is the parish food pantry? Publicize the St. Vincent de Paul Society's activities.
- Sponsor an inter-parish picnic at a neighborhood park. Continue the banquet
  in fellowship with others in the Body of Christ.
- For your consideration: Sprinkling Baptismal Water B; Alternative Opening
  Prayer; Intercessions for those who hunger, the poor, the distressed, the
  persecuted, openness to God's Word, hopefulness; Ordinary Sundays
  Preface VI (P34); Eucharistic Prayer III; Memorial Acclamation C; Ordinary
  Solemn Blessing I.

MUSIC

- Psalm 145
- *The Breaking of the Bread* (Feiten/Resource)
- *Come, My Children* (Dameans/NALR)
- *Come to the Water* (Jesuits/NALR)
- *Everyday I Will Praise You* (Gilsdorf/Resource)
- *Father, We Sing Your Praises* (Zsigray/NALR)
- *For Us To Live* (Weston Priory)
- *Gather Us In* (Haugen/GIA)
- *Give Us Living Water* (Dameans/NALR)
- *God and Man at Table* (Stamps/Dawn Treador)
- *I Am the Bread of Life*
- *If God is For Us* (Jesuits/NALR)
- *I Long for You* (Dameans/NALR)
- *Jesus, In Our Hands* (Wise/GIA)
- *Look Beyond* (Dameans/NALR)
- *Lord, to Whom Shall We Go* (Conry/NALR)
- *Morning Has Broken* (Farjeon)
- *New Life* (Landry/NALR)
- *O Healing River* (Traditional)
- *One Bread, One Body* (Jesuits/NALR)
- *Our Blessing Cup* (Joncas/NALR)
- *Praise the Lord, My Soul* (Parker/GIA)
- *Song of the Exile* (Haugen/GIA)
- *That There May Be Bread* (Weston Priory)
- *The Bread of Rejoicing* (Deiss/NALR)
- *To Be Your Bread* (Haas/Cooperative Ministries)
- *We're Going On a Picnic* (White/Resource)
- *You Will Draw Water* (Conry/NALR)

SUNDAY PLANNING SHEET

Date _____

Parish focus _____

Environment & art _____

Ritual notes _____

Faith development (eg., in newsletter/classes) _____

Children's faith experience _____

Prelude _____

Hymn of gathering _____

Sprinkling/Penitential rite _____

Hymn of praise _____

Opening Prayer _____

First reading _____ Responsory _____

Second reading _____ Gospel acclamation _____

Gospel _____ Profession of faith _____

General intercessions _____

At the preparation & presentation _____

Preface dialog _____ Preface _____

Preface acclamation _____

Eucharistic prayer _____ Memorial acclamation _____

Eucharistic amen _____

The Lord's prayer _____

Breaking of bread _____

The communion hymn _____

The post-communion hymn _____

Blessing _____ At the dismissal _____

Memoranda:

NINETEENTH SUNDAY OF THE YEAR

YEAR A

READINGS

First Kings (19:9,11-13)
The familiar story of Elijah's encounter with the Lord reiterates the theme of the previous Sundays: God is not to be found in the places where we might expect God to be. God is not bound by our limited perspective or short-sighted vision. God will be God.

Romans (9:1-5)
Paul relates that he has deep feeling for his Jewish kin. He acknowledges that they were the first bearers of salvation and, by implication, that Christians should praise God for the gift of Israel.

Matthew (14:22-33)
The impetuosity and love of Peter are seen in this reading. We also see that in the beginning Peter had many doubts which often caused him to sink. Still, he always managed to keep the Lord and God's forgiving love before his eyes. This proved to be the source of his deliverance.

FOCUS

Often the note of surprise involved in an experience of the Divine can be the very thing that causes us to lose balance and falter. The nation of Israel did this with Jesus, and Peter did it in the confrontation of the elements. If we keep our eyes on Jesus, even if we falter we will eventually be delivered from all difficulties and rest secure in him.

IDEA STARTERS

- *CCT Lectionary* (Proper 14): Ex 14:19-31; Ps 106:4-12; Rom 9:1-5; Mt 14:22-33.
- At the intercessions, use Peter's words as a response; "Lord, save us."
- A bulletin article raising the question about when God is most a part of our lives may be appropriate: Is it only in crisis situations?
- It may be appropriate to celebrate Baptism at today's Eucharist: the Lord saves us through the baptismal waters!
- Sponsor an afternoon of sailing or fishing at a neighborhood lake; have a picnic at a beach!
- Evaluate your use of silence during the Eucharist: at the Confession of Sin, following each reading and homily, at the Intercessions, at the Preparation of the Altar, after communion, and after each invitation.
- For your consideration: Sprinkling Baptismal Water B; Intercessions for our Jewish brethren, for those who work or live in overnight shelters, those afflicted by natural disaster, for justice and peace in the world, kindness and truth, consolation of the bereaved, for trust; Ordinary Sundays Preface III (P31); Memorial Acclamation D; Ordinary Solemn Blessing V.

MUSIC

- Psalm 85
- *Alleluia, Give Thanks* (Deiss/NALR)
- *Amazing Grace* (traditional)
- *Answer When I Call* (Jesuits/NALR)
- *Believe* (McGrath/Resource)
- *Blest Be the Lord* Jesuits/NALR)
- *Glory and Praise* (Jesuits/NALR)
- *The God of Abraham Praise* (ICEL)
- *How Can I Keep From Singing?* (traditional)
- *How Firm A Foundation* (ICEL)
- *I Believe In the Sun* (Landry/NALR)
- *Jesus is Lord* (Toolan/Resource)
- *On Eagles' Wings* (Joncas/NALR)
- *Praise the Lord, My Soul* (Jesuits/NALR)
- *Redeemer, Lord* (Jesuits/NALR)
- *Seek First His Kingdom Over You* (Mullins/Resource)
- *Speak, Lord* (Schoenbachler/PAA)
- *This Alone* (Jesuits/NALR)
- *Trust in the Lord* (Jesuits/NALR)
- *We Are Called* (Pattersen/Resource)
- *Yahweh, the Faithful One* (Jesuits/NALR)
- *You Are Near* (Jesuits/NALR)

SUNDAY PLANNING SHEET   Date _____

Parish focus _____

Environment & art _____

Ritual notes _____

Faith development (eg., in newsletter/classes) _____

Children's faith experience _____

Prelude _____

Hymn of gathering _____

Sprinkling/Penitential rite _____

Hymn of praise _____

Opening Prayer _____

First reading _____Responsory _____

Second reading _____Gospel acclamation _____

Gospel _____Profession of faith _____

General intercessions _____

At the preparation & presentation _____

Preface dialog _____Preface _____

Preface acclamation _____

Eucharistic prayer _____Memorial acclamation _____

Eucharistic amen _____

The Lord's prayer _____

Breaking of bread _____

The communion hymn _____

The post-communion hymn _____

Blessing _____At the dismissal _____

Memoranda:

TWENTIETH SUNDAY OF THE YEAR

YEAR A

READINGS
Isaiah (56:1,6–7)
Once again, we are presented with the familiar theme of the prophet Isaiah. Only when our rituals are validated by our thoughts and acts do they have any value in God's eyes.
Romans (11:13–15,29–32)
Paul states two things in this reading from Romans. One, he longs for the Jews to claim Jesus as Lord and Messiah, since this will further (and complete) the plan of salvation. His second point is that God's plan of salvation is beyond our understanding. Even disobedience can be turned into glory through God's saving power and gracious act of love in Jesus.
Matthew (15:21–28)
Faithful persistence is a key to salvation. As the Canaanite woman, we must persist in our humble, obedient, and faithful "waiting on the Lord" if his gift of salvation is to be effective in us. This is all we can give him: loving fidelity!

FOCUS
Lived (practiced) faith is what gives meaning to all our actions in response to God. Isaiah states this in regard to ritualized worship. Paul reminds the gentiles that all people are able to be recipients of God's saving grace if they will receive it. Matthew gives us an example. The Canaanite woman's faith is what is rewarded. This is all Jesus requires of his followers.

IDEA STARTERS
- *CCT Lectionary* (Proper 15): Ex 16:2-15; Ps 78:1-3,10-20; Rm 11:13-16,29-32; Mt 15: 21-28.
- The Gospel pericopes for these next Sundays give an opportunity for reflection upon some of the "marks of the church." Today's focus involves catholicity — the universality of Jesus' message.
- God's love is for all: Catholic, Protestant, Jewish, Buddhist, atheist, American, Soviet, Irish, Mexican, white, and black; all religions, all nationalities, and all colors. God has created us all.
- Be careful in explaining the Romans passage. How is God speaking to us in such a selection? Use your bulletin as an instructional aid.
- Have a neighborhood picnic sponsored by all the religious organizations in the community. Close with an interfaith prayer service as daylight fades.
- For your consideration: Alternative Opening Prayer; Intercessions for travellers, foreign visitors in the assembly, proper celebration of the Sabbath, the United Nations, Jews and Gentiles, healing, persistent faithfulness and prayer; Ordinary Sundays Preface V (P33); Eucharistic Prayer III; Memorial Acclamation D; Ordinary Solemn Blessing II.

MUSIC

- Psalm 67
- *All Our Joy* (Dameans/NALR)
- *All the Ends of the Earth* (Jesuits/NALR)
- *And the Father Will Dance* (Landry/NALR)
- *The Fullness of God* (Andersen/Resource)
- *Gather Us In* (Haugen/GIA)
- *Go Up to the Mountain* (Weston Priory)
- *Hasten the Appointed* (ICEL)
- *He is the Lord* (Haas/Cooperative Ministries)
- *Hymn to God's Love* (Mondoy/Resource)
- *I Will Praise You* (Wrynn/Resource)
- *I Have Loved You* (Joncas/NALR)
- *In Him We Live* (Landry/NALR)
- *Lord, Let Your Mercy Be On Us* (Culbreth/Resource)
- *May the Peoples Praise You* (Gilsdorf/Resource)

SUNDAY PLANNING SHEET   Date _____

Parish focus _____

Environment & art _____

Ritual notes _____

Faith development (eg., in newsletter/classes) _____

Children's faith experience _____

Prelude _____

Hymn of gathering _____

Sprinkling/Penitential rite _____

Hymn of praise _____

Opening Prayer _____

First reading _____Responsory _____

Second reading _____Gospel acclamation _____

Gospel _____Profession of faith _____

General intercessions _____

At the preparation & presentation _____

Preface dialog _____Preface _____

Preface acclamation _____

Eucharistic prayer _____Memorial acclamation _____

Eucharistic amen _____

The Lord's prayer _____

Breaking of bread _____

The communion hymn _____

The post-communion hymn _____

Blessing _____At the dismissal _____

Memoranda:

TWENTY-FIRST SUNDAY OF THE YEAR

YEAR A

READINGS

Isaiah (22:15,19-23)
Isaiah is sent to the master of the palace with a message from the Lord. A new official will be raised up by the Lord's own hand, and Shevna (the former official) will lose his authority. All authority is from the Lord.

Romans (11:33-36)
Paul praises the wisdom, knowledge, and mind of God. No one can perceive God's thoughts, no one acts as counselor, no one can make a claim on God. All we can do is glorify God.

Matthew (16:13-20)
Peter, speaking for the apostles, the community of belief, makes the basic act of faith. He proclaims Jesus Lord and Son of God. Jesus declares that this knowledge is a divine gift, and that Peter's openness to the Spirit enables him to assume a position of pre-eminence in the community of believers.

FOCUS
All authority has its origin in God. Rather than becoming irresponsible, leaders must be filled with a sense of service and humility. If they are not, like Shevna, they will quickly be replaced by those who will be responsive to the Lord's will. Paul praises this seeing and pervasive wisdom of God, a wisdom which we can only stand before and praise. In Matthew we see once again the living of God's wisdom. Peter acknowledges who Christ is through the work of the Spirit. His openness to this Spirit enables Jesus to place Peter in a position of authority, not because Peter deserves it, but simply because the Spirit will have it so.

IDEA STARTERS
- *CCT Lectionary* (Proper 16): Ex 17:1-7; Ps 95; Rm 11:33-36; Mt 16: 13-20.
- Today's adult forum or homily may address the apostolic nature of the church.
- Be what you celebrate. Hold a picnic for the diocesan church with her bishop; on cathedral grounds, at a park, or in the cathedral!
- Place your papal flag at the coffee hour table or in a VBS classroom. How do our Gospel and first lesson help us understand this emblem?
- How may visuals be used today, specifically keys and rocks?
- For your consideration: Opening Prayer; Intercessions for the pope and bishop, national leaders, fearless witness, forgiveness, those in any kind of authority; Ordinary Sundays Preface VIII (P36); Eucharistic Prayer I; Memorial Acclamation D; Solemn Blessing for Apostles' Days.

MUSIC

- Psalm 138
- *Anthem* (Conry/NALR)
- *Believe* (McGrath/Resource)
- *Beginning Today* (Dameans/NALR)
- *Church of God* (ICEL)
- *He Has Anointed Me* (Dameans/NALR)
- *Here I Am, Lord* (Jesuits/NALR)
- *How Beautiful on the Mountains* (Deiss/NALR)
- *I Will Give Thanks* (Blachura/Resource)
- *I In Them* (Gilsdorf/Resource)
- *Lord, To Whom Shall We Go?* (Joncas/NALR)
- *The Lord Blesses Me* (Hilliard/Resource)
- *Service* (Dameans/NALR)
- *We Thank You, Father* (Weston Priory)
- *Who Has Known* (Jesuits/NALR)
- *Sing Out In Thanksgiving* (Jabusch/NALR)

SUNDAY PLANNING SHEET   Date _____

Parish focus _____

Environment & art _____

Ritual notes _____

Faith development (eg., in newsletter/classes) _____

Children's faith experience _____

Prelude _____

Hymn of gathering _____

Sprinkling/Penitential rite _____

Hymn of praise _____

Opening Prayer _____

First reading _____Responsory _____

Second reading _____Gospel acclamation _____

Gospel _____Profession of faith _____

General intercessions _____

At the preparation & presentation _____

Preface dialog _____Preface _____

Preface acclamation _____

Eucharistic prayer _____Memorial acclamation _____

Eucharistic amen _____

The Lord's prayer _____

Breaking of bread _____

The communion hymn _____

The post-communion hymn _____

Blessing _____At the dismissal _____

Memoranda:

TWENTY-SECOND SUNDAY YEAR A OF THE YEAR

READINGS
Jeremiah (20:7-9)
Jeremiah, "seduced" by the Lord, cannot keep from proclaiming God's word. Though it costs him hardship, pain, ridicule, and scandal, still he is impelled to deliver the Lord's message.
Roman (12:1-2)
Paul pleads with the Romans to offer themselves as "the holocaust." This is accomplished by not compromising values "to this age" but by living as Jesus would have us. When we do this, we clearly see God's will for us.
Matthew (16:21-27)
Peter wishes to have Jesus spared the work of redemption. Jesus, however, points out that only through sacrifice do we share God's life. That sacrifice is the obligation of our own will.

FOCUS
Jeremiah did what Paul counselled the Romans to do. He opened himself to God's will. In so doing, he offered his own body to the redemptive process. He offered himself (in other words) to make the word of God concrete. As Paul says, he then understood what it was God asked of him. Peter in the Gospel does just the opposite. He subjects God's plan to the value judgment of the human perspective. Therefore, he misses "the hidden wisdom of God." Jesus reiterates that without the sacrifice of the will, no good can follow.

IDEA STARTERS
- *CCT Lectionary* (Proper 17): Ex 19:1-9; Ps 114; Rm 12:1-13; Mt 16:21-28.
- Today's homily or adult forum may address what it means to be church: not a people who claim to be perfect, but a people who claim to be optimists.
- Special use of the processional cross today presents to the Christian a recollection of Christ's command to follow him — with our crosses.
- The prediction of the paschal mystery (Gospel) makes sense only now that we know that "the Lord is risen indeed." Look at the gospel parallels in the synoptics. Only the disciples are told these things, though this wasn't the kind of Christ they expected. Their understanding came only after the Resurrection. Today, we (with the apostles) are witnesses to these things.
- The second reading provides a reflection upon the religious lifestyle. The three monastic vows help free a person to be a witness to the paschal mystery: poverty vs. consumerism and materialism, celibacy vs. hedonism, obedience vs. atheistic existentialism.
- For your consideration: Sprinkling Baptismal Water B; Opening Prayer; Intercessions for the deprived, oppressed, imprisoned, God's will in our lives, spiritual transformation, endurance, power against temptation; Ordinary Sundays Preface VII (P35); Eucharistic Prayer II; Memorial Acclamation C; Lenten Solemn Blessing.

MUSIC

- Psalm 65
- *Behold the Wood* (Jesuits/NALR)
- *Come to Me* (Weston Priory)
- *If With All Your Hearts* (Mullins/Resource)
- *Lift High the Cross* (PMB)

- *Like a Sunflower* (Landry/NALR)
- *May We Praise You* (Jesuits/NALR)
- *Only a Shadow* (Landry/NALR)
- *Only This I Want* (Jesuits/NALR)
- *The Seed That Falls* (Lisicky/Resource)
- *You Are My People* (Lisicky/Resource)

SUNDAY PLANNING SHEET   Date _____

Parish focus _____

Environment & art _____

Ritual notes _____

Faith development (eg., in newsletter/classes) _____

Children's faith experience _____

Prelude _____

Hymn of gathering _____

Sprinkling/Penitential rite _____

Hymn of praise _____

Opening Prayer _____

First reading _____ Responsory _____

Second reading _____ Gospel acclamation _____

Gospel _____ Profession of faith _____

General intercessions _____

At the preparation & presentation _____

Preface dialog _____ Preface _____

Preface acclamation _____

Eucharistic prayer _____ Memorial acclamation _____

Eucharistic amen _____

The Lord's prayer _____

Breaking of bread _____

The communion hymn _____

The post-communion hymn _____

Blessing _____ At the dismissal _____

Memoranda:

TWENTY-THIRD SUNDAY OF THE YEAR
YEAR A

READINGS

Ezekiel (33:7-9)
God tells Ezekiel that since he has been given responsibility for being a prophet to God's people, he shall be held accountable for his faithfully discharging that task.

Romans (13:8-10)
Paul tells the Romans that the law of love is the fulfillment and completion of the entirety of the Law.

Matthew (18:15-20)
The love Christians have for one another is sometimes confrontative. It points out to the other the areas which need development and growth. Since the body unified to Christ is one, bound together in his love, the love shared between one another is always supportive, and always emanates from compassionate concern.

FOCUS

All three readings point to love and the responsibility it carries with it. God, the author of all love, invests us with responsibility for one another. If we do not carry out our duties toward one another, we will be held responsible. The Gospel re-echoes this theme. In Romans Paul directly equates love, not only with the best in the Law, but the very completion of the Law.

IDEA STARTERS

- *CCT Lectionary* (Proper 18): Ex 19:16-24; Ps 115:1-11; Rm 13:1-10; Mt 18:15-20.
- The concept of fraternal correction is best understood in terms of church; the gathering of people who profess faith in the Risen Lord and live out his message (cf. Zanzig. T., *Understanding Your Faith*. St. Mary's Press, 1980).
- Why does the church take official stands not only on matters of faith but on those of morals as well?
- How is the paschal mystery the "fulfillment of the scriptures"?
- Does the assembly realize that when they confess their sins to a priest they are actually confessing to "almighty God and to their brothers and sisters"?
- For your consideration: Penitential Rite A; Alternative Opening Prayer; Intercessions for watchmen, sinner, guilt-ridden, neighbors (friend or foe), spirit of love, willingness to see and hear God in others, end to pride; Ordinary Sundays Preface I (P29); Eucharistic Prayer III; Ordinary Solemn Blessing III.

MUSIC

- Psalm 95
- *All That We Have* (Dameans/NALR)
- *All Those Who Love Me* (Weston Priory)
- *Come Down, O Love Divine* (PMB)
- *Father, We Sing Your Praises* (Zsigray/NALR)
- *Father We Thank Thee* (PMB)
- *For the Beauty of the Earth* (PMB)
- *Glorious In Majesty* (Cothran/GIA)
- *If Today You Hear His Voice* (Prochaska/Resource)
- *Oh, How Good* (Landry/NALR)
- *Send Us Your Spirit* (Haas/Coop Ministries)
- *Sholom* (Reagan/NALR)
- *Song of Gathering* (Wise/GIA)
- *Song of Peace* (Kreutz/PMB)
- *A Time for Building Bridges* (Landry/NALR)
- *Ubi Caritas* (Taize/NALR)
- *Where Two Or More* (Fisherfolk/Resource)
- *We Are Called* (Pattersen/Resource)
- *With All My Heart* (Lisicky/Resource)

SUNDAY PLANNING SHEET   Date _____

Parish focus _____

Environment & art _____

Ritual notes _____

Faith development (eg., in newsletter/classes) _____

Children's faith experience _____

Prelude _____

Hymn of gathering _____

Sprinkling/Penitential rite _____

Hymn of praise _____

Opening Prayer _____

First reading _____Responsory _____

Second reading _____Gospel acclamation _____

Gospel _____Profession of faith _____

General intercessions _____

At the preparation & presentation _____

Preface dialog _____Preface _____

Preface acclamation _____

Eucharistic prayer _____Memorial acclamation _____

Eucharistic amen _____

The Lord's prayer _____

Breaking of bread _____

The communion hymn _____

The post-communion hymn _____

Blessing _____At the dismissal _____

Memoranda:

TWENTY-FOURTH SUNDAY YEAR A OF THE YEAR

READINGS
Sirach (27:30-28:7)
As we treat others, in the Lord, we can expect similar treatment.
Romans (14:7-9)
We are the Lord's in life and death. We can never escape this. Christ died so that he might establish sovereignty over all.
Matthew (18:21-35)
The servant wished to be treated in a way (forgivingly) in which he refused to treat others. For this reason, he lost forgiveness and was judged according to his own standards.

FOCUS
The focal point for this Sunday's readings can be seen as the importance of forgiveness in the kingdom. Those who do not forgive cannot experience forgiveness, since they do not have the capacity to integrate so generous an act (forgiveness) into their persons.

IDEA STARTERS
- *CCT Lectionary* (Proper 19): Ex 20:1-20; Ps 19:7-14; Rm 14:5-12; Mt 18:21-35.
- The Penitential Rite and The Kiss of Peace should be highlighted today. The Lord's Prayer, with its powerful phrase, "forgive us our sin as we forgive those who sin against us," summarizes the Gospel.
- The celebration of Reconciliation is meaningless if one does not come with a sincere, contrite heart. We must want to change. "Go and sin no more."
- At a children's liturgy, have youngsters portray the forgiveness to which God calls us. Act out the Parable. Tell the parable as a story, possibly with slides.
- Adult forum: Double-standards: What are they? Why do they exist? How may we combat them?
- For your consideration: Penitential Rite A; Opening Prayer; Intercessions for the vengeful, ending injustice, forgiveness, kindness, compassion, submissiveness to God's will, national leaders, auditors; Reconciliation Eucharistic Prayer I; Memorial Acclamation B; highlight the *Comm(on)-union Rite;* Ordinary Solemn Blessing V.

MUSIC
- Psalm 103
- *As the Father Has Sent Me* (O'Brien/Resource)
- *Dwelling Place* (Jesuits/NALR)
- *Happy Are They* (Miffleton/Resource)
- *In Your Love Remember Me* (Kendzia/NALR)
- *I In Them* (Gilsdorf/Resource)
- *Keeping Festival* (Toolan/Resource)
- *No One Lives for Himself* (Oosterhuis/NALR)
- *Our God is Love* (Repp/K&R)
- *Service* (Dameans/NALR)
- *Share a Little Bit of Your Love* (Repp/K&R)
- *This is Our Prayer for You* (Repp/K&R)
- *Without Seeing You* (Deiss/NALR

SUNDAY PLANNING SHEET

Date _____

Parish focus _____

Environment & art _____

Ritual notes _____

Faith development (eg., in newsletter/classes) _____

Children's faith experience _____

Prelude _____

Hymn of gathering _____

Sprinkling/Penitential rite _____

Hymn of praise _____

Opening Prayer _____

First reading _____ Responsory _____

Second reading _____ Gospel acclamation _____

Gospel _____ Profession of faith _____

General intercessions _____

At the preparation & presentation _____

Preface dialog _____ Preface _____

Preface acclamation _____

Eucharistic prayer _____ Memorial acclamation _____

Eucharistic amen _____

The Lord's prayer _____

Breaking of bread _____

The communion hymn _____

The post-communion hymn _____

Blessing _____ At the dismissal _____

Memoranda:

TWENTY-FIFTH SUNDAY OF THE YEAR

YEAR A

READINGS

Isaiah (55:6-9)
Isaiah states that God's ways are transcendent, far beyond the comprehension of humanity.

Philippians (1:20-24,27)
Paul states that whether he is joined to Christ in death or continues to serve him in the body, he will always be in Christ since to do the will of Christ is to unite oneself to the risen Lord.

Matthew (20:1-16)
In this parable, Jesus points to the gracious gift of forgiveness God offers us. We cannot understand it; we can only rejoice and accept it.

FOCUS

The focus for today's readings seems quite clear. God's justice is directly relayed through not simply equanimity and fairness, but merciful love. This is a mystery the human mind will never fully comprehend. It doesn't need to understand, but simply to accept in joyful humility.

IDEA STARTERS

- *CCT Lectionary* (Proper 20): Ex 32:1-14; Ps 106:7-8, 19-23; Phil 1:21-27; Mt 20:1-16.
- What is God's grace? How is God's grace present in the sacraments? Do we accept God's grace?
- What are people's feelings about God's forgiveness which is freely given equally to the committed Christian and to the last minute penitent?
- If today's Gospel is taken literally, it may make a case for social injustice! What is the Gospel really saying about the church and her "eleventh hour" members?
- At a children's liturgy, act out the Gospel.
- A forum on suicide: "It is more urgent that I remain alive for your sake" (second reading).
- Does your parish encourage new membership (e.g.,through involvement hospitality)? When was the last time your community inspired an adult to be baptized or to be received into the church's full communion? How do we go about welcoming those who simply need God's initiative through us?
- For your consideration: Sprinkling Baptismal Water B; Alternative Opening Prayer; Intercessions for attentiveness to the Lord in our lives, generosity. Gospel living, realtors, employers, employees, labor unions, unemployed, mercy, forgiveness; Ordinary Sundays Preface VII (P35); Eucharistic Prayer III; Memorial Acclamation D; Ordinary Solemn Blessing IV.

MUSIC

- Psalm 145
- *All the Ends of the Earth* (Jesuits/NALR)
- *Anthem* (Conry/NALR)
- *Awake O Sleeper* (Dameans/NALR)
- *Everyday I Will Praise You* (Gilsdorf/Resource)
- *Glory and Praise* (Jesuits/NALR)
- *Hymn of Initiation* (Westendorf/NALR)
- *I Thank My God* (Andersen/Resource)
- *In Christ there is No East or West* (PMB)
- *Justice Shall Flourish* (Schoenbachler/Coop Ministries)
- *The Lord is Near* (Joncas/NALR)
- *O Lord You Know Our Weakness* (PMB)
- *Only in God* (Jesuits/NALR)
- *Praise and Honor* (Tucciarone/Resource)
- *The Sun is Rising* (Weston Priory)
- *Take, Lord, Receive* (Jesuits/NALR)

SUNDAY PLANNING SHEET   Date _____

Parish focus _____

Environment & art _____

Ritual notes _____

Faith development (eg., in newsletter/classes) _____

Children's faith experience _____

Prelude _____

Hymn of gathering _____

Sprinkling/Penitential rite _____

Hymn of praise _____

Opening Prayer _____

First reading _____Responsory _____

Second reading _____Gospel acclamation _____

Gospel _____Profession of faith _____

General intercessions _____

At the preparation & presentation _____

Preface dialog _____Preface _____

Preface acclamation _____

Eucharistic prayer _____Memorial acclamation _____

Eucharistic amen _____

The Lord's prayer _____

Breaking of bread _____

The communion hymn _____

The post-communion hymn _____

Blessing _____At the dismissal _____

Memoranda:

TWENTY-SIXTH SUNDAY YEAR A
OF THE YEAR

READINGS
Ezekiel (18:25-28)
Ezekiel challenges us with the mystery of the wisdom that is the Lord's. While we judge by appearances and other superficial criteria, the Lord probes to the center, to the deeper meaning of a person's mind and heart. What sometimes seems unjust is indeed the most authentic and integrated justice, for it is part of the very mind and justice that is God; a justice which is vital and lifegiving.
Philippians (2:1-11)
Paul, in the ancient Christian hymn to Christ, displays to our eyes God's conception of justice in action. It is oblational, self-sacrificing, and totally given. Such love, Paul says, is given to us as a model and for our justification.
Matthew (21:28-32)
Verbal responses mean nothing, Jesus tells us, unless they are underscored with lived reality. Those prompted by the Spirit of God who respond to the divine invitation to life, though they may have been resistant at first, can share in life in abundance.

FOCUS
With the model of Jesus as the suffering servant, obediently emptying himself not only of his divinity but of his very human life, Paul points the way of God's wisdom. As Ezekiel did, Paul demonstrates that wisdom and justice seen and lived from the divine perspective far surpass the superficialities of limited, darkened human vision. While it seems unfair from the human perspective, it is this very expansive quality of divine justice which results in salvation for sinners.

IDEA STARTERS
- *CCT Lectionary* (Proper 21): Ex 33:12-23; Ps 99; Phil 2:1-13; Mt 21:28-32.
- How may today's Gospel pericope be seen as a further elaboration of last Sunday's text?
- The first lesson is a powerful speech. How do you picture Ezekiel preaching this message? How will the reader proclaim the passage's urgency?
- Provide a background to the Philippians hymn we proclaim annually on Passion (Palm) Sunday, and sing weekly as a part of Sunday Evening Prayer.
- At a children's liturgy, make the Gospel into a contemporary story which they might actually experience.
- Do you ever hear the accusation: "It's always the same people who run things here"? Have people volunteer to participate in parish ministries at the liturgical, service oriented, and social levels today.
- For your consideration: Pentitential Rite A; Opening Prayer; Second Lesson (full form); Intercessions for justice, virtuous living, guidance, truth, compassion, joy, respect for the name of Jesus, parent-child relationships, tax collectors, prostitutes; Ordinary Sundays Preface VII (P35); Memorial Acclamation A; Ordinary Solemn Blessing II.

MUSIC

- Psalm 25
- *All Hail the Power of Jesus' Name* (PMB)
- *Bless this Bounteous Land of Freedom* (Senchur/PMB)
- *God and Man at Table* (Stamps)
- *He is the Lord* (Haas/Coop Ministries)
- *Jesus is Lord* (Toolan/Resource)

- *I Will Sing* (Dyer Celebration)
- *Look Toward Me* (Lisicky/Resource)
- *My Peace, My Joy, My Love* (Page/Resource)
- *Spare Us, Lord* (PMB)
- *Teach Me Your Ways* (Foster/Resource)

SUNDAY PLANNING SHEET   Date _____

Parish focus _____

Environment & art _____

Ritual notes _____

Faith development (eg., in newsletter/classes) _____

Children's faith experience _____

Prelude _____

Hymn of gathering _____

Sprinkling/Penitential rite _____

Hymn of praise _____

Opening Prayer _____

First reading _____Responsory _____

Second reading _____Gospel acclamation _____

Gospel _____Profession of faith _____

General intercessions _____

At the preparation & presentation _____

Preface dialog _____Preface _____

Preface acclamation _____

Eucharistic prayer _____Memorial acclamation _____

Eucharistic amen _____

The Lord's prayer _____

Breaking of bread _____

The communion hymn _____

The post-communion hymn _____

Blessing _____At the dismissal _____

Memoranda:

TWENTY-SEVENTH SUNDAY OF THE YEAR

YEAR A

READINGS

Isaiah (5:1-7)
Isaiah tells the story of the owner of the vineyard who expected a great yield from the vineyard he has so carefully tended and cared for. In response to the lack of yield, the owner of the vineyard disowns it and leaves it to certain ruin. The allusions to Judah and Jerusalem are clearly drawn.

Philippians (4:6-9)
Paul lists for the Philippians how they can be a responsive, productive "vineyard." Living lives that mirror the perfection of the Godhead will result in peaceful, tranquil lives.

Matthew (21:33-43)
The "vineyard theme" alters with the accent placed on the relationship between the owner of the vineyard and his tenants. The greed and malevolence of the tenants is the motivation for the violent, abusive, and murderous action even to the owner's son. Their behavior results in their being brought to a bad end. Jesus confronts the chief priests and elders with the fact that they too shall lose their inheritance for their rejection of him.

FOCUS

Philippians serves as the counterpoint to the Isaian and Matthean readings. Lives lived in the Lord's own light will result in peace and joy. Those who refuse to acknowledge their "poverty of spirit" will be like the failed gardens of the violent tenants. They will lose their inheritance and be left to the violence and destruction of their evil ways.

IDEA STARTERS

- *CCT Lectionary* (Proper 22): Nu 27:12-23; Ps 81:1-10; Phil 3:12-21; Mt 21:33-43.
- The autumn is here. It is almost time for the harvest. How attractive and up-to-date are the parish bulletin boards? How might your liturgical artists refurbish these communication centers with the remainder of the liturgical year and natural season in mind?
- How may your hospitality team celebrate the beginning of another "working year" with all parishioners?
- After worship, share conversation, coffee, cookies and grapes (cf. Gospel).
- The Gospel includes an excerpt from Easter Psalm 118. Every Sunday is a "little Easter."
- The Isaian prophecy may almost appear to be a text of a folk song. How might you bring this poetry to life?
- For your consideration: Sprinkling Baptismal Water A; Alternative Opening Prayer; Intercessions for farmers, inhabitants of Jerusalem, favorable weather, honesty, purity, decency, virtue, tenants, masons, Respect Life Sunday; Ordinary Sundays Preface V (P33); Eucharistic Prayer III; Memorial Acclamation B; Ordinary Solemn Blessing II.

MUSIC

- Psalm 80
- *Alleluia, My Word* (Wise/GIA)
- *All You Nations Clap Your Hands* (Lisicky/Resource)
- *All the Ends of the Earth* (Foster/Resource)
- *All You Lands* (Vessels/GIA)
- *City of God* (Jesuits/NALR)
- *I Am the Vine* (Hurd/FCC)
- *Journeys Ended, Journeys Begun* (Weston Priory)
- *Let All the Earth* (Haugen/GIA)
- *Lift Every Voice and Sing* (Johnson/PMB)
- *The Messenger Song* (Gilsdorf/Resource)
- *Restore Us* (Gilsdorf/Resource)
- *Thanks Be To You, O God* (Stuntz/PMB)
- *We Plow the Fields* (traditional/PMB)

SUNDAY PLANNING SHEET   Date _____

Parish focus _____

Environment & art _____

Ritual notes _____

Faith development (eg., in newsletter/classes) _____

Children's faith experience _____

Prelude _____

Hymn of gathering _____

Sprinkling/Penitential rite _____

Hymn of praise _____

Opening Prayer _____

First reading _____Responsory _____

Second reading _____Gospel acclamation _____

Gospel _____Profession of faith _____

General intercessions _____

At the preparation & presentation _____

Preface dialog _____Preface _____

Preface acclamation _____

Eucharistic prayer _____Memorial acclamation _____

Eucharistic amen _____

The Lord's prayer _____

Breaking of bread _____

The communion hymn _____

The post-communion hymn _____

Blessing _____At the dismissal _____

Memoranda:

TWENTY-EIGHTH SUNDAY OF THE YEAR

YEAR A

READINGS
Isaiah (25:6-10)
Isaiah foretells what the "Day of the Lord" will be like. It shall usher in the fullness of joy, peace, divine knowledge, and compassion. When this happens, all shall know it is the Lord's work and rejoice in it.

Philippians (4:12-14,19-20)
Paul states that though he has learned to rely alone on the Lord, he was touched that the Philippians should wish to share in his sufferings. He assures them that their reward awaits them in the Kingdom.

Matthew (22:1-14)
This parable of the wedding feast refers to the kingdom both now and in its future fulfillment.

FOCUS
Like Paul, those who wish to share in the Messianic Kingdom must be willing to prepare for the celebration of the "Wedding Feast" through disciplined acceptance of God's will. When this happens, the fullness of the Reign of God will appear. All tears shall be wiped from the faces of the believers.

IDEA STARTERS
- *CCT Lectionary* (Proper 23): Deut 34:1-12; Ps 135:1-14; Phil 4:1-9; Mt 22:1-14.
- The lessons celebrate that Christians (those given the baptismal garment) are sharers in God's Kingdom in our midst.
- The alb (worn by any baptized person usually in a liturgical leadership position: presider, acolyte, cantor, etc.) is nothing more than the baptismal garment.
- How is the Eucharist a foretaste of the feast to come? How can this be demonstrated in the Liturgy?
- Young children may be asked to illustrate Isaiah's prophecy through arts and crafts. Older children may act out the Gospel.
- The celebration of infant baptism may be appropriate today.
- Bulletin article: "The Baptismal Garment."
- For your consideration: Sprinkling Baptismal Water B; Alternate Opening Prayer; Gospel (full-form); Intercessions for mountain climbers, the hungry, alcoholics, international peace, the depressed, shepherds, stewardship of creation, hope, engaged couples, rulers of nations, criminals, Vocation Awareness Week; Ordinary Sundays Preface VI (P34); Eucharistic Prayer I; Memorial Acclamation D; Ordinary Solemn Blessing IV.

MUSIC

- Psalm 23
- *A Banquet is Prepared* (Jesuits/NALR)
- *Breaking of the Bread* (Feiten/Resource)
- *God and Man at Table* (Stamps/Treador Music)
- *In the Day of the Lord* (Gutfreund/NALR)

- *Jesus is Life* (Landry/NALR)
- *Praise the Lord* (Keyes/Resource)
- *Psalm 23* (Toolan/Resource)
- *Song of the Beatitudes* (Deiss/NALR)
- *Taste and See* (Haugen/GIA)
- *With Our Hearts Full Of Joy* (Patterson/Resource)

SUNDAY PLANNING SHEET   Date _____

Parish focus _____

Environment & art _____

Ritual notes _____

Faith development (eg., in newsletter/classes) _____

Children's faith experience _____

Prelude _____

Hymn of gathering _____

Sprinkling/Penitential rite _____

Hymn of praise _____

Opening Prayer _____

First reading _____Responsory _____

Second reading _____Gospel acclamation _____

Gospel _____Profession of faith _____

General intercessions _____

At the preparation & presentation _____

Preface dialog _____Preface _____

Preface acclamation _____

Eucharistic prayer _____Memorial acclamation ___

Eucharistic amen _____

The Lord's prayer _____

Breaking of bread _____

The communion hymn _____

The post-communion hymn _____

Blessing _____At the dismissal _____

Memoranda:

TWENTY-NINTH SUNDAY OF THE YEAR

READINGS

Isaiah (45:1,4-6)
Cyrus, without his knowledge, is blessed by the Lord, and used for the salvation and deliverance of God's people.

First Thessalonians (1:1-5)
Paul reminds the Thessalonians that they were chosen by God and bore fruit in that election. He indicates that this accomplishment (their faith response) is the work of the Holy Spirit.

Matthew (22:15-21)
Jesus indicates to the scheming Pharisees that for the person of faith priorities are clearly and honestly established. Things which belong to God are God's, and all others follow in their proper perspective.

FOCUS

It is God who ultimately establishes all those in a just and legitimate authority. God acts on virtue of God's own wisdom and knowledge and not that of people. Therefore, those who honor God's authority will honor the authority of others.

IDEA STARTERS

- *CCT Lectionary* (Proper 24): Ruth 1:1-19a; Ps 146; I Thes 1:1-10; Mt 22:15-22.
- Giving biblical background to First Thessalonians will provide guidance in understanding the second lessons during these last Ordinary Sundays.
- An adult forum might discuss this heated issue: "The Christian's *Obligation* to Withhold Taxes."
- A bulletin article may address stewardship.
- What part must God play in the lives of the married? the ordained? the business executive? the fourteen year old? the farmer?
- You may wish to seek out new volunteers to "prove their faith and labor in love." Thank those who have already volunteered.
- For your consideration: Opening Prayer; Intercessions for non-believers, worship in spirit and truth, all nationalities, in thanksgiving, dedication, for hypocrites, IRS workers, Mission Sunday; Ordinary Sundays Preface V (P33); Eucharistic Prayer III; Memorial Acclamation D; *The Lord's Prayer* sung; Ordinary Solemn Blessing III.

MUSIC

- Psalm 96
- *All That We Have* (Dameans/NALR)
- *I Believe in the Sun* (Landry/NALR)
- *If God is For Us* (Jesuits/NALR)
- *Like a Sunflower* (Landry/NALR)
- *May We Praise* (Jesuits/NALR)
- *A Mighty Fortress* (Luther/PMB)
- *My Refuge* (Vessels/GIA)
- *O God of Loveliness* (Westendorf/PMB)
- *Only A Shadow* (Landry/NALR)
- *Shout For Joy* (Byrne/Resource)
- *Today is Born A Savior* (Hilliard/Resource)
- *Worship and Praise* (Keyes/Resource)

SUNDAY PLANNING SHEET

Date _____

Parish focus _____

Environment & art _____

Ritual notes _____

Faith development (eg., in newsletter/classes) _____

Children's faith experience _____

Prelude _____

Hymn of gathering _____

Sprinkling/Penitential rite _____

Hymn of praise _____

Opening Prayer _____

First reading _____ Responsory _____

Second reading _____ Gospel acclamation _____

Gospel _____ Profession of faith _____

General intercessions _____

At the preparation & presentation _____

Preface dialog _____ Preface _____

Preface acclamation _____

Eucharistic prayer _____ Memorial acclamation _____

Eucharistic amen _____

The Lord's prayer _____

Breaking of bread _____

The communion hymn _____

The post-communion hymn _____

Blessing _____ At the dismissal _____

Memoranda:

THIRTIETH SUNDAY OF THE YEAR

YEAR A

READINGS
Exodus (22:20–26)
Israel is reminded of her captivity in Egypt and challenged to use this experience as a guide in her treatment of aliens, the oppressed, the poor, and the powerless. Her compassion must mirror that of the Lord's, who showed compassion to her in her need.
First Thessalonians (1:5–10)
By imitating Christ as modeled by Paul, the Thessalonians have become beacons of faith and purity for Christians everywhere.
Matthew (22:34–40)
Jesus discloses the greatest commandment: love of God with the totality of the person and love of neighbor and self.

FOCUS
When we follow the pattern of Jesus and live his great commandment of love, then there are no strangers, aliens, or others. All become brothers and sisters under the one gracious God. The more we grow in this fashion, the more we become beacons of light and hope for a darkened world.

IDEA STARTERS
- *CCT Lectionary* (Proper 25): Ruth 2:1–13; Ps 128; I Thes 2:1–8; Mt 22:34–46.
- We come to the final month of ordinary Sundays. Looking to the kingdom, today's lectionary reflects upon the law of the kingdom: Love.
- Gathering at church on Sunday should be motivated by the Great Commandments. Why are people present? How would you rate your parish's hospitality?
- Bulletin article: Who are the Pharisees and Sadducees? Compare their views to contemporary Jewish beliefs and practices.
- Does your parish have a human concerns group to educate and work in your community? Does your parish publicize its social outreach (faith in action)?
- At the Presentation, "gifts for the needs of the church and the poor" may be brought forward.
- For your consideration: Opening Prayer; Intercessions for visitors, widow(er)s, orphans, the poor, extortionists, garment workers, compassion, enemies, perseverence, the life of the world to come, lawyers, church authorities, Lutheran–RC dialogue; Ordinary Sundays Preface VIII (P36); Ordinary Solemn Blessing IV.

MUSIC

- Psalm 18
- *Arise, Come Sing in the Morning* (Zsigray/NALR)
- *Bless the Lord, You People* (Pinson/NALR)
- *By the Love* (Weston Priory)
- *Dwelling Place* (Jesuits/NALR)
- *Jesus In Our Hands* (Wise/GIA)
- *Grace and Peace* (Gilsdorf/Resource)
- *In You I Take Refuge* (Hilliard/Resource)
- *My Lord Is Alive* (Toolan/Resource)
- *Song of Thanksgiving* (Dameans/NALR)
- *That There May Be Bread* (Weston Priory)
- *Though the Mountains May Fall* (Jesuits/NALR)
- *A Time for Building Bridges* (Landry/NALR)
- *Ubi Caritas* (Taize/GIA)
- *You Shall Love the Lord* (Englert/PMB)

SUNDAY PLANNING SHEET

Date _____

Parish focus _____

Environment & art _____

Ritual notes _____

Faith development (eg., in newsletter/classes) _____

Children's faith experience _____

Prelude _____

Hymn of gathering _____

Sprinkling/Penitential rite _____

Hymn of praise _____

Opening Prayer _____

First reading _____Responsory _____

Second reading _____Gospel acclamation _____

Gospel _____Profession of faith _____

General intercessions _____

At the preparation & presentation _____

Preface dialog _____Preface _____

Preface acclamation _____

Eucharistic prayer _____Memorial acclamation _____

Eucharistic amen _____

The Lord's prayer _____

Breaking of bread _____

The communion hymn _____

The post-communion hymn _____

Blessing _____At the dismissal _____

Memoranda:

THIRTY-FIRST
SUNDAY OF THE YEAR

YEAR A

READINGS
Malachi (1:14-2:8-10)
Those who do not acknowledge the Lord as God and king are doomed to alienation and destruction. We know the unfaithful by the injustice of their deeds.
First Thessalonians (2:7-9,13)
Those who accept the Word of God into their lives perceive that it comes not as a human saying, but as the holy Word of God, which is at work within the hearts of all who believe.
Matthew (23:1-12)
Jesus reminds his followers that the greatest among them is the one who serves. Those who exalt themselves are always humbled.

FOCUS
The people of God are those who recognize the Word of God for what it is: God. In welcoming God into their lives, God becomes active in them, bringing them out of the alienation and isolation of egoism. They are able to become servants and so to share the life of the Master.

IDEA STARTERS
- *CCT Lectionary* (Proper 26): Ruth 4:7-17; I Thes 2:9-13,17-20; Mt 23:1-12.
- Today's Gospel gives us another illustration of the kingdom: God is our Father, and Jesus teaches us the law of the kingdom.
- Bulletin article: "Who are the scribes?"
- The lessons provide a study of authority in the church. Does your parish council take an active role (collegially)? Do parish leaders understand the authority of Jesus *and themselves* in terms of foot-washing (cf. John 13)?
- Honor coordinators, presidents, and leaders of parish activities at the coffee hour.
- November has traditionally been the month commemorating all the faithfully departed. How might your community observe this custom using the year round furnishings of the church (eg., font, paschal candle)?
- For your consideration: Opening Prayer; Intercessions for all nations, faithfulness, peace, children, parenting, hopefulness, friendships, evangelizers, teachers, manual laborers, rabbis; Eucharistic Prayer IV; *The Lord's Prayer* sung; Ordinary Solemn Blessing V.

MUSIC

- Psalm 131
- *As a Little Child* (Gilsdorf/Resource)
- *As the Father Has Sent Me* (O'Brien/Resource)
- *Calm and Quiet* (Walters/Resource)
- *In Him We Live* (Landry/NALR)
- *Love Consecrates the Humblest Act* (McManus/PMB)
- *The Messenger Song* (Gilsdorf/Resource)
- *One Bread, One Body* (Jesuits/NALR)
- *One Lord* (Haas/Cooperative Ministries)
- *Only This I Want* (Jesuits/NALR)
- *Peace Prayer* (Jesuits/NALR)
- *Song of the Exile* (Haugen/GIA)
- *Song of Wonder* (Deiss/NALR)
- *'Tis the Gift to be Simple* (Merman/PMB)
- *To Be Your Bread* (Haas/Cooperative Ministries)
- *Spirit of God* (Weston Priory)
- *You Are Near* (Jesuits/NALR)

SUNDAY PLANNING SHEET   Date _____

Parish focus _____

Environment & art _____

Ritual notes _____

Faith development (eg., in newsletter/classes) _____

Children's faith experience _____

Prelude _____

Hymn of gathering _____

Sprinkling/Penitential rite _____

Hymn of praise _____

Opening Prayer _____

First reading _____Responsory _____

Second reading _____Gospel acclamation _____

Gospel _____Profession of faith _____

General intercessions _____

At the preparation & presentation _____

Preface dialog _____Preface _____

Preface acclamation _____

Eucharistic prayer _____Memorial acclamation ___

Eucharistic amen _____

The Lord's prayer _____

Breaking of bread _____

The communion hymn _____

The post-communion hymn _____

Blessing _____At the dismissal _____

Memoranda:

THIRTY-SECOND SUNDAY OF THE YEAR

YEAR A

READINGS
Wisdom (6:12-16)
Wisdom readily comes to those who seek her. She never disappoints those who truly and honestly long for her and her knowledge. She is gracious, and solicitous to those who plead for her aid.
First Thessalonians (4:13-18)
All those who share Christ's life on the earth will share his resurrection. They will be raised to glory and reign with him in splendor forever.
Matthew (25:1-13)
The foolish bridesmaids do not heed the call of Wisdom to prudence and spiritual sense. They lose their place at the heavenly wedding banquet due to their lack of preparation and wisdom.

FOCUS
Those who live in Christ possess wisdom and act in prudent sensible ways. They prepare for the reign of God and are not caught unawares. They will enter into glory with the Bridegroom to share for eternity in the everlasting wedding banquet.

IDEA STARTERS
- *CCT Lectionary* (Proper 27): Amos 5:15-24; Ps 50:7-15; I Thes 4:13-18; Mt 25:1-13.
- The Christian symbol of marriage is exemplified in today's Gospel: Christ (bridegroom) and church (bride). Celebrate marriage at the Sunday Eucharist!
- The baptismal symbol of oil lamps (candle) is also in the Gospel. The Paschal Mystery is also recalled: the great nightwatch (Easter Vigil); we have been baptized into Christ's death; torches; Jesus the Gate. Celebrate infant baptism at the Eucharist!
- In the bulletin: Explain the traditional images (biblical-cultural symbols) representing the parousia as explained in Thessalonians.
- The first lesson personifies Wisdom. God shares Wisdom with us through the Holy Spirit: May She build a home in us!
- For your consideration: Sprinkling of Baptismal Water A; Opening Prayer A; Second Reading (full-form); Intercessions for wisdom, love, stewardship of creation, consolation, engaged couples, preparedness; Ordinary Sundays Preface IV (P32); Memorial Acclamation C; Ordinary Sundays Solemn Blessing I.

MUSIC

- Psalm 63
- *Awaken My Heart* (Deiss/NALR)
- *Canticle of the Sun* (Haugen/GIA)
- *The Dawn of the Day* (Deiss/NALR)
- *Eye Has Not Seen* (Haugen/GIA)
- *Good Morning, Zachary* (Gutfreund/NALR)
- *Happy Are They* (Miffleton/Resource)
- *I Have Loved You* (Joncas/NALR)
- *Let Heaven Rejoice* (Jesuits/NALR)
- *Let Us Walk in the Light of the Lord* (Haugen/GIA)
- *Lord of Glory* (Jesuits/NALR)
- *Mountains and Hills* (Jesuits/NALR)
- *Only In God* (Jesuits/NALR)
- *O Worship the King* (Grant/PMB)
- *Psalm 63* (Goglia/Resource)
- *Prodigal Son* (Culbreth/Resource)
- *Sing A New Song* (Jesuits/NALR)
- *Song of Gathering* (Wise/GIA)
- *Trust in the Lord* (Jesuits/NALR)
- *We Remember* (Haugen/GIA)
- *Yahweh* (Weston Priory)
- *You Will Draw Water* (Conry/NALR)

SUNDAY PLANNING SHEET   Date _____

Parish focus _____

Environment & art _____

Ritual notes _____

Faith development (eg., in newsletter/classes) _____

Children's faith experience _____

Prelude _____

Hymn of gathering _____

Sprinkling/Penitential rite _____

Hymn of praise _____

Opening Prayer _____

First reading _____Responsory _____

Second reading _____Gospel acclamation _____

Gospel _____Profession of faith _____

General intercessions _____

At the preparation & presentation _____

Preface dialog _____Preface _____

Preface acclamation _____

Eucharistic prayer _____Memorial acclamation _____

Eucharistic amen _____

The Lord's prayer _____

Breaking of bread _____

The communion hymn _____

The post-communion hymn _____

Blessing _____At the dismissal _____

Memoranda:

THIRTY-THIRD SUNDAY OF THE YEAR

YEAR A

READINGS
Proverbs (31:10-13,19-20,30-31)
In this reading from Proverbs, we see a development of the concept set forth in Genesis that husband and wife are helpmates for one another. A wife of honor is praised as precious and beyond all value!
First Thessalonians (5:1-6)
The "Day of the Lord" comes when people least expect it. Christians are always ready for his coming for they live in his light and belong to him.
Matthew (25:14-30)
The parable presents us with three servants, each entrusted with a particular sum of money by a stern master. Two, through investment, double their sums, but the third out of fear buries it and returns it without profit. While rewarding the other two, the master seizes the money of the third and presents it to the man with the most. In the Kingdom, those who use and develop the talents the Lord gives are rewarded, while those who do not lose everything.

FOCUS
As we near the end of the liturgical year, the readings have an eschatological vision. We begin to look to the time when the Lord shall come in glory. The symbol of a good wife serves as the sign of the person who, in touch with God's will, does what is right and rejoices in the right. The Matthean parable stresses the idea that to prepare for the Lord's Day, we must be willing to use what we have been given for the good of the kingdom. We must be willing to trust in the Spirit, who will guide all decisions and keep us in the safety of God's embrace.

IDEA STARTERS
- *CCT Lectionary* (Proper 28): Zeph 1:7, 12-18; Ps 76; I Thes 5:1-11; Mt 25:14-30.
- The readings today ask us to reflect upon personal stewardship: "Merciful Father, we offer with joy and thanksgiving what you have first given us our selves, our time, and our possessions, signs of your gracious love" (LBW).
- "Volunteer Sunday." Have all of your parish clubs, committees, and other groups provide a display of their work photos, programs, minutes at the coffee hour. Have a representative from every organization from pre-school to Golden Age club!
- Recognize all volunteers, especially new ones.
- Children may act out today's parable.
- An adult forum may address "Generativity" in the life of the Christian.
- Explain the scriptural image of the bride in terms of Christian submissiveness, in the example of Jesus Christ.
- Does your community effectively use all the talents of its members for the glory of God?
- For your consideration: Opening Prayer; Gospel (full-form); Intercessions for families, garment workers, the needy, the harvest, Jerusalem, new mothers, bankers, corporate executives; Ordinary Sundays Preface VII (P35); Eucharistic Prayer I; Memorial Acclamation A; Ordinary Solemn Blessing I.

MUSIC

- Psalm 128
- *Abba, Father* (Landry/NALR)
- *Alleluia, Sing to the Lord* (Fowler/Resource)
- *Anthem* (Conry/NALR)
- *For the Beauty of the Earth* (Pierpoint/PMB)
- *Gather Us In* (Haugen/GIA)
- *Happy Are They* (Miffleton/Resource)
- *Lord of the Dance* (Carter/Galliard Ltd.)
- *Lord, To Whom Shall We Go?* (Conry/NALR)
- *Play Before the Lord* (Jesuits/NALR)
- *Send Us Your Spirit* (Haas/Cooperative Ministries)
- *Sing to the Lord A Joyful Song* (Monsell/PMB)
- *A Song of Blessing* (Wise/GIA)
- *We Are Called* (Pattersen/Resource)

SUNDAY PLANNING SHEET   Date _____

Parish focus _____

Environment & art _____

Ritual notes _____

Faith development (eg., in newsletter/classes) _____

Children's faith experience _____

Prelude _____

Hymn of gathering _____

Sprinkling/Penitential rite _____

Hymn of praise _____

Opening Prayer _____

First reading _____ Responsory _____

Second reading _____ Gospel acclamation _____

Gospel _____ Profession of faith _____

General intercessions _____

At the preparation & presentation _____

Preface dialog _____ Preface _____

Preface acclamation _____

Eucharistic prayer _____ Memorial acclamation _____

Eucharistic amen _____

The Lord's prayer _____

Breaking of bread _____

The communion hymn _____

The post-communion hymn _____

Blessing _____ At the dismissal _____

Memoranda:

SOLEMNITY OF CHRIST THE KING THIRTY-FOURTH OR LAST SUNDAY OF THE YEAR

YEAR A

READINGS

Ezekiel (34:11-12,15-17)
The image of the shepherd tending his flock is presented to Ezekiel. Indeed, an ancient analogy for the caring and compassionate love the Lord has for us the sheep of God's heart.

First Corinthians (15:20-26,28)
Christ the Deliverer is the first fruit of those who have fallen asleep in death. His death, both necessary and proper, is the passage which enables us to come into life. At the end, he will restore the primal harmony of creation, receive the authority, and place it at the feet of God.

Matthew (25:31-46)
Service is the mark of those who dwell in the kingdom of the Lord. What we do to the least in the Kingdom is done to the Lord. God closely identifies with the poor.

FOCUS

Ezekiel reminds us that the Lord is a shepherd for God's people who cares for them and brings them to safety. Paul points to the ultimate deliverance from death to life. This passage Jesus has accomplished for us by showing us that in the kingdom we die to self, through service. As we serve others, indeed the very least of the kingdom, we gauge our progress over death and our advancement toward the Lord of life.

IDEA STARTERS

- *CCT Lectionary:* Ez 34:11-16, 20-24; Ps 23; I Cor 15:20-28; Mt 25: 31-46.
- What is the paradox of this festival's title? What does this say about the church, we who are Christ's ambassadors?
- The full realization of Christ's reign will be on the day of the Lord. What about the kingdom in our midst?
- At a children's liturgy, symbols of kingship may be explained in the light of Jesus' ministry.
- An image of Christ the King may be displayed and decorated in a prominent place.
- Sing a Hymn of Praise during today's introductory rites of gathering (eg. *'Gloria,* "This Is the Feast," *Te Deum).*
- Celebrate Ecumenical Vespers for today's final Sunday before Advent.
- Publicize community food pantries, clothing collection agencies, volunteer programs, etc.
- For your consideration: Sprinkling Baptismal Water A; Hymn of Praise sung; Opening Prayer; Intercessions for animal shelter personnel, the injured and ill, stewardship of creation, spiritually-based sovereignty, authority and power, the hungry, homeless, imprisoned, social workers; Christ the King Preface (P51); Eucharistic Prayer III; Memorial Acclamation.

B; *The Lord's Prayer* sung; Ordinary Solemn Blessing IV.

MUSIC

- Psalm 23
- *Alleluia, Sing to the Lord* (Fowler/Resource)
- *Glory to the Holy One* (Marchionda/PMB)
- *Go Up to the Mountain* (Weston Priory)
- *He is the Lord* (Haas/Cooperative Ministries)
- *I Will Sing* (Dyer/Celebration)
- *Jesus is Lord* (Toolan/Resource)
- *The Lord Is King* (Keyes/Resource)
- *The Lord is My Shepherd* (Wise/GIA)
- *Lord of Glory* (Jesuits/NALR)
- *Praise Canticle* (Haas/Cooperative Ministries)
- *Praise to the Holiest* (Newman/PMB)
- *Sing Alleluia Sing* (Dameans/NALR)

SUNDAY PLANNING SHEET
Date _____

Parish focus _____

Environment & art _____

Ritual notes _____

Faith development (eg., in newsletter/classes) _____

Children's faith experience _____

Prelude _____

Hymn of gathering _____

Sprinkling/Penitential rite _____

Hymn of praise _____

Opening Prayer _____

First reading _____ Responsory _____

Second reading _____ Gospel acclamation ____

Gospel _____ Profession of faith _____

General intercessions _____

At the preparation & presentation _____

Preface dialog _____ Preface _____

Preface acclamation _____

Eucharistic prayer _____ Memorial acclamation ___

Eucharistic amen _____

The Lord's prayer _____

Breaking of bread _____

The communion hymn _____

The post-communion hymn _____

Blessing _____ At the dismissal _____

Memoranda:

FIRST SUNDAY OF ADVENT   YEAR B

READINGS
Isaiah (63:16-17,19;64:2-7)
This reading incorporates a variety of emotions. The prophet moans over the fact that his people have wandered from the Lord. He pleads with God to redirect their vision and to call them back. Isaiah uses powerful imagery in comparing God's goodness to the deeds of the people. The reading ends with a humble declaration of God as the potter and men and women as the clay in God's hands.
First Corinthians (1:3-9)
Paul thanks God for the fidelity of the Corinthian community. He acknowledges that they have received the Word from God and brought it to fruition in their individual and corporate lives. The fragment ends with a declaration that God, who is the progenitor of the message, has called the Corinthians to life.
Mark (13:33-37)
Jesus warns his listeners that they should be ever watchful, on guard, awaiting the coming of the Kingdom. Their lives should be prepared and ordered as they await his return.

FOCUS
The readings for this first Sunday of Advent throb with the joy-filled expectations of the return of the Lord. The Isaian reading seems hardly able to contain the excitement that the Lord's return, with its liberating power, evokes. Paul indicates what can be expected from such a return. The spiritual gifts by which the Corinthians live are the fruits of the Lord's return. In the third reading, Jesus cautions us to be prepared for the day when he comes again.

IDEA STARTERS
- *CCT Lectionary:* Is 63:16-64:8; Ps 80:1-7; I Cor 1:3-9; Mk 13:32-37.
- Sponsor an ecumenical make-your-own Advent Wreath/Calendar/Jesse Tree on the eve of this day. Celebrate Evening Prayer, and close with a pot luck supper.
- The Advent Wreath is a family tradition which is often incorporated into the liturgy. The Advent Wreath blessing may be patterned after today's Alternative Opening Prayer.
- Advent has been called the season when God waits for us to wait for him. Explain this in light of today's first reading.
- For those inquirers who are ready, celebrate the Rite of Admission into the Catechumenate.
- Share stories about St. Nicholas with the children's class. Give your students chocolate coins.
- For your consideration: Penitential Rite C; omit *Hymn of Praise;* Opening Prayer; Intercessions for nomads, yearning for God, those suffering from natural disaster, our faithfulness, stewardship over God's creation, artists, shepherds and farmers, appropriate use of speech and knowledge, holiday travellers, catechumens, house-workers, acolytes; Advent Preface I (P1); Memorial Acclamation C; Advent Solemn Blessing.

MUSIC

- Psalm 80
- *Abba, Father* (Landry/NALR)
- *Blest Be the Lord* (Jesuits/NALR)
- *The Dawn of the Day* (Deiss/NALR)
- *Eye Has Not Seen* (Haugen/GIA)
- *Fill Us With Your Love* (Prezio/K&R)
- *Glory and Praise* (Jesuits/NALR)
- *I Have Loved You* (Joncas/NALR)
- *In Your Love Remember Me* (Kendzia/NALR)
- *The King Shall Come* (Brownlie/PMB)
- *Let Us Walk in the Light* (Haugen/GIA)
- *One Corinthians One* (Mullins/Resource)
- *Restore Us* (Gilsdorf/Resource)
- *Save Us, O Lord* (Jesuits/NALR)
- *Song of the Exile* (Haugen/GIA)
- *Though the Mountains May Fall* (Jesuits/NALR)
- *Till You* (Repp/K&R)
- *Worship and Praise* (Keyes/Resource)

ADVENT PLANNING SHEET   Date _____

Parish focus _____

Environment & art _____

Ritual notes _____

Faith development (eg., bulletin item) _____

Children's faith experience _____

Prelude _____

Hymn of gathering _____

Sprinkling baptismal water acclamation _____

Penitential rite_____Opening Prayer _____

Responsory _____Gospel acclamation _____

General intercessions _____

At the preparation & presentation _____

Preface dialogue _____Preface _____

Preface acclamation _____

Eucharistic prayer _____Memorial acclamation _____

Eucharistic amen _____

The Lord's prayer _____

Breaking of bread _____

The communion hymn _____

The post–communion hymn _____

Blessing _____At the dismissal _____

Memoranda:

SECOND SUNDAY OF ADVENT

YEAR B

READINGS

Isaiah (40:1-5,9-11)
The familiar Isaian theme of "Comfort, comfort my people" is placed before us today. Yahweh is seen as our comforter and deliverer, the one who straightens the crooked and smooths rough ways. He gently cares for the weak, tired, and small.

Second Peter (3:8-14)
Peter develops two main themes. The first is that of the Lord's experience of time, which is vastly different from our own. The Lord's perceptions of time and situations are different from those of human beings. What seems like delay to us is to God patient waiting for us to return.

Peter also points out the kind of lives we should live reflecting the goodness and purity of God.

Mark (1:1-8)
The beginning of Mark's Gospel picks up a theme touched on by Isaiah, that is, the position of the messenger sent before the Lord to announce his return. In the Gospel passage, we are introduced to the figure of the Baptist, who declares the glorious coming of the Lord and urges a purification of life as preparation to receive him and his kingdom.

FOCUS

The Baptist is the pivotal figure in this Sunday's set of readings. Isaiah introduces him as the one who announces the comforting news of the Lord's Day. The Gospel develops this theme, pointing to John and his ministry of repentance. He embodies the kind of person to whom Peter refers in his letter, vigilant and virtuous.

IDEA STARTERS

- *CCT Lectionary:* Is 40:1-11; Ps 85:8-13; II Pt 3:8-15a; Mk 1:1-8.
- The evangelization committee of your parish may invite regulars to bring non-churchgoers to worship today. Provide a free brunch for your guests!
- Today's Gospel from Mark is similar to next Sunday's text from John. Both introduce the character of the Baptizer.
- Give children an experience of a desert.
- Celebrate St. Lucy's Day (December 13) with old-country customs. Begin with ecumenical Vespers.
- What programs do you offer to comfort the bereaved, the alienated, and the lonely?
- For your consideration: Penitential Rite C; Opening Prayer; Intercessions for those in need of comfort, Jerusalem, evangelizers, kindness, peace, truth, justice, patience, messengers, desert-dwellers; Advent Preface I; Memorial Acclamation C; Advent Solemn Blessing.

MUSIC

- Psalm 85
- *And the Father Will Dance* (Landry/NALR)
- *Good Morning, Zachary* (Gutfreund/NALR)
- *Go Up to the Mountain* (Weston Priory)
- *If With All Your Hearts* (Mullins/Resource)
- *In the Day of the Lord* (Gutfreund/NALR)
- *Let the Valleys Be Raised* (Jesuits/NALR)
- *Like A Shepherd* (Jesuits/NALR)
- *O Lord of Light* (PMB)
- *The Lord, He Comes* (Keyes/Resource)
- *On Jordan's Bank* (Coffin/PMB)
- *Patience, People* (Jesuits/NALR)
- *Prepare Ye* (Prezio/K&R)
- *Seek the Lord* (Jesuits/NALR)
- *Take Comfort, God's People* (Westendorf/PMB)

ADVENT PLANNING SHEET   Date _____

Parish focus _____

Environment & art _____

Ritual notes _____

Faith development (eg., bulletin item) _____

Children's faith experience _____

Prelude _____

Hymn of gathering _____

Sprinkling baptismal water acclamation _____

Penitential rite_____Opening Prayer _____

Responsory _____Gospel acclamation _____

General intercessions _____

At the preparation & presentation _____

Preface dialogue _____Preface _____

Preface acclamation _____

Eucharistic prayer _____Memorial acclamation _____

Eucharistic amen _____

The Lord's prayer _____

Breaking of bread _____

The communion hymn _____

The post-communion hymn _____

Blessing _____At the dismissal _____

Memoranda:

THIRD SUNDAY OF ADVENT

YEAR B

READINGS
Isaiah (61:1-2,10-11)
Today's passage from Isaiah is one Jesus takes for himself as a description of his person and ministry. It also serves as a basis for the Magnificat (today's responsorial psalm). It describes the selection of the Lord's anointed by God, and the honor to which the Chosen One is raised.
First Thessalonians (5:16-24)
Paul exhorts the Thessalonian community to rejoice in the Lord always. Christians should be open to the Spirit, ready to experience many different things which the discernment of the Spirit will help believers to judge and choose between. The passage ends with the assurance that God is holy and trustworthy and, therefore, will provide all he has promised.
John (1:6-8,19-28)
We are given a fuller exposure to the person of the Baptist than we have had up to now. He is the one who prepares the way for the Lord. He announces repentance in preparation for Christ's return.

FOCUS
The readings today accent a mood of joy. Christians obtain joy by acknowledging their position vis-a-vis the Lord and attempting to carry out faithfully all he wishes for them. If we occupy this position, our hearts and minds will be open to everything, for we will be open to the Spirit's activity and discernment in our lives.

IDEA STARTERS
- *CCT Lectionary:* Is 61:1-4, 8-11; Lk 1:46b-55; I Thes 5:16-24; Jn 1:6-8, 19-28.
- At a Bible Study, compare last Sunday's Gospel with today's text from John.
- Publicize your outreach programs for the poor: clothing and food pantry, shelter for homeless, etc. Seek volunteers and donations.
- Bulletin article: "Mary's Song of Praise." Explain the meaning and usage of this canticle in the Liturgy of the Hours.
- How may you incorporate the "O" Antiphons through art and music in the liturgy?
- Celebrate the Anointing of the Sick at the Sunday Eucharist. The homebound will especially appreciate the holiday visit to the parish.
- For your consideration: Penitential Rite C; Alternative Opening Prayer; Intercessions for the lowly, brokenhearted, captives, vindication, salvation, married couples, hungry, attitude of prayer, holistic spirituality, witnessing; Eucharistic Prayer IV; Memorial Acclamation D; Advent Solemn Blessing.

MUSIC

- Luke 1:46-54 (Magnificat)
- *And the Father Will Dance* (Landry/NALR)
- *Before the Sun Burned Bright* (Jesuits/NALR)
- Be Glad, O People (Weston Priory)
- *The Cry of the Poor* (Jesuits/NALR)
- *Gather Us In* (Haugen/GIA)
- *God and Man at Table* (Stamps/Dawn Treador)
- *He Has Anointed Me* (Dameans/NALR)
- *How Beautiful on the Mountains* (Deiss/NALR)
- *Jubilate, Servite* (Taize/GIA)
- *Justice Shall Flourish* (Schoenbachler/Cooperative Ministries)
- *Kyrie, Eleison* (Clark/Celebration)
- *O Come, O Come Emmanuel* (Traditional/PMB)·
- *O, That I Had a Thousand Voices* (Mentzer/NALR)
- *Proclaim the Joyful Message* (PMB)
- *Rejoice in the Lord Always* (Traditional)
- *Rise Up, Jerusalem* (Schoenbachler/NALR)
- *Spirit, Come Forth* (Duesing/Resource)
- *The Spirit of God* (Deiss/PMB)
- *The Spirit of God* (Goglia/Resource)
- *We Were Strangers* (Deiss/NALR)

ADVENT PLANNING SHEET   Date _____

Parish focus _____

Environment & art _____

Ritual notes _____

Faith development (eg., bulletin item) _____

Children's faith experience _____

Prelude _____

Hymn of gathering _____

Sprinkling baptismal water acclamation _____

Penitential rite_____Opening Prayer _____

Responsory _____Gospel acclamation _____

General intercessions _____

At the preparation & presentation _____

Preface dialogue _____Preface _____

Preface acclamation _____

Eucharistic prayer _____Memorial acclamation _____

Eucharistic amen _____

The Lord's prayer _____

Breaking of bread _____

The communion hymn _____

The post-communion hymn _____

Blessing _____At the dismissal _____

Memoranda:

FOURTH SUNDAY OF ADVENT

YEAR B

READINGS
Second Samuel (7:1-5,8-11,16)
David is told that it is not he who will build the Lord a house, but rather the Lord who shall raise up a great house for David, Israel, and all people. From this house all shall be brought to live in the Lord's own light.
Romans (16:25-27)
Paul indicates the inclusiveness of the House of David by stating that salvation is the free gift of all, which is brought by Jesus, the Lord. For Paul this is the kernel of the Gospel message.
Luke (1:26-38)
The figure of the Virgin open, vulnerable, ready and willing to receive what the Lord will give, is placed before us today. This is the pattern for all Christians of all times.

FOCUS
God is the author of salvation. God extends this gift to all through the Son Jesus, the Christ. Our role in this process is to be open, vulnerable, and accepting we are to be virginal to God.

IDEA STARTERS
- *CCT Lectionary:* II Sam 7:8-16; Ps 89:1-4, 19-24; Rm 16:25-27; Lk 1:26-38.
- Do your parishioners understand the term "annunciation" illustrated in today's Gospel?
- Today you may focus upon Mary as an Advent role model. We await the return of the Lord as a mother prepares for the birth of her child. (The new Italian *Sacramentary* provides a third Advent Preface where Mary is referred to as the "New Eve.")
- The Samuel pericope stresses God's presence among us (Emmanuel). We do not make room for God. God makes himself at home in and with us.
- Liturgical Dance: "The Annunciation."
- Have an Advent Pageant based upon today's Lucan text for the parish children.
- Adult Education topic: "The Incarnation" (based upon the Gospel passage).
- For your consideration: Penitential Rite C; Alternative Opening Prayer; Intercessions for enemies, royal families, the Jewish people, faithfulness to God's covenant, preachers, wisdom, expectant mothers, end to fear; conclude the Intercessions with the "Hail Mary"; Advent Preface II (P2); Eucharistic Prayer II; Memorial Acclamation D; *The Lord's Prayer* sung; Advent Solemn Blessing.

MUSIC

- Psalm 89
- *And There Will Shine* (Repp/K&R)
- *Ave Maria*
- *Behold A Virgin Bearing Him* (Gannon/PMB)
- *Blessed is She* (Mullins/Resource)
- *Dear Maker of the Starry Skies* (Knox/PMB)
- *Dwelling Place* (Jesuits/NALR)
- *Exult You Just Ones* (Jesuits/NALR)
- *Hail Mary: Gentle Woman* (Landry/NALR)
- *The King of Glory* (Jabusch/PMB)
- *Let the King of Glory Come* (Joncas/NALR)
- *Lord of Glory* (Jesuits/NALR)
- *Lord, To Whom Shall We Go?* (Conry/NALR)
- *Maranatha* (Antioch/K&R)
- *May We Praise You* (Jesuits/NALR)
- *Song of Mary* (Aridas/Resource)
- *We Remember* (Haugen/GIA)
- *Who Has Known?* (Jesuits/NALR)
- *Yahweh, the Faithful One* (Jesuits/NALR)
- *You Are Near* (Jesuits/NALR)

ADVENT PLANNING SHEET   Date _____

Parish focus _____

Environment & art _____

Ritual notes _____

Faith development (eg., bulletin item) _____

Children's faith experience _____

Prelude _____

Hymn of gathering _____

Sprinkling baptismal water acclamation _____

Penitential rite_____Opening Prayer _____

Responsory _____Gospel acclamation _____

General intercessions _____

At the preparation & presentation _____

Preface dialogue _____Preface _____

Preface acclamation _____

Eucharistic prayer _____Memorial acclamation _____

Eucharistic amen _____

The Lord's prayer _____

Breaking of bread _____

The communion hymn _____

The post-communion hymn _____

Blessing _____At the dismissal _____

Memoranda:

THE SOLEMNITY OF CHRISTMAS

YEAR B

(See Year A For All Readings For All Masses)
The following commentary is for the Mass during the day.

READINGS

Isaiah (52:7-10)
Isaiah originally announced this good news when Jerusalem was in ruins and God's people were in exile. In the Hebrew understanding, the solemn proclamation of the word makes the event it signifies happen. In the very telling and hearing of the word, "Your God is king," God is acknowledged as king, and God's people are brought from ruin and destruction to victory and peace.

Hebrews (1:1-6)
The coming of Jesus Christ ushered in a new age, surpassing what went before but not repudiating its value. The person of Jesus Christ makes God fully present to humanity.

John (1:1-18)
This is poetry at its finest, and needs to be understood with the heart as much as with the head. The Word is not just God made present but God inserted into the innermost depths of our own beings.

FOCUS

Do not be embarrassed by the earthiness of this feast of the incarnation. Grace builds on nature; it does not run away from it. The Word of God meant what he said when he became flesh; he wasn't just play-acting.

"What can we do to make the Christmas celebration special?" Don't settle for liturgical glitter and tinsel display without substance. Look for substance first, then look for ways to unfold it. How do the dead of night and the precious few hours of daylight speak to us of the incarnation?

IDEA STARTERS

- *CCT Lectionary* (second proper): Is 62:6-7, 10-12; Ps 97; Ti 3:4-7; Lk 2:8-20.
- Note that all Christmas Eve/Day lections are interchangeable. Liturgy planners decide the texts you wish to focus upon this year.
- As the Hymn of Praise *(Gloria in excelsis)* is sung, have a procession to the creche: torchbearers leading someone who will place the image of the infant into the manger.
- During the Nicene Creed, especially highlight the words, "by the power of the Holy Spirit he became incarnate from the virgin Mary, and was made man," with the liturgical gesture of bowing.
- At a "Christmas Carol Liturgy," replace ordinary and proper chants with familiar hymns of the season.
- Incorporate your Christmas pageant into a children's Liturgy of the Word.
- Will today's visiting Christians (especially inactive or non-members) consider your parish welcoming and worth revisiting before Lent?
- For your consideration: Hymn of Praise (sung); Alternative Opening Prayer; Intercessions for the redeemed, cities, the forsaken, rulers, kindness, love, mercy, the newborn, the media; Christmas Preface III (P5); Eucharistic Prayer I (w/Christmas proper); Memorial Acclamation D; Christmas Solemn Blessing.

MUSIC

- Psalms 96, 97, 98
- *Angels' Proclamation* (Sessions/Resource)
- *A Savior is Born* (Lisicky/WLP)
- *The Beautiful Mother* (Jesuits/NALR)
- *Bright Stars* (Keyes/Resource)
- *Children, Run Joyfully* (Jesuits/NALR)
- *Emmanuel Is Born Tonight* (Johnston/WLP)
- *Gentle Night* (Jesuits/NALR)
- *God Rest Ye Merry Gentlemen* (Christmas Carol)
- *O Come, All Ye Faithful* (Christmas Carol)
- *Shout for Joy* (Byrne/Resource)
- *Shout for Joy, O You on Earth* (Smith/WLP)
- *Wake From Your Sleep* (Jesuits/NALR)

CHRISTMASTIME PLANNING SHEET   Date _____

Parish focus _____

Environment & art _____

Ritual notes _____

Faith development (eg., audit ed.) _____

Children's faith experience _____

Prelude _____

Hymn of gathering _____

Sprinkling baptismal water _____

Gloria in excelsis _____

Opening Prayer _____

Responsory _____

First reading _____ Responsory _____

Second reading _____ Gospel acclamation _____

Gospel _____ Profession of faith _____

General intercessions _____

At the preparation & presentation _____

Preface dialogue _____ Preface _____

Preface acclamation _____

Eucharistic prayer _____ Memorial acclamation _____

Eucharistic amen _____

The Lord's prayer _____

Breaking of bread _____

The communion hymn _____

The post-communion hymn _____

Blessing _____ At the dismissal _____

Memoranda:

FEAST OF THE HOLY FAMILY

(See Year A For First Two Readings And Further Commentary)

READINGS

Sirach (3:2-6,12-14)
When Sirach wrote, leaving the family home meant death. One could not ordinarily survive being cut off from one's roots. Today, mobility away from the family origins is the norm, not the exception. It is more difficult to hear this word today. And perhaps that makes it more urgent.

Colossians (3:12-21)
Paul sometimes gives the impression he enjoys telling people what to do. Underlying his practical commands and advice, however, is the firm awareness of who we are: "You are God's chosen ones, now live accordingly!"

Luke (2:22-40)
This Gospel places Jesus solidly within the Jewish tradition. Simeon looks backward and sees Jesus as the fulfillment of Israel's hopes. Anna bursts forth with the good news of deliverance.

FOCUS

Respect cannot be legislated; it has to be born out of an inner sense of rightness. In the past, society provided both motivation and support for family solidarity and parental respect. These are clouded and confused today. Our liturgy faces the challenge of renewing a sense of solidarity in our twofold identity as members of both the Christian and the human families.

IDEA STARTERS

- *CCT Lectionary:* Is 61:10-62:3; Ps 111; Gal 4:4-7; Lk 2:22-40.
- *The Roman Lectionary* (1981) provides alternative first and second readings for today's feast.
- Following today's homily, you may invite couples to reaffirm their marriage vows. Honor all married couples at the coffee hour.
- Adult Forum: "Marriage, Symbol of the Church." Discuss this concept in light of today's second lesson.
- Explain the scriptural background and the liturgical use of the "Canticle of Simeon" (Lk 2) in a bulletin article.
- Publicize programs for widow(er)s, singles, homosexuals, etc. All belong to the family of the Church.
- For your consideration: Hymn of Praise (sung); Alternative Opening Prayer; Gospel (full form); Intercessions for husbands, wives, children, openness to Emmanuel and spiritual gifts, holy/whole relationships, new parents, widow(er)s; Christmas Preface I (P3); Eucharistic Prayer I (w/proper); Memorial Acclamation D; The Lord's Prayer (sung); Christmas Solemn Blessing.

MUSIC

- Psalm 128
- *Come To the Lord* (Meyette/Resource)
- *Children At Your Feet* (Fisherfolk/Resource)
- *Emanuel* (Jesuits/NALR)
- *It Came Upon a Midnight Clear* (Christmas Carol)

- *The Lord Has Come* (Adrias/WLP)
- *O Thou Joyful Day* (Christmas Carol)
- *Prepare the Way for the Son of God* (Rodrigues/WLP)
- *Shepherd Boy of Bethlehem* (Reilly/WLP)

CHRISTMASTIME PLANNING SHEET Date _____

Parish focus _____

Environment & art _____

Ritual notes _____

Faith development (eg., audit ed.) _____

Children's faith experience _____

Prelude _____

Hymn of gathering _____

Sprinkling baptismal water _____

Gloria in excelsis _____

Opening Prayer _____

Responsory _____

First reading _____ Responsory _____

Second reading _____ Gospel acclamation _____

Gospel _____ Profession of faith _____

General intercessions _____

At the preparation & presentation _____

Preface dialogue _____ Preface _____

Preface acclamation _____

Eucharistic prayer _____ Memorial acclamation _____

Eucharistic amen _____

The Lord's prayer _____

Breaking of bread _____

The communion hymn _____

The post-communion hymn _____

Blessing _____ At the dismissal _____

Memoranda:

SOLEMNITY OF MARY, THE MOTHER OF GOD, JANUARY 1

YEARS A, B AND C

(See Year A For All Readings And Further Commentary)

READINGS

Numbers (6:22-27)
This Hebrew liturgical blessing is a reminder of Christ as the enduring blessing of God. In his favor, God brings us into active conformity with his will, and this is our peace.

Galatians (4:4-7)
What Jesus Christ is, as the Son of God, his spirit makes us to become. Paul calls us to recognize our dignity.

Luke (2:16-21)
This reading looks forward to the mission of Jesus as the incarnate Word. Circumcision signified participation in the covenant, and pledged allegiance to and cooperation with God's power to renew all things.

FOCUS

The Octave (eighth day) of Christmas expresses both rootedness in time and the opening of the natural order into eternity. Seven days (the week) signify natural completion of time. Seven plus one speaks of the first and never-ending day of the fulfillment beyond time. It is appropriate that today is both New Year's Day and Day of Prayer for World Justice and Peace.

IDEA STARTERS

- *CCT Lectionary:* Nu 6:22-27; Ps 67; Gal 4:4-7 or Phil 2:9-13; Lk 2:15-21.
- While Roman Catholics commemorate "Mary, Mother of God," Lutheran and Episcopalian calendars observe "The Name of Jesus." The Presbyterian calendar marks today's observance as "New Year." Roman Catholics may observe "World Day of Prayer for Peace."
- The Advent-Christmas season moves quickly. Take heed of the Gospel message: look at the Incarnation and "treasure all these things and reflect on them in your heart."
- Have a parish New Year's Eve party. Open the celebration with a Bible service (see *The Book of Occasional Services*).
- In a bulletin article explain Mary's title, "Mother of God."
- Explain the true meaning of "abba."
- For your consideration: Hymn of Praise (sung); Alternative Opening Prayer; Intercessions for the new year, continued hope to God's blessings, our relationship to God the Father, a spirit of life enveloped by God, respect for the name of Jesus; Christmas Preface III (P5); Eucharistic Prayer I (w/proper); Memorial Acclamation D; The Lord's Prayer (sung); Ordinary Solemn Blessing I.

MUSIC

- Psalm 67
- *Angels From the Realms of Glory* (Christmas Carol)
- *The Christmas Alleluia* (Blunt/WLP)
- *Exult You Just Ones* (Jesuits/NALR)
- *Hymn to the Virgin Mother* (Toolan/Resource)
- *I Give You My Son* (Dallman/WLP)
- *Just Begun* (Jesuits/NALR)
- *Let Your Mind Be That of Christ* (Miffleton/WLP)
- *Mother of Life* (Dicie/Resource)
- *Night Full of Stars* (Jabusch/WLP)
- *On the Birthday of the Lord* (Throm/WLP)
- *Renewal Song* (Anderson/Resource)
- *Sleep, Baby Jesus* (Tucciarone/WLP)
- *What Child is This?* (Christmas Carol)
- *What Marvels and Wonders* (Deiss/WLP)

CHRISTMASTIME PLANNING SHEET Date _____

Parish focus _____

Environment & art _____

Ritual notes _____

Faith development (eg., audit ed.) _____

Children's faith experience _____

Prelude _____

Hymn of gathering _____

Sprinkling baptismal water _____

Gloria in excelsis _____

Opening Prayer _____

Responsory _____

First reading _____Responsory _____

Second reading _____Gospel acclamation _____

Gospel _____Profession of faith _____

General intercessions _____

At the preparation & presentation _____

Preface dialogue _____Preface _____

Preface acclamation _____

Eucharistic prayer _____Memorial acclamation _____

Eucharistic amen _____

The Lord's prayer _____

Breaking of bread _____

The communion hymn _____

The post-communion hymn _____

Blessing _____At the dismissal _____

Memoranda:

SOLEMNITY OF THE EPIPHANY

(See Year A For All Readings And Further Commentary)

READINGS
Isaiah (60:1-6)
The exiled prophet's dream of a restored Jerusalem becoming the center of the world was never fulfilled literally, but was transformed into new meaning in Christ.
Ephesians (3:2-3,5-6)
The mission of the church, to call all humankind into union with God, is a "mystery" (secret plan), according to Paul. Union with God is impossible until the barriers to union with one another are broken down, so that different cultures and mentalities can realize their shared identity as one people in Christ.
Matthew (2:1-12)
This story echoes the coming of the Queen of Sheba to Solomon (I Kg 10:1-13), and shows Jesus as the "New Solomon" whose wisdom draws even the wisest of the world to acknowledge their true dignity in humble submission.

FOCUS
In ancient tradition, the Epiphany is more important than Christmas. As the climax of the Christmas season, it is the unfolding of the implications of the incarnation. Jesus is manifested as the savior of all peoples. The implications of this feast for liturgy are unsettling: does our celebration stimulate us to make the saving presence of Jesus available to all, or is it merely our own spiritual pacifier?

IDEA STARTERS
- *CCT Lectionary:* Is 60:1-6; Ps 72:1-14; Eph 3:1-12; Mt 2:1-12.
- Add the images of the Magi to your creche today.
- If it is customary, homes of parishioners may be blessed throughout this week (cf. *The Book of Occasional Services*).
- Use of gold vestments, paraments, and incense are appropriate today.
- At ecumenical vespers, sing the Canticle of Simeon.
- At a children's liturgy let the children experience the giftsof the magi. Have a drummer boy tell the story of the Magi as he remembers it.
- Publicize today as "Bring a Friend Sunday." Welcome all visitors; provide a special brunch.
- For your consideration: Hymn of Praise (sung); Opening Prayer; Intercessions for Jerusalem, all nationalities, travellers, seamen and women, judges, royalty, the poor, the lowly, the ordained, contemporary prophets, Jews, non-believers, road workers; Epiphany Preface (P6); Eucharistic Prayer I (w/proper); Memorial Acclamation D; Epiphany Solemn Blessing.

MUSIC

- Psalm 72
- *A Savior is Born* (Blunt/WLP)
- *The First Noel* (Christmas Carol)
- *The Journey* (Blunt/WLP)
- *This Night in Bethlehem* (Bates/WLP)
- *The People that Walk in Darkness* (Jesuits/NALR)
- *Rise Up, Zion* (Miffleton/WLP)
- *Rise Up, Jerusalem* (Jesuits/NALR)
- *Sing! Rejoice* (Marchionda/WLP)
- *This Is My Son* (Jabusch/WLP)
- *We Three Kings* (Christmas Carol)

CHRISTMASTIME PLANNING SHEET Date _____

Parish focus _____

Environment & art _____

Ritual notes _____

Faith development (eg., audit ed.) _____

Children's faith experience _____

Prelude _____

Hymn of gathering _____

Sprinkling baptismal water _____

Gloria in excelsis _____

Opening Prayer _____

Responsory _____

First reading _____ Responsory _____

Second reading _____ Gospel acclamation _____

Gospel _____ Profession of faith _____

General intercessions _____

At the preparation & presentation _____

Preface dialogue _____ Preface _____

Preface acclamation _____

Eucharistic prayer _____ Memorial acclamation _____

Eucharistic amen _____

The Lord's prayer _____

Breaking of bread _____

The communion hymn _____

The post-communion hymn _____

Blessing _____ At the dismissal _____

Memoranda:

SECOND SUNDAY AFTER CHRISTMAS

YEAR B

(See Year A For Commentary)

CHRISTMASTIME PLANNING SHEET Date _____

Parish focus _____

Environment & art _____

Ritual notes _____

Faith development (eg., audit ed.) _____

Children's faith experience _____

Prelude _____

Hymn of gathering _____

Sprinkling baptismal water _____

Gloria in excelsis _____

Opening Prayer _____

Responsory _____

First reading _____ Responsory _____

Second reading _____ Gospel acclamation _____

Gospel _____ Profession of faith _____

General intercessions _____

At the preparation & presentation _____

Preface dialogue _____ Preface _____

Preface acclamation _____

Eucharistic prayer _____ Memorial acclamation _____

Eucharistic amen _____

The Lord's prayer _____

Breaking of bread _____

The communion hymn _____

The post-communion hymn _____

Blessing _____ At the dismissal _____

Memoranda:

THE BAPTISM OF THE LORD

YEAR B

(See Year A For First Two Readings And Further Commentary)

READINGS

Isaiah (42:1-6,6-7)
The people of ancient Israel saw a reflection of their own mission to the world in this portrayal of God's chosen servant. We see this image as a pale foreshadowing of the mission of Christ, and of its continuation in his body, the church. This reading is a mirror for us to examine ourselves.

Acts of the Apostles (10:34-38)
We are nearly always wrong if we try to put limits on God. Even the apostles who were Jesus' intimate friends had to learn from experience the extent of God's loving impartiality.

Mark (1:7-11)
Mark's account of Jesus' baptism is the earliest and simplest version of the story. The dove, a symbol of love used in the Old Testament to depict God's beloved people, attests to Jesus' becoming the representative of God's new people in the Spirit.

FOCUS

What is said of Jesus is said of us all, the people who have been called by Christ and commissioned to continue his presence: "You are my beloved. On you my favor rests." The attitude of impartiality and universality that was Peter's hard-won lesson must be ours. The agenda of our ministry is itemized in the reading from Isaiah.

IDEA STARTERS

- *CCT Lectionary:* Gn 1:1-5; Ps 29; Acts 19:1-7; Mk 1:4-11.
- Today's feast is considered the last day of the Christmas season.
- It is appropriate to celebrate infant baptism or confirmation at today's principle Eucharist.
- Today begins the series of pericopes from Mark's Gospel. Provide a Bible study.
- Bulletin article: "Redeemed Redeemer?" Why was the Savior baptized?
- Why does the Father's voice in Mark's Gospel practically say the same thing later on in 9:6?
- Jesus was "ordained" at his baptism. What about us, at our baptism?
- For your consideration: Hymn of Praise (sung); Opening Prayer; Intercessions for those in mourning, justice, the blind, prisoners, the homebound, tailors and seamstresses, sovereigns, openness, fear of the Lord, the Jewish people, healers, evangelizers, the newly baptized; Baptism Preface (P7); Eucharistic Prayer I (w/Epiphany proper); Memorial Acclamation D; The Lord's Prayer (sung); Ordinary Solemn Blessing I.

MUSIC

- Psalm 29
- *All Those Who Love Me* (Weston Priory)
- *Banks of the Jordan* (Duesing/Resource)
- *Dedication Song* (Raffa/Resource)
- *Dwelling Place* (Jesuits/NALR)
- *Hymn of Praise* (Dicie/Resource)
- *The Goodness of God* (Weston Priory)
- *We Were Strangers* (Deiss/NALR)

CHRISTMASTIME PLANNING SHEET Date _____

Parish focus _____

Environment & art _____

Ritual notes _____

Faith development (eg., audit ed.) _____

Children's faith experience _____

Prelude _____

Hymn of gathering _____

Sprinkling baptismal water _____

Gloria in excelsis _____

Opening Prayer _____

Responsory _____

First reading _____Responsory _____

Second reading _____Gospel acclamation _____

Gospel _____Profession of faith _____

General intercessions _____

At the preparation & presentation _____

Preface dialogue _____Preface _____

Preface acclamation _____

Eucharistic prayer _____Memorial acclamation _____

Eucharistic amen _____

The Lord's prayer _____

Breaking of bread _____

The communion hymn _____

The post-communion hymn _____

Blessing _____At the dismissal _____

Memoranda:

ASH WEDNESDAY

(See Year A For Commentary)

LENTEN PLANNING SHEET

Date _____

Parish focus _____

Environment & art _____

Ritual notes _____

Faith development (eg., audit ed.) _____

Children's faith experience _____

Prelude _____

Hymn of gathering _____

Sprinkling baptismal water _____

Gloria in excelsis _____

Opening Prayer _____

Responsory _____

First reading _____ Responsory _____

Second reading _____ Gospel acclamation _____

Gospel _____ Profession of faith _____

General intercessions _____

At the preparation & presentation _____

Preface dialogue _____ Preface _____

Preface acclamation _____

Eucharistic prayer _____ Memorial acclamation _____

Eucharistic amen _____

The Lord's prayer _____

Breaking of bread _____

The communion hymn _____

The post-communion hymn _____

Blessing _____ At the dismissal _____

Memoranda:

FIRST SUNDAY OF LENT   YEAR B

READINGS

Genesis (9:8-15)
Christian tradition sees the flood as an image of the "waters of baptism that make an end of sin and a new beginning of goodness" (Blessing of Baptismal Water). The promise of the covenant new life in abundance grows out of the purifying destruction; the basic goodness of creation and of humankind are affirmed.

First Peter (3:18-22)
Peter is a baptismal instruction which describes the meaning of the Christian life for the newly initiated. In comparing baptism with the flood, the author emphasizes the positive union of the Christian with the risen Christ.

Mark (1:12-15)
Mark does not describe the temptations of Jesus in detail, but makes it clear that they follow the baptism in the Jordan and precede his ministry. Jesus' baptism signified his full acceptance of the human condition. He had to struggle with the human tendencies that would distort his mission as Messiah.

FOCUS

Lent begins with an emphasis on passage through water and through desert temptation. Jesus emerged from his baptism and struggled with the forces of evil having proven his fidelity to the Kingdom and its proclamation. This is the model for the baptismal passage of the Christian.

IDEA STARTERS

- *CCT Lectionary:* Gn 9:8-17; Ps 25:1-10; I Pt 3:18-22;Mk 1:9-15.
- Today the "Rite of Election" is celebrated with the catechumens who will be baptized at the Easter Vigil.
- Children's Liturgy: The readings give us the paradox of water: waters of the flood produce death; the yearning for water in the desert to continue life.
- Here are some ideas for bulletin articles: "Put to the Test by Satan," "Save Us From the Time of Trial," and "Deliver Us From Evil" (The Lord's Prayer, ICET translation).
- Sponsor a retreat during Lent following the example of Jesus (cf. Mk 1:12).
- The words concluding today's Gospel were used in the giving of ashes last Wednesday.
- For your consideration: Penitential Rite; omit "Hymn of Praise"; Opening Prayer; Intercessions for the Elect, ancestors, stewardship over creation, faithfulness, victims of natural disaster, teachers, compassion, kindness, humility, prisoners and prison workers, ship builders, sailors, Christian conscience, civil authorities, evangelists; Reconciliation Eucharistic Prayer II; Memorial Acclamation B; The Lord's Prayer (sung); Passion Solemn Blessing.

MUSIC

- Psalm 25
- *Fear Not* (Feiten/Resource)
- *Give Us Living Water* (Dameans/NALR)
- *Glory and Praise* (Jesuits/NALR)
- *In Your Love Remember Me* (Kendzia/NALR)
- *O Healing River* (Traditional)
- *Praise to the Holiest* (Newman/PMB)
- *Rainbow* (Dameans/NALR)
- *Thanks Be to You, O God* (Stuntz/PMB)
- *The Wonders He Has Done for You* (Anderson/Resource)
- *Yahweh* (Weston Priory)
- *You Will Draw Water* (Conry/NALR)

LENTEN PLANNING SHEET   Date _____

Parish focus _____

Environment & art _____

Ritual notes _____

Faith development (eg., midweek program) _____

Children's faith experience _____

Prelude _____

Hymn of gathering _____

Penitential rite _____

Opening Prayer _____

Reading cycle _____First reading _____

Responsory _____Second reading _____

Lenten gospel acclamation _____Gospel _____

RCIA rites & acclamations _____

General intercessions _____

At the preparation & presentation _____

Preface dialog _____Preface _____

Preface acclamation _____

Eucharistic prayer _____Memorial acclamation _____

Eucharistic amen _____

The Lord's prayer _____

Breaking of bread _____

The communion hymn _____

The post-communion hymn _____

Blessing _____At the dismissal _____

Memoranda:

SECOND SUNDAY OF LENT   YEAR B

READINGS
Genesis (22:1–2,9a,10–13,15–18)
The story of the sacrifice of Isaac emphasizes that true sacrifice lies in faith and obedience rather than in slaughter. It demonstrates also that the fulfillment of God's promise of descendants to Abraham does not depend on physical generation alone, but on the power of God.

Romans (8:31–34)
At the heart of faith is the confidence that, if God wills to save us, God does not will to accuse and condemn us. God's saving will is shown in raising Jesus up to be savior, not merely by his death, but by his continued presence with God, commending us to God.

Mark (9:2–10)
In the Gospels, the baptism and temptations of Jesus affirm his unity with humanity. The transfiguration affirms his divinity. This event marks the beginning of the disciples' awareness of the true nature of his mission.

FOCUS
Today, still at the beginning of Lent, we continue to ponder with the disciples the meaning of Jesus' death and resurrection. It is important that the initiated reflect on this together with the elect. In the journey to Easter they must support and nourish one another.

IDEA STARTERS
- *CCT Lectionary:* Gn 17:1–10, 15–19; Ps 105:1–11; Rm 4:16–25; Mk 8:31–38.
- It may be appropriate to present "the Beatitudes" to the Elect today.
- Bulletin article ideas: "The Messianic Secret"; "Sacrifice What You Love?"
- Examine Gospel parallels of the Transfiguration as well as of Easter morning.
- Have a winter olympics (eg., Parent-child, Big Brother-Little Brother teams) involving all parishioners.
- Invite inactive members to return and come back for Easter (and then keep coming!) How can we share with them our feeling that "it is good for us to be here"?
- For your consideration: Penitential Rite; Alternative Opening Prayer; Intercessions for the Elect, the Jewish people, family relationships, the afflicted, the deceased, vowed lifestyle, Jerusalem, enemies, judges and jurors, awe in God's presence; Transfiguration Preface (P50); Eucharistic Prayer II; Memorial Acclamation C; Passion Solemn Blessing.

MUSIC
- Psalm 116
- *All My Days* (Jesuits/NALR)
- *An Everlasting Song* (Sessions/Resource)
- *God, Our God of Distant Ages* (Westendorf/PMB)
- *God's Holy Mountain* (Westendorf/PMB)
- *He is the Lord* (Haas/Coop Music)
- *His Love Will Ever Be* (Fabing/NALR)
- *I Am Lord* (Duesing/Resource)
- *The Image of His Love* (Dicie/Resource)
- *Immortal, Invisible God* (Smith/PMB)
- *Jesus, Remember Me* (Taize/GIA)
- *O Worship the King* (Grant/PMB)
- *Transfiguration* (Landry/NALR)
- *We Are the Family* (Repp/K&R)
- *We Remember* (Haugen/GIA)

LENTEN PLANNING SHEET

Date _____

Parish focus _____

Environment & art _____

Ritual notes _____

Faith development (eg., midweek program) _____

Children's faith experience _____

Prelude _____

Hymn of gathering _____

Penitential rite _____

Opening Prayer _____

Reading cycle _____ First reading _____

Responsory _____ Second reading _____

Lenten gospel acclamation _____ Gospel _____

RCIA rites & acclamations _____

General intercessions _____

At the preparation & presentation _____

Preface dialog _____ Preface _____

Preface acclamation _____

Eucharistic prayer _____ Memorial acclamation _____

Eucharistic amen _____

The Lord's prayer _____

Breaking of bread _____

The communion hymn _____

The post-communion hymn _____

Blessing _____ At the dismissal _____

Memoranda:

THIRD SUNDAY OF LENT   YEAR B

READINGS
Exodus (20:1-17)
The commandments are in accord with natural law and any reasonable ethical system, but they rise above nature as expressions of the personal will of God. For the Christian, they are the first word, not the last word, the foundation upon which a life of Christian love, which goes beyond laws, is to be built.
First Corinthians (1:22-25)
Worldly wisdom focuses on one's rightness and gives rise to disputes and factions that destroy the unity of Christ's body, the Christian community. "God's folly" focuses on the cross of Christ, and allows nothing to disrupt our oneness with one another in the Crucified One.
John (2:13-25)
In one moment Jesus affirms the rightness of the whole Old Testament order by purifying the Temple of commercial defilement; in the next moment, he proclaims himself the New Temple, the fulfillment of everything the old order stands for.

FOCUS
Neither purification nor wisdom are ever ends in themselves. In personal life and in social life, those things that stand in the way of what we are called to become need to be rooted out. True wisdom focuses on the cross and new life of Christ.

IDEA STARTERS
- *CCT Lectionary:* Ex 20:1-17; Ps 19:7-14; I Cor 1:22-25; Jn 2:13-22.
- Celebrate the first "Scrutinies" with the Elect. Use lectionary cycle A, which presents the Easter/Baptism symbol of water. Present the words of the "Creed" to the Elect during the week.
- Include articles in the Sunday bulletin on "Justified by the Grace of Faith, Yet We Follow the Commandments," or "Sacred Images, Not Idols!"
- The Lord's purging of the Temple is a part of the inauguration of the Kingdom in our midst. Cleansing the temple of its defilement, Jesus then speaks about the Temple of his glorified body.
- For your consideration: Penitential Rite; Opening Prayer; First Lesson (full form); Intercessions for the Elect, Egypt, those oppressed, respect for God's name, parents, murderers, thieves, end to envy, for the divorced, separated and remarried, for wisdom, simplicity, enlightenment, fear of the Lord, true worship, pure hearts; Lenten Preface II (P9); Reconciliation Eucharistic Prayer I; Memorial Acclamation D; Passion Solemn Blessing.

MUSIC

- Psalm 19
- *All That We Have* (Dameans/NALR)
- *All the Days of My Life* (Goglia/Resource)
- *Anthem* (Conry/NALR)
- *Answer When I Call* (Jesuits/NALR)
- *Be With Me* (Haugen/GIA)
- *Come, My Children* (Dameans/NALR)
- *Dwelling Place* (Jesuits/NALR)
- *The House Built On a Rock* (Deiss/NALR)
- *How Can I Keep From Singing?* (Traditional)
- *Lord, To Whom Shall We Go?* (Conry/NALR)
- *Lord, To Whom Shall We Go?* (Joncas/NALR)
- *My Refuge* (Vessels/GIA)
- *1 Corinthians* (Mullins/Resource)
- *Only This I Want* (Jesuits/NALR)
- *Take, Lord, Receive* (Jesuits/NALR)
- *There is a River* (Cooney/Resource)
- *This Alone* (Jesuits/NALR)
- *Turn to Me* (Jesuits/NALR)

LENTEN PLANNING SHEET   Date _____

Parish focus _____

Environment & art _____

Ritual notes _____

Faith development (eg., midweek program) _____

Children's faith experience _____

Prelude _____

Hymn of gathering _____

Penitential rite _____

Opening Prayer _____

Reading cycle _____First reading _____

Responsory _____Second reading _____

Lenten gospel acclamation _____Gospel _____

RCIA rites & acclamations _____

General intercessions _____

At the preparation & presentation _____

Preface dialog _____Preface _____

Preface acclamation _____

Eucharistic prayer _____Memorial acclamation _____

Eucharistic amen _____

The Lord's prayer _____

Breaking of bread _____

The communion hymn _____

The post-communion hymn _____

Blessing _____At the dismissal _____

Memoranda:

FOURTH SUNDAY OF LENT   YEAR B

READINGS
Second Chronicles (36:14-16,19-23)
The "lost Sabbath" symbolized the whole infidelity of the Jewish people and leaders that led up to destruction and exile. The Sabbath as "day of rest" calls for both detachment from everyday pursuits and attention to the fundamental realities of our existence: we come from God and our destiny is with God.
Ephesians (2:4-10)
Our creation is not our own doing; neither is the restoration of creation in Christ our own doing. We cannot earn God's gift, but we must actively respond to it.
John (3:14-21)
Faith is not merely acceptance of a doctrine; it is intimate contact with Jesus the Christ in whom we touch God. The coming of God's word-made-flesh is itself judgment: acceptance in faith is itself rebirth to eternal life; rejection in disbelief is itself condemnation.

FOCUS
Light is not merely something we see; it is that by which we see everything else. Faith in Jesus transforms all reality by first transforming the way we look at reality.

IDEA STARTERS:
- *CCT Lectionary:* II Chron 36:14-23; Ps 137:1-6; Eph 2:4-10; Jn 3:14-21.
- The second "Scrutinies" is celebrated today with the Elect. Use lectionary cycle A which presents the Easter/Baptism symbol of light. Celebrate the "Ephphatha" with the Elect during the week.
- Use a crucifix during the homily.
- Ss. Patrick and Joseph are commemorated this week. Celebrate them according to custom within the lenten observance. Lift high the processional cross!
- For your consideration: Penitential Rite; Opening Prayer; Intercessions for the Elect, all nations, end to infidelity in relationships, contemporary prophets, end to war, for the aged and infirm, young adults, captives, faith in action, medical workers; Lent Preface I (P8); Eucharistic Prayer III; Memorial Acclamation D; Passion Solemn Blessing.

MUSIC
- Psalm 137
- *Awake, O Sleeper* (Dameans/NALR)
- *Come, Let's Build* (Repp/K&R)
- *Dedication Song* (Raffa/Resource)
- *Draw Near, O Lord* (Farrell/PMB)
- *For Us To Live* (Weston Priory)
- *I Am the Light* (Repp/K&R)
- *If I Forget You* (Cooney/Resource)
- *I Have Loved You* (Joncas/NALR)
- *Lift High the Cross* (Kitchin/PMB)
- *Light of the World* (Kendzia/NALR)
- *O Cross of Christ* (Stanbrook/PMB)
- *O Lord You Know Our Weakness* (Westendorf/PMB)
- *Only a Shadow* (Landry/NALR)
- *Redeemer Lord* (Jesuits/NALR)
- *Rise Up, Jerusalem* (Jesuits/NALR)
- *Servant Canticle* (Weston Priory)
- *Shout for Joy* (Byrne/Resource)
- *Speak for the Light* (Blunt/Resource)
- *There's a Wideness in God's Mercy* (Watts/PMB)
- *Till You* (Repp/K&R)
- *What Wondrous Love* (Means/PMB)

LENTEN PLANNING SHEET

Date _____

Parish focus _____

Environment & art _____

Ritual notes _____

Faith development (eg., midweek program) _____

Children's faith experience _____

Prelude _____

Hymn of gathering _____

Penitential rite _____

Opening Prayer _____

Reading cycle _____ First reading _____

Responsory _____ Second reading _____

Lenten gospel acclamation _____ Gospel _____

RCIA rites & acclamations _____

General intercessions _____

At the preparation & presentation _____

Preface dialog _____ Preface _____

Preface acclamation _____

Eucharistic prayer _____ Memorial acclamation _____

Eucharistic amen _____

The Lord's prayer _____

Breaking of bread _____

The communion hymn _____

The post-communion hymn _____

Blessing _____ At the dismissal _____

Memoranda:

FIFTH SUNDAY OF LENT YEAR B

READINGS
Jeremiah (31:31-34)
The old covenant was imperfect because it was essentially external and depended on repeated observance for its fulfillment. The new covenant would be eternal and unbreakable because it would depend on the fidelity and obedience of Jesus Christ, and would be fulfilled in all who cling to him in faith.
Hebrews (5:7-9)
Jesus is the perfect and only true priest because only he, as God-the-Son, can make God fully present and active in the world, and, as man-in-the-flesh, can fully respond in obedience.
John (12:20-33)
Glory is inner value. The glorification of Jesus is his suffering and death in which he manifests his true self in loving obedience to God. The resurrection is not merely a reward or a reversal of this death, but the loving acceptance of this self-gift by God.

FOCUS
It goes against the grain of human nature to look for glory in selfless obedience and fidelity to the point of an inglorious death. Yes, there is the promise of resurrection, but the difficulty posed by the example of Jesus is that the cross must be embraced, not merely endured.

IDEA STARTERS
- *CCT Lectionary:* Jer 31:31-34; Ps 51:10-17; Heb 5:7-10; Jn 12:20-33.
- The third "Scrutinies" is celebrated with the Elect. Use lectionary cycle A which presents the Easter/Baptism symbol of new life. Present the words of "The Lord's Prayer" to the Elect during the week.
- Using the symbol for the medical profession (serpent on a pole), discuss its symbolism (cf. Numbers 21:4-9, with today's Gospel).
- Lift high the processional crucifix.
- For your consideration: Penitential Rite; Alternative Opening Prayer; Intercessions for the Elect, the least to the greatest, Israel, our ancestors, Egypt, lawyers, forgiveness, a clean heart, reverence, obedience to the Lord; Passion Preface I (P17); Eucharistic Prayer I; Memorial Acclamation B; Passion Solemn Blessing.

MUSIC
- Psalm 51
- *Amazing Grace* (Traditional)
- *Ashes* (Conry/NALR)
- *Behold the Wood* (Jesuits/NALR)
- *Believe and Repent* (Meltz/PMB)
- *Benedicamus* (Repp/K&R)
- *Canon of the Seed* (Repp/K&R)
- *Grant to Us, Lord* (Deiss/PMB)
- *Heart of Christ* (Farrell/PMB)
- *I Am the Resurrection* (Dameans/NALR)
- *If With All Your Hearts* (Mullins/Resource)
- *Kyrie Eleison* (Clark/Celebration)
- *Let Us Walk in the Light* (Haugen/GIA)
- *Little Closer* (Sexton/Resource)
- *May the Deaths, Lord* (Weston Priory)
- *Our God is Love* (Repp/K&R)
- *Sing Out His Goodness* (Dameans/NALR)
- *Spare Us, Lord* (Westendorf/PMB)
- *The Sun is Rising* (Weston Priory)
- *Take Up Your Cross* (Everest/PMB)
- *A Time for Building Bridges* (Landry/NALR)
- *Will You Take the Time* (Weston Priory)
- *With Faith Grown* (Landry/NALR)

LENTEN PLANNING SHEET

Date _____

Parish focus _____

Environment & art _____

Ritual notes _____

Faith development (eg., midweek program) _____

Children's faith experience _____

Prelude _____

Hymn of gathering _____

Penitential rite _____

Opening Prayer _____

Reading cycle _____First reading _____

Responsory _____Second reading _____

Lenten gospel acclamation _____Gospel _____

RCIA rites & acclamations _____

General intercessions _____

At the preparation & presentation _____

Preface dialog _____Preface _____

Preface acclamation _____

Eucharistic prayer _____Memorial acclamation _____

Eucharistic amen _____

The Lord's prayer _____

Breaking of bread _____

The communion hymn _____

The post-communion hymn _____

Blessing _____At the dismissal _____

Memoranda:

PASSION/PALM SUNDAY   YEAR B

READINGS
Mark (11:1-10) or John (12:12-16) Gospel for the Procession
Either passage may be read for the procession with palms. Mark shows the authority of Jesus in the details. John bypasses details and emphasizes meaning: Jesus is entering glory through the approaching suffering.
Isaiah (50:4-7)
The suffering of God's chosen servant is seen to be the result of fidelity to God's word; it is not mere passive endurance but an active conformity to God's will.
Philippians (2:6-11)
Paul gives the passion (or better, passage) of Jesus as the pattern for Christians: Jesus emptied himself, God raised him up and enthroned him as Lord.
Mark (14:1-15,47)
Mark's passion account is in a lively style which relishes detail and does not shrink from what might appear offensive. Jesus is shown not so much in control of events as freely relinquishing control.

FOCUS
The triumph and glory of God's servant and the scandal of the cross are one and the same mystery. Our attentive listening and celebration must first bow before the mystery in order to begin to unlock it for our celebration. Understanding comes through the conscientious effort to live the mystery rather than analyze it.

IDEA STARTERS
- *CCT Lectionary:* Mk 11:1-11 (Palm); Is 50:4-9a; Ps 31:9-16; Phil 2:5-11; Mk 14:1-15:47.
- Be sure to include the Elect in the liturgies of Holy Week, especially the Chrism Eucharist at the cathedral.
- Be sure to celebrate the Liturgy of the Palms with a parade around the church (building or grounds). During the Liturgy of the Word, use only the Passion with a sung refrain throughout.
- When the Liturgy of the Palms is celebrated in the same area as the Eucharist (i.e., no procession of the assembly) consider having the presider wear a cope until the opening prayer of the Eucharist when the chasuble is worn.
- Avoid play acting the solemn proclamation. Have readers proclaim major portions, with a brief refrain to be sung by the assembly between each.
- For your consideration: Liturgy of Palms (omit Penitential Rite and Hymn of Praise); Opening Prayer; Passion (full form); Intercessions for preachers, the weary, openness to God's Word, enemies, equality, respect for Jesus' name, civil authorities; Passion Sunday Preface (P19); Reconciliation Eucharistic Prayer I; Memorial Acclamation C; Passion Solemn Blessing.

MUSIC

- Psalm 22
- *All Glory, Praise and Honor* (Neale/PMB)
- *All Hail the Power of Jesus' Name* (Perronet/PMB)
- *Glory to the Holy One* (Marchionda/PMB)
- *Hosanna!* (Dicie/Resource)
- *Hosanna* (Prezio/K&R)
- *Into Your Hands, Lord* (Goglia/Resource)
- *I See His Blood* (Joncas/Coop Music)
- *Jesus the New Covenant* (Deiss/PMB)
- *Jesus Shall Reign* (Watts/PMB)
- *Jesus Walked the Lonesome Valley* (Spiritual/PMB)
- *Let Heaven Rejoice* (Jesuits/NALR)
- *O Sacred Head* (Baker/PMB)
- *Out of the Depths* (Haugen/GIA)
- *Song of Abandonment* (Landry/NALR)

LENTEN PLANNING SHEET   Date _____

Parish focus _____

Environment & art _____

Ritual notes _____

Faith development (eg., midweek program) _____

Children's faith experience _____

Prelude _____

Hymn of gathering _____

Penitential rite _____

Opening Prayer _____

Reading cycle _____First reading _____

Responsory _____Second reading _____

Lenten gospel acclamation _____Gospel _____

RCIA rites & acclamations _____

General intercessions _____

At the preparation & presentation _____

Preface dialog _____Preface _____

Preface acclamation _____

Eucharistic prayer _____Memorial acclamation _____

Eucharistic amen _____

The Lord's prayer _____

Breaking of bread _____

The communion hymn _____

The post-communion hymn _____

Blessing _____At the dismissal _____

Memoranda:

HOLY THURSDAY: MASS OF THE LORD'S SUPPER

(See Year A For Commentary)

YEARS A, B AND C

TRIDUUM PLANNING SHEET

Date _____

Parish focus _____

Environment & art _____

Ritual notes _____

Faith development (eg., midweek program) _____

Children's faith experience _____

Prelude _____

Hymn of gathering _____

Penitential rite _____

Opening Prayer _____

Reading cycle _____ First reading _____

Responsory _____ Second reading _____

Lenten gospel acclamation _____ Gospel _____

RCIA rites & acclamations _____

General intercessions _____

At the preparation & presentation _____

Preface dialog _____ Preface _____

Preface acclamation _____

Eucharistic prayer _____ Memorial acclamation _____

Eucharistic amen _____

The Lord's prayer _____

Breaking of bread _____

The communion hymn _____

The post-communion hymn _____

Blessing _____ At the dismissal _____

Memoranda:

GOOD FRIDAY: CELEBRATION OF THE LORD'S PASSION

YEARS A, B AND C

(See Year A For All Commentary)

TRIDUUM PLANNING SHEET

Date _____

Parish focus _____

Environment & art _____

Ritual notes _____

Faith development (eg., midweek program) _____

Children's faith experience _____

Prelude _____

Hymn of gathering _____

Penitential rite _____

Opening Prayer _____

Reading cycle _____First reading _____

Responsory _____Second reading _____

Lenten gospel acclamation _____Gospel _____

RCIA rites & acclamations _____

General intercessions _____

At the preparation & presentation _____

Preface dialog _____Preface _____

Preface acclamation _____

Eucharistic prayer _____Memorial acclamation _____

Eucharistic amen _____

The Lord's prayer _____

Breaking of bread _____

The communion hymn _____

The post-communion hymn _____

Blessing _____At the dismissal _____

Memoranda:

THE EASTER VIGIL
(See Year A For Commentary)

TRIDUUM PLANNING SHEET

Date _____

Parish focus _____

Environment & art _____

Ritual notes _____

Faith development (eg., midweek program) _____

Children's faith experience _____

Prelude _____

Hymn of gathering _____

Penitential rite _____

Opening Prayer _____

Reading cycle _____ First reading _____

Responsory _____ Second reading _____

Lenten gospel acclamation _____ Gospel _____

RCIA rites & acclamations _____

General intercessions _____

At the preparation & presentation _____

Preface dialog _____ Preface _____

Preface acclamation _____

Eucharistic prayer _____ Memorial acclamation _____

Eucharistic amen _____

The Lord's prayer _____

Breaking of bread _____

The communion hymn _____

The post-communion hymn _____

Blessing _____ At the dismissal _____

Memoranda:

EASTER SUNDAY YEARS A, B AND C
(See Year A For All Readings And Further Commentary)

READINGS
Acts (10:34,37-43)
Jesus, the crucified one, is both Christ and Lord. Though innocent and generous he is betrayed and murdered by his own people. God, however, uses this tragedy to demonstrate God's own glory. God raises Jesus from the dead. Jesus then commissions his disciples to carry out the work of evangelization.

Colossians (3:1-4) or First Corinthians (5:6-8)
In the reading from Colossians, Paul underscores that the Christian dies and rises to New Life, with Christ, through Baptism. In the fragment from First Corinthians, Paul uses the analogy of yeast *(azymea)* to indicate the effect Christians have on the world. As the "yeast of sincerity and truth," we enrich and fill the earth with the very life of Christ.

John (20:1-9)
In the Gospel we hear once more the familiar story of Mary Magdalen, the first to receive the Good News of the Resurrection from the Risen Lord's own lips.

FOCUS
The Pentecost Experience is the stimulus which activates the yeast-like effect the church has on the world. The witnesses of Mary Magdalen, John, and Peter are necessary to raise not only the church, but all of creation to the unity of the Risen Lord.

IDEA STARTERS
- *CCT Lectionary:* Acts 10:34-43 or Col 3:1-4; Ps 118:14-24; I Cor 15:1-11 or Acts 10:34-43; Jn 20:1-18 or Mk 16:1-8.
- If the neophytes will participate in the day's Eucharist, bid them a warm welcome to the Sunday assembly.
- Readers should proclaim the first two readings as their personal messages to the assembly.
- Because of the renunciation of sin and sprinkling of Easter Water, it is appropriate to omit a Penitential Rite or Sprinkling Rite during today's gathering rites.
- Infant baptism is appropriate today.
- End the Easter Triduum with Solemn Easter Vespers.
- Find a musical setting of the Paschal *Sequence.*
- For your consideration: Hymn of Praise (sung); Reaffirmation of Baptismal Vows; Intercessions for neophytes, healing, witnessing, world peace and fellowship, preachers, grace, carpenters, sculptors, stone masons, pure hearts, bakers, cemetery workers; Easter Preface I (P21); Eucharistic Prayer I w/Easter proper; Memorial Acclamation B; Easter Season Solemn Blessing.

MUSIC

- Psalm 118
- *Alleluia, the Lord, My Strength* (Keyes/Resource)
- *Benedicamus* (Repp/K&R)
- *Christ, the Lord is Risen Today* (Traditional/PMB)
- *Easter Hymn* (Duesing/Resource)
- *Easter Sequence* (Traditional/PMB)
- *Hail Thee, Festival Day* (Fortunato/PMB)
- *Jesus is Life* (Landry/NALR)
- *Praise Canticle* (Haas/Cooperative Music)
- *Resurrection Song* (Sexton/Resource)
- *Singers, Sing* (Gannon/PMB)
- *Sing to the Mountains* (Jesuits/NALR)
- *This is the Day* (Deiss/PMB)
- *This is the Day* (Goglia/Resource)
- *This is the Day* (Haugen/GIA)

EASTER PLANNING SHEET   Date _____

Parish focus _____

Environment & art _____

Ritual notes _____

Faith development (eg., midweek program) _____

Children's faith experience _____

Prelude _____

Hymn of gathering _____

Sprinkling baptismal water acclamation _____

Opening Prayer _____

Reading cycle _____First reading _____

Responsory _____Second reading _____

Lenten gospel acclamation _____Gospel _____

RCIA rites & acclamations _____

General intercessions _____

At the preparation & presentation _____

Preface dialog _____Preface _____

Preface acclamation _____

Eucharistic prayer _____Memorial acclamation _____

Eucharistic amen _____

The Lord's prayer _____

Breaking of bread _____

The communion hymn _____

The post-communion hymn _____

Blessing _____At the dismissal _____

Memoranda:

SECOND SUNDAY OF EASTER

YEAR B

READINGS

Acts (4:32-35)
The presence of the church in the world is a sign of wonder and joy, yet it engenders fear. Peter, the Rock, is recognized as a powerful figure in the Body of Christ.

First John (5:1-6)
What makes a Christian Christian? Believing that Jesus is the Christ. Such a one is saved through his blood and is his vessel of Love. This love conquers the world through the power of the Spirit.

John (20:19-31)
Locked doors are no impediment to the glorified body of the Risen Lord, and fearful sin is no block to his body the Church. As instrument of his love, she frees all from the death-like shackles that bear down on them and keep them from the full experience of his life.

FOCUS

The Resurrection is God's ultimate sign of the freeing power of love. Today's readings show how Jesus' victory over death releases the Christian from the tyranny of death. The results of such freedom are the reception of our inheritance as the adopted Children of God, as well as the ability to free those caught in the chains of death (sin), through the healing power of Christ.

IDEA STARTERS

- *CCT Lectionary:* Acts 4:32-35; Ps 133; I Jn 1:1-2:2; Jn 20:19-31.
- Have a neophyte pray the Nicene Creed to which the entire assembly sings an acclamation of assent.
- Jesus shares his life with us, so we must share who we are and what we have with others.
- Topics for adult ed: Acts 4:32-35; Commune? Religious Community? Communism?
- "Peace be with you!" How do we react when we share Christ-in-us with others (cf. Jn 20:20b)?
- For your consideration: Sprinkling Easter Water; Hymn of Praise (sung); Opening Prayer; Intercessions for neophytes, unity among nations, Churches, families and neighbors, civil authorities and religious leaders, the needy, real estate agents, agnostics, atheists, non-Christians, faith through doubt; Easter Preface IV (P24); Eucharistic Prayer I w/proper; Memorial Acclamation A; Easter Sunday Solemn Blessing.

MUSIC

- Psalm 118
- *Everyone Moved by the Spirit* (Landry/NALR)
- *For Us To Live* (Weston Priory)
- *Glorious in Majesty* (Cothran/GIA)
- *Go Now in Peace* (Wise/GIA)
- *He is the Lord* (Haas/Cooperative Music)
- *I Danced in the Morning* (Carter/Galaxy Music)
- *O Sons and Daughters* (Neale/PMB)
- *Praised Be The Father* (Dameans/NALR)
- *Praise the Lord* (Dicie/Resource)
- *Shalom* (Reagan/NALR)
- *A Song of Blessing* (Wise/GIA)
- *That There May Be Bread* (Weston Priory)
- *There is Peace* (Goglia/Resource)
- *We Remember* (Haugen/GIA)
- *Will You Take the Time* (Weston Priory)
- *The Wonders He Has Done for You* (Anderson/Resource)
- *Ye Watchers and Ye Holy Ones* (Riley/PMB)

EASTER PLANNING SHEET   Date _____

Parish focus _____

Environment & art _____

Ritual notes _____

Faith development (eg., midweek program) _____

Children's faith experience _____

Prelude _____

Hymn of gathering _____

Sprinkling baptismal water acclamation _____

Opening Prayer _____

Reading cycle _____ First reading _____

Responsory _____ Second reading _____

Lenten gospel acclamation _____ Gospel _____

RCIA rites & acclamations _____

General intercessions _____

At the preparation & presentation _____

Preface dialog _____ Preface _____

Preface acclamation _____

Eucharistic prayer _____ Memorial acclamation ___

Eucharistic amen _____

The Lord's prayer _____

Breaking of bread _____

The communion hymn _____

The post-communion hymn _____

Blessing _____ At the dismissal _____

Memoranda:

THIRD SUNDAY
OF EASTER

YEAR B

READINGS
Acts of the Apostles (3:13–15,17–19)
Peter points out that, in their condemnation of Jesus, the people acted out of
ignorance. Not realizing who he was and what relationship he had to them,
they put to death the one who is the Source of Life. Yet God uses this as a
part of the great salvific plan.
First John (2:1–5)
Jesus is the one who saves us from our sins and acts as our intercessor with
God. If we keep his word and follow in his way, we can be sure that we know
him and live in his love.
Luke (24:35–48)
Jesus is truly risen in his human body now joined to God's Glory. In his name,
all sin is forgiven and the goodness of salvation is given to us.

FOCUS
From all time God has planned that humanity should share in divine life, the
free gift of God's Love. Jesus is the key figure in this plan uniting in himself
the nature of God and human beings. Through his obedience we are united
to God's life and freed from the death of sin.

IDEA STARTERS
- *CCT Lectionary:* Acts 3:12-19; Ps 4; I Jn 3:1-7; Lk 24:35-48.
- Have the neophytes share their initiation experiences with members of the
  community.
- First Eucharist for children may appropriately be celebrated today.
- Highlight the action of "Breaking the Bread and Pouring the Cup," if this
  is not already the custom. Use anthem 9 or 10 from the *Book of Occasional
  Services,* "Confractoria."
- Acts 3:15b and Lk 24:48 provide bases for a day of recollection, a homily,
  and a bulletin article-reflection.
- John's epistle provides food for thought: those who deny the reality of
  personal sin in essence deny the need for the Savior.
- For your consideration: Sprinkling Easter Water; Hymn of Praise (sung);
  Alternative Opening Prayer; Intercessions for neophytes, the Jewish people,
  justice in legal systems, spirit of knowledge and repentance, perseverence
  in prayer, joy and awe before the Lord; Easter Preface V (P25); Eucharistic
  Prayer I w/proper; Memorial Acclamation C; Breaking of Bread
  (highlighted); Easter Sunday Solemn Blessing.

MUSIC
- Psalm 4
- *All You On Earth* (Westendorf/PMB)
- *Are Not our Hearts* (Landry/NALR)
- *Breaking of the Bread* (Prezio/K&R)
- *Dedication Song* (Raffa/Resource)
- *How Beautiful* (Wise/GIA)
- *Jesus Christ is Risen Today* (Traditional/PMB)
- *Let All the Earth* (Dameans/NALR)
- *Praise the Lord, My Soul* (Parker/GIA)
- *Shout for Joy* (Byrne/Resource)
- *Something Which is Known* (Weston Priory)
- *Zephaniah's Song* (Anderson/Resource)

EASTER PLANNING SHEET   Date _____

Parish focus _____

Environment & art _____

Ritual notes _____

Faith development (eg., midweek program) _____

Children's faith experience _____

Prelude _____

Hymn of gathering _____

Sprinkling baptismal water acclamation _____

Opening Prayer _____

Reading cycle _____First reading _____

Responsory _____Second reading _____

Lenten gospel acclamation _____Gospel _____

RCIA rites & acclamations _____

General intercessions _____

At the preparation & presentation _____

Preface dialog _____Preface _____

Preface acclamation _____

Eucharistic prayer _____Memorial acclamation ____

Eucharistic amen _____

The Lord's prayer _____

Breaking of bread _____

The communion hymn _____

The post-communion hymn _____

Blessing _____At the dismissal _____

Memoranda:

FOURTH SUNDAY OF EASTER

YEAR B

READINGS
Acts of the Apostles (4:8–12)
Jesus, rejected and spurned by his own, has become the foundation of the world's salvation.
First John (3:1–2)
Divine love transforms us into God's children. The power of this is so great that someday we shall share the very essence of the Godhead, since we shall see God in the face.
John (10:11–18)
Jesus is the Shepherd who lovingly cares for his sheep. He knows them and they respond to him. He has concern for and calls to other sheep, who are not in his flock, but who need his guidance. Someday all shall be united to God through the Good Shepherd.

FOCUS
Those who accept Christ as the cornerstone open the possibility of sharing the life of God, since they become God's children. They do this by acknowledging Jesus as Shepherd of the flock.

IDEA STARTERS
- *CCT Lectionary:* Acts 4:8–12; Ps 23; I Jn 3:8–24; Jn 10:11–18.
- Today is "Good Shepherd Sunday."
- Examine the process of naming in Scripture. Find out more about patron saints.
- Have the children of the parish act out the story of the Good Shepherd vs. the Hired Hand.
- Examine what's in a name relationship: done in the name of Jesus; the Shepherd knows his sheep; we are called children of God.
- For your consideration: Sprinkling Easter Water; Hymn of Praise (sung); Opening Prayer; Intercessions for neophytes, those in leadership roles, healing, respect for the name of Jesus, hope, farmers and farmworkers, sacrificial love; Easter Preface II (P22); Eucharistic Prayer I w/proper; Memorial Acclamation B; Easter Sunday Solemn Blessing.

MUSIC
- Psalm 118
- *Canticle of Mary* (Magnificat)
- *Eye Has Not Seen* (Haugen/GIA)
- *I Will Sing* (Dyer/Celebration)
- *Jesus, the Lord* (Keyes/Resource)
- *Lift High Your Hearts* (Patterson/Resource)
- *The Lord is My Shepherd* (Wise/GIA)
- *Morning Has Broken* (Farjeon)
- *Shepherd's Alleluia* (Landry/NALR)

EASTER PLANNING SHEET

Date _____

Parish focus _____

Environment & art _____

Ritual notes _____

Faith development (eg., midweek program) _____

Children's faith experience _____

Prelude _____

Hymn of gathering _____

Sprinkling baptismal water acclamation _____

Opening Prayer _____

Reading cycle _____ First reading _____

Responsory _____ Second reading _____

Lenten gospel acclamation _____ Gospel _____

RCIA rites & acclamations _____

General intercessions _____

At the preparation & presentation _____

Preface dialog _____ Preface _____

Preface acclamation _____

Eucharistic prayer _____ Memorial acclamation _____

Eucharistic amen _____

The Lord's prayer _____

Breaking of bread _____

The communion hymn _____

The post-communion hymn _____

Blessing _____ At the dismissal _____

Memoranda:

FIFTH SUNDAY OF EASTER

YEAR B

READINGS

Acts of the Apostles (9:26-31)
Saul, a powerful gift from the Lord, is initially misunderstood and feared by the early church. He also proves a burr in the side to the Hellenic Jews, who try to kill him. Despite adversity the church grows and develops in the Spirit.

First John (3:18-24)
The same Spirit that kept the early church in peace and strengthened her is the Spirit that makes us recognize that Jesus is alive and dwelling with us. This Spirit helps us to live God's love and then to share God's life.

John (15:1-8)
Without our vital, life-giving connection to Jesus, we, like vines cut off from the branch, wither, dry out, and die.

FOCUS

The church, whether in the apostolic age or in the twentieth century, needs to stay connected to the Risen Lord. If we do not cut ourselves off from him, we shall recognize and appreciate his gifts, live his commandment of love, not be subjected to the tyranny of an isolated, ego-centered conscience and will one day share his life fully.

IDEA STARTERS

- *CCT Lectionary:* Acts 8:26-40; Ps 22:25-31; I Jn 4:7-12; Jn 15:1-8.
- Begin talking about the need for the Sacrament of Penance w/the neophytes based on today's epistle.
- Have children bring in pictures of themselves, and tape them to a vine banner.
- Saul is one of our Lord's branches trimmed clean.
- Volunteers needed? "Let us love in deed and truth."
- Have a parish outing to an orchard.
- For your consideration: Sprinkling Easter Water; Hymn of Praise (sung); Alternative Opening Prayer; Intercessions for neophytes, fellowship among believers, contemporary prophets and martyrs, families, vinegrowers; Easter Preface IV (P24); Eucharistic Prayer I w/proper; Memorial Acclamation D; Easter Season Solemn Blessing.

MUSIC

- Psalm 22
- *Anthem* (Conry/NALR)
- *Be Not Afraid* (Jesuits/NALR)
- *Call to Me* (Byrne/Resource)
- *Christ is Alive* (Wren/PMB)
- *Faith in Action* (Blunt/Resource)
- *Go Up to the Mountain* (Weston Priory)
- *Hymn of Joy* (Wordsworth/PMB)
- *Jubilate, Servite* (Taize/GIA)
- *Lord, To Whom Shall We Go?* (Joncas/NALR)
- *Love is Come Again* (Crum/PMB)
- *Something Beautiful for God* (Mullins/Resource)
- *Spirit of Promise* (Gilsdorf/Resource)
- *Ubi Caritas* (Taize/GIA)

EASTER PLANNING SHEET

Date _____

Parish focus _____

Environment & art _____

Ritual notes _____

Faith development (eg., midweek program) _____

Children's faith experience _____

Prelude _____

Hymn of gathering _____

Sprinkling baptismal water acclamation _____

Opening Prayer _____

Reading cycle _____ First reading _____

Responsory _____ Second reading _____

Lenten gospel acclamation _____ Gospel _____

RCIA rites & acclamations _____

General intercessions _____

At the preparation & presentation _____

Preface dialog _____ Preface _____

Preface acclamation _____

Eucharistic prayer _____ Memorial acclamation _____

Eucharistic amen _____

The Lord's prayer _____

Breaking of bread _____

The communion hymn _____

The post-communion hymn _____

Blessing _____ At the dismissal _____

Memoranda:

SIXTH SUNDAY OF EASTER   YEAR B

READINGS
Acts of the Apostles (10:25-26,34-35,44-48)
The Spirit moves where it will. Not bound by human regulation or rule, it spontaneously, freely inhabits any human heart, setting it alive and pulsing with divine life. Peter wisely realizes this in the manifestation of the outpouring of the Spirit on Cornelius and his family. As a Spirit-filled witness to Christ himself, Peter proclaims the obvious to the surprised and a happy community of believers.

First John (4:7-10)
God is Love! God's power, his *elan vital,* is the power and energy of charity. The proof of this love is the Incarnation and Redemption. While we were yet in our sin, the Lord loved us enough to enter our condition, and seal the covenant of love with us in Christ's Blood.

John (15:9-17)
The love to which John refers in his First Letter is pointed to by the Lord in the Farewell Discourses of John's Gospel. Jesus reminds us that his love is the love of God. This love impels Jesus to give the greatest gift, his life. It also calls the community of the church, the new body of Christ, into being.

FOCUS
The divine nature is perfectly explained by one word, love. This love which longs to share itself is the love which impelled the Lord to offer his sacrifice of self. It is the self-same love which filled Cornelius and his family, moving them to acknowledge the Lord. Finally, it is the same love which enables the community to perceive and accept the spontaneous work of the Spirit in the affairs of humanity.

IDEA STARTERS
- *CCT Lectionary:* Acts 10:44-48; Ps 98; I Jn 5:1-6; Jn 15:9-17.
- "You have not chosen me; I have chosen you."
- Use the song, "O How I Love Jesus" in a talk with the children about John's epistle.
- The days between Ascension and Pentecost are traditional days of ecumenical prayer in preparation for the commemoration of the Spirit's descent upon God's people. Use the motto, "From Death to Life with Christ" (cf. Eph 2:4-7).
- For your consideration: Sprinkling Easter Water; Hymn of Praise (sung); Opening Prayer; Intercessions for neophytes, mothers, equality, unity, believers and non-believers, unconditional love, joy, spirit of sacrifice; Easter Preface II (P22); Eucharistic Prayer I w/proper; Memorial Acclamation D; Easter Sunday Solemn Blessing.

MUSIC

- Psalm 98
- *Alleluia No. 1* (Fishel/PMB)
- *By Love* (Repp/K&R)
- *God So Loved the World* (Antioch/K&R)
- *I Have Loved You* (Joncas/NALR)
- *In Honor of the Holy Cross*
  (Dicie/Resource)
- *Keep In Mind* (Deiss/PMB)
- *A Living Hope* (Jones/PMB)
- *Lord of Glory* (Jesuits/NALR)
- *Love is Come Again* (Crum/PMB)
- *Love Song* (Westendorf/PMB)
- *Resurrection Song* (Sexton/Resource)
- *Shout for Joy* (Byrne/Resource)
- *This is the Day* (Deiss/PMB)
- *Without Seeing You* (Deiss/PMB)
- *You Are My Friends* (Regan/NALR)

EASTER PLANNING SHEET
Date _____

Parish focus _____

Environment & art _____

Ritual notes _____

Faith development (eg., midweek program) _____

Children's faith experience _____

Prelude _____

Hymn of gathering _____

Sprinkling baptismal water acclamation _____

Opening Prayer _____

Reading cycle _____First reading _____

Responsory _____Second reading _____

Lenten gospel acclamation _____Gospel _____

RCIA rites & acclamations _____

General intercessions _____

At the preparation & presentation _____

Preface dialog _____Preface _____

Preface acclamation _____

Eucharistic prayer _____Memorial acclamation _____

Eucharistic amen _____

The Lord's prayer _____

Breaking of bread _____

The communion hymn _____

The post-communion hymn _____

Blessing _____At the dismissal _____

Memoranda:

THE SOLEMNITY OF THE ASCENSION

YEAR B

(See Year A For All Readings And Commentary Except:)

Mark (16:15–20)
The ending of Mark's Gospel shows how Jesus remains with his church. When the church proclaims and lives the Gospel, the Lord himself is at work.

EASTER PLANNING SHEET

Date _____

Parish focus _____

Environment & art _____

Ritual notes _____

Faith development (eg., midweek program) _____

Children's faith experience _____

Prelude _____

Hymn of gathering _____

Sprinkling baptismal water acclamation _____

Opening Prayer _____

Reading cycle _____ First reading _____

Responsory _____ Second reading _____

Lenten gospel acclamation _____ Gospel _____

RCIA rites & acclamations _____

General intercessions _____

At the preparation & presentation _____

Preface dialog _____ Preface _____

Preface acclamation _____

Eucharistic prayer _____ Memorial acclamation ___

Eucharistic amen _____

The Lord's prayer _____

Breaking of bread _____

The communion hymn _____

The post-communion hymn _____

Blessing _____ At the dismissal _____

Memoranda:

SEVENTH SUNDAY OF EASTER

YEAR B

READINGS

Acts of the Apostles (1:15-17,20-26)
Moved and guided by the Spirit, the apostolic college supported by the prayers of the whole believing community call Matthias to the vocation of apostle.

First John (4:11-16)
Those who live in a loving, compassionate manner point to the God who lives in their midst who brings them to life. Since God has given us himself in love, we must give ourselves to others in the same way.

John (17:11-19)
It is the Spirit sent out on us by the Lord which keeps us whole and complete. The Spirit protects the church from error. This protection and guidance is vitally important since the church is set apart from and against the spirit of the world, the spirit of self-centeredness and death.

FOCUS

Those who choose Jesus are consecrated by his Spirit and called out of the clasp of death, the spirit of the world. Like Matthias, they fill the role that the Spirit specifically calls them to occupy. Anointed in the Spirit of Love, they live in the reality of trinitarian communion and are impelled to compassion in the same fashion the Godhead is.

IDEA STARTERS

- *CCT Lectionary:* Acts 1:15-17, 21-26; Ps 1; I Jn 5:9-13; Jn 17:11b-19.
- RCIA: "Consecrated by the Word of God for the Sake of the World."
- What happens when being (acting) Christian makes us unpopular?
- Continue ecumenical daily prayer.
- Bulletin article: Parish Council Elections ("May Another Take Office")
- A Rogation Procession may be held today (cf. *Book of Occasional Services,* NY: Church Hymnal Corp., 1979).
- For your consideration: Sprinkling Easter Water; Hymn of Praise (sung); Alternative Opening Prayer; Intercessions for neophytes, church leaders, life centered in God, reverence for God's name, realization of the world as the kingdom of God; Ascension Preface I (P26); Eucharistic Prayer I w/Ascension *Communicates* & Easter *Hanc Igitur;* Memorial Acclamation D; The Lord's Prayer (sung); Ascension Solemn Blessing.

MUSIC

- Psalm 103
- *Anthem* (Conry/NALR)
- *Christ is Alive* (Wren/PMB)
- *Eye Has Not Seen* (Haugen/GIA)
- *For I Shall See You Again* (Weston Priory)
- *Let the Earth Rejoice and Sing* (Farrell/PMB)
- *The Lord Who Lives Inside of Me* (Pattersen/Resource)
- *One Bread, One Body* (Jesuits/NALR)
- *Peace Song* (Stenson/Resource)
- *Praise the Lord, My Soul* (Parker/GIA)
- *Something Which is Known* (Weston Priory)
- *That All Be One* (Somerville/PMB)
- *Ubi Caritas* (Taize/GIA)
- *Zephaniah's Song* (Andersen/Resource)

EASTER PLANNING SHEET

Date _____

Parish focus _____

Environment & art _____

Ritual notes _____

Faith development (eg., midweek program) _____

Children's faith experience _____

Prelude _____

Hymn of gathering _____

Sprinkling baptismal water acclamation _____

Opening Prayer _____

Reading cycle _____ First reading _____

Responsory _____ Second reading _____

Lenten gospel acclamation _____ Gospel _____

RCIA rites & acclamations _____

General intercessions _____

At the preparation & presentation _____

Preface dialog _____ Preface _____

Preface acclamation _____

Eucharistic prayer _____ Memorial acclamation _____

Eucharistic amen _____

The Lord's prayer _____

Breaking of bread _____

The communion hymn _____

The post-communion hymn _____

Blessing _____ At the dismissal _____

Memoranda:

SOLEMNITY OF PENTECOST

YEARS A, B AND C

(See Year A For All Readings and Further Commentary)

READINGS

Acts of the Apostles (2:1-11)
The Spirit reverses the ancient curse of Babel. All people are brought to unity and a close sense of the wonder of God's great love through the activity of the Spirit. All the artificial barriers which block our efforts at eucharistic unity are melted in the furnace of the Spirit's love.

First Corinthians (12:3-7,12-13)
The Spirit reconciles all differences so that unity is achieved in diversity. Rather than homogeneity, there is harmony. It is the Spirit which moves us to confess the Lordship of Jesus. It is the Spirit which calls the body of Christ, the church, into being.

John (20:19-23)
The Spirit is the breath of God. In this divine life force, we are freed from the chains of death that bind us. The various functions of Christ's body are set to their tasks and brought to life in the activity of the Spirit.

FOCUS

The Spirit is the life force of the church, the new body of Christ. The Spirit is responsible for bringing the love of God into being in our lives.

IDEA STARTERS

- *CCT Lectionary:* Acts 2:1-21 *or* Ez 37:1-14; Ps 104:24-34; Rm 8:22-27 *or* Acts 2:1-21; Jn 15:26-27, 16:4b-15.
- Any of the Elect who were unable to be presented for Initiation at the Easter vigil may do so at the Pentecost vigil.
- Scriptural symbols provide many opportunities for a children's liturgy (eg.,Tower of Babel, dry bones, fire, spiritual gifts, breath, wind).
- Have a parish picnic for the beginning of summer. Ask people to bring a friend who does not usually come to church.
- Use of foreign tongues in familiar parts of the liturgy may give the assembly a sense of amazed understanding. Use short Greek or Latin refrains.
- The Acts lection may lend itself to choral proclamation.
- Sponsor an observance of Peace Pentecost.
- For your consideration: Sprinkling Easter Water; Hymn of Praise (sung); Opening Prayer; Golden Sequence (sung); Intercessions for neophytes, charismatic prayer groups, those suffering from natural disasters, spiritual gifts, love, forgiveness, understanding, travellers; Pentecost Preface (P28); Reconciliation Eucharistic Prayer II; Memorial Acclamation D; Holy Spirit Solemn Blessing.

MUSIC

- Psalm 104
- *Pentecost Sequence* (Traditional/PMB)
- *Alleluia, People of God* (Deiss/NALR)
- *Come Holy Ghost* (Caswell/PMB)
- *Gifts for Our Lord* (Cohen/NALR)
- *Hail Thee, Festival Day!* (Fortunatus/PMB)
- *May We Praise* (Jesuits/NALR)
- *O Holy Spirit, By Whose Breath* (Grant/PMB)
- *O Holy Spirit, Come to Us* (Farrell/PMB)
- *Send Us Your Spirit* (Haas/Cooperative Music)
- *Spirit Come Forth* (Duesing/Resource)
- *The Spirit is A-Movin'* (Landry/NALR)
- *Spirit of God* (Weston Priory)
- *Spirit of Promise* (Gilsdorf/Resource)
- *We Are Many Parts* (Haugen/GIA)
- *We Thank You, Father* (Weston Priory)
- *Veni Sancte Spiritus* (Taize/GIA)

EASTER PLANNING SHEET   Date _____

Parish focus _____

Environment & art _____

Ritual notes _____

Faith development (eg., midweek program) _____

Children's faith experience _____

Prelude _____

Hymn of gathering _____

Sprinkling baptismal water acclamation _____

Opening Prayer _____

Reading cycle _____First reading _____

Responsory _____Second reading _____

Lenten gospel acclamation _____Gospel _____

RCIA rites & acclamations _____

General intercessions _____

At the preparation & presentation _____

Preface dialog _____Preface _____

Preface acclamation _____

Eucharistic prayer _____Memorial acclamation _____

Eucharistic amen _____

The Lord's prayer _____

Breaking of bread _____

The communion hymn _____

The post-communion hymn _____

Blessing _____At the dismissal _____

Memoranda:

SOLEMNITY OF
THE HOLY TRINITY

YEAR B

READINGS
Deuteronomy (4:32-34,39-40)
As the ancient Hebrews were reminded of the greatness of God's love,
Christians by virtue of Jesus' incarnation and work of salvation are brought
to a heightened awareness of the wonder of the Lord's presence in trinitarian
love. This presence resides in the church, the body of Christ.
Romans (8:14-17)
The Spirit leads us to recognize our position as heirs to the kingdom of God
with Christ. It also moves us to acknowledge God as Father and to cry to
God as "Abba," daddy.

Matthew (28:16-20)
Jesus commends us to spread the Good News to all people, incorporating them
into his body in the name of the Trinity. He leaves us with the promise that
God will be with us always.

FOCUS
The Spirit moved the ancient Hebrews to acknowledge the greatness of God
and now moves the church to acknowledge Jesus as Lord, the one who makes
us heirs to the Kingdom. The same Spirit allows us to recognize God as Father
and as little children to cry out to God "daddy."

IDEA STARTERS
- *CCT Lectionary:* Is 6:1-8; Ps 29; Rm 8:12-17; Jn 3:1-17.
- Why is today's alternative opening prayer alien to the traditional form of
  Christian prayer?
- Use the "Glory to God" as the hymn of praise, the "Glory to the Father"
  (ICET translation) as the Gospel Alleluia, the "Athanasian Creed" (LBW
  translation) as the profession of faith, The Lord's Prayer (ICET) and the
  Te Deum (ICET text/LBW music) as the post-communion hymn.
- Infant baptism may be celebrated with today's readings.
- For your consideration: Sprinkling Baptismal Water; Hymn of Praise (sung);
  Opening Prayer; Intercessions for stewardship of creation, hope, adopted
  children & families, evangelism; Trinity Preface (P43); Eucharistic Prayer
  IV; Memorial Acclamation B; The Lord's Prayer (sung); Easter Season
  Solemn Blessing.

MUSIC

- Psalm 33
- *Abba, Father* (Landry/NALR)
- *Be Glad, O People* (Weston Priory)
- *Call to Me* (Byrne/Resource)
- *Eagles' Wings* (Andersen/Resource)
- *For Us To Live* (Weston Priory)
- *Glory and Praise* (Jesuits/NALR)
- *How Beautiful on the Mountains* (Deiss/NALR)
- *Let All the Earth* (Haugen/GIA)
- *The Messenger Song* (Gilsdorf/Resource)
- *My Friends, I Bless You* (Weston Priory)
- *Praise! Praise the Lord* (Sessions/Resource)
- *Remember Your Love* (Dameans/NALR)
- *Sing Praise to our Creator* (Westendorf/PMB)
- *Song of Gathering* (Wise/GIA)
- *Song to the God We Love* (Meyette/Resource)
- *There is Peace* (Goglia/Resource)
- *Wonderful and Great* (Deiss/PMB)
- *Yahweh* (Weston Priory)
- *You Are My Witness* (Fisherfolk/Resource)

SUNDAY PLANNING SHEET   Date _____

Parish focus _____

Environment & art _____

Ritual notes _____

Faith development (eg., in newsletter/classes) _____

Children's faith experience _____

Prelude _____

Hymn of gathering _____

Sprinkling/Penitential rite _____

Hymn of praise _____

Opening Prayer _____

First reading _____Responsory _____

Second reading _____Gospel acclamation _____

Gospel _____Profession of faith _____

General intercessions _____

At the preparation & presentation _____

Preface dialog _____Preface _____

Preface acclamation _____

Eucharistic prayer _____Memorial acclamation _____

Eucharistic amen _____

The Lord's prayer _____

Breaking of bread _____

The communion hymn _____

The post-communion hymn _____

Blessing _____At the dismissal _____

Memoranda:

SOLEMNITY OF CORPUS CHRISTI

YEAR B

(In USA Sunday after Trinity)

READINGS
Exodus (24:3-8)
It is the blood of the covenant/sacrifice which seals the contract between God and humanity.
Hebrews (9:11-15)
Christ, mediator of the new covenant, who enters the tabernacle and rends the veil which separates God from humanity, accomplishes this feat through his blood. The sacrificial character of his death saves us from death and molds us into the life of his own body.
Mark (14:12-16,22-26)
Jesus inaugurates the work of salvation completed on the cross with the sacred meal of the new Pasch. By eating the gift of his body and drinking his blood we build ourselves up into his body and blood.

FOCUS
The blood of goats and calves was only a sign of the efficacy of the blood of the true Lamb of God. This sacrificial lamb, immolated on the altar of the cross, provides the deliverance from death we need to reconnect with God. By eating his flesh and blood, we are knit together into his body and then share in the banquet of heaven now eternity in time.

IDEA STARTERS
- *CCT Lectionary* (proper 5): I Sm 16:14-23; Ps 57; II Cor 4:13-5:1; Mk 3:20-35.
- First Eucharist may be celebrated today.
- Eucharistic Ministers may be installed today.
- Bakers of the Bread minister to the assembly by providing bread that looks like bread. Honor these ministers at the coffee hour.
- Exposition of the Holy Eucharist may be celebrated with another parish or with Vespers tonight (cf. *Holy Communion and Worship of the Eucharist Outside Mass,* nos. 79-108).
- Add an acclamation to be sung throughout the Eucharistic Prayer (in the style of the Children's Prayers).
- Omit the *Sequence* and sing "Thee We Adore, O Hidden Savior" (LBW) after communion.
- For your consideration: Sprinkling Baptismal Water; Opening Prayer from Votive Mass of Eucharist B; Intercessions for healing, grace, honor for God's name, the hungry, homeless, friendless, the Jewish people, bakers & winery workers; Holy Eucharist Preface I (P47); Eucharistic Prayer II; Memorial Acclamation C; Ordinary Solemn Blessing IV.

MUSIC

- Psalm 116
- *Alleluia! Sing to Jesus* (Dix/PMB)
- *The Bread of Our Days* (Goglia/Resource)
- *Father, We Sing Your Praises* (Zsigray/NALR)
- *Gift of Finest Wheat* (Westendorf/PMB)
- *O Healing River* (Traditional)
- *I Am the Living Bread* (Mullins/Resource)
- *I See His Blood* (Joncas/Cooperative Music)
- *Look Beyond* (Dameans/NALR)
- *One Bread, One Body* (Jesuits/NALR)
- *Our Blessing Cup* (Joncas/NALR)
- *Song of the Lamb* (Fabing/NALR)
- *The Son of God Proclaim* (Bridge/PMB)
- *There is One Bread* (Deiss/PMB)
- *This is My Body* (Jesuits/NALR)
- *To Be Your Bread* (Haas/Cooperative Music)
- *We Remember* (Haugen/GIA)
- *Wondrous Gift* (Shade/K&R)

SUNDAY PLANNING SHEET   Date _____

Parish focus _____

Environment & art _____

Ritual notes _____

Faith development (eg., in newsletter/classes) _____

Children's faith experience _____

Prelude _____

Hymn of gathering _____

Sprinkling/Penitential rite _____

Hymn of praise _____

Opening Prayer _____

First reading _____Responsory _____

Second reading _____Gospel acclamation _____

Gospel _____Profession of faith _____

General intercessions _____

At the preparation & presentation _____

Preface dialog _____Preface _____

Preface acclamation _____

Eucharistic prayer _____Memorial acclamation _____

Eucharistic amen _____

The Lord's prayer _____

Breaking of bread _____

The communion hymn _____

The post-communion hymn _____

Blessing _____At the dismissal _____

Memoranda:

SOLEMNITY OF THE SACRED HEART (Friday After Second Sunday After Pentecost)

READINGS

Hosea (11:1,3-4,8-9)
As Hosea continued to love, pursue and forgive his unfaithful wife, God does the same with regard to an unfaithful Israel.
Ephesians (3:8-12,14-19)
The goal of redemption is that we together "attain the fullness of God himself."
John (19:31-37)
The blood and water from the side of Jesus allude to the sacramental presence of Jesus' redemption in the church.

FOCUS

Christ is the Lamb of God who pours out his blood (life) for us, even when we are unfaithful. What does it mean, then, for the gathered community to be Christ?

IDEA STARTERS

• Symbols: Lamb, blood, water
• With the symbols of blood and water, this feast connects the end of the life with the beginning.
• This feast recalls the Passover. Consider a lamb dinner or barbecue now rather than at Passover (when most Jews no longer serve lamb).

MUSIC

• Isaiah 12:2-6
• *In Your Midst* (Keyes/Resource)
• *The Lord Is Kind and Merciful* (Haugen/GIA)
• *The Fullness of God* (Andersen/Resource)
• *Spirit of the Promise* (Gilsdorf/Resource)

PLANNING SHEET

Date _____

Parish focus _____

Environment & art _____

Ritual notes _____

Faith development (eg., in newsletter/classes) _____

Children's faith experience _____

Prelude _____

Hymn of gathering _____

Sprinkling/Penitential rite _____

Hymn of praise _____

Opening Prayer _____

First reading _____ Responsory _____

Second reading _____ Gospel acclamation _____

Gospel _____ Profession of faith _____

General intercessions _____

At the preparation & presentation _____

Preface dialog _____ Preface _____

Preface acclamation _____

Eucharistic prayer _____ Memorial acclamation _____

Eucharistic amen _____

The Lord's prayer _____

Breaking of bread _____

The communion hymn _____

The post-communion hymn _____

Blessing _____ At the dismissal _____

Memoranda:

SECOND SUNDAY OF THE YEAR

YEAR B

READINGS
First Samuel (3:3–10,19)
This story of God's call to Samuel prefigures the call by Christ to discipleship. God's word in itself does not confer power or privilege. It simply calls and invites. Insight and spirit are endowed upon the prophet only as a result of attentive obedience.
First Corinthians (6:13–15,17–20)
Morality is not empty rules, but the necessary result of a life in union with Christ. Immorality is wrong, not because of any laws but because it enslaves us to something that is incompatible with following Christ.
John (1:35–42)
The Christian vocation is not an order that demands mindless obedience. In the call of the apostles we see a step-by-step dialogue of inquiry and invitation. Others are led to Jesus through our response as well.

FOCUS
Christians are not self-made people. We are what we are only as a result of God's call and gift. In liturgy we hear the call again, and celebrate the gift realizing that the call is to carry the cross following Christ, and the heart of the gift is a share in his sacrifice.

IDEA STARTERS
- *CCT Lectionary:* I Sm 3:1–20; Ps 63:1–8; I Cor 6:12–20; Jn1:35–42.
- This is the Sunday within Christian Unity Week. Celebrate ecumenical evening prayer.
- Have children discuss the ark of the covenant in religion class. Use a drawing or model of the covenant box when explaining or role playing the first lesson.
- Today our Lord's manifestation is by preaching. How does your parish invite people to "come and see"?
- Today begins the series of second readings from First Corinthians. Conduct a Bible study, adult forum, or write a bulletin article about the letter. Also, John's Gospel will be used periodically throughout the year (especially Lent/Easter and Sundays in the summer). Plan to provide some background about this Gospel which is much older than and different in style from Mark, from whom we customarily hear during this liturgical year.
- Evaluate your use of silence during the liturgy: at the Penitential Rite, at the invitations "Let us Pray," after the readings, and after communion.
- For your consideration: Alternative Opening Prayer; Intercessions for parents, perseverence in prayer, open hearts, glorifying God in our bodies, catechumens and inquirers; Sundays Preface VI (P34); Eucharistic Prayer II, Memorial Acclamation D; Breaking of Bread Litany ("Lamb of God"); Ordinary Solemn Blessing V.

MUSIC

- Psalm 40
- *Beginning Today* (Dameans/NALR)
- *For Us to Live* (Weston Priory)
- *God So Loved the World* (Antioch/K&R)
- *Here Am I, Lord* (Reagan/PMB)
- *Here I Am, Lord* (Jesuits/NALR)
- *Mountains and Hills* (Jesuits/NALR)
- *One Lord* (Haas/Cooperative Music)
- *Praise the Lord, My Soul* (Parker/GIA)
- *Say the Word Again* (Repp/K&R)
- *Sing A New Song* (Jesuits/NALR)
- *Song of the Lamb* (Fabing /NALR)
- *Speak, Lord* (Dameans/NALR)

SUNDAY PLANNING SHEET   Date _____

Parish focus _____

Environment & art _____

Ritual notes _____

Faith development (eg., in newsletter/classes) _____

Children's faith experience _____

Prelude _____

Hymn of gathering _____

Sprinkling/Penitential rite _____

Hymn of praise _____

Opening Prayer _____

First reading _____Responsory _____

Second reading _____Gospel acclamation _____

Gospel _____Profession of faith _____

General intercessions _____

At the preparation & presentation _____

Preface dialog _____Preface _____

Preface acclamation _____

Eucharistic prayer _____Memorial acclamation _____

Eucharistic amen _____

The Lord's prayer _____

Breaking of bread _____

The communion hymn _____

The post-communion hymn _____

Blessing _____At the dismissal _____

Memoranda:

THIRD SUNDAY
OF THE YEAR

YEAR B

READINGS
Jonah (3:1-5,10)
This short passage does not do justice to the message of the book of Jonah. God assures us that he loves our enemies, even if we don't. Yet God challenges us to show them love, not hatred; to care for their conversion, not their punishment.
First Corinthians (7:29-31)
Time is always short. Our sense of urgency may not come from an expectation of Christ's immediate return, but it should come from realizing that the particular moment of grace that passes does not come again. The eternal Kingdom of God puts all our activities into a new perspective.

Mark's account of the call of the first disciples emphasizes the decisiveness of their response. Both the proclamation of the Kingdom with its call to repentance and the invitation of the disciples carry a sense of urgency.

FOCUS
Urgency. Even though it's early and we have the whole year before us, the word of God comes upon us with an urgent demand to place the Kingdom of God before all else.

IDEA STARTERS
- *CCT Lectionary:* Jonah 3:1-5, 10; Ps 62:5-12; I Cor 7:29-35; Mk 1:14-20.
- Martin Luther called penance nothing more than a return to our baptismal call. The first and third lessons illustrate this.
- Discuss the sacrament of reconciliation in terms of God manifesting grace to those who have faith in Jesus.
- At a children's liturgy show pictures of fishermen casting their nets as well as hauling in their catch. If possible, show the children one of these large nets (place it over them, if this won't frighten them!) Explain how we symbolically walked into these nets at Baptism, and how Jesus continues to pull us along the road of the Kingdom in our midst.
- Bulletin articles: "The Biblical Significance of the number Forty".
- Mark 1:15 is the text used for the giving of ashes on Ash Wednesday, and will be used again on the First Sunday in Lent.
- For your consideration: Sprinkling Baptismal Water B; Opening Prayer; Intercessions for cities, true spirit of repentance, teachers and students, compassion, kindness, humility, married couples, fishermen and women, vocations to ordained ministry, religious life and to lay ministry in the Church; Reconciliation Eucharistic Prayer I; Memorial Acclamation B; Ordinary Solemn Blessing III.

MUSIC

- Psalm 25
- *The Apostle's Song* (Shade/K&R)
- *By the Love* (Weston Priory)
- *Earthen Vessels* (Jesuits/NALR)
- *Glorious in Majesty* (Cothran/NALR)
- *The Kingdom of God* (Deiss/NALR)

- *The Messenger Song* (Gilsdorf/Resource)
- *Remember Your Love* (Dameans/NALR)
- *Seek the Lord* (Jesuits/NALR)
- *Teach Me Your Ways* (Foster/Resource)
- *This Is The Day* (Goglia/Resource)
- *We Are Called* (Patterson/Resource)

SUNDAY PLANNING SHEET   Date _____

Parish focus _____

Environment & art _____

Ritual notes _____

Faith development (eg., in newsletter/classes) _____

Children's faith experience _____

Prelude _____

Hymn of gathering _____

Sprinkling/Penitential rite _____

Hymn of praise _____

Opening Prayer _____

First reading _____Responsory _____

Second reading _____Gospel acclamation _____

Gospel _____Profession of faith _____

General intercessions _____

At the preparation & presentation _____

Preface dialog _____Preface _____

Preface acclamation _____

Eucharistic prayer _____Memorial acclamation _____

Eucharistic amen _____

The Lord's prayer _____

Breaking of bread _____

The communion hymn _____

The post-communion hymn _____

Blessing _____At the dismissal _____

Memoranda:

FOURTH SUNDAY OF THE YEAR

YEAR B

READINGS
Deuteronomy (18:15-20)
The prophet, as God's true representative, has the power to proclaim God's will in such a way that his words bring about the deeds they signify.
First Corinthians (7:32-35)
Paul here presents virginity as a sign of detachment from the ways of the world, not as its only means of fulfillment. The important thing in any state in life is to keep our eyes firmly fixed on the Beyond and not to let ourselves become hopelessly entangled in the concerns of here and now.
Mark (1:21-28)
This passage contains a nutshell summary of the whole mission of Jesus: to free humankind from enslavement to the forces of evil. Those who hear his word experience his power. His teaching cannot be separated from his person. He is what he teaches.

FOCUS
Insipid liturgies, hand-in-hand with dull and weak Christian communities, come from lack of faith in the power of the word. If we really believed the Word of God has the power to bring about the new life it promises, we would proclaim and preach it with the sense of that power, and allow its power to overcome the demonic obstacles we face in our Christian mission to the world.

IDEA STARTERS
- *CCT Lectionary:* Deut 18:15-20; Ps 111; I Cor 8:1-13; Mk 1:21-28.
- Today, Jesus is manifested to the people of Capernaum by his preaching style.
- How attentive are we to the teaching of Christ?
- How about a bulletin article on "The Teaching Authority of the Church."
- February 3 is the commemoration of St. Blase. If observed: following the post-communion prayer, read an appropriate reading, say a communal prayer of praise, the collect of St. Blase, simple blessing and dismissal. During a hymn, members of the assembly may either come forward for the St. Blase blessing or leave directly.
- For your considersation: Alternative Opening Prayer; Intercessions for contemporary prophets, worship of the true God alone, vowed lifestyle, the magisterium, the sick; Sunday Preface I (P29); Eucharistic Prayer IV; Memorial Acclamation B.

MUSIC

- Psalm 95
- *For You Are My God* (Jesuits/NALR)
- *Glory to the Holy One* (Marchionda/PMB)
- *His Love Will Ever Be* (Fabing/NALR)
- *Holy, Holy, Holy Lord, God Almighty* (Heber/PMB)
- *I Believe in the Sun* (Landry/NALR)
- *I Danced in the Morning* (Carter/Galliard)
- *Like Cedars They Shall Stand* (Jesuits/NALR)
- *Lord, To Whom Shall We Go?* (Joncas/NALR)
- *Lord, Your Almighty Word* (Marriott/PMB)
- *Our Life and Our Song* (Conry/NALR)
- *Praise the Name* (Kendzia/NALR)
- *Psalm 8* (Pulkingham/Resource)
- *Something Which is Known* (Weston Priory)
- *We Praise You* (Dameans/NALR)
- *Won't You Come?* (Porter/Resource)

SUNDAY PLANNING SHEET   Date _____

Parish focus _____

Environment & art _____

Ritual notes _____

Faith development (eg., in newsletter/classes) _____

Children's faith experience _____

Prelude _____

Hymn of gathering _____

Sprinkling/Penitential rite _____

Hymn of praise _____

Opening Prayer _____

First reading _____Responsory _____

Second reading _____Gospel acclamation _____

Gospel _____Profession of faith _____

General intercessions _____

At the preparation & presentation _____

Preface dialog _____Preface _____

Preface acclamation _____

Eucharistic prayer _____Memorial acclamation _____

Eucharistic amen _____

The Lord's prayer _____

Breaking of bread _____

The communion hymn _____

The post-communion hymn _____

Blessing _____At the dismissal _____

Memoranda:

FIFTH SUNDAY OF THE YEAR

READINGS

Job (7:1-4,6-7)
Do not expect too much from this reading. Like the whole book of Job, it makes sense only if it is allowed to set the scene for a fuller revelation of God's plan and power. Let this reading pose the question, and seek the answer in the Gospel.

First Corinthians (9:16-19,22-23)
If we are aware that God's word is a treasure generously lavished upon us, we cannot fail to feel compelled to share this great gift. The price of discipleship is fidelity to making the Good News of Christ alive and active.

Mark (1:29-39)
Success, even in performing the work of God's Kingdom, brings with it its own demon, the temptation to stop growing and keep repeating old successful patterns. Jesus could have stayed and become a successful village doctor and left unfulfilled his true mission, to proclaim the universality of God's Kingdom.

FOCUS
Each new insight into the human condition calls for a renewed commitment to bringing the power of the Kingdom of God to bear upon human needs. Jesus accomplished his work as the enfleshed Word of God. Now the same powerful Word is enfleshed among us. This is the mystery we come to terms with as we celebrate liturgy.

IDEA STARTERS
- *CCT Lectionary:* Job 7:1-7; Ps 147:1-11; I Cor 9:16-23; Mk 1:29-39.
- Today's Gospel marks three important parts of Jesus' ministry: healing, personal prayer, preaching.
- Bulletin articles: "Jesus' Healing Ministry in Mark's Gospel", "Prepare for Lent: Centers where you may go to be absorbed in prayer."
- Celebrate Anointing of the Sick at today's Eucharist.
- Be sure members of the assembly understand the Job pericope in context of the entire book.
- Is it healthy for a person to try to be "all things for all people"?
- For your consideration: Opening Prayer; Intercessions for peace of mind, hopefulness, the brokenhearted, those in hospitals, wisdom, evangelists, the weak, cloistered religious; Sunday Preface III (P31); Eucharistic Prayer IV; Memorial Acclamation B; Ordinary Solemn Blessing IV.

MUSIC

- Psalm 147
- *All Our Joy* (Dameans/NALR)
- *And the Father Will Dance* (Landry/NALR)
- *The Bread of Rejoicing* (Deiss/NALR)
- *Dona Nobis Pacem* (Repp/K&R)
- *Dance in the Darkness* (Landry/NALR)
- *The Dawn of the Day* (Deiss/NALR)
- *Eye Has Not Seen* (Haugen/GIA)
- *Fill Us With Your Love* (Prezio/K&R)
- *Glory* (Wood/Resource)
- *He Has Anointed Me* (Dameans/NALR)
- *How Beautiful* (Wise/GIA)
- *How Can I Keep From Singing?* (Traditional)
- *Into Your Hands* (Boecker/Resource)
- *Kyrie Eleison* (Clark/Celebration)
- *Lay Your Hands* (Landry/NALR)
- *My Refuge* (Vessels/GIA)
- *Out of the Depths* (Haugen/Quiet Breeze)
- *Redeemer. Lord* (Jesuits/NALR)
- *There is a River* (Cooney/Resource)
- *There is Peace* (Goglia/Resource)

SUNDAY PLANNING SHEET   Date _____

Parish focus _____

Environment & art _____

Ritual notes _____

Faith development (eg., in newsletter/classes) _____

Children's faith experience _____

Prelude _____

Hymn of gathering _____

Sprinkling/Penitential rite _____

Hymn of praise _____

Opening Prayer _____

First reading _____ Responsory _____

Second reading _____ Gospel acclamation _____

Gospel _____ Profession of faith _____

General intercessions _____

At the preparation & presentation _____

Preface dialog _____ Preface _____

Preface acclamation _____

Eucharistic prayer _____ Memorial acclamation _____

Eucharistic amen _____

The Lord's prayer _____

Breaking of bread _____

The communion hymn _____

The post–communion hymn _____

Blessing _____ At the dismissal _____

Memoranda:

SIXTH SUNDAY OF THE YEAR

READINGS
Leviticus (13:1-2,44-46)
Again the Old Testament reading testifies to the impotence of human means to address human needs. This emphasizes that the full depth of compassion and breadth of vision necessary to overcome the evil that afflicts and divides the human race is the gift of the Kingdom.
First Corinthians (10:31-11:1)
God's glory is that all humanity be united as one in Christ. We celebrate and profess this unity in liturgy. We are called live as church passionately committed to bringing this unity about in mutual compassion and acceptance.
Mark (1:40-45)
More than any other disease, leprosy symbolized alienation, making its victim an outcast to be shunned by society. Compassion, a sense of solidarity with the suffering person, is the key to healing.

FOCUS
The themes of compassion and unity as signs that the Kingdom of God is present lead well into Lent. We need, however, to keep asking ourselves the question, why is there so little healing of alienation visible among us? What does this say about the depth of our commitment to live the mystery we celebrate?

IDEA STARTERS
- *CCT Lectionary* (last Sunday after Ephiphany): II Kgs 2:1-12a; Ps 50:1-6; II Cor 4:3-6; Mk 9:2-9.
- Many Christian churches observe the "Transfiguration of Our Lord" today, similar to the CCT texts specified above.
- Do not let the Leviticus lesson go unexplained! God does not punish us with sickness, "God's will" has nothing to do with it.
- The healed person, saved from his leprosy, could not hold back telling the Good News. How about us?
- You may announce your Lenten program using the quote from First Corinthians: "Do All for the Glory of God."
- For your consideration: Intercessions for the sick, lepers, forgiveness, racial peace and unity, medical advances, nomads, joy in believing in Jesus; Sunday Preface VIII (P36); Eucharistic Prayer III; Memorial Acclamation B; Ordinary Solemn Blessing II.

MUSIC
- Psalm 32
- *Anthem* (Conry/NALR)
- *In Christ there is no East or West* (Spiritual/PMB)
- *Praise the Lord, My Soul* (Jesuits/NALR)
- *Psalm 57* (Adrias/Resource)
- *Save Us, O Lord* (Jesuits/NALR)
- *Sing to the Mountains* (Jesuits/NALR)
- *Song of Gathering* (Wise/GIA)
- *Spirit, Come Forth* (Duesing/Resource)
- *Till You* (Repp/K&R)
- *We Are Many Parts* (Haugen/GIA)
- *Yahweh* (Weston Priory)

SUNDAY PLANNING SHEET

Date _____

Parish focus _____

Environment & art _____

Ritual notes _____

Faith development (eg., in newsletter/classes) _____

Children's faith experience _____

Prelude _____

Hymn of gathering _____

Sprinkling/Penitential rite _____

Hymn of praise _____

Opening Prayer _____

First reading _____ Responsory _____

Second reading _____ Gospel acclamation _____

Gospel _____ Profession of faith _____

General intercessions _____

At the preparation & presentation _____

Preface dialog _____ Preface _____

Preface acclamation _____

Eucharistic prayer _____ Memorial acclamation _____

Eucharistic amen _____

The Lord's prayer _____

Breaking of bread _____

The communion hymn _____

The post-communion hymn _____

Blessing _____ At the dismissal _____

Memoranda:

SEVENTH SUNDAY OF THE YEAR

READINGS

Isaiah (43:18-19,21-22,24b-25)
The prophet delivers God's message to a people blinded by their own expectations. God is bringing something new and unexpected to Israel. He is leading his people into new territory. What is required of the people is to forget the past and to let go of what they expect to happen.

Second Corinthians (6:13-15,17-20)
Paul assures the Corinthians that, although he will not visit them, he cares deeply about them. He takes the opportunity to tell them that it is Christ, no mortal preacher, who assures them of life.

Mark (2:1-12)
Jesus comes with a new law of love and forgiveness. It is there for those free enough to experience and accept it.

FOCUS

The Kingdom breaks in on the world in the least expected ways. Today's readings call us to break out of our old patterns of thinking and behavior. Those whose security is tied up with the status quo will not be able to hear God's Word.

IDEA STARTERS

- *CCT Lectionary:*Is 43:18-25; Ps 41; 2 Cor 1:18-22; Mt 2:1-12.
- Jesus often healed through the forgiveness of sin. Use the Penitential Rite to highlight the connection between our physical, spiritual and mental health.
- God is full of surprises. Try something new and unexpected today.
- An article in the bulletin could address the question, "What do I think God is?"
- For your consideration: Alternative Opening Prayer; Intercessions for openness to the unexpected in our lives, for therapists and other healers, for health for our families.

MUSIC

- Psalm 41
- *All Praise the Power of Jesus' Name* (Perronet/PMB)
- *God Dwells in the Hearts* (Jabusch/Resource)
- *Jesus the New Covenant* (Diess/PMB)
- *Our God is Love* (Repp/K&R)
- *Praise the Lord* (Dicie/Resource)
- *Say the Word Again* (Repp/K&R)
- *Sing A New Song* (Jesuits/NALR)
- *There's a Wideness in God's Mercy* (Watts/PMB)
- *Speak, Lord* (Dameans/NALR)
- *You Are My Witnesses* (Fisherfolk/Resource)

SUNDAY PLANNING SHEET

Date _____

Parish focus _____

Environment & art _____

Ritual notes _____

Faith development (eg., in newsletter/classes) _____

Children's faith experience _____

Prelude _____

Hymn of gathering _____

Sprinkling/Penitential rite _____

Hymn of praise _____

Opening Prayer _____

First reading _____ Responsory _____

Second reading _____ Gospel acclamation ___

Gospel _____ Profession of faith ___

General intercessions _____

At the preparation & presentation _____

Preface dialog _____ Preface _____

Preface acclamation _____

Eucharistic prayer _____ Memorial acclamation __

Eucharistic amen _____

The Lord's prayer _____

Breaking of bread _____

The communion hymn _____

The post-communion hymn _____

Blessing _____ At the dismissal _____

Memoranda:

EIGHTH SUNDAY OF THE YEAR

YEAR B

READINGS

Hosea (2:16-17,21-22)
The image of God as the bridegroom of Israel is nowhere more richly presented than in the Book of Hosea.

Second Corinthians (3:1-6)
Paul confronts division in the early church by calling on the people to transcend personality cults and focus on the author of the Good News rather than its messengers. He emphasizes that his authority to teach them comes directly from God.

Mark (2:18-22)
In Jewish culture fasting is traditionally associated with waiting for the Messiah. By not observing religious fasts Jesus and his disciples symbolized the messianic nature of Jesus' ministry.

FOCUS

The greatest obstacle to living the fullness of faith in Christ is lack of openness to the new and unexpected. Such openness involves the possibility that the way things are might require change. This is a difficult reality for us to face, but necessary for a life in Christ.

IDEA STARTERS

- *CCT Lectionary:* Hs 2:14-20; Ps 103:1-13; 2 Cor 3:1-6; Mk 2:18-22.
- How do we resist change in our lives? In the life of our parish? In the life of our community?
- Today's liturgy provides an appropriate context for an ecumenical service emphasizing our oneness in Christ Jesus.
- Children are naturally open to the new and unexpected. How can this fact be incorporated into today's liturgy?
- Bulletin article: "What divides our parish community?"
- For your consideration: Opening Prayer; Intercessions for Christian unity, open hearts, the hungry.

MUSIC

- Psalm 103
- *Believe* (McGrath/Resource)
- *Gather Round* (Page/Resource)
- *I Believe in the Sun* (Landry/NALR)
- *One Lord* (Haas/Cooperative Music)

- *Sing a New Song* (Jesuits/NALR)
- *There is One Lord* (Deiss/NALR)
- *The Messenger Song* (Gilsdorf/Resource)
- *We Are Called* (Patterson/Resource)

SUNDAY PLANNING SHEET

Date _____

Parish focus _____

Environment & art _____

Ritual notes _____

Faith development (eg., in newsletter/classes) _____

Children's faith experience _____

Prelude _____

Hymn of gathering _____

Sprinkling/Penitential rite _____

Hymn of praise _____

Opening Prayer _____

First reading _____ Responsory _____

Second reading _____ Gospel acclamation _____

Gospel _____ Profession of faith _____

General intercessions _____

At the preparation & presentation _____

Preface dialog _____ Preface _____

Preface acclamation _____

Eucharistic prayer _____ Memorial acclamation _____

Eucharistic amen _____

The Lord's prayer _____

Breaking of bread _____

The communion hymn _____

The post-communion hymn _____

Blessing _____ At the dismissal _____

Memoranda:

NINTH SUNDAY
OF THE YEAR

YEAR B

READINGS
Deuteronomy (5:12-15)
The origins of the Sabbath involved the need to rest from labor. In our society where the pace of life accelerates at a dizzying pace, less and less time is set aside for pursuing higher or lasting goals.
Second Corinthians (4:6-11)
Paul is an apostle though he was not part of the twelve selected by Jesus. It is because of his weakness that God has been able to make him an apostle. Paul underscores an essential point by describing the power of God in his life: God takes our weaknesses and works his strength through them.
Mark (2:23-3:6)
The Law was given for the benefit of God's people. God did not create humans to serve the Law. Jesus came into a religious environment where the importance of the Law had grown out of proportion. His message involved a reordering of priorities regarding the Law.

FOCUS
We live in a society where life never seems to slow down, much less to stop. We value hard work as much as amount of work. We compete with one another as to who works more. In such a life there is little opportunity for real rest and little space to let God or other people in.

This was the original purpose of the sabbath, not to impose more obligations, but to create sacred space and sacred rest.

IDEA STARTERS
- *CCT Lectionary:* 1 Sm 16:1-13; Ps 20; 2 Cor 4:5-12; Mk 2:23-3:6.
- Today is a good day to educate the community about different parts of the liturgy. Where do they come from? What is their meaning?
- Give special attention to the post-liturgy coffee. Invite those who never stay after church to make an exception today. "Don't rush off."
- How about a bulletin article on "The Law was made for us not we for the Law".
- For your considersation: Alternative Opening Prayer; Intercessions for lawyers, laborers, farmers.

MUSIC
- Psalm 81
- *Be Glad, O People* (Weston Priory)
- *Gather Us In* (Haugen/GIA)
- *Give Thanks* (Gilsdorf/Resource)
- *Go Up To the Mountain* (Jesuits/NALR)
- *Let Us All Rejoice* (Toolan/Resource)
- *The House Built On a Rock* (Deiss/NALR)
- *Song of Gathering* (Wise/GIA)
- *Praise the Name of the Lord* (Patterson/Resource)

SUNDAY PLANNING SHEET

Date _____

Parish focus _____

Environment & art _____

Ritual notes _____

Faith development (eg., in newsletter/classes) _____

Children's faith experience _____

Prelude _____

Hymn of gathering _____

Sprinkling/Penitential rite _____

Hymn of praise _____

Opening Prayer _____

First reading _____ Responsory _____

Second reading _____ Gospel acclamation _____

Gospel _____ Profession of faith _____

General intercessions _____

At the preparation & presentation _____

Preface dialog _____ Preface _____

Preface acclamation _____

Eucharistic prayer _____ Memorial acclamation _____

Eucharistic amen _____

The Lord's prayer _____

Breaking of bread _____

The communion hymn _____

The post-communion hymn _____

Blessing _____ At the dismissal _____

Memoranda:

TENTH SUNDAY OF THE YEAR

READINGS

Genesis (3:9-15)
When we flee from the fact of our sinfulness we lose sight of God and so lose touch with who we are. It is not our weakness, but only our refusal to admit it that is our downfall.

Second Corinthians (4:13-5:1)
We cannot avoid dealing with the mundane issues of survival, but keeping God as our goal helps us to maintain a proper perspective. Paul instructs us about priorities in our lives.

Mark (3:20-35)
The unforgiveable sin — blaspheming the Holy Spirit — is traditionally thought of as having to do with an ultimate hardening of heart against God. This Gospel is not an easy one to understand. It calls for much prayerful meditation.

FOCUS

Sin and hope are the themes of today's readings. The focus is not so much on not sinning as on the assurance that all of our sins will be forgiven as long as we keep our hearts open and our lives moving. It is only when we put on the brakes and decide we aren't going to give, to change anymore that there is no hope for us.

IDEA STARTERS

- *CCT Lectionary:* I Sm 16:4-23; Ps 57; 2 Cor 4:13-5:1; Mk 3-20-35.
- The Penitential Rite can serve as a centerpiece to the Liturgy of the Word. Can it be spread throughout the first half of the Mass?
- Today would be a good day for a communal celebration of Penance.
- Celebrate Anointing of the Sick at today's Eucharist.
- Emphasize God's merciful love throughout the liturgy.
- For your consideration: Opening Prayer; Intercessions for peace of mind, hopefulness, addicts, criminals, those in prisons.

MUSIC

- Psalm 130
- *Amazing Grace* (Traditional)
- *Earthen Vessels* (Jesuits/NALR)
- *The Image of His Love* (Dicie/Resource)
- *Let Us Walk in the Light* (Haugen/GIA)
- *Redeemer Lord* (Jesuits/NALR)
- *Remember Your Love* (Dameans/NALR)
- *Kyrie Eleison* (Clark/Celebration)

SUNDAY PLANNING SHEET

Date _____

Parish focus _____

Environment & art _____

Ritual notes _____

Faith development (eg., in newsletter/classes) _____

Children's faith experience _____

Prelude _____

Hymn of gathering _____

Sprinkling/Penitential rite _____

Hymn of praise _____

Opening Prayer _____

First reading _____ Responsory _____

Second reading _____ Gospel acclamation _____

Gospel _____ Profession of faith _____

General intercessions _____

At the preparation & presentation _____

Preface dialog _____ Preface _____

Preface acclamation _____

Eucharistic prayer _____ Memorial acclamation _____

Eucharistic amen _____

The Lord's prayer _____

Breaking of bread _____

The communion hymn _____

The post-communion hymn _____

Blessing _____ At the dismissal _____

Memoranda:

ELEVENTH SUNDAY OF THE YEAR

YEAR B

READINGS
Ezekiel (17:22–24)
From the most unusual source the Lord raises up a tree to himself. In the process he humbles all that are considered great. Those that are abundant become empty, the fertile barren, and the green wither away.
Second Corinthians (5:6–10)
Our confidence is strong. We build it upon the Lord, and though we do not see him, we believe in him through the gift of faith.
Mark (4:26–34)
Jesus presents us with the sense of mystery in the Kingdom by the use of two parables. The mysterious process of the growth of the seed from sprout to blade, ear to ripened wheat; and the image of the Church as mustard seed grown to maturity, are presented by the Lord to indicate the element of the "topsy-turvy" nature of God and its activity in time.

FOCUS
The Lord uses whom he wishes to accomplish his plan on earth. Our part in the process is to cooperate, to praise his name, and to acknowledge our obedience to him. If we do this, we will be like the seed of mustard — a joyful surprise, blooming before the Lord.

IDEA STARTERS
- *CCT Lectionary* (Proper 6): II Sm 1:1; Ps 46; II Cor 5:5-10, 14-17; Mk 4:26-34.
- Show a film depicting the growth of a mustard seed at a children's liturgy.
- Sponsor a community gardening party. Take pride in your parish grounds.
- Today is Father's Day.
- For your consideration: Opening Prayer; Intercession for fathers, grand-fathers, "big brothers," uncles, gardeners, hope and confidence in God; Sunday Preface V (P33); Eucharistic Prayer III; Ordinary Time Solemn Blessing IV.

MUSIC
- Psalm 92
- *All My Day* (Jesuits/NALR)
- *Amen, We Live For You* (Sexton/Resource)
- *Arise! Come Sing In the Morning* (Zsigray/NALR)
- *Awaken, My Heart* (Deiss/NALR)
- *Beginning Today* (Dameans/NALR)
- *Dedication Song* (Raffa/Resource)
- *Just Like A Mustard Seed* (Repp/K&R)
- *Till I Love* (Sexton/Resource)

SUNDAY PLANNING SHEET
Date _____

Parish focus _____

Environment & art _____

Ritual notes _____

Faith development (eg., in newsletter/classes) _____

Children's faith experience _____

Prelude _____

Hymn of gathering _____

Sprinkling/Penitential rite _____

Hymn of praise _____

Opening Prayer _____

First reading _____ Responsory _____

Second reading _____ Gospel acclamation _____

Gospel _____ Profession of faith _____

General intercessions _____

At the preparation & presentation _____

Preface dialog _____ Preface _____

Preface acclamation _____

Eucharistic prayer _____ Memorial acclamation _____

Eucharistic amen _____

The Lord's prayer _____

Breaking of bread _____

The communion hymn _____

The post-communion hymn _____

Blessing _____ At the dismissal _____

Memoranda:

TWELFTH SUNDAY OF THE YEAR

YEAR B

READINGS
Job (38:1,8-11)
The power of the Lord calls order from the primal chaos. His dynamic vitality brings life from death.
Second Corinthians (5:14-17)
In the redemption we have become a new creation. It is through the love of Christ that this has been accomplished. By taking upon himself our sin and suffering, he has made us come to life, in his life.
Mark (4:35-41)
Jesus is the same God who called order from the chaos in the beginning. All of creation still responds to his word. Only human beings disturb the harmony of creation by a lack of faith and a deficiency of love.

FOCUS
Jesus, the image of the Father, Alpha and Omega, was in the beginning breathing over the primal water and calling it into order. He controls all of creation, visible and invisible. Through his death, he has purchased us and recreated us in his image.

IDEA STARTERS
- *CCT Lectionary* (Proper 7): II Sm 5:1-12; Ps 48; 2 Cor 5:18-6:2; Mk 4:35-41.
- Have a liturgy by the lake, on the beach, etc. (weather permitting!)
- Topic for an Adult Forum: "Christian Judgment" (cf. 2 Cor 5:16).
- Infant baptism may be appropriate today.
- For your consideration: Sprinkling Baptismal Water; Alternative Opening Prayer; Intercessions for peace with the earth, navy men and women, shiphands, those distressed, perseverance in prayer; Sunday Preface III (P31); Eucharistic Prayer IV; Memorial Acclamation D; Ordinary Time Solemn Blessing I.

MUSIC
- Psalm 107
- *All Flesh is Grass* (Haugen/GIA)
- *All That We Have* (Dameans/NALR)
- *Be Not Afraid* (Jesuits/NALR)
- *Eagles Wings* (Andersen/Resource)
- *Glorious in Majesty* (Cothran/GIA)
- *The Wonders He Has Done* (Andersen/Resource)
- *You Are Near* (Jesuits/NALR)

SUNDAY PLANNING SHEET
Date _____

Parish focus _____

Environment & art _____

Ritual notes _____

Faith development (eg., in newsletter/classes) _____

Children's faith experience _____

Prelude _____

Hymn of gathering _____

Sprinkling/Penitential rite _____

Hymn of praise _____

Opening Prayer _____

First reading _____Responsory _____

Second reading _____Gospel acclamation _____

Gospel _____Profession of faith _____

General intercessions _____

At the preparation & presentation _____

Preface dialog _____Preface _____

Preface acclamation _____

Eucharistic prayer _____Memorial acclamation _____

Eucharistic amen _____

The Lord's prayer _____

Breaking of bread _____

The communion hymn _____

The post-communion hymn _____

Blessing _____At the dismissal _____

Memoranda:

THIRTEENTH SUNDAY OF THE YEAR — YEAR B

READINGS
Wisdom (1:13–15,2:23–24)
God is the author of life. He does not contain death and wills life to all. Creation mirrors this vitality. Death is the result of envy of evil and is experienced by those who embrace evil.
Second Corinthians (8:7,9,13–15)
Since Christ has given in such abundance to us we should likewise give cheerfully and with generosity to others.
Mark (5:21–43)
Jesus displays divine generosity in the healing of the woman with a hemorrhage and the raising of Jairus' daughter. Gifts given freely to those who display faith in him.

FOCUS
The dynamic quality of life impels it to share itself freely with all who seek it. All that is needed is loving faith.

IDEA STARTERS
- *CCT Lectionary* (Proper 8):II Sm 6:1-15; Ps 24; II Cor 8-7-15; Mk 5:21-43.
- Anointing of the Sick may be celebrated communally with today's readings.
- Topic for an Adult Forum: "God did not make death."
- Publicize support groups for the bereaved in your area.
- For your consideration: Sprinkling Baptismal Water A; Gospel (full form); Intercession for those near death, the deceased, justice, spiritual awakening, the mournful, the impoverished, children, the ill, faith; Sunday Preface I (P29); Children's Eucharistic Prayer I; Memorial Acclamation B; Solemn Blessing For Funerals.

MUSIC
- Psalm 30
- *Awake, O Sleeper* (Dameans/NALR)
- *Be With Me* (Haugen/GIA)
- *Blest Be the Lord* (Jesuits/NALR)
- *Return All Things* (Dicie/Resource)
- *Sing To God a Brand New Canticle* (Quinlan/NALR)
- *Sing To the Mountains* (Jesuits/NALR)
- *Strong and Constant* (Andersen/Resource)

SUNDAY PLANNING SHEET

Date _____

Parish focus _____

Environment & art _____

Ritual notes _____

Faith development (eg., in newsletter/classes) _____

Children's faith experience _____

Prelude _____

Hymn of gathering _____

Sprinkling/Penitential rite _____

Hymn of praise _____

Opening Prayer _____

First reading _____ Responsory _____

Second reading _____ Gospel acclamation _____

Gospel _____ Profession of faith _____

General intercessions _____

At the preparation & presentation _____

Preface dialog _____ Preface _____

Preface acclamation _____

Eucharistic prayer _____ Memorial acclamation ____

Eucharistic amen _____

The Lord's prayer _____

Breaking of bread _____

The communion hymn _____

The post-communion hymn _____

Blessing _____ At the dismissal _____

Memoranda:

FOURTEENTH SUNDAY OF THE YEAR

YEAR B

READINGS
Ezekiel (2:2-5)
The presence of Ezekiel and his message of judgment make the presence of God a fact for the community of Israel.
Second Corinthians (12:7-10)
Paul knows and experiences the divine presence in his own pain and weakness. He recounts for the Corinthian community, the various gifts the Lord has used to make him aware of his power.
Mark (6:1-6)
A false sense of knowledge regarding who the Lord is becomes the power that Jesus can work in our lives when we humbly acknowledge our need for his light in our lives.

FOCUS
Today's readings point to the various revelations of God's presence among his people. This presence is seen in the individuals he sends to instruct, admonish, and guide. In the Corinthian fragment and the Gospel, our attention is directed to the fact that God's presence is manifested in our weakness before him and upon his wisdom.

IDEA STARTERS
- *CCT Lectionary* (Proper 9): II Sm 7:1-17; Ps 89-20-37; II Cor 12:1-10; Mk 6:1-6.
- What are today's prophets saying?
- Thurifer, torchbearers and possibly the crucifer lead the deacon to proclaim the Good News in the center of the assembly. Has your community ever seen this?
- The Sunday experience is the gathering of ordinary people baptized to be priests, prophets and kings.
- For your consideration: Intercession for contemporary prophets, to see God more clearly, strength in times of dehumanizing temptations, openness to all people, perseverance; Sunday Preface III (P31); Eucharistic Prayer IV; Ordinary Time Solemn Blessing II.

MUSIC
- Psalm 123
- *Amazing Grace* (Traditional)
- *Glory and Praise* (Jesuits/NALR)
- *Good Morning, Zachary* (Gutfreund/NALR)
- *I Have Loved You* (Joncas/NALR)
- *Our Life and Our Song* (Conry/NALR)
- *Praise the Lord* (Keyes/Resource)
- *Song For the Masses* (Schonbachler/NALR)
- *Song Of Thanksgiving* (Dicie/Resource)

SUNDAY PLANNING SHEET

Date _____

Parish focus _____

Environment & art _____

Ritual notes _____

Faith development (eg., in newsletter/classes) _____

Children's faith experience _____

Prelude _____

Hymn of gathering _____

Sprinkling/Penitential rite _____

Hymn of praise _____

Opening Prayer _____

First reading _____ Responsory _____

Second reading _____ Gospel acclamation _____

Gospel _____ Profession of faith _____

General intercessions _____

At the preparation & presentation _____

Preface dialog _____ Preface _____

Preface acclamation _____

Eucharistic prayer _____ Memorial acclamation _____

Eucharistic amen _____

The Lord's prayer _____

Breaking of bread _____

The communion hymn _____

The post-communion hymn _____

Blessing _____ At the dismissal _____

Memoranda:

FIFTEENTH SUNDAY OF THE YEAR

READINGS

Amos (7:12-15)
Amos proclaims his call to the prophetic office as coming not from some "school" of prophets, or due to the interpretation of any person — rather receiving its impetus from God alone.

Ephesians (1:3-14)
Paul states that it is in Christ that the Christian receives the call to live a life, filled with the love of God. We are given this vocation as children of God, not through any merit of our own, but rather as an outgrowth of the divine love.

Mark (6:7-13)
Jesus commissions the Twelve and through the power of his word enables them to be the emissaries of his healing and life-giving message.

FOCUS

Any valid vocation comes from the "Divine Impetus." The most dramatic and "final" form of this happened in the Incarnation, Jesus, the God-man. He is the perfect vessel, communicating God's life to his people, the "first payment against all redemption." To respond to his call results in the communication of God's healing power to humanity.

IDEA STARTERS

- *CCT Lectionary* (Proper 10): II Sm 7:18-29; Ps 132-11-18: Eph 1:1-10; Mk 6:7-13.
- Every spiritual blessing has been bestowed on us in Christ. God has chosen us; he bids us "Go forth into the world rejoicing in the power of his Spirit!" We are disciples and apostles at the same time!
- Send out those visiting the sick during the dismissal rites of the liturgy.
- Scripture sharing and witnessing over today's Gospel can help form Christian community.
- For your consideration: Sprinkling Baptismal Water B; Alternative Opening Prayer; Second Reading (full form); Intercessions for pastors, and all the ordained, social justice activists & martyrs, rich harvest, holy & blameless living, wisdom, the hungry, travellers, the poor, homeless, repentance, healing; Children's Eucharistic Prayer I; Memorial Acclamation D; Ordinary Solemn Blessing III.

MUSIC

- Psalm 85
- *And the Father Will Dance* (Landry/NALR)
- *Anthem* (Conry/NALR)
- *Before the Sun Burned Bright* (Jesuits/NALR)
- *The Church's One Foundation* (Stone/PMB)
- *Come Unto Me, All Who Are Weary* (Jesuits/NALR)
- *Dwelling Place* (Jesuits/NALR)
- *He Has Anointed Me* (Dameans/NALR)
- *Here I Am, Lord* (Jesuits/NALR)
- *How Beautiful* (Wise/GIA)
- *How Beautiful on the Mountains* (Deiss/NALR)
- *In Him We Live* (Landry/NALR)
- *In the Day of the Lord* (Gutfreund/NALR)
- *Kyrie Eleison* (Clark/Celebration)
- *Lay Your Hands* (Landry/NALR)
- *May the People Praise You* (Gilsdorf/Resource)
- *The Messenger Song* (Gilsdorf/Resource)
- *Praised Be the Father* (Dameans/NALR)
- *Sing Out His Goodness* (Dameans/NALR)
- *Song of Thanksgiving* (Dameans/NALR)

SUNDAY PLANNING SHEET   Date _____

Parish focus _____

Environment & art _____

Ritual notes _____

Faith development (eg., in newsletter/classes) _____

Children's faith experience _____

Prelude _____

Hymn of gathering _____

Sprinkling/Penitential rite _____

Hymn of praise _____

Opening Prayer _____

First reading _____ Responsory _____

Second reading _____ Gospel acclamation _____

Gospel _____ Profession of faith _____

General intercessions _____

At the preparation & presentation _____

Preface dialog _____ Preface _____

Preface acclamation _____

Eucharistic prayer _____ Memorial acclamation _____

Eucharistic amen _____

The Lord's prayer _____

Breaking of bread _____

The communion hymn _____

The post-communion hymn _____

Blessing _____ At the dismissal _____

Memoranda:

SIXTEENTH SUNDAY OF THE YEAR

READINGS

Jeremiah (23:1-6)
The Lord will deliver his people from the shepherds who abuse and mistreat his flock. He will provide new shepherds who will unite the flock and bring it to God himself, in loving obedience.

Ephesians (2:13–18)
Jesus, the Christ, unites humanity through the blood of his cross, by his obedience he receives authority to become the shepherd who leads the flock back to the arms of the Father.

Mark (6:30–34)
The desire for a true shepherd results in the people seeking out the Lord in even out-of-the-way places. Since he is the Good Shepherd, he listens and responds to their needs.

FOCUS

The Lord lovingly provides for our needs. Through the care of messengers who, responding to the invitation to serve the people of God, guide and care for them, God shows his mercy and compassion. Finally, through his son, who in his person is the embodiment of the Good Shepherd, the Father extends his compassionate love fully to his people.

IDEA STARTERS

- *CCT Lectionary* (Proper 11): II Sm 11:1-15; Ps 53: Eph 11-22; Mk 6:30-34.
- Jesus was so moved by the faith of the people that he refrained from "a little rest" and began to teach them. He believes in us!
- You may ask for Religious Education volunteers today.
- Vacation Bible Schoolers may illustrate some teaching(s) of Jesus during worship or at the coffee hour.
- Celebrate the liturgy by the lake today.
- For your consideration: Opening Prayer "for the Church D"; Intercessions for faithful teachers/leaders in church & society, justice for the sake of Christ, refreshment from the Lord, trust, peace & reconciliation, retreat master & spiritual directors; Sunday Preface VIII (P36); Eucharistic Prayer IV; Ordinary Solemn Blessing I.

MUSIC

- Psalm 23
- *Alleluia, People of God* (Deiss/NALR)
- *Be Glad, O People* (Weston Priory)
- *Come, My Children* (Dameans/NALR)
- *Come to Me* (Weston Priory)
- *I Lift Up My Soul* (Jesuits/NALR)
- *In Your Presence* (Byrne/Resource)
- *Jesus is Life* (Landry/NALR)
- *Let All the Earth* (Haugen/GIA)
- *Like a Shepherd* (Jesuits/NALR)
- *The Lord is My Shepherd* (Wise/GIA)
- *Lord of Glory* (Jesuits/NALR)
- *Lord, This is the People* (Byrne/Resource)
- *May We Praise* (Jesuits/NALR)
- *Only a Shadow* (Landry/NALR)
- *Redeemer Lord* (Jesuits/NALR)
- *Save Us, O Lord* (Jesuits/NALR)
- *Shepherd's Alleluia* (Landry/NALR)
- *A Time for Building Bridges* (Landry/NALR)
- *Trust in the Lord* (Jesuits/ NALR)
- *We Remember* (Haugen/GIA)
- *We Were Strangers* (Deiss/NALR)

SUNDAY PLANNING SHEET

Date _____

Parish focus _____

Environment & art _____

Ritual notes _____

Faith development (eg., in newsletter/classes) _____

Children's faith experience _____

Prelude _____

Hymn of gathering _____

Sprinkling/Penitential rite _____

Hymn of praise _____

Opening Prayer _____

First reading _____ Responsory _____

Second reading _____ Gospel acclamation _____

Gospel _____ Profession of faith _____

General intercessions _____

At the preparation & presentation _____

Preface dialog _____ Preface _____

Preface acclamation _____

Eucharistic prayer _____ Memorial acclamation _____

Eucharistic amen _____

The Lord's prayer _____

Breaking of bread _____

The communion hymn _____

The post-communion hymn _____

Blessing _____ At the dismissal _____

Memoranda:

SEVENTEENTH SUNDAY OF THE YEAR

YEAR B

READINGS

Second Kings (4:42-44)
Elisha is so filled with the Spirit that his very word is enough to produce a miraculous multiplication of food to feed the hungry.

Ephesians (4:1-6)
The one God binds his people together in a spirit of love and unites them in his peace.

John (6:1-15)
Jesus satisfies his people feeding not only their physical hunger but their deepest longings and desires.

FOCUS

If we live in God, then our every need will be taken care of and we will never want for anything that is good for us.

IDEA STARTERS

- *CCT Lectionary* (Proper 12): II Sm 12: 1-14; Ps 32; Eph 3:14-21; Jn 6:1-15.
- During the five Sundays of John's Gospel, study the structure of the Eucharistic Celebration today, the "Assembly Gathers."
- St. Vincent DePaul Society: Fill 12 baskets with food and clothing today or through the next few Sundays.
- How is John's Gospel different from Mark's? How is today's Gospel different from Mk 6:33-44?
- For your consideration: Opening Prayer; Intercessions for bakers, storeowners, sharing necessities, the hungry, faith in ourselves/others/God, hope prisoners & workers, spiritual gifts, unity among Christians, the Jewish people, children, world leaders; Holy Eucharist Preface II (P48); Eucharistic Prayer III; Memorial Acclamation C; The Lord's Prayer (sung); Breaking of Bread (highlighted); Ordinary Solemn Blessing III.

MUSIC

- Psalm 145
- *Abba, Father* (Landry/NALR)
- *Anyone Who Eats This Bread* (Weston Priory)
- *Be Still My Friends* (Andersen/Resource)
- *The Bread of Rejoicing* (Deiss/NALR)
- *Father We Sing Your Praises* (Zsigray/NALR)
- *Father, We Thank Thee* (Tucker/PMB)
- *Gloria III* (Taize/GIA)
- *God & Man at Table* (Stamps/Dawn Treader)
- *The Hand of the Lord* (Landry/NALR)
- *Let Heaven Rejoice* (Jesuits/NALR)
- *The Lord is Near* (Dameans/NALR)
- *One Lord* (Haas/Cooperative Music)
- *Send Us Your Spirit* (Kendzia/NALR)
- *Sing Out in Thanksgiving* (Jabusch/NALR)
- *Song of Gathering* (Wise/GIA)
- *That There May Be Bread* (Weston Priory)
- *There is One Lord* (Dameans/NALR)
- *There is One Lord* (Deiss/PMB)

SUNDAY PLANNING SHEET

Date _____

Parish focus _____

Environment & art _____

Ritual notes _____

Faith development (eg., in newsletter/classes) _____

Children's faith experience _____

Prelude _____

Hymn of gathering _____

Sprinkling/Penitential rite _____

Hymn of praise _____

Opening Prayer _____

First reading _____ Responsory _____

Second reading _____ Gospel acclamation _____

Gospel _____ Profession of faith _____

General intercessions _____

At the preparation & presentation _____

Preface dialog _____ Preface _____

Preface acclamation _____

Eucharistic prayer _____ Memorial acclamation _____

Eucharistic amen _____

The Lord's prayer _____

Breaking of bread _____

The communion hymn _____

The post-communion hymn _____

Blessing _____ At the dismissal _____

Memoranda:

EIGHTEENTH SUNDAY OF THE YEAR

YEAR B

READINGS
Exodus (16:2-4,12-15)
The grumbling Israelite community questions the fidelity of the Lord in their lack of food as they wander through the desert. The gifts of quail in the evening and dewy manna in the morning are demonstrations of the Lord's continuing desire to strengthen a people who so often question God's gift of love.
Ephesians (4:17, 20-24)
Paul exhorts the Ephesians that, having heard the Good News of Christ's redemption, they must live a new life, putting aside their old ways, their old selves, and putting on the "new man" of Christ Jesus. Having done so, they will live in the Lord's justice and truth.
John (6:24-35)
Jesus confronts the crowd with their hunger and the deeper and more profound meaning which lies behind it. He invites them, in a typical Johannine fashion, to put aside the things that are perishable and to seek the food which will last forever and deliver them from their nagging hunger and thirst.

FOCUS
If we put on Christ, if our concerns are his concerns, then we shall not "miss the forest for the trees." When we eat his body and drink his blood, not only will our hunger be satiated, but we ourselves shall grow into his body, and therefore be food for a hungry world, which longs for the message, the "meat" of the good news of Jesus' risen glory.

IDEA STARTERS
- *CCT Lectionary* (Proper 13): II Sm 12:15b-24; Ps 34:11-22; Eph 4:1-6; Jn 6:24-35.
- The Assembly Listens, "The Liturgy of the Word" (Hearing the Word of the One come down from heaven).
- Eucharistic Ministers may be installed on any of these Johannine Sundays.
- Have a parish picnic at a neighborhood park. Meet by the lake.
- A Gospel Procession may illustrate the fact that God in Christ walked in our midst and is in our midst.
- For your consideration: Alternative Opening Prayer; Intercessions for nomads, the hungry, homeless, soup kitchen worker, a spiritual way of thinking, faith; Sunday Preface III (P31); Eucharistic Prayer III; Memorial Acclamation C; The Lord's Prayer (sung); Ordinary Solemn Blessing II.

MUSIC
- Psalm 78
- *All the Ends of the Earth* (Foster/Resource)
- *Eye has Not Seen* (Haugen/GIA)
- *For Us To Live* (Weston Priory)
- *Give Thanks to God* (Lisicki/Resource)
- *His Love Will Ever Be* (Fabing/NALR)
- *I Am the Bread of Life* (Toolan/GIA)
- *I Believe In the Sun* (Landry/NALR)
- *In Memory of Jesus* (Landry/NALR)
- *It's a New Day* (Wise/GIA)
- *Jesus in Our Hands* (Wise/GIA)
- *Light of the World* (Kendzia/NALR)
- *Mighty Lord* (Jesuits/NALR)
- *Mountains and Hills* (Jesuits/NALR)
- *Only in God* (Jesuits/NALR)

SUNDAY PLANNING SHEET

Date _____

Parish focus _____

Environment & art _____

Ritual notes _____

Faith development (eg., in newsletter/classes) _____

Children's faith experience _____

Prelude _____

Hymn of gathering _____

Sprinkling/Penitential rite _____

Hymn of praise _____

Opening Prayer _____

First reading _____ Responsory _____

Second reading _____ Gospel acclamation _____

Gospel _____ Profession of faith _____

General intercessions _____

At the preparation & presentation _____

Preface dialog _____ Preface _____

Preface acclamation _____

Eucharistic prayer _____ Memorial acclamation _____

Eucharistic amen _____

The Lord's prayer _____

Breaking of bread _____

The communion hymn _____

The post-communion hymn _____

Blessing _____ At the dismissal _____

Memoranda:

NINETEENTH SUNDAY OF THE YEAR

YEAR B

READINGS
First Kings (19:4–8)
At the point of despair, Elijah is supported with food and drink delivered by an angel. He is thus encouraged to continue his journey to encounter the Lord God on Horeb.
Ephesians (4:30–5:2)
Paul exhorts the Ephesians to become imitators of Christ through the way of love. Self sacrifice is the method through which we accomplish this task.
John (6:41–51)
Jesus, the reflection of God's glory, is the true bread come down from heaven. Those who eat this living bread will never taste death but will possess the fullness of the Lord's life.

FOCUS
Elijah, exhausted in his struggle to "pour himself out" in service to the Lord, is sustained by an angel bearing heavenly food. Strengthened, he is able to continue his journey to meet the God of love on Horeb. Jesus makes it clear that he is the Bread of Heaven, giving all who eat this bread life eternal.

IDEA STARTERS
- *CCT Lectionary* (Proper 14): II Sm 18:1,5,9-15; Ps 143: 1-8; Eph 4:25-5:2; Jn 6:35, 41-51.
- Walk Humbly With Your God: Plan a day, evening, or weekend of recollection on relationships with God and neighbor.
- Ritual: Use an incense of "pleasing fragrance."
- Draw parallels between Jesus as the staple of life and bread as the staple of life in a bulletin article.
- For your consideration: Alternative Opening Prayer; Intercessions for travellers, perseverance, the suicidal, the hungry, Christ-like living, openness to spiritual gifts, the Jewish people, faith; Sunday Preface III (P31); Reconciliation Eucharistic Prayer I; Memorial Acclamation C; The Communion Rite (highlighted); Ordinary Solemn Blessing V.

MUSIC
- Psalm 34
- *Be Glad, Be Happy* (Gilsdorf/Resource)
- *Father We Sing Your Praises* (Zsigray/NALR)
- *Here Is My Life* (Wise/GIA)
- *I Am the Bread of Life* (Toolan/GIA)
- *Jesus Loves Me As I Am* (Mierzwa/Resource)
- *Let All Mortal Flesh* (Moultrie/PMB)
- *Look Beyond* (Dameans/NALR)
- *May We Praise You* (Jesuits/NALR)
- *On Eagles' Wings* (Joncas/NALR)
- *Our God is Love* (Repp/K&R)
- *Praise the Lord, My Soul* (Parker/GIA)
- *To Be Your Bread* (Haas/GIA)
- *Yahweh* (Weston Priory)

SUNDAY PLANNING SHEET

Date _____

Parish focus _____

Environment & art _____

Ritual notes _____

Faith development (eg., in newsletter/classes) _____

Children's faith experience _____

Prelude _____

Hymn of gathering _____

Sprinkling/Penitential rite _____

Hymn of praise _____

Opening Prayer _____

First reading _____Responsory _____

Second reading _____Gospel acclamation _____

Gospel _____Profession of faith _____

General intercessions _____

At the preparation & presentation _____

Preface dialog _____Preface _____

Preface acclamation _____

Eucharistic prayer _____Memorial acclamation _____

Eucharistic amen _____

The Lord's prayer _____

Breaking of bread _____

The communion hymn _____

The post-communion hymn _____

Blessing _____At the dismissal _____

Memoranda:

TWENTIETH SUNDAY OF THE YEAR

YEAR B

READINGS

Proverbs (9:1-6)
In this reading, Wisdom (personified in feminine form) prepares a table filled with the food of knowledge and understanding. Those who seek truth, wishing to forsake foolishness, eat and drink from her table.

Ephesians (5:15-20)
Paul points to the food the Ephesians should seek in order to become thoughtful, spirit-filled people. Prayer and praise, quiet joy, and a thankful heart, in short a eucharistic spirit, is the food of God's children.

John (6:51-58)
Continuing his eucharistic discourse, Jesus points to God's life and his own life as the foundation of the lives of all who believe in him. This divinized life is nurtured by the constant and consistent nourishment provided by the flesh and blood of the Lord.

FOCUS

The food of wisdom, foretold in the Old Testament, is brought to its fullness in the new, in the very word, flesh, and blood of the Lord Jesus. This food is the only source of nourishment for the believer. Those who feast on the Lord grow in his light, love, and life.

IDEA STARTERS

- *CCT Lectionary* (Proper 15): II Sm 18:24-33; Ps 102: 1-12; Eph 5:15-20; Jn 6:51-58.
- Sharing the Bread and Cup: The readings provide a background for catechesis about communion under both kinds.
- Music ministries may be acknowledged, recruited and honored at today's coffee hour, in the bulletin, etc. (cf. Eph 5:19).
- Sponsor a potluck brunch (agape).
- For your consideration: Opening Prayer; Intercessions for wisdom, the poor and hungry, speaking uprightly, peace and goodness, stewardship over creation, singers and composers; Sunday Preface VI (P34); Eucharistic Prayer I; Memorial Acclamation C; Communion Rite (highlighted); Ordinary Solemn Blessing III.

MUSIC

- Psalm 34
- *Anyone Who Eats this Bread* (Weston Priory)
- *Come, My Children* (Dameans/NALR)
- *Come to My Table* (Vickers/NALR)
- *Father, We Thank Thee* (Tucker/PMB)
- *Glorious Praise* (Hilliard/Resource)

- *The Hand of the Lord* (Landry/NALR)
- *Hymn of the Lord's Supper* (Ivancic/GIA)
- *Jesus Is My Saving Lord* (Johnson/Resource)
- *Shout With God* (Tucciarone/Resource)
- *When in our Music God Is Glorified* (Green/PMB)

SUNDAY PLANNING SHEET

Date _____

Parish focus _____

Environment & art _____

Ritual notes _____

Faith development (eg., in newsletter/classes) _____

Children's faith experience _____

Prelude _____

Hymn of gathering _____

Sprinkling/Penitential rite _____

Hymn of praise _____

Opening Prayer _____

First reading _____ Responsory _____

Second reading _____ Gospel acclamation _____

Gospel _____ Profession of faith _____

General intercessions _____

At the preparation & presentation _____

Preface dialog _____ Preface _____

Preface acclamation _____

Eucharistic prayer _____ Memorial acclamation ____

Eucharistic amen _____

The Lord's prayer _____

Breaking of bread _____

The communion hymn _____

The post-communion hymn _____

Blessing _____ At the dismissal _____

Memoranda:

TWENTY-FIRST SUNDAY OF THE YEAR

YEAR B

READINGS

Joshua (24:1-2,15-18)
The covenant, made with the patriarchs, sealed on Horeb with Moses, is renewed at Shechem, the site of ancient contacts between God and Israel, by Joshua. This ritual action is done in the name of the whole people.

Ephesians (5:21-32)
Paul discusses how the new covenant should be lived and mirrored in the relationship of the community of the church. The chief characteristic of this relational bond is loving compassionate concern, built on trust.

John (6:60-69)
To reject Jesus catapults a person on a course which can only lead farther and farther away from God. Those who profess God as Lord and feed on the Lord are led to the same confession as Peter and the Twelve: "We are convinced that you are God's holy one."

FOCUS
The right order of things seems to be a preoccupation of today's readings. Joshua publicly confesses for himself and his family the relational pattern of the covenant — "I will be your God, you will be my people." Israel follows his lead and accepts the covenant. Paul reiterates the pattern of the relationship of the New Israel: compassionate, loving concern built on intimate trust between God and God's people. Jesus, in the close of the Johannine eucharistic discourse, demonstrates the results of those who accept and those who reject this pattern.

IDEA STARTERS
- *CCT Lectionary* (Proper 16): II Sm 23:1-7; Ps 67: Eph 5:21-33; Jn 6:55-69.
- Celebrate "Becoming a Catechumen" at today's liturgy with interested inquirers.
- Readers: missalettes in the USA use the *New American Bible* translation. Note that all other English speaking countries use the *Jerusalem Bible*. In light of the second reading, which version says it best?
- Honor those who faithfully "serve the Lord" in your community. Appeal for new servants of the Word as worship leaders, catechists, social outreachers, etc.
- For your consideration: Rite of Becoming a Catechumen; Alternative Opening Prayer; Intercessions for those in leadership (Church, national, business, parish), faithfulness to the Lord, summer travellers, the bereaved, the engaged and married, openness to God's grace; Sunday Preface VIII (P36); Eucharistic Prayer I; Memorial Acclamation C; Communion Rite (highlighted); Ordinary Solemn Blessing II.

MUSIC

- *Psalm 34*
- *Canticle of the Sun* (Haugen/GIA)
- *The Church's One Foundation* (Stone/PMB)
- *Do You Really Love Me?* (Landry/NALR)
- *Go Forth People of God* (Barbara/Resource)
- *Hosanna* (Weston Priory)
- *If Anyone Loves Me* (Weston Priory)
- *Look Toward Me* (Lisicky/Resource)
- *Lord Of Glory* (Jesuits/NALR)
- *Lord Be With Us Now* (Lawrence/Resource)
- *Lord, to Whom Shall We Go?* (Conry/NALR)
- *Lord, to Whom Shall We Go?* (Joncas/NALR)
- *Sent Forth by God's Blessing* (Westendorf/PMB)

SUNDAY PLANNING SHEET   Date _____

Parish focus _____

Environment & art _____

Ritual notes _____

Faith development (eg., in newsletter/classes) _____

Children's faith experience _____

Prelude _____

Hymn of gathering _____

Sprinkling/Penitential rite _____

Hymn of praise _____

Opening Prayer _____

First reading _____Responsory _____

Second reading _____Gospel acclamation _____

Gospel _____Profession of faith _____

General intercessions _____

At the preparation & presentation _____

Preface dialog _____Preface _____

Preface acclamation _____

Eucharistic prayer _____Memorial acclamation _____

Eucharistic amen _____

The Lord's prayer _____

Breaking of bread _____

The communion hymn _____

The post-communion hymn _____

Blessing _____At the dismissal _____

Memoranda:

TWENTY-SECOND SUNDAY   YEAR B OF THE YEAR

READINGS

Deuteronomy (4:1-2,6-8)
To accept the Law and live by it brings the fullness of life which only the Lord can give. Those who live the Law possess justice and peace.

James (1:17-18,21-22,27)
All things that are good come from the Lord. Through the creative word, God has brought all things into existence. If we accept God's lordship, our lives will echo this ordered, created, and loving pattern.

Mark (7:1-8,14-15,21-23)
True impurity is manufactured within the hearts of people. This sinfulness is the result of not humbly accepting the lordship of Jesus and lovingly doing his will. All the ceremonies, rituals, and traditions people can devise cannot remove this sin, which can only be cleansed through humble, loving obedience.

FOCUS

How can we remain pure, that is, remain in God's life? Being open to the spirit, recognizing that all things are gifts, showered on us from God, and living the Law, God's life communicated to us — these are the ways we keep God's life alive in us. The first and third readings draw parallels as to what the Lord's law is. The second reading describes the fruit of living in such a fashion.

IDEA STARTERS

- *CCT Lectionary* (Proper 17): I Kgs 2:1-4, 10-12; Ps 121; Eph 6:10-20: Mk 7:1-8, 14-15, 21-23.
- We come together celebrating the New Heart and the New Spirit (cf. Ez 36:26) we were given in Baptism.
- Adult Forum: "The Roman Catholic Church — Scripture and Tradition."
- Bulletin Article: "Does eating meat on Fridays in Lent make a person unclean?"
- Ecumenical Forum: What role does tradition play in the many Christian denominations? (in Jewish denominations, too?)
- Have a summer's end picnic with activities for the young, the married, the single, and the seniors on Labor Day!
- For your consideration: Opening Prayer; Intercessions for fidelity of God's will and Word, honesty, faith-in-action, orphans, widow(er)s, the world; Sunday Preface VII (P35); Reconciliation Eucharistic Prayer II; Memorial Acclamation B; Ordinary Solemn Blessing V.

MUSIC

- Psalm 15
- *Blessed Be God* (Lawrence/Resource)
- *I Lift Up My Soul* (Jesuits/NALR)
- *One Lord* (Haas/Cooperative Music)
- *Path of Life* (Dameans/NALR)
- *Praise the Lord* (Keyes/Resource)
- *Show Us the Path of Life* (Haugen/GIA)

SUNDAY PLANNING SHEET

Date _____

Parish focus _____

Environment & art _____

Ritual notes _____

Faith development (eg., in newsletter/classes) _____

Children's faith experience _____

Prelude _____

Hymn of gathering _____

Sprinkling/Penitential rite _____

Hymn of praise _____

Opening Prayer _____

First reading _____ Responsory _____

Second reading _____ Gospel acclamation _____

Gospel _____ Profession of faith _____

General intercessions _____

At the preparation & presentation _____

Preface dialog _____ Preface _____

Preface acclamation _____

Eucharistic prayer _____ Memorial acclamation _____

Eucharistic amen _____

The Lord's prayer _____

Breaking of bread _____

The communion hymn _____

The post-communion hymn _____

Blessing _____ At the dismissal _____

Memoranda:

TWENTY-THIRD SUNDAY OF THE YEAR

YEAR B

READINGS

Isaiah (35:4-7)
Isaiah describes in vivid imagery what the messianic age will be like. All the bonds will be broken, all handicaps and limitations brooked, and all that is incomplete will be brought to fullness.

James (2:1-5)
God's love is inclusive. It breaks the chains of discrimination and shortsightedness and opens the way to loving acceptance. It provides us with eyes to see as the Lord sees.

Mark (7:31-37)
Jesus loosens the tongue and unstops the ears of a deaf man with a speech impediment. His command to open not only restores the man's physical powers, but allows him to declare the Lord's greatness.

FOCUS

Isaiah foretells the messianic age in the first reading. In the third, Jesus fulfills it. The gifts of this age, however, not only restore and renew the physical. The Messiah inaugurates an age where all of us are released from the blindness which keeps us from seeing things in their true perspective, the way God sees them. Blessed with this restored vision, we are kept from the exclusive, discriminating behavior, so antithetical to the Christian lifestyle referred to by James.

IDEA STARTERS

- *CCT Lectionary* (Proper 18): Ecc 5:8-15 or Prv 2:1-8; Ps 119:129-136; Jas 1:17-27; Mk 7:31-37.
- Discuss the "Ephphatha" of the Gospel without revealing too much of the mysteries (i.e.,RCIA rites to come!) If the "Rite of Becoming a Catechumen" is celebrated, highlight the signing of the senses (no. 85).
- Discuss how your parish might reach out to church members in the area who feel alienated from the church. How does your parish reach out to all in your community without distinctions and prejudices?
- "The Lord protects strangers." What do we do to welcome visitors to our church?
- Bible Study: The Epistle of James.
- For your consideration: Alternative Opening Prayer; Intercessions for the fearful, the handicapped, the oppressed, the hungry, hostages, welcome the strangers, widow(er)s, orphans, end to discrimination of all kinds, visitors, alienated Christians; Sunday Preface (Italian Sacramentary); Eucharistic Prayer IV; Memorial Acclamation D; Ordinary Solemn Blessing V.

MUSIC

- Psalm 146
- *Amazing Grace* (Traditional)
- *Believe* (McGrath/Resource)
- *Be Not Afraid* (Jesuits/NALR)
- *Gather Us In* (Haugen/GIA)
- *God's Blessing Sends Us Forth* (Westendorf/PMB)
- *I Will Sing, I Will Sing* (Dyer/Celebration)
- *Jesus, Heal Us* (Ellis/NALR)
- *May We Grow* (Repp/K & R)
- *One Bread, One Body* (Jesuits/NALR)
- *Praise The Name of the Lord* (Patterson/Resource)
- *Praise to the Lord* (Winkworth/PMB)
- *Song of Gathering* (Wise/GIA)
- *Yahweh* (Weston Priory)

SUNDAY PLANNING SHEET   Date _____

Parish focus _____

Environment & art _____

Ritual notes _____

Faith development (eg., in newsletter/classes) _____

Children's faith experience _____

Prelude _____

Hymn of gathering _____

Sprinkling/Penitential rite _____

Hymn of praise _____

Opening Prayer _____

First reading _____Responsory _____

Second reading _____Gospel acclamation _____

Gospel _____Profession of faith _____

General intercessions _____

At the preparation & presentation _____

Preface dialog _____Preface _____

Preface acclamation _____

Eucharistic prayer _____Memorial acclamation _____

Eucharistic amen _____

The Lord's prayer _____

Breaking of bread _____

The communion hymn _____

The post-communion hymn _____

Blessing _____At the dismissal _____

Memoranda:

TWENTY-FOURTH SUNDAY YEAR B OF THE YEAR

READINGS

Isaiah (50:4-9)
The Messiah retains his faith in God even when he is sorely pressed and seemingly abandoned by God. Confidently, he challenges all who would dispute his right to be God's witness to confront him before the Lord. In his faithfulness he is sure of the Lord's loving protection.

James (2:14-18)
A faith not translated into action is a lifeless sham, unworthy of the name faith. To be truly faithful, one must act lovingly toward those in the body of the Lord.

Mark (8:27-35)
The Messiah must suffer persecution, rejection, and death to fulfill his mission and enter his glory. Those who follow him can and must expect to replicate the same pattern in their own lives.

FOCUS

The first and third readings outline for us the vocation of the suffering servant of Yahweh. Through faithful love, manifested through pain and rejection, glory is obtained. This is both the scandal and paradox of the cross. James spells out how this is related to each believer. A faith which makes no demands, which does not involve death to self so others might live, is no faith at all. Recognition of the Messiah is not enough. If we do not walk with him in the shadow of the cross, we are an impediment to the growth of the Kingdom.

IDEA STARTERS

- *CCT Lectionary* (Proper 19): Prv 22:1-2, 8-9; Ps 125; Jas 2:1-5,8-10,14-17; Mk 8:27-38.
- Share personal answers to Jesus' questions: "Who do people say I am?" "Who do you say I am?"
- How do we carry the cross of Christ in our lives?
- Ecumenical Forum: "Justification by the grace of faith calls forth good deeds."
- For your consideration: Opening Prayer; Intercessions for just courts (judges, jurors, lawyers, defendants, witnesses), the homeless, fidelity despite temptation, gospel priorities; Sunday Preface II (P30); Memorial Acclamation D; Passion Solemn Blessing.

MUSIC

- Psalm 116
- *For You Are My God* (Jesuits/NALR)
- *Lift High the Cross* (Kitchin/PMB)
- *Now Let Us From the Table Rise* (Kaan/PMB)
- *O God of Loveliness* (Vaughan/PMB)
- *Only This I Want* (Jesuits/NALR)
- *Our Blessing Cup* (Joncas/NALR)
- *This Is the People* (Keyes/Resource)
- *What Great Marvels* (Gilsdorf/Resource)
- *With Faith Grown in Suffering* (Landry/NALR)
- *You Are Near* (Jesuits/NALR)

SUNDAY PLANNING SHEET

Date _____

Parish focus _____

Environment & art _____

Ritual notes _____

Faith development (eg., in newsletter/classes) _____

Children's faith experience _____

Prelude _____

Hymn of gathering _____

Sprinkling/Penitential rite _____

Hymn of praise _____

Opening Prayer _____

First reading _____ Responsory _____

Second reading _____ Gospel acclamation _____

Gospel _____ Profession of faith _____

General intercessions _____

At the preparation & presentation _____

Preface dialog _____ Preface _____

Preface acclamation _____

Eucharistic prayer _____ Memorial acclamation _____

Eucharistic amen _____

The Lord's prayer _____

Breaking of bread _____

The communion hymn _____

The post-communion hymn _____

Blessing _____ At the dismissal _____

Memoranda:

TWENTY-FIFTH SUNDAY OF THE YEAR

YEAR B

READINGS

Wisdom (2:12,17-20)
This reading seems to be the opposite perspective of the Isaian reading from last Sunday. Here we see the persecutors of the Lord's servant. We feel the anger and hatred toward the just one. His integrity is completely offensive to them, and testing his fidelity is their pleasure.

James (3:16-4:3)
James describes the characteristics of wisdom. He then turns his attention to contrasting these characteristics with the difficulties and ruptures his community faces. These are traced to a lack of wisdom which produces vile behavior and malicious desires.

Mark (9:30-37)
The child is the paradigm for the person who wishes to enter the Kingdom. Such an individual will give himself or herself over to the work of the cross, trusting that the Lord will lovingly protect God's children under the most adverse situations.

FOCUS

It is the very childlike innocence of the virtuous, discussed in Mark, which sets the teeth of the wicked on edge, as described in Wisdom. This innocence does not relent to the cravings of envy and greed that characterize the godless. While sustaining severe persecution, the just lovingly place their trust in God and cast their care upon the Lord.

IDEA STARTERS

- *CCT Lectionary* (Proper 20): Job 28:20-28; Ps 27:1-6; Jas 3:13-18; Mk 9:30-37.
- Children's Liturgy: The image of the child in the gospel shows us one of complete dependence upon God's grace of adoption given to us at baptism.
- Appeal for new greeters, ushers, host(ess)s. "Those who welcome, welcome me!"
- James gives good directions for committee communications as well as daily living.
- Take the gospel in the context of its post-Transfiguration setting (cf., Mk 9:2-10ff).
- For your consideration: Intercessions for trust in God, justice and peace, personal and communal holiness, those in leadership positions, hospitality, children; Sunday Preface VII (P35); Memorial Acclamation D; Passion Solemn Blessing.

MUSIC

- Psalm 54
- *Blest Be the Lord* (Jesuits/NALR)
- *Come, My Friend* (Page/Resource)
- *Come, My Children* (Dameans/NALR)
- *Eye Has Not Seen* (Haugen/GIA)
- *Glorious Praise* (Hilliard/Resource)
- *In Your Love Remember Me* (Kendzia/NALR)
- *Kyrie Eleison* (Clark/Celebration)
- *Let Us Walk in the Light* (Haugen/GIA)
- *Love Consecrates the Humblest Act* (McManus/PMB)
- *Service* (Dameans/NALR)

SUNDAY PLANNING SHEET

Date _____

Parish focus _____

Environment & art _____

Ritual notes _____

Faith development (eg., in newsletter/classes) _____

Children's faith experience _____

Prelude _____

Hymn of gathering _____

Sprinkling/Penitential rite _____

Hymn of praise _____

Opening Prayer _____

First reading _____ Responsory _____

Second reading _____ Gospel acclamation _____

Gospel _____ Profession of faith _____

General intercessions _____

At the preparation & presentation _____

Preface dialog _____ Preface _____

Preface acclamation _____

Eucharistic prayer _____ Memorial acclamation _____

Eucharistic amen _____

The Lord's prayer _____

Breaking of bread _____

The communion hymn _____

The post-communion hymn _____

Blessing _____ At the dismissal _____

Memoranda:

TWENTY-SIXTH SUNDAY OF THE YEAR

YEAR B

READINGS

Numbers (11:25-29)
Moses, who is imbued with the Lord's spirit, shares that spirit with the elders of Israel. Since he is not ego-oriented but God-centered, he rejoices to discover others also received this outpouring. His selflessness enables him to rejoice at this furthering of the Kingdom.

James (5:1-6)
The rich (those who perceive they have no need of God) mourn to discover the tragedy of their mistake and their foolish independence. In their fury they attack the just one and attempt to put an end to him. Relying on the Lord, the just one does not resist.

Mark (9:38-43,45,47-48)
All who work for the Lord are on the side of the Kingdom. Nothing should act as a deterrent in keeping us from the Kingdom. Only the life of God is of value.

FOCUS

Those who recognize the centrality of the Lord's life and Kingdom have their priorities set well. They place God's life first and all else second. Even in times of adversity they are faithful since they recognize God is their support.

IDEA STARTERS

- *CCT Lectionary* (Proper 21): Job 42:1-6; Ps 27:7-14; Jas 4:13-17, 5:7-11; Mk 9:38-50.
- Discuss recent letters by the American bishops on peace and economics in light of the James pericope.
- How does the James passage apply to me? If not "rich," what term may I put in its place?
- All Christians are baptized into a common ministry.
- Paraments: Autumn is upon us! A deep evergreen may be appropriate as we approach the winter.
- For Your Consideration: Opening Prayer, Intercessions for contemporary prophets, those preparing for Confirmation, the rich and poor, farmers, ecumenical relations, handicapped, respect for God's creation of our body; Reconciliation Eucharistic Prayer II; Memorial Acclamation D; Dedication of a Church; Solemn Blessing (adapted).

MUSIC

- Psalm 19
- *Alleluia* (Culbreth/Resource)
- *A Song of Blessing* (Wise/GIA)
- *The Cry of the Poor* (Jesuits/NALR)
- *How Beautiful* (Wise/GIA)
- *Like a Sunflower* (Landry/NALR)
- *Lord Jesus, Come* (Dicie/Resource)
- *Share As One in the Lord* (Tucciarone/Resource)
- *The Spirit Is A-Movin'* (Landry/NALR)
- *Spirit of God* (Weston Priory)
- *Thanks Be to You, O God* (Stuntz/PMB)
- *'Tis a Gift to Be Simple* (Traditional)
- *There, Let Me Bring in My Love* (Repp/K & R)
- *We Are Many Parts* (Haugen/GIA)

SUNDAY PLANNING SHEET

Date _____

Parish focus _____

Environment & art _____

Ritual notes _____

Faith development (eg., in newsletter/classes) _____

Children's faith experience _____

Prelude _____

Hymn of gathering _____

Sprinkling/Penitential rite _____

Hymn of praise _____

Opening Prayer _____

First reading _____ Responsory _____

Second reading _____ Gospel acclamation _____

Gospel _____ Profession of faith _____

General intercessions _____

At the preparation & presentation _____

Preface dialog _____ Preface _____

Preface acclamation _____

Eucharistic prayer _____ Memorial acclamation _____

Eucharistic amen _____

The Lord's prayer _____

Breaking of bread _____

The communion hymn _____

The post-communion hymn _____

Blessing _____ At the dismissal _____

Memoranda:

TWENTY-SEVENTH OF THE YEAR

YEAR B

READINGS

Genesis (2:18–24)
The second story of creation is presented to us today. We see the creation of man and woman as the Lord's greatest act of creative activity. They serve as a complement to one another and as sharers in his divine creativity.

Hebrews (2:9–11)
In the letter to the Hebrews, we are told that Jesus, our deliverer and the new Adam, was perfected through suffering so that he might completely identify with us. It is through this incarnational identification that we are able to claim the same Father.

Mark (10:2–16)
In the reading from Mark, Jesus sets the model of marriage under the new dispensation firmly in the spirit of the primeval situation. Since two are one flesh, they cannot be separated. More important, Jesus sets the standard of the little child as that for all believers. Anyone who trusts the Father with the same calm, childlike spirit, will be welcome as part of the Kingdom.

FOCUS

The three readings today hinge on the reading from Hebrews. The Genesis reading presents us with the primal relationship between human beings and God. The Gospel reading sets Jesus before us, telling his apostles that childlike obedience and trust are the pattern for the new creation (i.e. those born under the New Dispensation). This is the way it was in the beginning. Hebrews tells us that such obedience is achieved through suffering, suffering endured faithfully and in trust. This pattern was set by Jesus himself.

IDEA STARTERS

- *CCT Lectionary* (Proper 22): Gn 2:18; Ps 128; Heb 1:1-4, 2:9-11; Mk 10:2-16.
- Explore church beliefs regarding marriage.
- Sponsor a one-day workshop on annulments.
- Today begins seven pericopes from Hebrews.
- Respect Life Sunday is observed today.
- Today's readings are appropriate for a marriage.
- For your consideration: Opening Prayer; Gospel (full form); Intercessions for acceptance of interdependence, fidelity in all lifestyle commitments, families, children, diocesan tribunals; Marriage Preface II (P73); Eucharistic Prayer III; Memorial Acclamation C; Ordinary Solemn Blessing I.

MUSIC

- Psalm 128
- *Choose Life* (Weston Priory)
- *Let the Children Come to Me* (Sessions/Resource)
- *One Bread, One Body* (Jesuits/NALR)
- *Our Hearts Are One* (Lucas/Resource)
- *Path of Life* (Dameans/NALR)
- *Song of Thanksgiving* (Dicie/Resource)
- *The Wonders He Has Done For You* (Andersen/Resource)

SUNDAY PLANNING SHEET

Date _____

Parish focus _____

Environment & art _____

Ritual notes _____

Faith development (eg., in newsletter/classes) _____

Children's faith experience _____

Prelude _____

Hymn of gathering _____

Sprinkling/Penitential rite _____

Hymn of praise _____

Opening Prayer _____

First reading _____Responsory _____

Second reading _____Gospel acclamation _____

Gospel _____Profession of faith _____

General intercessions _____

At the preparation & presentation _____

Preface dialog _____Preface _____

Preface acclamation _____

Eucharistic prayer _____Memorial acclamation _____

Eucharistic amen _____

The Lord's prayer _____

Breaking of bread _____

The communion hymn _____

The post-communion hymn _____

Blessing _____At the dismissal _____

Memoranda:

TWENTY-EIGHTH SUNDAY OF THE YEAR

READINGS
Wisdom (7:7-11)
For the person who possesses wisdom, God's Spirit of understanding, nothing else is necessary. Wisdom is sufficient unto Herself.
Hebrews (4:12-13)
Jesus, the Word of God, probes and knows the heart of each person. Nothing is concealed from his effective, penetrating gaze.
Mark (10:17-30)
Those who throw in their lot with Jesus will inherit everything in the end. First, however, they must be prepared to sacrifice all for Him.

FOCUS
Once again, the Gospel reading gives an "enfleshment" of the preceding two readings. In the wisdom section, we are told that nothing is of greater value than wisdom. One should be happy to give all for her. In the fragment from Hebrews, Jesus is presented as God's wisdom, his effective Word. This word is searing, severing bone from marrow. Mark's story presents a rich young man. He recognizes Jesus as being the gift of God. When this gift asks the young man to pay the price, all he has, for this "best possession," the young man cannot. Jesus reminds Peter that only one who casts himself to the care of God can pay such a high price. Nothing is impossible to God.

IDEA STARTERS
- *CCT Lectionary* (Proper 23): Gn 3:8-19; Ps 90:1-12; Heb 4:1-3, 9-13; Mk 10:17-30.
- Observe Vocations Awareness Week in light of today's Gospel.
- Explore the evangelical counsels and how people have lived them (e.g. Francis of Assissi, Dorothy Day).
- Study the pastoral on the economy. Is it faithful to Christ's teachings?
- Today's readings are appropriate for religious profession.
- At the coffee hour, honor those who have vowed to live the evangelical counsels.
- For your consideration: Opening Prayer; Gospel (full form); Intercessions for prudence, stewardship of personal resources, Christian motivation for action, the rich and poor, vowed religious, perseverance; Sunday Preface V (p33); Eucharistic Prayer IV; Memorial Acclamation B; Ordinary Solemn Blessing II.

MUSIC
- Psalm 90
- *Alleluia, Your Word* (Deiss/NALR)
- *Dedication Song* (Raffa/Resource)
- *Follow Me* (Repp/K&R)
- *The Image of His Love* (Dicie/Resource)
- *Like a Sunflower* (Landry/NALR)
- *Won't You Come* (Porter/Resource)

SUNDAY PLANNING SHEET

Date _____

Parish focus _____

Environment & art _____

Ritual notes _____

Faith development (eg., in newsletter/classes) _____

Children's faith experience _____

Prelude _____

Hymn of gathering _____

Sprinkling/Penitential rite _____

Hymn of praise _____

Opening Prayer _____

First reading _____ Responsory _____

Second reading _____ Gospel acclamation _____

Gospel _____ Profession of faith _____

General intercessions _____

At the preparation & presentation _____

Preface dialog _____ Preface _____

Preface acclamation _____

Eucharistic prayer _____ Memorial acclamation _____

Eucharistic amen _____

The Lord's prayer _____

Breaking of bread _____

The communion hymn _____

The post-communion hymn _____

Blessing _____ At the dismissal _____

Memoranda:

TWENTY-NINTH SUNDAY OF THE YEAR
YEAR B

READINGS
Isaiah (53:10-11)
The suffering servant offers himself in his innocence as a sin offering for the salvation of all.
Hebrews (4:14-16)
Jesus, our Great High Priest, is familiar with our weaknesses, since he has endured them. The only thing he has not shared with us is sin. Since he has experienced our weakness, yet did not sin, we can confidently cling to him and our profession of faith in him as our Savior.
Mark (10:35-45)
From the impertinence of Zebedee's sons' request, the apostles learn an important lesson. Those who would follow the Lord must be prepared to serve, to the point of death. This is the mark of the true disciple.

FOCUS
Jesus the suffering servant, the High Priest who offers the innocent sacrifice, himself, is our advocate. His reign is lived in service, oblationary service which drains itself to death. Those who follow him can expect to act in no other way.

IDEA STARTERS
- *CCT Lectionary:* Is 53:7-12; Heb 4:14-16; Mk 10:35-45.
- If there is a season in your parish today is a good day to show appreciation for his work at a coffee after liturgy.
- It is unlikely that we will literally be asked to give up our lives for the Gospel. How does the scriptural theme of giving up our lives for the Lord apply to us?
- How can our parish community serve the wider community in the spirit of Christ?

MUSIC
- Psalm 33
- *Choose Life* (Weston Priory)
- *Let the Children Come to Me* (Sessions/Resource)
- *One Bread, One Body* (Jesuits/NALR)
- *Our Hearts Are One* (Lucas/Resource)
- *Path of Life* (Dameans/NALR)
- *Song of Thanksgiving* (Dicie/Resource)
- *The Wonders He Has Done For You* (Andersen/Resource)

SUNDAY PLANNING SHEET

Date _____

Parish focus _____

Environment & art _____

Ritual notes _____

Faith development (eg., in newsletter/classes) _____

Children's faith experience _____

Prelude _____

Hymn of gathering _____

Sprinkling/Penitential rite _____

Hymn of praise _____

Opening Prayer _____

First reading _____Responsory _____

Second reading _____Gospel acclamation _____

Gospel _____Profession of faith _____

General intercessions _____

At the preparation & presentation _____

Preface dialog _____Preface _____

Preface acclamation _____

Eucharistic prayer _____Memorial acclamation _____

Eucharistic amen _____

The Lord's prayer _____

Breaking of bread _____

The communion hymn _____

The post-communion hymn _____

Blessing _____At the dismissal _____

Memoranda:

THIRTIETH SUNDAY OF THE YEAR

YEAR B

READINGS

Jeremiah (31:7-9)
Christ, chosen by God to be our High Priest, identifies with our weakness. In his humanity, he shared our weakness and through this weakness, won glory by obedience.

Mark (10:46-52)
Jesus demonstrates he has inaugurated the messianic age by restoring the sight of the blind Bartimeaus.

FOCUS

Jeremiah describes the Lord's Day as a time when the deaf would hear, the blind see, the dumb speak, and all people will be united as God's family. Christ, High Priest by divine election, delivers us by sacrificing himself. "You have nothing whatever to fear from him." This statement can be directed toward each of us. He knows us and loves us in spite of, and because of, what we are. "He is calling you."

IDEA STARTERS

- *CCT Lectionary* (Proper 25): Jer 31:7-9; Ps 126; Heb 5:1-6; Mk 10:46-52.
- Act out today's miracle story at a children's liturgy.
- What role do Christians play in showing the Kingdom in our midst (cf. Jer 31)?
- Anointing of the Sick may be celebrated with today's readings.
- Liturgical Dance may capture the emotion of today's readings.
- Ecumenical Vespers marking Reformation-Reconciliation Sunday may be celebrated tonight.
- For your consideration: Penitential Rite C-iii; Alternative Opening Prayer; Intercessions for all nations, the handicapped, those preparing for child birth, the sorrowful, for laughter & joy, the harvest, for beggars, Christian unity; Eucharistic Prayer IV; Memorial Acclamation B; Ordinary Solemn Blessing V.

MUSIC

- Psalm 126
- *And the Father Will Dance* (Landry/NALR)
- *Be Still My Friends* (Andersen/Resource)
- *Call to Me* (Byrne/Resource)
- *The Cry of the Poor* (Jesuits/NALR)
- *Depending on Your Love* (Sexton/Resource)
- *How Beautiful* (Wise/GIA)
- *I Have Loved You* (Joncas/NALR)
- *I Have Waited* (Gilsdorf/Resource)
- *Let All the Earth* (Haugen/NALR)
- *May We Praise You* (Jesuits/NALR)
- *Mighty Lord* (Jesuits/NALR)
- *Shout for Joy* (Byrne/Resource)
- *Son of David* (Jesuits/NALR)
- *Till You* (Repp/K&R)
- *We Thank You, Father* (Weston Priory)

SUNDAY PLANNING SHEET

Date _____

Parish focus _____

Environment & art _____

Ritual notes _____

Faith development (eg., in newsletter/classes) _____

Children's faith experience _____

Prelude _____

Hymn of gathering _____

Sprinkling/Penitential rite _____

Hymn of praise _____

Opening Prayer _____

First reading _____Responsory _____

Second reading _____Gospel acclamation _____

Gospel _____Profession of faith _____

General intercessions _____

At the preparation & presentation _____

Preface dialog _____Preface _____

Preface acclamation _____

Eucharistic prayer _____Memorial acclamation _____

Eucharistic amen _____

The Lord's prayer _____

Breaking of bread _____

The communion hymn _____

The post-communion hymn _____

Blessing _____At the dismissal _____

Memoranda:

THIRTY-FIRST SUNDAY OF THE YEAR

READINGS

Deuteronomy (6:2-6)
The Shema is presented as the core and basis of covenanted faith. The Lord is One and our God. We must love him with our whole being.
Hebrews (7:23-28)
God's word has made Jesus the eternal High Priest. Thus his sacrifice is final and effective.
Mark (12:28-34)
Jesus points to the simple faith of the scribe as being proof that he is close to the Lord's Day.

FOCUS

Total love of God and love of neighbor which emanates from this is the foundation of faith. This faith is the stuff by which we are joined to Christ and therefore participate in his salvific act of faith.

IDEA STARTER

- *CCT Lectionary* (Proper 26): Dt 6:1-9; Ps 119:33-48; Heb 7:23-28; Mk 12:28-34.
- Theme for a children's liturgy: "When we show our love for ourselves and others, we show our love for God."
- The Eucharist joins us to participation in the one sacrifice of love Jesus offered on Good Friday.
- Bulletin article: "Types of Love" (cf. C.S. Lewis, *The Four Loves*).
- For your consideration: Opening Prayer; Intercessions for the Jewish people, steadfast hearts, holiness, spiritual sacrifice, increase in love; Sunday Preface VI (P34); Eucharist Prayer I; Memorial Acclamation C; Ordinary Solemn Blessing III.

MUSIC

- Psalm 18
- *Amen, We Sing to You* (Sexton/Resource)
- *By Love* (Repp/K&R)
- *Lord, We Are Sorry* (Raffa/Resource)
- *Share a Little Bit of Your Love* (Repp/K&R)
- *Song of Gathering* (Wise/GIA)
- *Spirit of God* (Weston Priory)
- *Strong and Constant* (Andersen/Resource)
- *That There May Be Bread* (Weston Priory)
- *This Alone* (Jesuits/NALR)
- *To Be Your Bread* (Haas/Cooperative Music)
- *Ubi Caritas* (Taize/GIA)

SUNDAY PLANNING SHEET

Date _____

Parish focus _____

Environment & art _____

Ritual notes _____

Faith development (eg., in newsletter/classes) _____

Children's faith experience _____

Prelude _____

Hymn of gathering _____

Sprinkling/Penitential rite _____

Hymn of praise _____

Opening Prayer _____

First reading _____Responsory _____

Second reading _____Gospel acclamation _____

Gospel _____Profession of faith _____

General intercessions _____

At the preparation & presentation _____

Preface dialog _____Preface _____

Preface acclamation _____

Eucharistic prayer _____Memorial acclamation _____

Eucharistic amen _____

The Lord's prayer _____

Breaking of bread _____

The communion hymn _____

The post-communion hymn _____

Blessing _____At the dismissal _____

Memoranda:

THIRTY-SECOND SUNDAY YEAR B
OF THE YEAR

READINGS
Kings (17:10-16
The widow's generosity to Elijah results in her deliverance. Her faith in his word eventuates in the deliverance of her son and herself.
Hebrews (9:24-28)
Christ offers his sacrifice once and for all. He entered heaven itself and opened it so that we might share God's Light. When he returns a second time, he will bring all who trust him into the glory of the Father.
Mark (12:38-44)
The widow is praised because she gave generously out of her need. Doing so, she demonstrates her faith in the promise of divine care and compassion.

FOCUS
Those who trust in the Lord's love act generously, as he is generous. It is this trustful, loving posture which identifies them with Jesus and so gives them the opportunity to share his life for eternity.

IDEA STARTER
- *CCT Lectionary* (Proper 27): I Kgs 18:8-16; Ps 146; Heb 9:24-28; Mk 12:38-44.
- Share a true spirit of sacrifice.
- Publicize food and clothing drives for the coming holidays.
- Elevate the Rite of Preparing the Altar and the Gifts (see "General Instruction of the Roman Missal," nos. 49-53).
- If the coffee hour is usually gratis, have a special offering cup for the poor. the poor.
- For your consideration: Alternative Opening Prayer; Gospel (full form); Intercessions for widow(er)s, prophets, bakers, the dying, abundant harvest, the hungry, oppressed, blind, orphans, hospitality, humility; Sunday Preface VI (P34); Eucharist Prayer III; Memorial Acclamation C; Ordinary Solemn Blessing III.

MUSIC
- Psalm 146
- *Beatitudes* (Dameans/NALR)
- *Blessed is the Name of Love* (Repp/K&R)
- *I Am the Light* (Repp/K&R)
- *Lord, We Are Sorry* (Raffa/Resource)
- *Justice Shall Flourish* (Schonbachler/Coop Music)
- *The Kingdom of God* (Deiss/NALR)
- *Praise the Lord, My Soul* (Parker/GIA)
- *Psalm of Rest* (Raffa/Resource)

SUNDAY PLANNING SHEET

Date _____

Parish focus _____

Environment & art _____

Ritual notes _____

Faith development (eg., in newsletter/classes) _____

Children's faith experience _____

Prelude _____

Hymn of gathering _____

Sprinkling/Penitential rite _____

Hymn of praise _____

Opening Prayer _____

First reading _____ Responsory _____

Second reading _____ Gospel acclamation _____

Gospel _____ Profession of faith _____

General intercessions _____

At the preparation & presentation _____

Preface dialog _____ Preface _____

Preface acclamation _____

Eucharistic prayer _____ Memorial acclamation _____

Eucharistic amen _____

The Lord's prayer _____

Breaking of bread _____

The communion hymn _____

The post-communion hymn _____

Blessing _____ At the dismissal _____

Memoranda:

THIRTY-THIRD SUNDAY OF THE YEAR

YEAR B

READINGS
Daniel (12:1-3)
Those who are "Michael," like God and point to him alone, shall live in his Kingdom together.
Hebrews (10:11-14, 18)
Jesus' sacrifice sanctifies us to share in the glory of the Father.
Mark (13:24-32)
Jesus prophesizes the Danielian Apocalyptic Vision, using the image of the Son of Man. This Divine Messenger will come at end of time to bring all of the just into the Kingdom.

FOCUS
In the last days, those who have been sanctified by Jesus, the High Priest, will be led to the glory of the Father's Kingdom. There they will live in his life for all eternity.

IDEA STARTERS
- *CCT Lectionary* (Proper 28): Dn 7:9-14; Ps 145:8-13; Heb 10:11-189; Mk 13:24-32.
- Have the children role play the Daniel pericope at their children's liturgy.
- How did Jesus, in his humanity, understand God the Father?
- Bible Study of ancient and contemporary interpretations of Mark's recollections of Jesus' words in today's text.
- For your consideration: Opening Prayer; Intercessions for guards, those in distress, virtue, justice, true sacrifice, confidence, holiness, creation; Sunday Preface IV (P32).

MUSIC
- Psalm 16
- *All Flesh is Grass* (Haugen/GIA)
- *And There Will Shine* (Repp/K&R)
- *Benedicamus* (Repp/K&R)
- *The Dawn of Day* (Deiss/NALR)
- *Little Closer* (Sexton/Resource)
- *Lord, This is the People* (Byrne/Resource)
- *Praise the Lord, My Soul* (Parker/GIA)
- *Resurrection Song* (Sexton/Resource)

SUNDAY PLANNING SHEET

Date _____

Parish focus _____

Environment & art _____

Ritual notes _____

Faith development (eg., in newsletter/classes) _____

Children's faith experience _____

Prelude _____

Hymn of gathering _____

Sprinkling/Penitential rite _____

Hymn of praise _____

Opening Prayer _____

First reading _____ Responsory _____

Second reading _____ Gospel acclamation _____

Gospel _____ Profession of faith _____

General intercessions _____

At the preparation & presentation _____

Preface dialog _____ Preface _____

Preface acclamation _____

Eucharistic prayer _____ Memorial acclamation _____

Eucharistic amen _____

The Lord's prayer _____

Breaking of bread _____

The communion hymn _____

The post-communion hymn _____

Blessing _____ At the dismissal _____

Memoranda:

THE SOLEMNITY OF CHRIST THE KING

READINGS
Daniel (7:13-14)
Once again, the image of the Son of Man is set before us. This Divine Messenger is the medium through which judgment is brought to earth and the Kingdom is visited on humanity.
Revelations (1:5-8)
Jesus Christ, Alpha and Omega, is God's faithful witness. He is the first of the new creation and as such, consecrates all who accept Him as the Lord to the service of the Father.
John (18:33-37)
Jesus testifies that he is a King and that his subjects are all those who commit themselves to the truth.

FOCUS
Jesus is judge, Lord, the beginning and the end. His faithfulness presents all with the opportunity to be faithful. All who cherish truth and sincerity are linked to Christ as their Lord. He will bring them home to the Father where they will live forever.

IDEA STARTERS
- *CCT Lectionary* (Proper 29): Jer 23:1-6; Ps 93; Rv 1:4b-8; Jn 18:33-37.
- Guide the children in building a picture of the Kingdom of God on earth.
- What is the truth of Jesus Christ for you?
- Ecumenically celebrate this last Sunday of the Church year with Evening Prayer.
- For your consideration: Hymn of Praise (*Te Deum* sung); Opening Prayer; Intercessions for all nations, nationalities, world leaders, just laws, truth, witnessing, openness to God; Christ the King Preface (P51); Eucharistic Prayer III; Memorial Acclamation D; Lord's Prayer (sung); Ordinary Solemn Blessing V.

MUSIC
- Psalm 93
- *All You Lands* (Vessels/GIA)
- *Alpha and Omega* (Repp/K&R)
- *Come, Let's Build* (Repp/K&R)
- *Hymn of Praise* (Dicie/Resource)
- *In Your Presence* (Byrne/Resource)
- *Lift High Your Hearts* (Pattersen/Resource)
- *Worthy Is the Lamb* (Jesuits/NALR)
- *You Are My Witness* (Fisherfolk/Resource)

SUNDAY PLANNING SHEET

Date _____

Parish focus _____

Environment & art _____

Ritual notes _____

Faith development (eg., in newsletter/classes) _____

Children's faith experience _____

Prelude _____

Hymn of gathering _____

Sprinkling/Penitential rite _____

Hymn of praise _____

Opening Prayer _____

First reading _____Responsory _____

Second reading _____Gospel acclamation _____

Gospel _____Profession of faith _____

General intercessions _____

At the preparation & presentation _____

Preface dialog _____Preface _____

Preface acclamation _____

Eucharistic prayer _____Memorial acclamation _____

Eucharistic amen _____

The Lord's prayer _____

Breaking of bread _____

The communion hymn _____

The post-communion hymn _____

Blessing _____At the dismissal _____

Memoranda:

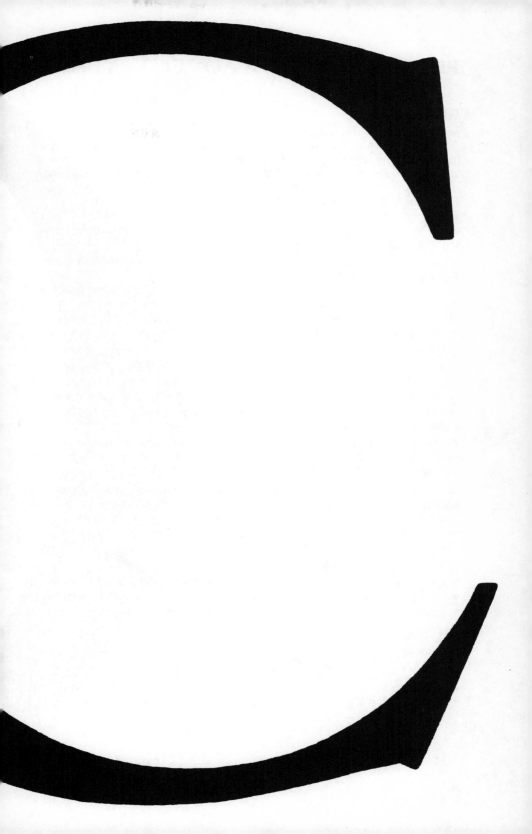

FIRST SUNDAY OF ADVENT   YEAR C

READINGS
Jeremiah (33:14-16)
As a young harpist, David was brought to the court of Saul to help alleviate his melancholy. As King David, he continued to bring hope in the midst of adversity by knitting the nation together and by meeting the many challenges to Israel.
First Thessalonians (3:12-14:2)
The word "heart" in Hebrew is not the organ of feeling but the controlling center of the personality. It is the center of human life, coordinating senses, will, and intellect.

Also in this text, "saints" refers to all people who belong to God.
Luke (21:25-28,34-36)
In this passage, constructed from quotes of Old Testament prophets, redemption should be understood as liberation. God, the source of this liberation, then "possessed" the freed people. The Holy Spirit of Jesus is in us as the promise and the first fruits of this full liberation.

FOCUS
In this beginning of the church year, we return to the roots of our rich past and our heritage. These days are an opportunity to connect our parish life to the larger human family. The focus for today might include stories or pictures of all races and types of people and might dwell on the earth as our common home.

As people of a common life in God, we mark our days and decisions with the works of our hearts. Try to demonstrate ways that the personal decisions and life-styles of our community connect with people globally.

While the word "redemption" can connote a more passive, waiting posture, liberation bespeaks personal action. When our roots are in our hearts, our nourishment and our strength springs from there. How can our families, our communities liberate each other, liberate the oppression of the larger world? How can we create the new world?

IDEA STARTERS
- *CCT Lectionary:* Jer 33:14-16; Ps 25:1-10; 1 Th 3:9-13; Lk 21:25-36.
- Plan a community celebration of the Anointing of the Sick during Advent.
- Make a "growing" Advent banner: one that is progressive.

MUSIC
- Psalm 25
- *Creator of the Stars of Night* (ICEL)
- *Little Closer* (Sexton/Resource)
- *Like the Dawn* (Sexton/Resource)
- *I Have Waited* (Gilsdorf/Resource)

- *In Your Love Remember Me* (Kendzia/NALR)
- *Help Me Lord* (Culberth/Resource)
- *Lord of Light* (Lisicky/Resource)
- *O Lord Of Life* (Lisicky/Resource)

ADVENT PLANNING SHEET

Date _____

Parish focus _____

Environment & art _____

Ritual notes _____

Faith development (eg., bulletin item) _____

Children's faith experience _____

Prelude _____

Hymn of gathering _____

Sprinkling baptismal water acclamation _____

Penitential rite_____Opening Prayer _____

Responsory _____Gospel acclamation _____

General intercessions _____

At the preparation & presentation _____

Preface dialogue _____Preface _____

Preface acclamation _____

Eucharistic prayer _____Memorial acclamation _____

Eucharistic amen _____

The Lord's prayer _____

Breaking of bread _____

The communion hymn _____

The post-communion hymn _____

Blessing _____At the dismissal _____

Memoranda:

SECOND SUNDAY OF ADVENT

YEAR C

READINGS

Baruch (5:1-9)
Working as a scribe for Jeremiah, Baruch produced this vision of life as Jerusalem clothed in glory.

Philippians (1:4-6,8-11)
Paul's theme is built around thanksgiving for and partnership with the community. He urges inward preparation. You can develop this in a way which de-emphasizes our sinfulness and guilt and focuses more on the beauty of a life prepared for Christ.

Luke (3:1-6)
Luke contrasts the powers we recognize with the authority and power of the Word of God. He urges a renewal of moral and spiritual arenas, leading to new power in God.

FOCUS

This theme seeks to develop the inward preparations for the season. In realizing our global connectedness, we also look inwardly for connectedness psychically, spiritually, physically, and communally. This inward renewal is symbolized here by the bloom of the Christmas Poinsettia.

Focus could include personal qualities such as integrity, peace, honor, and devotedness. How do we bring these into the larger community?

Who are the "authorities" of our lives — governmental, medical, educational, hierarchical. Can any of these match the personal power Christ brings in us?

The development of this theme has the opportunity to be positive and based on a bright and attractive future from renewal rather than a dour repentance theme.

IDEA STARTERS

- *CCT Lectionary:* Bar 5:1-9 or Mac 3:1-4; Ps 126; Ph 1:3-11; Lk 3:1-6.
- Announce a vigil service of prayers and hymns for the Feast of the Immaculate Conception.
- As the eve of St. Nicholas' feast, this Sunday could be a special celebration for the children.
- Bless expectant women this Sunday. Plan to bless them and their newborns as each "appears," emphasizing the need of waiting.

MUSIC

- Psalm 126
- *Abba, Father* (Landry/NALR)
- *Go Up To the Mountain* (Weston Priory)
- *Prepare Ye The Way* (Johnson/Resource)
- *Prepare! The Lord Is Near* (Amann/Resource)
- *Consolation* (Gilsdorf/Resource)

ADVENT PLANNING SHEET

Date _____

Parish focus _____

Environment & art _____

Ritual notes _____

Faith development (eg., bulletin item) _____

Children's faith experience _____

Prelude _____

Hymn of gathering _____

Sprinkling baptismal water acclamation _____

Penitential rite_____Opening Prayer _____

Responsory _____Gospel acclamation _____

General intercessions _____

At the preparation & presentation _____

Preface dialogue _____Preface _____

Preface acclamation _____

Eucharistic prayer _____Memorial acclamation _____

Eucharistic amen _____

The Lord's prayer _____

Breaking of bread _____

The communion hymn _____

The post-communion hymn _____

Blessing _____At the dismissal _____

Memoranda:

THIRD SUNDAY
OF ADVENT

YEAR C

READINGS

Zephaniah (3:14–18a)
Like the prophetic line to which he belongs, Zephaniah writes a story of salvation, promising joy and restoration to Jerusalem. This would be a good time to show the ways we trust in the Lord in our times that will bring us into the future.

Philippians (4:4–7)
Within our time the Lord is present to us and in all our activities. We can celebrate the life of the community and the diverse ways we show God's love in educational, ministerial or justice projects; personal counseling, socials, youth and elderly work, etc.

Luke (3:10–18)
Luke in describing "good news" here really describes a message of forgiveness and the beginning of a new relationship between God and humanity. He is very prescriptive, telling us what precisely to do within this new relationship.

FOCUS

The development of these Advent readings leads us from connection to the global community, and connection within ourselves, to connections with our immediate neighbors. This could be a good week to celebrate the accomplishments of the community and to suggest new areas in which we do not now respond.

At a time of world-wide economic plight, we give not from our extra, but from our sustenance. The need to look inward and to connect with those outside us will put us in touch with the wealth we have.

This could be a good time to recall the alternative Christmas movement and highlight ways to recycle goods and services as gifts. We could create from our homes and our skills rather than to continue the exploitations of the marketplace.

IDEA STARTERS

- *CCT Lectionary:* Zeph 3:14–20; Is 12:2–6; Ph 4:4–9; Lk 3:7–18.
- This is Gaudete Sunday. Have a special hospitality time after Mass, perhaps with games and activities for families.
- Instead of the Penitential Rite, use the Rite of Blessing and Sprinkling of Water this Sunday.

MUSIC

- Psalm Isaiah 12
- *And the Father Will Dance* (Landry/NALR)
- *Eye Has Not Seen* (Haugen/GIA)
- *Zephaniah's Song* (Andersen/Resource)
- *Nothing Is Greater* (Toolan/Resource)
- *Shout For Joy* (Byrne/Resource)
- *Joyful Dawning* (Davis/Resource)
- *The Lord Is Coming* (Tucciarone/Resource)

ADVENT PLANNING SHEET

Date _____

Parish focus _____

Environment & art _____

Ritual notes _____

Faith development (eg., bulletin item) _____

Children's faith experience _____

Prelude _____

Hymn of gathering _____

Sprinkling baptismal water acclamation _____

Penitential rite_____Opening Prayer _____

Responsory _____Gospel acclamation _____

General intercessions _____

At the preparation & presentation _____

Preface dialogue _____Preface _____

Preface acclamation _____

Eucharistic prayer _____Memorial acclamation _____

Eucharistic amen _____

The Lord's prayer _____

Breaking of bread _____

The communion hymn _____

The post-communion hymn _____

Blessing _____At the dismissal _____

Memoranda:

FOURTH SUNDAY OF ADVENT

YEAR C

READINGS

Micah (5:1-4)
The prophecy is considered a vision in which, like David, the Shepherd-King will come from Bethlehem and a lesser clan of Israel.

Hebrews (10:5-10)
Rather than the formal sacrifices that were traditionally offered to please God, here Christ offers himself, dedicating his life to the will of God.

Luke (1:39-45)
The visitation of Mary is from the Jewish tradition of Midrash, or narrative storytelling. It is used here to explain the correlated missions of John the Baptist and Jesus. Mary's faith and courage are in direct contrast to the disbelief of Zachariah.

FOCUS

As we remember the spirit of Christ, incarnate in this season, the challenge of fidelity to his message meets us. We need to dwell on those things which sustain us personally and in the community this year.

The symbol of the holly-berry wreath is a cue to celebrate actions of your community which model fidelity: the anniversaries of priests, married couples, long-term justice projects the community maintains, building projects, etc.

Christmas, beyond the child Christ, also connects us to the joy and hope we hold for building a renewed life, a new earth.

IDEA STARTERS

- *CCT Lectionary:* Mk 5:2-5a; Ps 80:1-7; Heb 10:5-10; Lk 1:39-55.
- Announce the night this week when the parish Christmas Tree will be decorated. Invite each family to bring a homemade ornament. After decorating is done, bless the tree.
- A little research could provide ample material for a bulletin article on the meaning and origins of some of the many symbols of Christmas.

MUSIC

- Psalm 80
- *Amazing Grace* (Traditional)
- *Canticle of the Sun* (Haugen/GIA)
- *Earthen Vessels* (Jesuits/NALR)

- *You Shall Stand Fast* (Toolan/Resource)
- *In Your Presence* (Byrne/Resource)
- *Here I Am* (Lisicky/Resource)
- *Advent Song* (Prochaska/Resource)

ADVENT PLANNING SHEET

Date _____

Parish focus _____

Environment & art _____

Ritual notes _____

Faith development (eg., bulletin item) _____

Children's faith experience _____

Prelude _____

Hymn of gathering _____

Sprinkling baptismal water acclamation _____

Penitential rite_____ Opening Prayer _____

Responsory _____ Gospel acclamation _____

General intercessions _____

At the preparation & presentation _____

Preface dialogue _____ Preface _____

Preface acclamation _____

Eucharistic prayer _____ Memorial acclamation _____

Eucharistic amen _____

The Lord's prayer _____

Breaking of bread _____

The communion hymn _____

The post-communion hymn _____

Blessing _____ At the dismissal _____

Memoranda:

CHRISTMAS MASS VIGIL

YEARS A,B AND C

(See Year A For All Readings And Commentary)

CHRISTMASTIME PLANNING SHEET Date _____

Parish focus _____

Environment & art _____

Ritual notes _____

Faith development (eg., audit ed.) _____

Children's faith experience _____

Prelude _____

Hymn of gathering _____

Sprinkling baptismal water _____

Gloria in excelsis _____

Opening Prayer _____

Responsory _____

First reading _____ Responsory _____

Second reading _____ Gospel acclamation _____

Gospel _____ Profession of faith _____

General intercessions _____

At the preparation & presentation _____

Preface dialogue _____ Preface _____

Preface acclamation _____

Eucharistic prayer _____ Memorial acclamation ____

Eucharistic amen _____

The Lord's prayer _____

Breaking of bread _____

The communion hymn _____

The post-communion hymn _____

Blessing _____ At the dismissal _____

Memoranda:

CHRISTMAS MASS AT MIDNIGHT

YEAR C

(See Year A For Further Commentary)

READINGS

Isaiah (9:1-7)
While this passage was probably written to celebrate the ascendency of an Israelite king, here it describes the coming Messiah as our ideal king. He contains all the best qualities of our heroes and his reign will be known by justice and peace. The passage is a joyful, celebrational one because light and freedom have won.

Titus (2:11-14)
Since we read this at Christmas, the sense of the arrival of grace can sometimes be overshadowed by the arrival of Jesus. We can live in hope, in spite of the evils of our times, because grace shows us the ways of faith.

Luke (2:1-14)
For Luke this is the centralpiece of the narrative of Christ's birth and it firmly places Christ within the lines of Davidic origin. Luke portrays the shepherds as welcoming and hospitable, while the villagers are not, in order to set up the context of this gospel as addressed to the Gentile community. The angelic song of praise is directed both to God and to people in order to show God's favor.

FOCUS:

Jesus' birth story connects us each year to the revelation of God's word and wisdom. Our task is to reflect on where God's wisdom is present in our community and in our personal lives. What insights, awarenesses or knowledge have come to us this year? What activities have given birth to a fuller presence of God? What "Light and Freedom" do we celebrate?

CHRISTMASTIME PLANNING SHEET Date _____

Parish focus _____

Environment & art _____

Ritual notes _____

Faith development (eg., audit ed.) _____

Children's faith experience _____

Prelude _____

Hymn of gathering _____

Sprinkling baptismal water _____

Gloria in excelsis _____

Opening Prayer _____

Responsory _____

First reading _____Responsory _____

Second reading _____Gospel acclamation _____

Gospel _____Profession of faith _____

General intercessions _____

At the preparation & presentation _____

Preface dialogue _____Preface _____

Preface acclamation _____

Eucharistic prayer _____Memorial acclamation _____

Eucharistic amen _____

The Lord's prayer _____

Breaking of bread _____

The communion hymn _____

The post-communion hymn _____

Blessing _____At the dismissal _____

Memoranda:

CHRISTMAS MASS AT DAWN

YEARS A,B AND C

(See Year A For All Readings And Commentary)

CHRISTMASTIME PLANNING SHEET   Date _____

Parish focus _____

Environment & art _____

Ritual notes _____

Faith development (eg., audit ed.) _____

Children's faith experience _____

Prelude _____

Hymn of gathering _____

Sprinkling baptismal water _____

Gloria in excelsis _____

Opening Prayer _____

Responsory _____

First reading _____ Responsory _____

Second reading _____ Gospel acclamation _____

Gospel _____ Profession of faith _____

General intercessions _____

At the preparation & presentation _____

Preface dialogue _____ Preface _____

Preface acclamation _____

Eucharistic prayer _____ Memorial acclamation _____

Eucharistic amen _____

The Lord's prayer _____

Breaking of bread _____

The communion hymn _____

The post-communion hymn _____

Blessing _____ At the dismissal _____

Memoranda:

(See Year A For Further Commentary)

READINGS

Isaiah (52:7-10)
The story told here is literally a picture of Israel returning from exile and the joy at her restoration. For us it symbolizes the birth of Jesus and the peace we have in the revelation of God's word.

Hebrews (1:1-6)
This opening of Hebrews may be part of a primitive hymn to the wisdom of God. Here it is used to describe Jesus as a reflection and representation of God. Jesus' stature above angels places him, as word and wisdom, present in the creation of the universe.

John (1:1-18)
Again, the importance of wisdom to the Jewish people is emphasized by the style of this poem. God is portrayed as an active, dynamic reality and the Son is captured by the four figures of word, life, light and son.

CHRISTMASTIME PLANNING SHEET Date _____

Parish focus _____

Environment & art _____

Ritual notes _____

Faith development (eg., audit ed.) _____

Children's faith experience _____

Prelude _____

Hymn of gathering _____

Sprinkling baptismal water _____

Gloria in excelsis _____

Opening Prayer _____

Responsory _____

First reading _____Responsory _____

Second reading _____Gospel acclamation _____

Gospel _____Profession of faith _____

General intercessions _____

At the preparation & presentation _____

Preface dialogue _____Preface _____

Preface acclamation _____

Eucharistic prayer _____Memorial acclamation _____

Eucharistic amen _____

The Lord's prayer _____

Breaking of bread _____

The communion hymn _____

The post-communion hymn _____

Blessing _____At the dismissal _____

Memoranda:

FEAST OF THE HOLY FAMILY

YEAR C

(See Year A For First Two Readings And Further Commentary)

READINGS

Sirach (3:3-7,14-17)
Sirach, who ran an academy for young men, collected the sayings or "wisdom" of the people into this book. Wisdom was a practical approach to life within a religious or moral context. Here the example is of the expectations of children in family life and the rewards for such action.

Colossians (3:12-21)
Paralleling the Sirach expectations, this piece highlights the role of the Christian family. Arising from the teachings of Christ, these practical suggestions were signs of spiritual maturity. Paul's wisdom speaks to the family relations of his times.

Luke (2:41-52)
While this story serves as a conclusion to Luke's Infancy Narrative and as a transition to the recording of Jesus' public life, it also continues to highlight the symbol of wisdom and of family expectations. The concentration of wisdom in the child is special, yet he remains within the correct actions of the Law.

FOCUS

Focus for today might include how we live the message of Christ's wisdom. Include more than the traditional family in your planning. Family today means also the homes of singles and single parents, and couples who have no children. At its broadest, family could be talked about as human family or global family, and include our actions toward folks everywhere on earth.

IDEA STARTERS

- *CCT Lectionary:* Is 63:7-9; Ps 11; Heb 2:10-18; Mt 2:13-15, 19-23.
- Today's readings lend themselves to special developments, such as: members of a family proclaiming them, or a family delivering the homily. Let grandparent/grandchildren combinations carry gifts or lead the Prayers of the Faithful.
- This Sunday's infamous second reading is very poetic. Its meaning and background need to be shared (perhaps in your parish bulletin).
- Would a ritual of reaffirming marriage vows following the homily be appropriate today?
- For your consideration: omit the penitential rite and sing a simple (brief) setting of the *Glory to God* throughout the Christmas season; have an alternative opening prayer; include prayers for single people, priests and religious, as well as for families in the intercession; Christmas Preface II (P4); Eucharistic Prayer I w/proper; Prayer Over the People No.2, 8, 9, 20, 22 or 23.

MUSIC

- Psalm 128
- *As a Family* (Page/Resource
- *As a Little Child* (Gilsdorf/Resource)
- *Dwelling Place* (Jesuits/NALR)
- *Happy are the Ones* (Jesuits/NALR)

- *In a Lowly Manger Born* (Yuki/LBW)
- *Hark the Herald Angels Sing* (Christmas carol)
- *In Love We Gather* (Schafer/WLP)
- *Like Olive Branches* (Deiss/WLP)

CHRISTMASTIME PLANNING SHEET Date _____

Parish focus _____

Environment & art _____

Ritual notes _____

Faith development (eg., audit ed.) _____

Children's faith experience _____

Prelude _____

Hymn of gathering _____

Sprinkling baptismal water _____

Gloria in excelsis _____

Opening Prayer _____

Responsory _____

First reading _____ Responsory _____

Second reading _____ Gospel acclamation _____

Gospel _____ Profession of faith _____

General intercessions _____

At the preparation & presentation _____

Preface dialogue _____ Preface _____

Preface acclamation _____

Eucharistic prayer _____ Memorial acclamation _____

Eucharistic amen _____

The Lord's prayer _____

Breaking of bread _____

The communion hymn _____

The post-communion hymn _____

Blessing _____ At the dismissal _____

Memoranda:

SOLEMNITY OF MARY THE MOTHER OF GOD

YEARS A, B, AND C

(See Year A For All Readings And Further Commentary)

READINGS
Numbers (6:22–27)
Galatians (4:4–7)
Luke (2:16–21)

FOCUS
In the past God spoke to the people of old by the prophets, but now He speaks to us in the Eternal Word, who became incarnate from the Virgin Mary, and was Jesus.

And by being born of a woman, the Son has transformed all creation, graciously blessing all that the Father has designed.

Idea Starters:
- The first reading with its appointed psalm may provide background for a "New Year's Day Homily."
- For your consideration in planning the Marian feast: sung *Glory to God;* alternate Opening Prayer; prayers for future mothers, all mothers, the new year, respect for the name of Jesus, and peace in the intercessions; Christmas Preface I (P3); Eucharistic Prayer I w/Christmas proper; Solemn Blessing of Christmas or St. Mary.
- For your consideration in planning the Mass for Peace: sung *Glory to God;* Christmas Preface II (P4); Solemn Blessing for the New Year.

MUSIC
- *The Beautiful Mother* (Jesuits/NALR)
- *Hail Mary: Gentle Woman* (Landry/NALR)
- *The Lord Bless You* (Scholtes/FEL)
- *Mary's Canticle* (any setting)
- *What Child Is This—*

CHRISTMASTIME PLANNING SHEET Date _____

Parish focus _____

Environment & art _____

Ritual notes _____

Faith development (eg., audit ed.) _____

Children's faith experience _____

Prelude _____

Hymn of gathering _____

Sprinkling baptismal water _____

Gloria in excelsis _____

Opening Prayer _____

Responsory _____

First reading _____Responsory _____

Second reading _____Gospel acclamation _____

Gospel _____Profession of faith _____

General intercessions _____

At the preparation & presentation _____

Preface dialogue _____Preface _____

Preface acclamation _____

Eucharistic prayer _____Memorial acclamation _____

Eucharistic amen _____

The Lord's prayer _____

Breaking of bread _____

The communion hymn _____

The post-communion hymn _____

Blessing _____At the dismissal _____

Memoranda:

SOLEMNITY OF EPIPHANY

YEARS A,B AND C

(See Year A For All Readings And Further Commentary)

READINGS
Isaiah (60:1-6)
Ephesians (3:2-3,5-6)
Matthew (2:1-12)

FOCUS
By faith, "we have seen this star in the east" and have had our path of life illuminated by our gracious God. Now, living the life of faith, we witness to the universality of God's love, that every person may come to adore the Lord.

IDEA STARTERS
- The professional cross might have a "star" designed around it, for if we follow the star, it leads us to the cross of Christ, our glorious salvation.
- Is the *Epiphany Day Home Blessing* a cherished custom by members in your parish? This might be a good opportunity for pastoral outreach during this final week of the Christmas season. (See *Book of Occasional Services,* published by the Church Hymnal Corporation, New York.)

CHRISTMASTIME PLANNING SHEET Date _____

Parish focus _____

Environment & art _____

Ritual notes _____

Faith development (eg., audit ed.) _____

Children's faith experience _____

Prelude _____

Hymn of gathering _____

Sprinkling baptismal water _____

Gloria in excelsis _____

Opening Prayer _____

Responsory _____

First reading _____ Responsory _____

Second reading _____ Gospel acclamation _____

Gospel _____ Profession of faith _____

General intercessions _____

At the preparation & presentation _____

Preface dialogue _____ Preface _____

Preface acclamation _____

Eucharistic prayer _____ Memorial acclamation _____

Eucharistic amen _____

The Lord's prayer _____

Breaking of bread _____

The communion hymn _____

The post-communion hymn _____

Blessing _____ At the dismissal _____

Memoranda:

SECOND SUNDAY AFTER CHRISTMAS

YEARS A,B AND C

(See Year A For All Readings And Commentary)

CHRISTMASTIME PLANNING SHEET Date _____

Parish focus _____

Environment & art _____

Ritual notes _____

Faith development (eg., audit ed.) _____

Children's faith experience _____

Prelude _____

Hymn of gathering _____

Sprinkling baptismal water _____

Gloria in excelsis _____

Opening Prayer _____

Responsory _____

First reading _____Responsory _____

Second reading _____Gospel acclamation _____

Gospel _____Profession of faith _____

General intercessions _____

At the preparation & presentation _____

Preface dialogue _____Preface _____

Preface acclamation _____

Eucharistic prayer _____Memorial acclamation _____

Eucharistic amen _____

The Lord's prayer _____

Breaking of bread _____

The communion hymn _____

The post-communion hymn _____

Blessing _____At the dismissal _____

Memoranda:

FEAST OF THE
BAPTISM OF THE LORD

YEAR C

(See Year A For First Two Readings And Further Commentary)

READINGS

Isaiah (42:1-4,6-7)
Called the first servant song, this passage can be read as the individual's or the nation's role as a servant. To be a servant was the response of the humble person to God's occurrence in life. This response was characterized by teaching and restoring justice.

Acts of the Apostle (10:34-38)
The core message of Jesus' life is capsulized here and this was probably used for teaching. Also this message was extended to all people and not just the Jewish community.

Luke (3:15-16,21-22)
As the last of the major prophets, John stands on the edge of a new time like Moses on the edge of the promised land. The community which formed as a result of John's preaching became the place of entry for Jesus and the new relationship he brought with God. Note the reference to prayer, a part of many major stories of Jesus and for us a symbol of connectedness to the divine will.

FOCUS

The wisdom of connections could be explored this week. Seeking connections is a way to understand how our decisions and attitudes affect others in our neighborhoods, and others globally. Seeking the connections between our work lives and our home lives, between our public and private selves, between our personal, individual experiences of life and community life. How do we become whole? How do we become integrated persons in a destructive and isolating society?

IDEA STARTERS

- *CCT Lectionary:* Is 61:1-4; Ps 29; Acts 8:14-17; Lk 3:15-17, 21-22.
- Does your parish truly celebrate this day as the last day of the Christmas season?.
- The public celebration of baptism has long been associated with the theme of this liturgy. How might our planning team demonstrate the relationship between the Paschal mystery and the Christmas "epiphany"?
- Have members of your assembly experienced a festive "infant" baptism in the context of the Sunday eucharist? How about today?
- Would a baptism vigil with parents and sponsors of children to be baptized, joined by the celebrating assembly and any catechumens to be baptized at the Easter Vigil, be an effective Saturday evening liturgy? (See *Book of Occasional Services.*) Follow the celebration with a potluck supper.
- For your consideration: *Rite of Baptism for Children;* Sprinkling Baptismal Water; sung *Glory to God;* alternate opening prayer; prayers for those preparing for baptism, the newly baptized, and all the baptized in the intercessions.

MUSIC
- Psalm 29
- *The Church's One Foundation* (Traditional)
- *Beginning Today* (Dameans/NALR)
- *For Us To Live* (Weston Priory)
- *Lift Up Your Heads* (Keyes/Resource)
- *Here I Am, Lord* (Jesuits/NALR)
- *Lord, You Have Probed Me* (Gilsdorf/Resource)

CHRISTMASTIME PLANNING SHEET Date _____

Parish focus _____

Environment & art _____

Ritual notes _____

Faith development (eg., audit ed.) _____

Children's faith experience _____

Prelude _____

Hymn of gathering _____

Sprinkling baptismal water _____

Gloria in excelsis _____

Opening Prayer _____

Responsory _____

First reading _____Responsory _____

Second reading _____Gospel acclamation _____

Gospel _____Profession of faith _____

General intercessions _____

At the preparation & presentation _____

Preface dialogue _____Preface _____

Preface acclamation _____

Eucharistic prayer _____Memorial acclamation _____

Eucharistic amen _____

The Lord's prayer _____

Breaking of bread _____

The communion hymn _____

The post-communion hymn _____

Blessing _____At the dismissal _____

Memoranda:

ASH WEDNESDAY

(See Year A For All Readings And Commentary)

YEARS A,
B AND C

LENTEN PLANNING SHEET

Date _____

Parish focus _____

Environment & art _____

Ritual notes _____

Faith development (eg., midweek program) _____

Children's faith experience _____

Prelude _____

Hymn of gathering _____

Penitential rite _____

Opening Prayer _____

Reading cycle _____First reading _____

Responsory _____Second reading _____

Lenten gospel acclamation _____Gospel _____

RCIA rites & acclamations _____

General intercessions _____

At the preparation & presentation _____

Preface dialog _____Preface _____

Preface acclamation _____

Eucharistic prayer _____Memorial acclamation ____

Eucharistic amen _____

The Lord's prayer _____

Breaking of bread _____

The communion hymn _____

The post-communion hymn _____

Blessing _____At the dismissal _____

Memoranda:

FIRST SUNDAY OF LENT   YEAR C

READINGS
Deuteronomy (26:4-10)
The setting of this Scripture is a festival where the first fruits of the year are brought to the sanctuary. It tells the story of God's power in the Exodus. Note the key transition where the story switches from a tale of the father to the first person. It points to the transition from historical to personal faith.
Romans (10:8-13)
For the Christian Church, the focus of our belief changes from the Exodus to Jesus. His resurrection forms the basis of our belief in salvation.
Luke (4:1-13)
Traveling in a desert of demons, Jesus has a personal exodus. The temptation serves as a focus for his role as Messiah. He chooses not the political and material leadership that is offered, but rather, a more humble faithful path.

FOCUS
In the passage to life which is Lent, the Exodus is the initial symbol. These scriptures depict both the individuals and the community in the passage. What is common is the virtue of courage needed by both to move from the traps of easy political, material, or psychically safe solutions.

Begin with courage in your planning. What are modern symbols of it in your community? Tell stories of people you have met who have met life with noticable courage. How is individual courage different from that of a community when it faces a problem?

How can we help people review their lives as they face the renewal asked for in Lent? Traditional services of the stations of the cross, vespers, and novenas are best for only part of our congregations. For others to confront the "easy" solutions, widely differing events may be needed.

IDEA STARTERS
- *CCT Lectionary:* Dt. 26:1-11; Ps 91:9-16; Rm 10:86-13; Lk 4:1-13
- The "Rite of Election" from the *Rite of Christian Initiation of Adults* may appropriately be celebrated at today's liturgy.
- Lent is a time for becoming free again in God's spirit by purifying and cleansing our lives. How might the decor of your worship area reflect this?
- Have chant-like melodies fallen into disuse in your parish? Their power to evoke meditation and reflection are most appropriate during this season.
- For your consideration: a Penitential Rite, with a Greek *Kyrie* (throughout the season); omit *Glory to God* (throughout the season); Opening Prayer; Lenten Gospel Acclamation; Intercession for conversion, for just governments, and for faith in God's promise; First Lenten Sunday Preface (P12) or Reconciliation Eucharistic Prayer I; Memorial Acclamation "D"; Prayer Over the People 5.

MUSIC
- Psalm 91
- *Be Not Afraid* (Jesuits/NALR)
- *Forty Days and Forty Nights* (Traditional)
- *Hosea* (Weston Priory)
- *Like the Dawn* (Sexton/Resource)
- *New Life* (Lawrence/Resource)
- *Trust In the Lord* (Jesuits/NALR)
- *Like Olive Branches* (Deiss/WLP)|

LENTEN PLANNING SHEET

Date _____

Parish focus _____

Environment & art _____

Ritual notes _____

Faith development (eg., midweek program) _____

Children's faith experience _____

Prelude _____

Hymn of gathering _____

Penitential rite _____

Opening Prayer _____

Reading cycle _____ First reading _____

Responsory _____ Second reading _____

Lenten gospel acclamation _____ Gospel _____

RCIA rites & acclamations _____

General intercessions _____

At the preparation & presentation _____

Preface dialog _____ Preface _____

Preface acclamation _____

Eucharistic prayer _____ Memorial acclamation ____

Eucharistic amen _____

The Lord's prayer _____

Breaking of bread _____

The communion hymn _____

The post-communion hymn _____

Blessing _____ At the dismissal _____

Memoranda:

SECOND SUNDAY OF LENT   YEAR C

READINGS
Genesis (15:5-12,17-18)
Abraham's covenant may be the strongest symbol of Old Testament assurance of God's continued concern. The ancient covenant ritual depicts the severed animals as the fate of the two parties who break it, while the birds of prey are the dangers that threaten it. And all the elements of God's power are present in the setting sun, the deep and tremor and darkness.
Philippians (3:17-4:1)
This urging from Paul asks us to remain faithful to the gift from God. He talks about the rewards of such steadiness and seeks the example of Christians for those about him.
Luke (9:28-36)
The Transfiguration begins as a prayer event for the disciples, but it quickly turns into a religious experience. This repeats the message of the baptismal scene in which God confirms the power of Jesus. He is seen here as the fulfillment of these Old Testament figures.

FOCUS
A second major symbol of the passage to life is the covenant. It functions for us as the promise of God's presence and attention. It reassures us of our specialness and uniqueness (consciousness) in a world full of the common (unconsciousness).

The covenant also represents the agreement, conscious and unconscious, which we make with ourselves and our families. An exploration of these agreements is essential to any process of renewal. How can we liturgically assist this beyond the traditional reconciliation rites of the season?

What are the major promises within your parish community? What covenants have been set up between the people and the church, between the church and its employees?

IDEA STARTERS
- *CCT Lectionary:* Gn 15:1-12, 17-18; Ps 127; Ph 3:17-4:1; Lk 13:31-35 or Lk 9:28-36.
- Are the Sundays in Lent truly celebrated as "little Easters"? How are the Lenten Sundays uniquely celebrated?
- Does your parish celebrate weekly Sunday evening prayer? Use Genesis 15:17 as a title for an explanatory bulletin article inviting your assembly to celebrate Vespers.
- "...went up to a mountain to pray." Do you have a list of retreat centers and monasteries in your area available for the asking?
- How is the symbol of the cross (representing our Lord's passion) used throughout Lent?
- For your consideration: Intercessions for parents, a firm faith in the Lord, and unfearful proclamation of the good news; Second Lenten Sunday Preface (P13); Eucharistic Prayer III; Memorial Acclamation "B"; Prayer Over the People 7.

MUSIC

- Psalm 27
- *Abba Father* (Landry/NALR)
- *Abba, Father* (Gilsdorf/Resource)
- *I Am the Light* (Repp/A&V Music)

- *The Lord is My Light* (Jesuits/NALR)
- *Taste and See* (Gilsdorf/Resource)
- *Transfiguration* (Landry/NALR)
- *Immortal, Invisible God Only Wise* (Traditional)

LENTEN PLANNING SHEET

Date _____

Parish focus _____

Environment & art _____

Ritual notes _____

Faith development (eg., midweek program) _____

Children's faith experience _____

Prelude _____

Hymn of gathering _____

Penitential rite _____

Opening Prayer _____

Reading cycle _____First reading _____

Responsory _____Second reading _____

Lenten gospel acclamation _____Gospel _____

RCIA rites & acclamations _____

General intercessions _____

At the preparation & presentation _____

Preface dialog _____Preface _____

Preface acclamation _____

Eucharistic prayer _____Memorial acclamation _____

Eucharistic amen _____

The Lord's prayer _____

Breaking of bread _____

The communion hymn _____

The post-communion hymn _____

Blessing _____At the dismissal _____

Memoranda:

THIRD SUNDAY OF LENT   YEAR C

READINGS
Exodus (3:1-8,13-15)
In the polytheistic Middle East, it was important for Moses to know the name of the God he encountered. The overwhelming power of God was dangerous to mere mortals; hence Moses responded with the ancient custom of removing his sandles. "I Am Who Am" may be better translated as "I am the cause of what comes into existence." Knowing God's name opens up the possibility of relationship.

First Corinthians: (10:1-6,10-12)
Paul may be connecting the sacraments of baptism and eucharist to the Exodus events. The protection of God, seen here as a cloud, is now extended to the Christians. He warns against making the same mistake of overconfidence as the Jews.

Luke (13:1-9)
Repentance is clearly the goal of Luke in this scripture. God's mercy is like that of the tender gardener with patience for the slow ones. But, there is also the underlying theme that failure to repent leads to destruction.

FOCUS
If we move through Lent as a passage to life and if we have explored the covenants we act by, the next major step is to seek repentance for the barriers we have created.

To explore the "phony" places of our world, involve your parish's teenagers. No one is more keenly in touch with what is real and precious as adolescents. Their critique of the world is painful and easy to disregard as the misunderstanding of the young.

Young people are also aware of the power and presence of God in life. In nature, in relationships, in personal dreams, they see the wonder that is God. Use their talents this Sunday. They could prepare a skit about the Gospel or the story of Moses meeting God. They could design the reconciliation service focusing on the phoniness of the world.

IDEA STARTERS
- *CCT Lectionary:* Ex 3:1-15; Ps 103:1-13; 1 Cor 16:1-13; Lk 13:1-9.
- If you have catechumens to be baptized at Easter, have them gather at the day's principal eucharist, using readings and chants from cycle A of the Lectionary.
- What is our attitude toward the Lord when we approach him?
- The Lord's mercy is more than simple forgiveness. How might a more versatile understanding of God's mercy be presented?
- As we come to the midpoint of Lent is our lenten discipline taking root and bearing fruit?
- For your consideration: Intercessions for the stewardship of God's creation, the descendants of Abraham, Isaac and Jacob, and for the victims of natural disasters; Lenten Preface II or Reconciliation Eucharistic Prayer I; Prayer Over the People 6.

MUSIC

- Psalm 103
- *Magnificat* (Schoenbachler/NALR)
- *Hosea* (Weston Priory)
- *On the Road* (Wood/Resource)
- *Penitential Hymn* (Conry/NALR)
- *Praise the Lord, My Soul* (Jesuits/NALR)
- *Song of Thanksgiving* (Dicie/Resource)
- *Turn to Me* (Jesuits/NALR)

LENTEN PLANNING SHEET

Date _____

Parish focus _____

Environment & art _____

Ritual notes _____

Faith development (eg., midweek program) _____

Children's faith experience _____

Prelude _____

Hymn of gathering _____

Penitential rite _____

Opening Prayer _____

Reading cycle _____First reading _____

Responsory _____Second reading _____

Lenten gospel acclamation _____Gospel _____

RCIA rites & acclamations _____

General intercessions _____

At the preparation & presentation _____

Preface dialog _____Preface _____

Preface acclamation _____

Eucharistic prayer _____Memorial acclamation _____

Eucharistic amen _____

The Lord's prayer _____

Breaking of bread _____

The communion hymn _____

The post-communion hymn _____

Blessing _____At the dismissal _____

Memoranda:

FOURTH SUNDAY OF LENT   YEAR C

READINGS
Joshua (5:9,10–12)
This covenant story is about the community rather than one individual. It takes place just before entering the promised land and Joshua completes a circumcision ceremony on those not previously circumcised. It symbolizes full membership in the community and membership in the covenant with God.
Second Corinthians: (5:12–17)
Jesus is the cause of a new creation, a new way of being in the world. His redemptive life brings everyone into the community. The world is reconciled to God through him.
Luke (15:1–3,11–32)
A keen distinction is made here between the God who forgives warmly and those who do not understand love. Jesus is the symbolic son who restores unity with God; God is given the qualities of patience and forgiveness.

FOCUS
When we remove our barriers, when we forgive ourselves, we can move on to the forgiveness of those in our lives. Their inclusion in our world is modeled twice by these scriptures; inclusion in the community and inclusion in interpersonal relationships.

The test of our renewal is our ability to extend warmth to everyone. Too often we limit ourselves to those who look like us, act like us, vote like us. Who needs to be brought into our community? Within the RCIA process the catechumenate will enter our church during this time. How does the community prepare for them? Who has left us that could be invited back at this time?

The return of the son who left is the archetypal story of forgiveness. It reminds us to search our lives for the unforgiven, for the unsettled people and events.

IDEA STARTERS
- *CCT Lectionary:* Josh 5:9–12; Ps 34:1–8; 2 Cor 5:16–21; Lk 15:1–3, 11–32.
- When catechumens are present, use readings from cycle A of the Lectionary.
- Is it possible to preach about today's gospel without "identifying" the prodigal son, the self-righteous son, or the forgiving father?
- What was the runaway son's motivation to return? (See Luke 15:17)
- How might a catechesis on the revised rites of reconciliation flow out of today's readings?
- For your consideration: Intercessions for the early harvest, the hungry, for landowners, and for the reconciliation of all peoples; Lenten Preface I or Reconciliation Eucharistic Prayer II; Prayer Over the People 4.

MUSIC
- Psalm 34
- *Amazing Grace* (Traditional)
- *Hosea* (Weston Priory)
- *My Son Has Gone Away* (Jesuits/NALR)
- *Prodigal Children* (Schoenbachler/NALR)
- *Prodigal Son* (Culbreth/Resource)
- *Taste And See* (Huges/Resource)
- *Yes, I Shall Arise* (Deiss, WLP)

LENTEN PLANNING SHEET

Date _____

Parish focus _____

Environment & art _____

Ritual notes _____

Faith development (eg., midweek program) _____

Children's faith experience _____

Prelude _____

Hymn of gathering _____

Penitential rite _____

Opening Prayer _____

Reading cycle _____ First reading _____

Responsory _____ Second reading _____

Lenten gospel acclamation _____ Gospel _____

RCIA rites & acclamations _____

General intercessions _____

At the preparation & presentation _____

Preface dialog _____ Preface _____

Preface acclamation _____

Eucharistic prayer _____ Memorial acclamation _____

Eucharistic amen _____

The Lord's prayer _____

Breaking of bread _____

The communion hymn _____

The post-communion hymn _____

Blessing _____ At the dismissal _____

Memoranda:

FIFTH SUNDAY OF LENT YEAR C

READINGS
Isaiah (43:16-21)
Isaiah's theme centers on a new "exodus." Like the original one God is portrayed as leading the people to redemption and love.
Philippians (3:8-14)
Paul's race is to know Christ and to participate fully in his power. Living like Christ, and possibly dying like him, brings the hope of resurrection.
John (8:1-11)
Here the Pharisees use a common trick: they try to trap the rabbi Jesus in a technicality of the law. He responds in a practical rather than a legal sense, and shows by it his constant forgiveness.

Juxtaposed before the sinless one is a person filled with sin. In this way, the challenge to repentance is issued.

FOCUS
The final step of the passage to life is commitment. Though we may have examined our lives and renewed our ways of living, the future will require doing this again and again. The resolve to begin a race leads us to a new kind of attention for its completion.

The passage to life is really a cycle — a cycle we will repeat many times. We need to help people to see freshness and new life in the cycle. In most areas of the country some signs of Spring can be found by this time, which make great symbols for the liturgy. Poetry which depicts hope and success after human trial can be another source of important symbols.

IDEA STARTERS
- *CCT Lectionary:* Is 43:16-21; Ps 126; Ph 3:8-14; Jn 12:1-8.
- When catechumens celebrate today's liturgy, use Lectionary cycle A.
- What are the "new things" that the Lord is doing for us today — and tomorrow?
- What is "the justice we possess...that comes to us through faith in Christ"?
- Why is the un-named woman in the gospel associated with Mary Magdelane?
- What is Jesus' attitude toward the sinner?
- For your consideration: Intercession for exiles, runners, for the proper living out of our sexuality, and for those bereaved; Lenten Preface II or Reconciliation Eucharistic Prayer I; Prayer Over the People 2.

MUSIC
- Psalm 126
- *Be Not Afraid* (Jesuits, NALR)
- *For You Are My God* (Jesuits/NALR)
- *Lenten Psalm* (Keyes/Resource)
- *Lord, Have Mercy* (Olivier/Resource)
- *Only This I Want* (Jesuits/NALR)
- *Prodigal Children* (Schoenbachler/NALR)
- *Remember Your Love* (Dameans/NALR)
- *This is the People* (Keyes/Resource)

LENTEN PLANNING SHEET

Date _____

Parish focus _____

Environment & art _____

Ritual notes _____

Faith development (eg., midweek program) _____

Children's faith experience _____

Prelude _____

Hymn of gathering _____

Penitential rite _____

Opening Prayer _____

Reading cycle _____ First reading _____

Responsory _____ Second reading _____

Lenten gospel acclamation _____ Gospel _____

RCIA rites & acclamations _____

General intercessions _____

At the preparation & presentation _____

Preface dialog _____ Preface _____

Preface acclamation _____

Eucharistic prayer _____ Memorial acclamation _____

Eucharistic amen _____

The Lord's prayer _____

Breaking of bread _____

The communion hymn _____

The post-communion hymn _____

Blessing _____ At the dismissal _____

Memoranda:

PASSION/PALM SUNDAY

YEARS A, B AND C

READINGS

Isaiah (50:4-7)
In what is called the Third Servant Song, Isaiah describes the one trained with God's words to bring comfort to the community. The suffering encountered by this messenger is unjust and here foretells Jesus' own passion and death.

Philippians (2:6-11)
This Pauline letter contains four instructions to the community. Here humility is illustrated. This passage is actually a hymn or a poem of very early Jewish-Christian liturgical usage. It is a primitive confession of belief and contains the following six parts: Jesus' pre-existence with God; Jesus' choice of humility through the Incarnation; death as the ultimate humility; God who exalts Jesus; adoration by the universe; and the new title given Jesus.

Luke (22:14-23:56)
The passion narrative may be the most familiar part of scripture. Luke gives the hearer easy access to the images of suffering, allowing any of us to "become" Peter, or Simon, or the good thief.

FOCUS

Palm Sunday depicts in the most graphic terms the limits of Christian humility. Paul tells us that Jesus gave up his state with God to become incarnate and then ultimately to die. The Passion leaves us in total amazement at the pain done to a human body and the disregard of the friends around Jesus.

How would you define humility in contemporary terms? The identity we guard so closely must occasionally be given up. We don't give up easily. Think of taxes, water rights or vacations. What seems deserved or owed to us is the last to go.

IDEA STARTERS

- *CCT Lectionary:* Is 50:4-9A; Ps 18:19-29; Ph 2:5-11; Lk 19:28-40 or Lk 22:14-23:56 or Lk 23:1-49.
- At today's principle Eucharist be sure to celebrate the Liturgy of Palms with procession (in place of Introductory Rites).
- The Liturgy of the Palms may be a suitable occasion for an Ecumenical Service. *The Roman Sacramentary, Book of Common Prayer* (Episcopal) and *Lutheran Book of Worship (Minister's Edition)* each contain a similar order of service to be celebrated prior to the Liturgy of the Word. Choose which rite you will use and have a pastor preside over the service. Choose a location central to the parishes involved so that, afterwards, all may go in procession to their own churches.
- Adorn the processional cross with palms and scarlet fabric. Use incense.
- The Passion according to Luke: Avoid using "script" versions of the reading. Do not have the assembly read along and say their part. An effective way to proclaim the Passion account is to divide the text into major sections and have a different reader proclaim each. The assembly may be seated during the reading. After each section all may join in singing a hymn or refrain,

corresponding to the mood of the section read immediately beforehand. (The assembly may stand to sing.) See *Proclaiming the Passion* (Office of Worship, Box 69, LaCrosse, WI 54601).

MUSIC

- Psalm 22
- *Glory, Laud and Honor* (ICEL)
- *Crown Him With Many Crowns* (ICEL)
- *Hosanna* (Weston Priory)
- *Look For the Saviour* (Page/Resource)

- *The King of Glory* (Jabusch)
- *At the Name of Jesus (ICEL)*
- *Praise Song* (Page/Resource)
- *Behold the Wood* (Jesuits/NALR)
- *Sacred Heart* (ICEL)

LENTEN PLANNING SHEET   Date _____

Parish focus _____

Environment & art _____

Ritual notes _____

Faith development (eg., midweek program) _____

Children's faith experience _____

Prelude _____

Hymn of gathering _____

Penitential rite _____

Opening Prayer _____

Reading cycle _____First reading _____

Responsory _____Second reading _____

Lenten gospel acclamation _____Gospel _____

RCIA rites & acclamations _____

General intercessions _____

At the preparation & presentation _____

Preface dialog _____Preface _____

Preface acclamation _____

Eucharistic prayer _____Memorial acclamation ____

Eucharistic amen _____

The Lord's prayer _____

Breaking of bread _____

The communion hymn _____

The post-communion hymn _____

Blessing _____At the dismissal _____

Memoranda:

HOLY THURSDAY: MASS OF THE LORD'S SUPPER

YEARS A, B AND C

(See Year A For All Readings And Commentary)

TRIDUUM PLANNING SHEET

Date _____

Parish focus _____

Environment & art _____

Ritual notes _____

Faith development (eg., midweek program) _____

Children's faith experience _____

Prelude _____

Hymn of gathering _____

Penitential rite _____

Opening Prayer _____

Reading cycle _____ First reading _____

Responsory _____ Second reading _____

Lenten gospel acclamation _____ Gospel _____

RCIA rites & acclamations _____

General intercessions _____

At the preparation & presentation _____

Preface dialog _____ Preface _____

Preface acclamation _____

Eucharistic prayer _____ Memorial acclamation _____

Eucharistic amen _____

The Lord's prayer _____

Breaking of bread _____

The communion hymn _____

The post–communion hymn _____

Blessing _____ At the dismissal _____

Memoranda:

GOOD FRIDAY: CELEBRATION OF THE LORD'S PASSION

YEARS A, B AND C

(See Year A For All Readings And Commentary)

TRIDUUM PLANNING SHEET

Date _____

Parish focus _____

Environment & art _____

Ritual notes _____

Faith development (eg., midweek program) _____

Children's faith experience _____

Prelude _____

Hymn of gathering _____

Penitential rite _____

Opening Prayer _____

Reading cycle _____ First reading _____

Responsory _____ Second reading _____

Lenten gospel acclamation _____ Gospel _____

RCIA rites & acclamations _____

General intercessions _____

At the preparation & presentation _____

Preface dialog _____ Preface _____

Preface acclamation _____

Eucharistic prayer _____ Memorial acclamation ____

Eucharistic amen _____

The Lord's prayer _____

Breaking of bread _____

The communion hymn _____

The post-communion hymn _____

Blessing _____ At the dismissal _____

Memoranda:

EASTER VIGIL   YEARS A, B AND C
(See Year A For Other Readings And Commentary)

READINGS
Luke (24:1-12)
The early church needed to give clear witness to resurrection of Jesus. Luke's account includes the eyewitness testimony of women, proving that resurrection was not a story made up by the apostles; the presence of two "legal" witnesses in the form of the heavenly men; and the eyewitness testimony of Peter, assuring believers that the resurrection is at the heart of the faith of the whole church.

TRIDUUM PLANNING SHEET

Date _____

Parish focus _____

Environment & art _____

Ritual notes _____

Faith development (eg., midweek program) _____

Children's faith experience _____

Prelude _____

Hymn of gathering _____

Sprinkling baptismal water acclamation _____

Opening Prayer _____

Reading cycle _____First reading _____

Responsory _____Second reading _____

Lenten gospel acclamation _____Gospel _____

RCIA rites & acclamations _____

General intercessions _____

At the preparation & presentation _____

Preface dialog _____Preface _____

Preface acclamation _____

Eucharistic prayer _____Memorial acclamation _____

Eucharistic amen _____

The Lord's prayer _____

Breaking of bread _____

The communion hymn _____

The post-communion hymn _____

Blessing _____At the dismissal _____

Memoranda:

EASTER SUNDAY YEARS A,B AND C
(See Year A For All Readings And Further Commentary)

READINGS
Acts of the Apostles (10:34,37–43)
With his characteristic enthusiasm, Peter here gives us a recounting of the ministry and life of Jesus. This message forms the basic text that is taught to all in the new church.

Colossians (3:1–4) or First Corinthians (5:6–8)
Either of these may be chosen on this Sunday. Though using different metaphors, both point to the new life we have because of Jesus. We are now one with him and because of him we are freed from death.

John (20:1–9)
In minute detail we hear of the events surrounding the empty tomb: the day, the time, the rock, the shroud. John illustrates the actual resurrection rather than using a lot of images of immortality. He gives us the ability to also "see" and "understand" that which was hidden until Jesus' resurrection.

FOCUS
No one can hear the Easter Sunday morning story without being amazed at the energy and awareness in the event. Just look at the verbs John uses: ran, taken, entered, observed, believed. There are details here in such vividness that any of us could have been present.

We are told that now the disciples understood what was taught to them. The event of the tomb created for them the "Aha" moment. These are the times when clarity and understanding finally came. Here are fresh connections and new ways to use old words and understandings.

In addition to the central theme of Christ's resurrection, this Easter can focus on awareness. How and where are we conscious of God, or life? How does our community promote life? How can your liturgy bring to awareness the symbols of life in your community: children, water, seeds, flowers, food?

IDEA STARTERS
- *CCT Lectionary:* Acts 10:34–43 or Is 65:17–25; Ps 118:14–24; 1 Cor 15:19–26 or Acts 10:34–43; Jn 20:1–18 or Lk 24:1–12.
- Celebrate Evening Prayer on Holy Saturday in the late afternoon. After the reading, celebrate a rite of blessing Easter foods (cf. *Book of Occasional Services.* NY: The Church Hymnal Corporation).
- Are Easter flowers gracing the ambo and altar, paschal candle and processional cross, baptismal font and tabernacle?
- Use the paschal candle in procession (instead of the processional cross) throughout the fifty days.
- During the season, where it is customary, pastors may visit homes to share an Easter Blessing with their parishioners—especially the homes and families, of the neophytes!
- For your consideration: Opening Prayer (Evening Mass: Alternative Prayer); sing the Sequence; Gospel Luke 24:1–12 (Evening Luke 24:13–35); Reaffirmation of Baptismal Vows with Sprinkling; Intercessions of neophytes, evangelization, the rejected, suffering and the hopeless; Easter Preface I (P 21); Eucharistic Prayer I (w/Easter propers); Memorial Acclamation B or D; Easter Solemn Blessing; Dismissal w/Alleluias.

- Throughout the Easter season replace the customary greeting ("The grace of our Lord...") with the traditional Easter greeting: Minister: "Alleluia! Christ is risen!" Assembly: "The Lord is risen indeed! Alleluia!" Say it with feeling! Also, replace the "Lamb of God," with the acclamation, "Christ our passover is sacrificed for us; therefore let us keep the feast, alleluia!"
- How might the baptismal water from the Great Vigil of Easter be acknowledged in its use after the reaffirmation of baptismal vows (following the homily)?

MUSIC

- Psalm 118
- *Christ the Lord is Risen Today* (ICEL)
- *Alleluia* (Page/Resource)
- *Hail Thee Festival Day* (LBW)

- *Jesus is Life* (Landry/NALR)
- *Resurrection Song* (Sexton/Resource)
- *This is the Day* (Haugen/GIA)
- *This is the Day* (Schoenbachler/PAA)

EASTER PLANNING SHEET   Date _____

Parish focus _____

Environment & art _____

Ritual notes _____

Faith development (eg., midweek program) _____

Children's faith experience _____

Prelude _____

Hymn of gathering _____

Sprinkling baptismal water acclamation _____

Opening Prayer _____

Reading cycle _____First reading _____

Responsory _____Second reading _____

Lenten gospel acclamation _____Gospel _____

RCIA rites & acclamations _____

General intercessions _____

At the preparation & presentation _____

Preface dialog _____Preface _____

Preface acclamation _____

Eucharistic prayer _____Memorial acclamation _____

Eucharistic amen _____

The Lord's prayer _____

Breaking of bread _____

The communion hymn _____

The post-communion hymn _____

Blessing _____At the dismissal _____

Memoranda:

SECOND SUNDAY OF EASTER

YEAR C

READINGS

Acts of the Apostles (5:12–16)
With great boldness, the Apostles meet in the Temple and are not intimidated by the power of its keepers. They take God as their guide. The miracles performed by the Apostles reinforced the power of Jesus in their ministry.

Revelation (1:9–13,17–19)
Exiled to Patmos, John chooses to write of the wonders of God which he can no longer witness to personally. The seven lampstands represent seven churches of the first century and in the center of the church stands the risen Christ. Jesus' presence in life is so strong that he even controls the keys of death.

John (20:19–31)
The assembled disciples are witness to the presence of the risen Jesus and are commissioned by him to bring others to a similar faith. The exclamation by Thomas is a statement of Jesus' oneness with God as he uses an ancient name for God. Jesus' bequest of the Spirit empowers the Apostles' ministry.

FOCUS

To believe without seeing can often be the essence of forgiving. It is hard to renew trust without any proof of change. Forgiveness is usually based on promises rather than facts.

To understand forgiveness as the essence of life is to understand the cycle of life. Nature gives us the easy model of life to death to life again. Jesus has given us a human model. We have merely to see our personal growth as tied to the small moments of forgiveness.

This Sunday would be the ideal time to concentrate on personal forgiveness of family and friends. We could attend to the healing memories from our pasts.

IDEA STARTERS

- *CCT Lectionary:* Acts 5:27–32; Ps 2; Rv 1:4–8; Jn 20:19–31.
- For the season: Throughout the fifty days, use the Easter greeting followed by the Sprinkling Rite (adapted so that you may use water from the Easter Vigil) and a simple musical setting of the "Glory of God" or other hymn of praise. Sing the same "Alleluia" you sang at the Vigil for the Gospel Acclamation. At the Breaking of the Bread, use the verse "Alleluia! Christ our Passover..." See the Easter Solemn Blessing. The *Gradual Romanum* (1974) appoints the "double alleluia" to follow the deacon's dismissal for all fifty days of Easter.
- For homily or bulletin: What role does doubt play in one's own system of belief?
- Be sure that the neophytes are still attending the Eucharist as a group for this time of post–baptismal catechesis (cf. RCIA, nos. 235–236).
- You may wish to highlight the Profession of Faith at today's liturgy by having the assembly sing a brief refrain before (and after) each of the three sections is proclaimed by the presider or other minister. Use the new translation of the Nicene Creed (*Prayers We Have In Common, Revised Edition.* Philadelphia: Fortress Press).

- For your consideration: Alternative Opening Prayer; intercessions for the neophytes, the sick and troubled, those who doubt God, and for forgiveness; Easter Preface I(p21); Eucharistic Prayer I (w/Easter Propers).

MUSIC
- Psalm 118
- *Mighty Lord* (Jesuits/NALR)
- *O Sons and Daughters* (ICEL)
- *Sing With All the Sons of Glory* (ICEL)
- *Alpha and Omega* (Schoenbachler/NALR)
- *Christ the Lord is Risen Again* (ICEL)
- *Sing a Song of Praise* (Page/Resource)
- *Sing To the Lord* (Gilsdorf/Resource)

EASTER PLANNING SHEET   Date _____

Parish focus _____

Environment & art _____

Ritual notes _____

Faith development (eg., midweek program) _____

Children's faith experience _____

Prelude _____

Hymn of gathering _____

Sprinkling baptismal water acclamation _____

Opening Prayer _____

Reading cycle _____First reading _____

Responsory _____Second reading _____

Lenten gospel acclamation _____Gospel _____

RCIA rites & acclamations _____

General intercessions _____

At the preparation & presentation _____

Preface dialog _____Preface _____

Preface acclamation _____

Eucharistic prayer _____Memorial acclamation ____

Eucharistic amen _____

The Lord's prayer _____

Breaking of bread _____

The communion hymn _____

The post-communion hymn _____

Blessing _____At the dismissal _____

Memoranda:

THIRD SUNDAY OF EASTER

YEAR C

READINGS
Acts of the Apostles (5:27-32,40-41)
The disciples identify with the life of their Master and count themselves proud to be reprimanded for teaching about Jesus. Peter manages here to turn the encounter into another opportunity to tell the story of Jesus' life and message.
Revelation (5:11-14)
This vision of John describes a scene of adulation for God and the Redeemer. These two equally gain the praise of all creation. Note the seven words in the angel's doxology. These describe the dimensions of the glory deserving God and Jesus: power, riches, wisdom, strength, honor, glory, and praise.
John (21:1-19)
This addendum to John's Gospel repeats the story of Jesus appearing to the disciples but moves the location to Galilee from Jerusalem. The meal he prepares on shore is reminiscent of the loaves and fishes miracle. Peter is established as first among the Apostles and his death is foretold.

FOCUS
From the fishing boat to the special meal to the commissioning of Peter, this Gospel speaks of stewardship. Sharing food, work, companionship, and responsibilites of the community are some examples of the Christian role in stewardship.

How is responsibility promoted to the laity in your community? Who contributes the resources needed for the church? When leadership is required, upon whom does the community call?

Is the parish planning for its future? It is training the leadership to take over current and future ministries? Who sets long range goals for the parish? How are resources of money, time, and space divided?

Often parishes are "run" by the willing ones who come forward. This would be a good time to explore how a community can abdicate its responsibility. Rather than leading by abdication, encourage a way for the community to be involved in your parish.

IDEA STARTERS
- *CCT Lectionary:* Acts 9:1-20; Ps 30:4-12; Rev 5:11-14; Jn 21:1-19; Jn 21:15-19.
- For your bulletin: A brief article explaining the background of the Acts of the Apostles and (especially) Revelation may guide your assembly's understanding of the Easter lectionary.
- Today's Gospel may be viewed in a "Eucharistic" light. Why is it so important that Jesus not only appears to his disciples, but sits down to have a meal with them as well?
- On Passion Sunday, the second reading began, "Your attitude must be Christ's." How do today's three readings illustrate that famous Philippians passage?
- Today's Gospel calls for community (pastors and people) gathering. Communion breakfast? Coffee and cake after worship? You decide.

- For your consideration: Opening Prayer; Intercessions for love of enemies, honor and glory to Jesus, the Kingdom of God in our midst, the hungry, the pope, bishops, and neophytes, for fishermen, chefs, waiters, and waitresses; Easter Preface III (P23). See also Second Easter Sunday.

MUSIC

- Psalm 30
- *At the Name of Jesus* (ICEL)
- *Do You Really Love Me* (Landry/NALR)
- *Give Thanks* (Gilsdorf/Resource)
- *Let Me, Lord* (Page/Resource)

- *To Be Your Bread* (Haas/Coop Ministries)
- *We Remember* (Haugen/PAA)
- *Worthy Is The Lamb* (Jesuits/NALR)
- *Worship and Praise* (Keyes/Resource)

EASTER PLANNING SHEET

Date _____

Parish focus _____

Environment & art _____

Ritual notes _____

Faith development (eg., midweek program) _____

Children's faith experience _____

Prelude _____

Hymn of gathering _____

Sprinkling baptismal water acclamation _____

Opening Prayer _____

Reading cycle _____First reading _____

Responsory _____Second reading _____

Lenten gospel acclamation _____Gospel _____

RCIA rites & acclamations _____

General intercessions _____

At the preparation & presentation _____

Preface dialog _____Preface _____

Preface acclamation _____

Eucharistic prayer _____Memorial acclamation _____

Eucharistic amen _____

The Lord's prayer _____

Breaking of bread _____

The communion hymn _____

The post-communion hymn _____

Blessing _____At the dismissal _____

Memoranda:

FOURTH SUNDAY OF EASTER

READINGS

Acts of the Apostles (13:14,43–52)
In traveling to Antioch, Paul seeks to bring the message to the Jews first. While the Jews reject him, his preaching is well received by many joyful Gentiles. Leaving behind the responsibility for the Jews, the mission becomes directed to the Gentile community.

Revelation (7:9,14–17)
This passage is inserted between visions of great trial on earth. It describes the wonder of heaven and the people of God who will be safe from earthly trials because of their righteousness. The verbs in future tense describe this as a promise.

John (10:27–30)
The heart of Good Shepherd Sunday is a theme of oneness. The relationship of the leader and his disciples is modeled on the oneness of Jesus and God. This oneness is further cemented by the rejection of the Jews.

FOCUS

A final quality of life is seen in collaboration. Any leader–group situation can be characterized by various values: authoritarianism, competition, training, or collaboration.

Collaboration is working together characterized by cooperation and by using the best talents of people available. In a parish setting collaboration could be the value we are seeking between different groups, between leadership and parishioners, and between the parish and larger community.

Good Shepherd Sunday is a time to explore this value in the decisions and responsibilities of your parish. What relationships exist between leaders and people? Between different parish groups? How does the community cooperate in the larger issues in your neighborhood? With other churches?

IDEA STARTERS

- *CCT Lectionary:* Acts 13:15–16, 26–23; Ps 23; Rv 7:9–17; Jn 10:22–30.
- Today had been called "Good Shepherd Sunday." Reference to this ancient symbol and title for our Lord may be made in the bulletin or homily.
- Today's first reading speaks about preaching to the Gentiles. How do people today feel about evangelization for the sake of conversion? How should the church proclaim the message of the Risen Lord to the non-believer?
- How are the Easter flowers and decorations holding up? Are the hymns still resounding with "alleluias" and messages of Christ Risen? (There are four more weeks of Easter rejoicing to go.)
- For your consideration: Opening Prayer; Intercessions for missionaries and non-believers, for neophytes and vocations to the ministries, for shepherds and farmers; Easter Preface II (P22); Memorial Acclamation D. See also Second Easter Sunday.
- Do your parish children see "the country" very often? An outing to a farm (to see cows, hens, sheep, etc.) may be an enjoyable activity for a spring

afternoon, especially if the farmer shares his/her own enthusiasm for caring over God's creation.

MUSIC

- Psalm 100
- *At the Lamb's High Feast* (ICEL)
- *Come To The Water* (Gilsdorf/Resource)
- *Come You Faithful Raise The Strain* (ICEL)
- *I Am The Light* (Repp/K&R)

- *Jesus Christ Is Risen Today* (ICEL)
- *The Lord Is My Shepherd, Alleluia* (Wise/Fontaine-GIA)
- *Shepherd's Alleluia* (Landry/NALR)
- *Sing A New Song* (Blachura/Resource)
- *You Will Draw Water* (Conry/NALR)

EASTER PLANNING SHEET   Date _____

Parish focus _____

Environment & art _____

Ritual notes _____

Faith development (eg., midweek program) _____

Children's faith experience _____

Prelude _____

Hymn of gathering _____

Sprinkling baptismal water acclamation _____

Opening Prayer _____

Reading cycle _____ First reading _____

Responsory _____ Second reading _____

Lenten gospel acclamation _____ Gospel _____

RCIA rites & acclamations _____

General intercessions _____

At the preparation & presentation _____

Preface dialog _____ Preface _____

Preface acclamation _____

Eucharistic prayer _____ Memorial acclamation ____

Eucharistic amen _____

The Lord's prayer _____

Breaking of bread _____

The communion hymn _____

The post-communion hymn _____

Blessing _____ At the dismissal _____

Memoranda:

FIFTH SUNDAY OF EASTER

YEAR C

READINGS

Acts (14:21-27)
This passage reports on Paul and Barnabas' first missionary journey. Following the ancient traditions of Hebrew clans, they appoint elders to guide each of the communities they have left behind. With elders as guides, the churches can continue the newly discovered faith.

Revelations (21:1-5)
The stories of earth's trial give way here to promises of glory. In the only place in Revelations where God is the ascribed speaker, the promise of full life is laid out in its entirety. Here we see all life made new, transformed by the power of God. The wondrous city which is described is symbolic of our church in the Easter season.

John (13:31-33,34-35)
The Last Supper discourse focuses for us the essence of the relationship between Jesus and God; that of love. This charity marks the lives of the disciples and reveals the power of the new church. Such power foretells the Spirit who reveals love in its depths. A hallmark theme of the Old Testament, love here is offered to all peoples and communities.

FOCUS

The primary key to Christ's revelation is love. Jesus clearly describes this as the essence of his relationship to God. His wish for us to know God in a like way is modeled by his love of the disciples. Our personal lives and our Church communal life repeats Christ's model of love through the power of the Spirit.

Twisting a popular quip, we can say that we are what we love. This could be a prime time to examine the people and place and objects into which we pour our affections and energies.

IDEA STARTERS

- *CCT Lectionary:* Acts 14:8-18; Ps 145:13b-21; Rev 21:1-6; Jn 13:31-35.
- The readings of this Easter season continue to unfold the mystery of being an "Easter person," especially to the neophytes. How does Jesus' command of love correlate with the promise of the "new Jerusalem" and the kingdom of God in our midst?
- Why are gospel selections from John's Last Supper discourse used during the days of Easter?
- The month of May traditionally has been a month honoring Mary, Mother of our Risen Lord. Church documents call for devotions to be in harmony with the seasons of the church year. The Marian hymn/prayer of Easter is *Regina Coeli* (Queen of Heaven), paraphrased in the hymn "Be Joyful Mary." At Eucharist, this hymn is best sung at the Presentation of the Gifts or at the Dismissal.
- Seasonal Reminders for the Great Fifty Days: Easter flowers should continue to adorn the Paschal candle, baptismal font, altar and ambo. Use the Easter greeting — "Alleluia, Christ is risen!" Response: "He is risen indeed,

Alleluia!" — with the Sprinkling of Baptismal Water (using the water from the Easter Vigil) followed by a festive hymn of praise (e.g., Gloria at the rites of gathering). At the breaking of the bread sing the antiphon "Christ, our passover, is sacrificed for us, therefore, let us keep the feast! Alleluia!" Following the Easter Solemn Blessing, the deacon's dismissal should include the double alleluia. Let alleluias resound during your hymn singing!

- For your consideration: Opening Prayer; Intercessions for nonbelievers, preachers, Jerusalem and other "international" cities, the environment and all God's creation; Easter Preface IV (P24); Eucharistic Prayer III; Memorial Acclamation D.

MUSIC

- Psalm 145
- *All I Ask Of You* (Weston Priory)
- *For I Shall See You Again* (Weston Priory)
- *Gather Round* (Page/Resource)
- *Gentle Spirit* (Stenson/Resource)
- *Our God Is Love* (Repp/K&R)
- *Praise The Lord, My Soul* (Parker/GIA)
- *Sing A New Song To The Lord* (Wilson/GIA)
- *Simple Gifts* (Page/Resource)

EASTER PLANNING SHEET   Date _____

Parish focus _____

Environment & art _____

Ritual notes _____

Faith development (eg., midweek program) _____

Children's faith experience _____

Prelude _____

Hymn of gathering _____

Sprinkling baptismal water acclamation _____

Opening Prayer _____

Reading cycle _____First reading _____

Responsory _____Second reading _____

Lenten gospel acclamation _____Gospel _____

RCIA rites & acclamations _____

General intercessions _____

At the preparation & presentation _____

Preface dialog _____Preface _____

Preface acclamation _____

Eucharistic prayer _____Memorial acclamation ____

Eucharistic amen _____

The Lord's prayer _____

Breaking of bread _____

The communion hymn _____

The post-communion hymn _____

Blessing _____At the dismissal _____

Memoranda:

SIXTH SUNDAY OF EASTER

YEAR C

READINGS

Acts of the Apostles (15:1-2,22-29)
In preaching to the Gentiles, the apostles must confront the questions of observance of Jewish Law. From this conciliar decree onward, the Jewish dietary and sexual observances are waived. What is required is to practice charity. The common good is given precedence before all other considerations.

Revelations (21:10-14,22-23)
John's description of the wonders of heaven call directly on the Old Testament symbols, especially those of Ezekiel. John's vision of the church as the city of Jerusalem reflects both the twelve apostles and the twelve tribes. God's presence is so total in this church that all other illumination seems pale.

John (14:23-29)
As the Last Supper discourse continues Jesus explains his work and his relationship to the Father and Spirit. The three values of love, peace, and understanding become vivid and are reflected in the church. Love of God yields a peace and tranquility which brings understanding and wisdom to life.

FOCUS
The coming of the Spirit leaves the church confident since this presence assures the fulfillment of its mission. This confidence and strength is unknown in worldly terms and can only come through living God's life of love. The surest sign of the presence of love in us is the manifestation of peace.

The dimensions of peace in contemporary life are hard to name. Explore the differences between internal and external peace. How do we serve the common good of our community? What is the difference between active peace and mere tolerance of quiet? What do we worry about? Do we make decisions and act as confident representations of life, love?

IDEA STARTERS
- *CCT Lectionary:* Acts 15:1-2, 22-29; Ps 67; Rv 21:10, 22-27; Jn 14:23-29.
- Today's readings speak of the power and the promise: the power of the Spirit promised to Jesus' disciples. How do people use the power Jesus promised?
- The Spirit of Jesus gives us a peace that frees us from mindless adherence to others' expectations. How do we express this when we share "the peace of the Lord" at Mass?
- The reading from Revelations gives an opportunity for reflection upon the meaning of the building used for worship, *domus ecclesiae* meaning the House of the Church (cf. *Environment and Art,* no. 28). As God is the temple of the heavenly Jerusalem, we are called to be the temple of God in this world (cf. 1 Corinthians 3:9-17).
- For your consideration: Opening Prayer; Intercessions for the neophytes, those who make laws, appropriate use of government funds, those who will be returning home from college, and for personal reflection upon God's will for us; Easter Preface III (P22); Eucharistic Prayer III; Memorial Acclamation C. See also "Seasonal Reminders" (cf. Fifth Sunday, above).

MUSIC

- Psalm 67
- *And There Will Shine* (Repp/K&R)
- *Come, Holy Spirit* (Culbreth/Resource)
- *Come, My Friend* (Page/Resource)
- *Dwelling Place* (Jesuits/NALR)
- *Gather Us In* (Haugen/GIA)
- *Glory And Praise* (Jesuits/NALR)
- *I Am The Light* (Repp/K&R)
- *If Anyone Loves Me* (Weston Priory)
- *Something Which Is Known* (Weston Priory)

EASTER PLANNING SHEET   Date _____

Parish focus _____

Environment & art _____

Ritual notes _____

Faith development (eg., midweek program) _____

Children's faith experience _____

Prelude _____

Hymn of gathering _____

Sprinkling baptismal water acclamation _____

Opening Prayer _____

Reading cycle _____First reading _____

Responsory _____Second reading _____

Lenten gospel acclamation _____Gospel _____

RCIA rites & acclamations _____

General intercessions _____

At the preparation & presentation _____

Preface dialog _____Preface _____

Preface acclamation _____

Eucharistic prayer _____Memorial acclamation _____

Eucharistic amen _____

The Lord's prayer _____

Breaking of bread _____

The communion hymn _____

The post-communion hymn _____

Blessing _____At the dismissal _____

Memoranda:

SOLEMNITY OF THE ASCENSION

YEAR C

(See Year A For First And Second Readings And Further Commentary)

John (14:23–29)
The farewell which signals the end of one sort of presence of Jesus on earth also spells the beginning of a new presence — that of the Holy Spirit within the church.

EASTER PLANNING SHEET

Date _____

Parish focus _____

Environment & art _____

Ritual notes _____

Faith development (eg., midweek program) _____

Children's faith experience _____

Prelude _____

Hymn of gathering _____

Sprinkling baptismal water acclamation _____

Opening Prayer _____

Reading cycle _____ First reading _____

Responsory _____ Second reading _____

Lenten gospel acclamation _____ Gospel _____

RCIA rites & acclamations _____

General intercessions _____

At the preparation & presentation _____

Preface dialog _____ Preface _____

Preface acclamation _____

Eucharistic prayer _____ Memorial acclamation _____

Eucharistic amen _____

The Lord's prayer _____

Breaking of bread _____

The communion hymn _____

The post-communion hymn _____

Blessing _____ At the dismissal _____

Memoranda:

SEVENTH SUNDAY OF EASTER

YEAR C

READINGS

Acts (7:55-60)
While the circumstances surrounding Stephen's death are obscure, there are many parallels to the death of Jesus. What is key here is the presence of the Spirit transforming Stephen and clarifying the relationship of Jesus to the Father.

Revelations (22:12-14,16-17,20)
In the conclusion to both Revelations and the Bible, Jesus undertakes a conversation with the church. He assures the church of the validity of these visions and urges the church to not only await the return but to actually approach him. This prayer for reunion may be the essence of Revelations.

John (17:20-26)
Jesus' prayer as he leaves the church behind is for unity. The relationship has shown between the Father-Son-Spirit is to be the guide for the relationship to the church. In reflecting this unity the church continues the mission of Christ.

FOCUS

Finally, the coming of the Spirit of Christ yields an understanding unlike any other knowledge. The true mission of Jesus and the intimacy of his relationship to God becomes clear. Jesus' revelation is assured by the Spirit and we glimpse the truth of his life.

The challenge of understanding Jesus and his message is still with us today. The simplicity of the words belie the complexity of applying their truth on our lives. The reunion sought by the church and foretold in Revelations will happen most surely when Christ's teaching is made alive in the world.

IDEA STARTERS

- *CCT Lectionary:* Acts 16:16-34; Ps 97; Rv 22:12-14, 16-17, 20; Jn 17:20-26.
- This Sunday after the Ascension includes Jesus' prayer for unity among his followers. These days between Ascension Day and Pentecost are observed as days of prayer for Christian Unity in the same dedicated way that Mary and the apostles prayed for the coming of Jesus' Spirit into their lives. Guest preachers and ecumenical liturgies/paraliturgies are appropriate throughout Ascensiontide.
- We continue to reflect upon the meaning of the Ascension as we recall St. Stephen's martyrdom, and we look forward to the final coming of Christ. Is there a relationship among the Revelations reading (with its Advent-like theme), St. Stephen (a Christmas feast, Dec. 26) and this Sunday before Pentecost?
- For your further consideration: Alternative Opening Prayer; Intercessions for the neophytes, the oppressed and contemporary martyrs, justice and peace, unity among nations, races and churches; Ascension Preface I (P26); Eucharistic Prayer I (w/proper); Ascension Solemn Blessing. See also "Seasonal Reminders" (cf. Fifth Sunday above).

MUSIC

- Psalm 97
- *Alpha And Omega* (Schoenbachler/NALR)
- *Glorious In Majesty* (Cothran/GIA)
- *Let Us Walk In The Light* (Haugen/Quiet Breeze Music)
- *Love Is Forever* (Dameans/NALR)
- *Peace* (Weston Priory)
- *Praise Canticle* (Haas/Cooperative Ministries)
- *Song Of Thanksgiving* (Dicie/Resource)
- *The Sun Is Rising* (Weston Priory)
- *We Remember* (Haugen/PAA)
- *We Come To You* (Page/Resource)

EASTER PLANNING SHEET   Date _____

Parish focus _____

Environment & art _____

Ritual notes _____

Faith development (eg., midweek program) _____

Children's faith experience _____

Prelude _____

Hymn of gathering _____

Sprinkling baptismal water acclamation _____

Opening Prayer _____

Reading cycle _____First reading _____

Responsory _____Second reading _____

Lenten gospel acclamation _____Gospel _____

RCIA rites & acclamations _____

General intercessions _____

At the preparation & presentation _____

Preface dialog _____Preface _____

Preface acclamation _____

Eucharistic prayer _____Memorial acclamation ___

Eucharistic amen _____

The Lord's prayer _____

Breaking of bread _____

The communion hymn _____

The post-communion hymn _____

Blessing _____At the dismissal _____

Memoranda:

THE SOLEMNITY OF PENTECOST

YEARS A, B AND C

(See Year A For All Readings And Further Commentary)

READINGS

Acts (2:1-11)
The Pentecost occurrence is not a random date. It is a traditional Jewish feast day falling the fiftieth day after Passover. As a feast of pilgrimage, it celebrated the harvest. In the new church, fifty days after the culmination of Christ's life was the time to begin the work of the church. Wind and fire are two major symbols of Pentecost and are ancient symbols of the power of God.

First Corinthians (12:3-7,12-13)
The center of personal and communal giftedness is the Spirit. Nothing given for the use of anyone is given without the common good in mind. The image of body reminds us of our unity through Christ's Spirit and mission.

John (20:19-23)
There is a tight linkage here between the resurrection event and the conferring of the Spirit on the Church. Now the gathered body takes over the mission which is captured by the symbol of spirit. A new relationship is in place. No longer is it Christ but now the church who acts in the world.

FOCUS

Ruah, pneuma, spiritus, air, wind, breath: whatever we choose to name it, it remains the essence of life. Throughout both the Old and New Testaments, the Spirit brings hope and promise. People long for it continuously, wishing to bring newness to the world.

We might ask about the efforts to which we bring life. To what people or concerns do we concentrate our promise? At this seasonal time of graduations and other celebrations, what hopes await our lives? How do we enliven others?

IDEA STARTERS

- *CCT Lectionary:* Acts 2:1-21 or Gn 11:1-9; Ps 104:24-34; Rm 8:14-17; Acts 2:1-2; Jn 14:8-17, 25-27.
- This is a special day for the whole Church, but most especially the neophytes baptized at the Easter Vigil.
- Celebrate a Vigil of Pentecost honoring the neophytes. Design a paraliturgy similar to Christmastide's Lessons and Carols using prayers from a Service of Light (Evening Prayer), the six Lectionary readings for the vigil of Pentecost, the Office of Readings for Pentecost, a profession of faith by the neophytes with a prayer of assent by the assembly. A simple dinner honoring the neophytes (and the festival of Pentecost) may appropriately be held this night (cf. *Rite of Christian Initiation of Adults,* nos. 235-237).
- Pentecost is the second great holy day of the Church Year (the first being the parent feast of Easter). At today's principle Eucharist, use banners (from Easter, and now add "red" ones) with bells and incense. Have everyone wear something red! Put some red flowers among the Easter lilies. This final day of Easter should be what Epiphany has traditionally been to Christmas.
- A Charismatic Mass is appropriately celebrated today.

- An ecumenical liturgy Evening Prayer would be a suitable way to close the season of Easter.
- For your further consideration: sing the Sequence (standing) after the Homily, before the Profession of Faith; intercessions for neophytes, people of all nations, God's creation, proper use of the gifts of the Spirit, and the forgiveness of our sins; Pentecost Preface (P28); Eucháristic Prayer I (w/propers); Memorial Acclamation D; Holy Spirit Solemn Blessing. See also "Seasonal Reminders" (cf. Fifth Sunday, above).

MUSIC
- Psalm 104
- *Come Holy Spirit* (Repp/K&R)
- *Let All The Earth* (Dameans/NALR)
- *Lord, Send Out Your Spirit* (any setting)
- *Morning Has Broken* (Farjeon)
- *Pentecost Sequence* (Aslott/Today's Missal)
- *Send Us Your Spirit* (Haas/Cooperative Ministries)
- *Shout Out Your Joy* (Dameans/NALR)
- *The Spirit Is A-Movin'* (Landry/NALR)
- *Spirit Of God* (Weston Priory)
- *The Spirit Song* (Dameans/PAA)
- *We Are Many Parts* (Haugen/PAA)

EASTER PLANNING SHEET   Date _____

Parish focus _____

Environment & art _____

Ritual notes _____

Faith development (eg., midweek program) _____

Children's faith experience _____

Prelude _____

Hymn of gathering _____

Sprinkling baptismal water acclamation _____

Opening Prayer _____

Reading cycle _____ First reading _____

Responsory _____ Second reading _____

Lenten gospel acclamation _____ Gospel _____

RCIA rites & acclamations _____

General intercessions _____

At the preparation & presentation _____

Preface dialog _____ Preface _____

Preface acclamation _____

Eucharistic prayer _____ Memorial acclamation _____

Eucharistic amen _____

The Lord's prayer _____

Breaking of bread _____

The communion hymn _____

The post-communion hymn _____

Blessing _____ At the dismissal _____

Memoranda:

THE SOLEMNITY OF
THE HOLY TRINITY

YEAR C

READINGS
Proverbs (8:22–31)
Proverb's beginning chapters are a recounting of the wisdom of God. Natural creation is especially seen as God's wisdom. Christ's life activities are also linked to wisdom. He is seen as present in the creation of the world.
Romans (5:1–5)
In Paul's description of faith, God's grace offers us peace and harmony. And the second effect of faith is a hope that all the promises of Christ's message will come true. The divine Trinity is at work in the faithful person through love, peace, hope.
John (16:12–15)
Having described the relationship to the Father, Jesus here also outlines the relationship to the Spirit. The vital role of the Spirit is to bring understanding. While Jesus revealed the love of the Father, the Spirit enables the church to reveal the work of the Son to the world. The Spirit is a guarantee of the future of the church.

FOCUS
While God is the source of love of which Jesus is the revelation, it takes the Spirit to bring true understanding to use. The multi-faceted power of the Trinity reminds us of the many places and events in our own lives where God's love could be conveyed.

Examine the relationships of families and neighborhoods. Where do we reflect love, peace, understanding? The trinity symbol reminds us to open out any bonds we form whether between people or in a community. We look to reproduce our caring relationships with the good of others.

IDEA STARTERS
- *CCT Lectionary*: Pr 8:22–31; Ps 8; Rm 5:1–5; Jn 16:12–15.
- This festival of the Church Year opens the second part of the Sundays in Ordinary Time.
- Rather than dedicating the homily to an explanation of what the Trinity is, use the Athanasian Creed for the Profession of Faith. A good translation of this prayer may be found in *Lutheran Book of Worship* (1978).
- The homily and bulletin articles may focus on prayer and spirituality. How do we relate to Yahweh, to the Father, to the Son, to the Holy Spirit? What do the trinitarian endings of our liturgical prayers mean? What should the Sign of the Cross mean to the believer? How do people feel about this adaptation of the prayer: "In the name of God the Creator, the Redeemer, and the Sanctifier. Amen."
- For your consideration: Sprinkling Baptismal Water prayer A; sung *Gloria;* Opening Prayer; *Athanasian Creed;* Intercessions for craftsmen, the sick, truthfulness among the nations and neighbors, and a right spirit and approach to God; Holy Trinity Preface (P43); Eucharistic Prayer III; Memorial Acclamation D; Ordinary Time Solemn Blessing I.

Whoever wishes to be saved must, first of all, hold the Catholic faith, for, unless he keeps it whole and inviolate, he will undoubtedly perish for ever.

Now this is the Catholic faith: We worship one God in the Trinity and the Trinity in unity, without either confusing the persons or dividing the substance; for the person of the Father is one, the Son's is another, the Holy Spirit's another; but the Godhead of Father, Son and Holy Spirit is one, their glory equal, their majesty equally eternal.

Such as the Father is, such is the Son, such also the Holy Spirit; uncreated is the Father, uncreated the Son, uncreated the Holy Spirit; infinite (*immensus*) is the Father, infinite the Son, infinite the Holy Spirit; eternal is the Father, eternal the Son, eternal the Holy Spirit; yet, they are not three eternal beings but one eternal, just as they are not three uncreated beings or three infinite beings but one uncreated and one infinite. In the same way, almighty is the Father, almighty the Son, almighty the Holy Spirit; yet, they are not three almighty beings but one almighty. Thus, the Father is God, the Son is God, the Holy Spirit is God; yet, they are not three gods but one God. Thus, the Father is Lord, the Son is Lord, the Holy Spirit is Lord; yet, they are not three lords but one Lord. For, as the Christian truth compels us to acknowledge each person distinctly as God and Lord, so too the Catholic religion forbids us to speak of three gods or lords.

The Father has neither been made by anyone, nor is He created or begotten; the Son is from the Father alone, not made nor created but begotten; the Holy Spirit is from the Father and the Son, not made nor created nor begotten, but proceeding. So there is one Father, not three Fathers; one Son, not three Sons; one Holy Spirit, not three Holy Spirits. And in this Trinity

there is no before or after, no greater or lesser, but three persons are equally eternal with each other fully equal. Thus, in all things, as has already bee stated above, both unity in the Trinity and Trinity the unity must be worshipped. Let him therefore wishes to be saved think this of the Trinity.

For his eternal salvation it is necessary, howev that he should also faithfully believe in the incarn of our Lord Jesus Christ. Here then is the right fait believe and confess that our Lord Jesus Christ, the of God, is both and equally God and man. He is G from the substance of the Father, begotten before ages, and He is man from the substance of a moth born in time; perfect God and perfect man, comp of a rational soul and a human body; equal to the Father as to His divinity, less than the Father as to humanity. Although He is God and man, He is nev theless one Christ, not two; however, not one becau the divinity has been changed into a human body, because the humanity has been assumed into God entirely one, not by a confusion of substance but by unity of personhood. For, as a rational soul and a b are a single man, so God and man are one Christ. F suffered for our salvation, went down to the underworld (*ad infernos*), rose again from the dead on th third day, ascended to the heavens, is seated at the right hand of the Father, wherefrom He shall come judge the living and the dead. At His coming all me are to rise again with their bodies and to render an account of their own deeds; those who have done g will go to eternal life, but those who have done evil eternal fire.

This is the Catholic faith. Unless one believes it faithfully and firmly, he cannot be saved.

MUSIC

- Psalm 8
- *All My Days* (Jesuits/NALR)
- *Bless The Lord, O My Soul* (Jesuits/NALR)
- *Glory And Praise* (Jesuits/NALR)
- *He Is The Lord* (Haas/Cooperative Ministries)
- *Jubilate, Servite* (Taize/GIA)
- *The Living God* (Temple/PAA)
- *Praise The Lord* (Dicie/Resource)
- *Praise! Praise The Lord* (Sessions/Resource)
- *A Song Of Blessing* (Wise/GIA)
- *Taste and See* (Cunningham/Resource)
- *We Thank You, Father* (Weston Priory)
- *Where Can I Go?* (Dameans/PAA)
- *Yahweh* (Weston Priory)

SUNDAY PLANNING SHEET   Date _____

Parish focus _____

Environment & art _____

Ritual notes _____

Faith development (eg., in newsletter/classes) _____

Children's faith experience _____

Prelude _____

Hymn of gathering _____

Sprinkling/Penitential rite _____

Hymn of praise _____

Opening Prayer _____

First reading _____Responsory _____

Second reading _____Gospel acclamation _____

Gospel _____Profession of faith _____

General intercessions _____

At the preparation & presentation _____

Preface dialog _____Preface _____

Preface acclamation _____

Eucharistic prayer _____Memorial acclamation _____

Eucharistic amen _____

The Lord's prayer _____

Breaking of bread _____

The communion hymn _____

The post-communion hymn _____

Blessing _____At the dismissal _____

Memoranda:

SOLEMNITY OF CORPUS CHRISTI

YEAR C

READINGS

Genesis (14:18–20)
Melchizedek is a priest in the tradition of the Canaanite religions. His blessing of Abraham includes the use of bread and wine. This may have been a covenant meal between two tribes.

First Corinthians (11:23–26)
This passage may be among the earliest recorded comments on the Eucharist. Here it is recorded as a ritual of a Presence which is unseen, yet powerfully active. In repeating Christ's actions we remember the death of the past and the promise of the future.

Luke (9:11–17)
In the only miracle to appear in all four Gospels, we see the peak of Jesus' Galilean mission. Hereafter Jesus spends more time on the preparation of the Apostles. The sheep without a shepherd theme is a common one. Note the words spoken at the Eucharist and the ones at the Emmaus supper. These are the same words, spoken in the same sequence.

FOCUS

Following closely on all the weeks of themes of Christ's revelation of love by the Spirit, comes the Eucharist. This celebration of remembrance reconnects us in timely ways to the unity of a triune God. Like the model provided by the Trinity, we live in a community connected by care.

What are the ways we are a body of people? Where is our power as a body? How could we act as a unified force for good in our neighborhoods? How do we feed others? In what ways do we bring life and hope to them?

IDEA STARTERS

- Today's festival is appropriately called the Solemnity of the Body and Blood of our Lord.
- This cycle's emphasis is upon the use of two elements, namely the bread and wine. Where and when do various ethnic groups in your parish use bread and wine?
- If your parish is interested in the ministry of "bakers of the bread" this feast would be a good time to begin using bread that looks like bread. Explain the symbolism in the homily and in the bulletin. Have the family who bakes the bread present it at Mass during the procession with the gifts.
- Be sure to highlight the "breaking of the bread" in an extra special way today.
- You may decide to (re)commission Eucharistic Ministers for another year of service during today's liturgy.
- In the past, great Eucharistic devotions were celebrated this day. Consult the new directives and prayers for processions and Benediction in the official text of *Holy Communion and Worship of the Eucharist Outside of Mass.*
- For your consideration: sung Hymn of Praise (eg. *Gloria*); Alternative Opening Prayer; sing the Sequence after the homily (or omit); Intercessions

for the hungry, ministers of the Eucharist, reverence for Holy Communion, for the Church as "Body of Christ"; Holy Eucharist Preface I (P47); Eucharistic Prayer I; Memorial Acclamation C; Ordinary Time Solemn Blessing II.

MUSIC

- Psalm 110
- *Breaking of the Bread* (Feiten/Resource)
- *The Bread of Life* (Dicie/Resource)
- *The Bread of Our Days* (Goglia/Resource)
- *Here Is My Life* (Wise/GIA)
- *Hymn Of The Lord's Supper* (Ivancic/GIA)
- *I Am The Bread Of Life* (Toolan/GIA)
- *Jesus In Our Hands* (Wise/GIA)
- *Taste And See The Goodness Of The Lord* (any setting)
- *This Is My Body* (Jesuits/NALR)
- *To Be Your Bread* (Haas/Cooperative Ministries)

EASTER PLANNING SHEET   Date _____

Parish focus _____

Environment & art _____

Ritual notes _____

Faith development (eg., midweek program) _____

Children's faith experience _____

Prelude _____

Hymn of gathering _____

Sprinkling baptismal water acclamation _____

Opening Prayer _____

Reading cycle _____First reading _____

Responsory _____Second reading _____

Lenten gospel acclamation _____Gospel _____

RCIA rites & acclamations _____

General intercessions _____

At the preparation & presentation _____

Preface dialog _____Preface _____

Preface acclamation _____

Eucharistic prayer _____Memorial acclamation ____

Eucharistic amen _____

The Lord's prayer _____

Breaking of bread _____

The communion hymn _____

The post-communion hymn _____

Blessing _____At the dismissal _____

Memoranda:

SOLEMNITY OF THE SACRED HEART
(Friday After Second Sunday After Pentecost)

YEAR C

READINGS
Ezekiel (34:11-16)
Seeing his people scattered into exile because of incompetent leadership, Ezekiel looks forward to the day when God himself will draw the people back together.
Romans (5:5-11)
God's love embraced us even when we were unmindful and straying.
Luke (15:3-7)
Jesus addresses in parable a mentality that restricts salvation to a legalistic observance of certain norms, and which thereby excludes thoase who cannot fulfill those norms precisely.

FOCUS
Jesus does not affirm that the sinner is loved more than the faithful, but that the shepherd has an obligation to seek out the lost. What is our attitude toward those outside the fold?

IDEA STARTERS
- Gather your evangelism team together for a planning session and Evening Prayer.
- For discussion: Who are the lost sheep within the parish? Who are the lost sheep in the immediate neighborhood? How do you seek them out.
- Hold a communal reconciliation service for the Order of Penitents (or consider beginning an Order of Penitents process for Catholics who want to re-enter the active life of the church.

MUSIC
- Psalm 23
- *Shepherd, Redeemer* (Keyes/Resource)
- *Psalm 23* (Brown/NALR)
- *All My Days* (Farney/Resource)
- *The Lord Is My Shepherd* (Gelineau/GIA)
- *My Shepherd Is the Lord* (Toolan/Resource)
- *The Lord's My Shepherd* (Lynch/Raven)

PLANNING SHEET

Date _____

Parish focus _____

Environment & art _____

Ritual notes _____

Faith development (eg., in newsletter/classes) _____

Children's faith experience _____

Prelude _____

Hymn of gathering _____

Sprinkling/Penitential rite _____

Hymn of praise _____

Opening Prayer _____

First reading _____ Responsory _____

Second reading _____ Gospel acclamation _____

Gospel _____ Profession of faith _____

General intercessions _____

At the preparation & presentation _____

Preface dialog _____ Preface _____

Preface acclamation _____

Eucharistic prayer _____ Memorial acclamation _____

Eucharistic amen _____

The Lord's prayer _____

Breaking of bread _____

The communion hymn _____

The post-communion hymn _____

Blessing _____ At the dismissal _____

Memoranda:

SECOND SUNDAY OF THE YEAR

YEAR C

READINGS

Isaiah (62:1-5)
Isaiah paints here the dream of Israel rebuilt and renewed. A new name and new status mark her; God pledges in her his faithfulness and delight.

First Corinthians (12:4-11)
In this early church, ministry arose from spiritual gifts or charisms. These abilities, whose source was God, were to be used for the whole community. Enthusiasm was not the indication of God's giftedness but the person's contribution to the common good.

John (2:1-12)
This event is called a nature miracle and telling the stories of Jesus' miracles served to model faith responses for the hearer. This faith pointed to an integration of God's revelation and a new wholeness in the person.

FOCUS

The wisdom of faithfulness and rebirth weaves through these readings. Celebrate ways the local church is faithful to its mission in the larger community.

Who are the gifted people in our churches who awe us and deepen our belief in life? Where are the gifts manifest among us that cause "small miracles" to occur? Could this be a time to call forth the gifts of others in the church or invite the use of our gifts for the common good of the larger community?

IDEA STARTERS

- *CCT Lectionary:* Is 62:1-5; Ps 36:5-10; 1 Cor 12:1-11; Jn 2:1-11.
- Water has been a symbol of rebirth, freshness, new life. An asperges or sprinkling ceremony could be used in place of the Penitential Rite.
- Is it possible to plan this liturgy without dwelling on the sacrament of marriage or Mary's words, "Do whatever he tells you"?
- Would a reaffirmation of marriage vows appropriately follow the homily?
- Today begins the series of readings from the later chapters of First Corinthians. Brief biblical background is appropriate for inclusion in the parish bulletin.
- Today's second reading can be used to point toward the observance of Christian Unity Week (beginning January 18).
- For your consideration: Opening Prayers; prayers for the married, the separated, divorced and remarried, for Christian Unity, for different ministries, for wine-makers in the Intercessions; Ordinary Sundays Preface III (P31); Ordinary Time Solemn Blessing III.

MUSIC

- Psalm 96
- *All Praise to You, O Lord* (Beadon/LBW)
- *Happy Are They* (Miffleton/Resource)
- *Mighty Lord* (Jesuits/NALR)

- *One Bread, One Body* (Jesuits/NALR)
- *Proclaim His Marvelous Deeds* (Zsigray/NALR)
- *The Spirit of God* (Deiss/WLP)
- *Sing To the Lord* (Gilsdorf/Resource)

SUNDAY PLANNING SHEET

Date _____

Parish focus _____

Environment & art _____

Ritual notes _____

Faith development (eg., in newsletter/classes) _____

Children's faith experience _____

Prelude _____

Hymn of gathering _____

Sprinkling/Penitential rite _____

Hymn of praise _____

Opening Prayer _____

First reading _____ Responsory _____

Second reading _____ Gospel acclamation _____

Gospel _____ Profession of faith _____

General intercessions _____

At the preparation & presentation _____

Preface dialog _____ Preface _____

Preface acclamation _____

Eucharistic prayer _____ Memorial acclamation _____

Eucharistic amen _____

The Lord's prayer _____

Breaking of bread _____

The communion hymn _____

The post-communion hymn _____

Blessing _____ At the dismissal _____

Memoranda:

THIRD SUNDAY
OF THE YEAR

YEAR C

READINGS
Nehemia (8:1-4,5-6,8-10)
This story tells of the return of the exiled community to Jerusalem, the renewal of the temple and their life as a community. The weeping was joyous — for the Law and the hearing of it restored the people.
First Corinthians (12:12-30)
The word "body" in this context refers to the group of believers. In a literal way the church is the incarnation of Christ. In a metaphoric sense, Christ is the unifying presence for the church.
Luke (1:1-4,4:14-21)
The composition of this reading suggests the importance of justice in Christ's life. As God's prophet he addressed the poor and oppressed. These were the foci of its saving activity. Most important the justice was to be brought about by the believing community. Love and care seek to do justice in the world.

FOCUS
The wonder of the bible itself is symbolized in the first reading where the people wept for joy at its presence. The psalm suggests for us six qualities of the biblical word: perfect, trustworthy, upright, clear, pure and true. What are the ways our community honors the biblical word? Are these qualities alive in our church? Does the word bring joy to our hearts and highlight wisdom for our lives? How could we celebrate or reverence the word in our liturgy this week?

IDEA STARTERS
- *CCT Lectionary:* Neb 8:1-4a, 5-6, 8-10; Ps 19:14-17; 1 Cor 12:12-30; Lk 4:14-21.
- How might you lure members of your assembly to see what happens next in today's gospel reading (after verse 21)?
- Would today be a good day to call for or commission new readers?
- When was the last time your parish sponsored a communal celebration of the anointing of the sick? Today's second and third readings lend themselves to such a liturgy.
- Today is the Sunday within the Week of Prayer for Christian Unity.
- How do the ministry of reader, the sacramental anointing of the sick, and the Christian Unity observance fit into these weeks of "unfolding manifestation of Jesus Christ"?
- For your consideration: Opening Prayers; prayers for the ministers of the word, missionaries, teachers, the sick, healers, Christian Unity in the Intercessions; Ordinary Sundays Preface III (P31); Ordinary Time Solemn Blessing III.

MUSIC
- Psalm 19
- *Call To Me* (Byrne/Resource)
- *In Christ There Is No East or West*
- *Let Us See Your Kindness* (Lisicky/Resource)
- *Give Thanks* (Page/Resource)
- *One Bread, One Body* (Jesuits/NALR)
- *Speak Lord* (Schoenbachler/PAA)
- *You Have Anointed Me* (Dameans/PAA)
- *The Spirit of God* (Deiss/WLP)

SUNDAY PLANNING SHEET

Date _____

Parish focus _____

Environment & art _____

Ritual notes _____

Faith development (eg., in newsletter/classes) _____

Children's faith experience _____

Prelude _____

Hymn of gathering _____

Sprinkling/Penitential rite _____

Hymn of praise _____

Opening Prayer _____

First reading _____ Responsory _____

Second reading _____ Gospel acclamation _____

Gospel _____ Profession of faith _____

General intercessions _____

At the preparation & presentation _____

Preface dialog _____ Preface _____

Preface acclamation _____

Eucharistic prayer _____ Memorial acclamation ____

Eucharistic amen _____

The Lord's prayer _____

Breaking of bread _____

The communion hymn _____

The post-communion hymn _____

Blessing _____ At the dismissal _____

Memoranda:

FOURTH SUNDAY OF THE YEAR

READINGS

Jeremiah (1:4–5,17–19)
The story of Jeremiah's calling and God's support in his prophetic role is a reminder to us of our call and support. The verb "knew" shows us the depth and the intricacy of God's knowledge of Jeremiah, whose entire life is absorbed in this role.

First Corinthians (12:31–13:13)
The gift from God which outdoes all others is love. It is the gift which guides the use of other gifts and which lasts longest because it is an attribute of God. Faith and hope are the responses we give to God's gift of love. Agape requires a radical response to this originating love of God.

Luke (4:21–30)
Israel's story is a continuing story of faithfulness and this theme is repeated in Jesus' life and message. As was his custom, Jesus taught in the Temple and the rejection of his message sets up Luke's Gospel to the Gentiles.

FOCUS
Where wisdom is rooted in love we are able to see rightly and to speak of what we see. How does love support the members of our community: the youth, the elderly, the singles, the unemployed, the hurting, etc. Do we call forth the gifts of the young to love? Can our senior members still contribute to us?

IDEA STARTERS
- *CCT Lectionary:* Jer 1:4–10; Ps 71:1–6; 1 Cor 13:1–13; Lk 4:21–30.
- Don't disassociate today's Gospel from last Sunday's. Note that the last verse of last week's gospel is the first for today.
- Does your parish have "coffee and ..." after the liturgy for those wishing to remain that they might meet new and old friends? Perhaps today would be a good day to start such a practice in the spirit of agape.
- For your consideration: Prayers for the prophets biblical and non-biblical, for people of every religion, for victims of injustice in the Intercessions; Ordinary Sundays Preface VII (P35); Ordinary Time Solemn Blessing II.

MUSIC
- Psalm 71
- *Before the Sun Burned Bright* (Jesuits/NALR)
- *Be Not Afraid* (Jesuits/NALR)
- *Believe* (McGrath/Resource)
- *Lord You Have Probed Me* (Gilsdorf/Resource)
- *Love is Patient* (Haugen/PAA)
- *You Are Near* (Jesuits/NALR)

SUNDAY PLANNING SHEET

Date _____

Parish focus _____

Environment & art _____

Ritual notes _____

Faith development (eg., in newsletter/classes) _____

Children's faith experience _____

Prelude _____

Hymn of gathering _____

Sprinkling/Penitential rite _____

Hymn of praise _____

Opening Prayer _____

First reading _____ Responsory _____

Second reading _____ Gospel acclamation _____

Gospel _____ Profession of faith _____

General intercessions _____

At the preparation & presentation _____

Preface dialog _____ Preface _____

Preface acclamation _____

Eucharistic prayer _____ Memorial acclamation ___

Eucharistic amen _____

The Lord's prayer _____

Breaking of bread _____

The communion hymn _____

The post-communion hymn _____

Blessing _____ At the dismissal _____

Memoranda:

FIFTH SUNDAY OF THE YEAR

YEAR C

READINGS

Isaiah (6:1-2,3-8)

This passage is filled with symbols for the majesty of God: The Ark of the Covenant, the Seraphim, the house filled with smoke, the coal, the three greetings of "holy." The power of God is juxstaposed with the sinfulness and unworthiness of Isaiah. It is only God's concern that Isaiah is cleansed and sent forth.

First Corinthians (15:1-11)

For the Christians of the Corinth Church, this passage is the core of their belief. The substance of Paul's preaching focuses on the passion, death and resurrection of Christ.

Luke (5:1-11)

While the mountain is the primary symbol for communication between God and people, the lake is the primary symbol for revealing the power of Christ. Peter's response to Jesus reveals single-minded strength: when encountering life's crises, Peter always impetuously chooses faithfulness.

FOCUS

The fifth and sixth Sundays of the year focus on the call to life. Isaiah and Peter are models of people in crisis who respond with faith and commitment.

Some questions to explore include: How are we called today to faith and commitment? What problems or crises face our community? How can we as a community respond to larger crises?

What individual crises need to be supported? How do we aid the divorced, ill, unemployed, grieving?

The presence of God's power is very obvious in these scriptures. How can you illustrate contemporary sites of God's power? What people or situations leave us in awe at God's presence? What signs of Spring are evident which remind us of God? What events give us hope? Could these be acted out in church?

IDEA STARTERS

- *CCT Lectionary:* Is 6:1-8 (9-13); Ps 138; 1 Cor 15:1-11; Lk 5:1-11.
- All will probably recognize Isaiah 6:3 (holy, holy...). At today's Eucharist have an acolyte stand at the side of the sanctuary and incense the altar and the gifts during the first half of the Preface Acclamation (Sanctus). Let the house of the church be filled with smoke. (See Isaiah 6:4.)
- The epiphanies in today's readings move from the power of God upon us to the power of God within us (Emmanuel), which causes meatnoia, conversion.
- What are "hosts"? (See Isaiah 6:3.) Also examine Paul's words, "I have worked harder than all others..." (I Corinthians 15:10.)
- Themes for purification, the Easter mystery and Jesus' forgiving call give an opportunity for you to begin publicizing your Lenten program.

- For your consideration: Sprinkling baptismal water prayer "A"; intercessions for victims of disasters, for missionaries, and for the conversion of heart; Ordinary Sundays Preface V (P33);Memorial Acclamation "A"; Ordinary Time Solemn Blessing I.

MUSIC

- Psalm 138
- *Anthem* (Conry/NALR)
- *Here I Am, Lord* (Jesuits/NALR)
- *Here I Am, Lord* (Schoenbachler/PAA) (Jesuits/NALR)
- *Sing to the Lord* (Gilsdorf/Resource)
- *We Are Called* (Patterson/Resource)
- *In Praise of His Name* (Jesuits/NALR)

SUNDAY PLANNING SHEET

Date _____

Parish focus _____

Environment & art _____

Ritual notes _____

Faith development (eg., in newsletter/classes) _____

Children's faith experience _____

Prelude _____

Hymn of gathering _____

Sprinkling/Penitential rite _____

Hymn of praise _____

Opening Prayer _____

First reading _____Responsory _____

Second reading _____Gospel acclamation _____

Gospel _____Profession of faith _____

General intercessions _____

At the preparation & presentation _____

Preface dialog _____Preface _____

Preface acclamation _____

Eucharistic prayer _____Memorial acclamation _____

Eucharistic amen _____

The Lord's prayer _____

Breaking of bread _____

The communion hymn _____

The post-communion hymn _____

Blessing _____At the dismissal _____

Memoranda:

SIXTH SUNDAY OF THE YEAR

READINGS
Isaiah (17:5–8)
Using the literary form of blessings and curses, Jeremiah repeats a common Old Testament theme: the just person is full of life while the godless person is like a fruitless desert. People of true faith pin their hopes on God alone.
First Corinthians (15:12,16–20)
The Resurrection of Christ is the source of life and freedom to the Christian believer. Those who believe in his victory over death participate in that victory.
Luke (6:17,20–26)
While on the surface this may look like Matthew's Sermon on the Mount, it differs in substantial ways. Jesus actually comes down from the mountain to speak to the disciples, the poor and the disabled. The group is mixed with Jews and Gentiles. And the "woes" are unique to this passage characterizing Jesus as a prophet. These sayings were probably collected from a variety of situations in Jesus' life and entered here as one teaching. "Blessed" here is not a literal blessing but better translated as "happy."

FOCUS
This Sunday focuses on the life to which we are called. It is a paradoxical life in that it promises happiness and fullness, yet asks for simpleness and humbleness. It is certainly not the life sold through the modern media.

What are the ways we can define life for the modern person? What will happiness and fullness mean in a time of less: jobs, money, resources, etc.? How do we overcome a sense of being cheated out of what we were promised by our dreams?

What suggestions can be made for our community to simplify?

IDEA STARTERS
- *CCT Lectionary:* Jer 17:5–10; Ps 1; 1 Cor 15:12–20; Lk 6:17–26.
- How do people use "blessing and curses" today?
- Today is the final Sunday before Lent. Careful use of "alleluias" during today's liturgies will mark its final use until the Easter Vigil. As a final hymn, *Alleluia, Song of Gladness* (the Hymnal — 1940) might put the assembly in a Lenten direction.
- Communities with musicians willing to "create" music for the words of the Ambrosian Rite's farewell to the Alleluia (enclose and seal up the word "alleluia"...) may want to see *Manual on the Liturgy* by Philip Pfactteicher and Carlos Messerli (Minneapolis: Augsburg Publishing House, 1979) page 307.
- St. Paul's reading emphasizes the importance of believing in the resurrection of our Saviour. In your Sunday bulletin stress the importance of understanding our Christian beliefs — especially by attending the parish Lenten programs.
- Might a *mardi gras* celebration be in order today or on Tuesday evening?

MUSIC

- Psalm 1
- *Beatitudes* (Page/Resource)
- *I Will Raise Him Up* (Toolan/GIA)
- *Happy Are They* (Miffleton/Resource)
- *O Happy Is the Just* (Weston Priory)
- *We Are the Light of the World* (Grief/Venacular)
- *The Cry of the Poor* (Jesuits/NALR)

SUNDAY PLANNING SHEET   Date _____

Parish focus _____

Environment & art _____

Ritual notes _____

Faith development (eg., in newsletter/classes) _____

Children's faith experience _____

Prelude _____

Hymn of gathering _____

Sprinkling/Penitential rite _____

Hymn of praise _____

Opening Prayer _____

First reading _____Responsory _____

Second reading _____Gospel acclamation _____

Gospel _____Profession of faith _____

General intercessions _____

At the preparation & presentation _____

Preface dialog _____Preface _____

Preface acclamation _____

Eucharistic prayer _____Memorial acclamation _____

Eucharistic amen _____

The Lord's prayer _____

Breaking of bread _____

The communion hymn _____

The post-communion hymn _____

Blessing _____At the dismissal _____

Memoranda:

SEVENTH SUNDAY OF THE YEAR

READINGS
First Samuel (26:2,7–9,12–13,22–23)
Here is a record of one of two opportunities David had to kill Saul, who had failed to lead his people properly. By sparing Saul, David exhibited a compassion based on faith in God.
First Corinthians (15:45–49)
We are earthly and heavenly, body and soul. We are heirs of Adam and of Christ. It is this integration of the human and the divine that Christ came to proclaim.
Luke (6:27–38)
Loving our enemies is the ultimate criterion of love. To help those who will not reciprocate simply for the sake of their good is the true measure of compassion. Love of enemy is not something that comes naturally. It must be learned by habit, and it must be aided by grace.

FOCUS
As Fr. John Hugo says: We love God as much as we love the person whom we love the least. As David showed compassion to Saul, so we are called by Jesus to love our enemies. This is possible for us because we have in us a spark of the divine.

IDEA STARTERS
- *CCT Lectionary:* Gn 45:3–11, 15; Ps 37:1–11; 1 Cor 15:35–38, 42–50; Lk 6:27–38.
- How does the law of "Love your enemy" translate into a world on the verge of nuclear annihilation?
- Where do we see contemporary examples of love of one's enemies in action?
- Use the Penitential Rite to talk about forgiveness of our enemies.

MUSIC
- Psalm 103
- *Beatitudes* (Page/Resource)
- *God is Love* (Hutson/Resource)
- *Love is Forever* (Dameans/NALR)
- *If Anyone Loves Me* (Weston Priory)
- *Seek First His Kingship* (Mullins/Resource)
- *Our God Is Love* (Repp/K&R)

SUNDAY PLANNING SHEET

Date _____

Parish focus _____

Environment & art _____

Ritual notes _____

Faith development (eg., in newsletter/classes) _____

Children's faith experience _____

Prelude _____

Hymn of gathering _____

Sprinkling/Penitential rite _____

Hymn of praise _____

Opening Prayer _____

First reading _____ Responsory _____

Second reading _____ Gospel acclamation _____

Gospel _____ Profession of faith _____

General intercessions _____

At the preparation & presentation _____

Preface dialog _____ Preface _____

Preface acclamation _____

Eucharistic prayer _____ Memorial acclamation _____

Eucharistic amen _____

The Lord's prayer _____

Breaking of bread _____

The communion hymn _____

The post-communion hymn _____

Blessing _____ At the dismissal _____

Memoranda:

EIGHTH SUNDAY OF THE YEAR

YEAR C

READINGS
Sirach (27:4–7)
The power of the spoken word is a power for good or evil. What is the balance like in our own lives?
First Corinthians (15:54–58)
Paul praises God for having overcome death in Jesus Christ. This is a hymn of victory and assurance of the fulfillment of salvation.
Luke (6:39–45)
This group of sayings of Jesus is a call to integrity. Jesus speaks here against hypocrisy and for humility and wholeness.

Again we see the theme of the power of words. Here Jesus refers to the power of words to reveal the true nature of the speaker.

FOCUS
God's love for us is mediated through words. We are a people of words. Speech is what separates us from the rest of the cosmos. It is what allows us to reflect on who we are.

The power of speech is a power to build up or destroy; to give life or take it.

IDEA STARTERS
- *CCT Lectionary:* Eu 27:4–7 or Is 55:10–13; Ps 92:1–4, 12–15; 1 Cor 15:51–58; Lk 6:39–49.
- How much of our speech is constructive and how much foolish or wasteful? This is a question that merits some attention.
- The great Muslim mystic, Al Gazzali, speaks of how difficult it is to fast from foolish or harmful speech. Much easier to fast from food!
- Today is a good day to honor greeters of the parish who offer hospitality through kind words.

MUSIC
- Psalm 92
- *Alpha and Omega* (Schoenbachler/NALR)
- *Be a New Man* (Wise/GIA)
- *How Firm a Foundation* (ICEL)
- *In Him We Live* (Landry/NALR)
- *In Your Presence* (Byrne/Resource)
- *Hear Us, Almighty Lord* (ICEL)
- *The Spirit of God* (Goglia/Resource)

SUNDAY PLANNING SHEET

Date _____

Parish focus _____

Environment & art _____

Ritual notes _____

Faith development (eg., in newsletter/classes) _____

Children's faith experience _____

Prelude _____

Hymn of gathering _____

Sprinkling/Penitential rite _____

Hymn of praise _____

Opening Prayer _____

First reading _____ Responsory _____

Second reading _____ Gospel acclamation _____

Gospel _____ Profession of faith _____

General intercessions _____

At the preparation & presentation _____

Preface dialog _____ Preface _____

Preface acclamation _____

Eucharistic prayer _____ Memorial acclamation _____

Eucharistic amen _____

The Lord's prayer _____

Breaking of bread _____

The communion hymn _____

The post-communion hymn _____

Blessing _____ At the dismissal _____

Memoranda:

NINTH SUNDAY OF THE YEAR

YEAR C

READINGS

First Kings (8:41–43)
In this reading the people of Israel reflect an understanding that their election as God's chosen priesthood involves a mission to shine as a light to the nations. The restoration of the Temple was to serve as a sign of God's presence to the entire world.

Galatians (1:1–2,6–10)
Paul addresses those who continue to make the Law the center of their spiritual lives. The only appropriate center is Christ Jesus. Paul himself keeps the Law but does not require other believers (non-Jews) to do so.

Luke (7:1–10)
The healing of the centurion dramatizes the concern of Jesus beyond the confines of the Jewish people. Although Jesus' ministry was confined to the Jews this event points to a wider application which is to begin with Pentecost.

FOCUS
Israel was chosen to be the vehicle of God's salvation to all nations. By its nature the church is called to include everyone who comes. Even more, to go out and seek to bring the Good News to others. Our belief that we are favored by God because we are church members is a risky assumption.

IDEA STARTERS
- *CCT Lectionary:* 1 Kg 8:22-23, 41-43; Ps 100; Gal 1:1-10; Lk 7:1-10.
- Today's readings provide an excellent context for an ecumenical service.
- Use the Penitential Rite to examine the community's failure to reach out to the wider community.
- Honor the Greeters and those who work in community outreach at a special coffee.

MUSIC
- Psalm 117
- *And There Will Shine* (Repp/K&R)
- *Dwelling Place* (Jesuits/NALR)
- *Gather Round* (Page/Resource)
- *Arise, Shine Out* (Bennet/Resource)
- *One Bread, One Body* (Jesuits/NALR)
- *Shout With God* (Tucciarone/Resource)

SUNDAY PLANNING SHEET

Date _____

Parish focus _____

Environment & art _____

Ritual notes _____

Faith development (eg., in newsletter/classes) _____

Children's faith experience _____

Prelude _____

Hymn of gathering _____

Sprinkling/Penitential rite _____

Hymn of praise _____

Opening Prayer _____

First reading _____ Responsory _____

Second reading _____ Gospel acclamation _____

Gospel _____ Profession of faith _____

General intercessions _____

At the preparation & presentation _____

Preface dialog _____ Preface _____

Preface acclamation _____

Eucharistic prayer _____ Memorial acclamation ____

Eucharistic amen _____

The Lord's prayer _____

Breaking of bread _____

The communion hymn _____

The post-communion hymn _____

Blessing _____ At the dismissal _____

Memoranda:

TENTH SUNDAY OF THE YEAR

YEAR C

READINGS

First Kings (17:17-24)
The miracles of Elija are a sign of God's presence and power in the ministry of the prophet. Here he is vindicated among the wicked.

Galatians (1:11-19)
In his argument against those who would insist on strict adherence to the Jewish Law by all believers, Paul establishes himself as a strict and upright keeper of the Law himself.

Luke (7:11-17)
Jesus raises the dead to life. This is not a resurrection in the sense of Jesus' resurrection, but rather a resuscitation.

FOCUS
The Gospel reading alludes to the miracle of Elija as described in today's first reading. There are similarities in the two events. Jesus both echoes and surpasses the work of the prophets.

IDEA STARTERS
- *CCT Lectionary:* 1 Kg 17:17-24; Ps 113; Gal 1:11-24; Lk 7:11-17.
- Today's readings provide an obvious context for the Anointing of the Sick.
- How do the miracles of Elija and Jesus differ?
- The raising of the widow's son was not simply a show of power. It was an act of compassion on the behalf of Jesus. Do our acts of compassion contain such power?

MUSIC
- Psalm 30
- *O Healing River* (Traditional)
- *He Fulfilled the Promise* (Page/Resource)
- *Give Thanks* (Lisicky/Resource)
- *Praise the Lord, My Soul* (Parker/GIA)
- *For Us To Live* (Weston Priory)
- *Into Your Hands* (Boecker/Resource)

SUNDAY PLANNING SHEET

Date _____

Parish focus _____

Environment & art _____

Ritual notes _____

Faith development (eg., in newsletter/classes) _____

Children's faith experience _____

Prelude _____

Hymn of gathering _____

Sprinkling/Penitential rite _____

Hymn of praise _____

Opening Prayer _____

First reading _____ Responsory _____

Second reading _____ Gospel acclamation _____

Gospel _____ Profession of faith _____

General intercessions _____

At the preparation & presentation _____

Preface dialog _____ Preface _____

Preface acclamation _____

Eucharistic prayer _____ Memorial acclamation _____

Eucharistic amen _____

The Lord's prayer _____

Breaking of bread _____

The communion hymn _____

The post-communion hymn _____

Blessing _____ At the dismissal _____

Memoranda:

ELEVENTH SUNDAY OF THE YEAR

READINGS
Second Samuel (12:7-10,13)
The prophet Nathan chides David for the taking of Bathsheba and death of Uriah. Their child, rather than David, will eventually suffer the consequences. It is David's penitence and faithfulness to God which wins him forgiveness and continued love.

Galatians (2:16,19-21)
In the second major theme of this letter, Paul distinguishes between law and faithfulness to the Gospel. The Spirit of God alive in us supersedes the law and eliminates the need for its burden. We find freedom in Christ's lifestyle and Spirit.

Luke (7:36-8:3)
This story of forgiveness is a story of courage. Here the woman knows well the obligations which the host overlooked. To Luke, Jesus renews and reorders by forgiving the sins of the community. The freedom which comes with the lifting of sin's burden may match the weight of courage. The women who followed and aided Jesus during his ministry are the ones who complete the ministry with him at his death.

FOCUS
Forgiveness is a primary theme for our faith. We are reminded of the loving God who puts aside severe and small errors. We are reminded of the humble person who must seek freedom from the patterns which are causing the errors.

Key to forgiveness is courage. It is the response to the offer of loving forgiveness. Courage triggers a resolve to pick up and move on: to renew our lives.

While forgiveness is most easily talked about in the context of home and personal life, we need more and more to remember the reconnection we need with other countries, peoples, places. This courage may be the most dramatic of all.

IDEA STARTERS
- *CCT Lectionary:* 1 Kg 19:1-18; Ps 42; Gal 2:15-21; Lk 7:36-8:3.
- Today's readings provide an opportunity for catechesis about the three rites of sacramental reconciliation.
- What role do women play in Luke's gospel? in our society? in the Church today?
- What is the relationship between the Galatians reading and Jesus' words in Luke 7:50?
- The lesson from Samuel speaks about sexual sin. (The Lucan excerpt implies it.) How does the contemporary church view human sexuality?
- For your consideration: Penitential Rite A; Alternative Opening Prayer; intercessions for forgiveness, proper sexual expression, living for God, religious leaders, judges and lawyers; Reconciliation Eucharistic Prayer I; Memorial Acclamation D; *Lord's Prayer* sung; Ordinary Solemn Blessing V.

MUSIC

- Psalm 32
- *All That We Have* (Dameans/NALR)
- *Ashes* (Conry/NALR)
- *Dwelling Place* (Jesuits/NALR)
- *Eye Has Not Seen* (Haugen/GIA)
- *Go Now In Peace* (Wise/GIA)
- *Hosea* (Weston Priory)
- *I Have Loved You* (Joncas/NALR)
- *My Refuge* (Vessels/GIA)
- *Praise The Lord* (Keyes/Resource)
- *Praise The Lord, Alleluia* (Page/Resource)
- *Remember Your Love* (Dameans/NALR)
- *Said Judas To Mary* (Carter/Galliard)
- *Seek The Lord* (Jesuits/NALR)
- *Son Of David* (Jesuits/NALR)
- *Though The Mountains May Fall* (Jesuits/NALR)

SUNDAY PLANNING SHEET   Date _____

Parish focus _____

Environment & art _____

Ritual notes _____

Faith development (eg., in newsletter/classes) _____

Children's faith experience _____

Prelude _____

Hymn of gathering _____

Sprinkling/Penitential rite _____

Hymn of praise _____

Opening Prayer _____

First reading _____Responsory _____

Second reading _____Gospel acclamation _____

Gospel _____Profession of faith _____

General intercessions _____

At the preparation & presentation _____

Preface dialog _____Preface _____

Preface acclamation _____

Eucharistic prayer _____Memorial acclamation _____

Eucharistic amen _____

The Lord's prayer _____

Breaking of bread _____

The communion hymn _____

The post-communion hymn _____

Blessing _____At the dismissal _____

Memoranda:

TWELFTH SUNDAY OF THE YEAR

YEAR C

READINGS

Zechariah (12:10-11)
Compassion sets the tone of this passage. Though the identity of the martyred person is obscure, we can understand it as the Christ. Hadad-rimmon is a fertility god mourned as the seasons change.

Galatians (3:26-29)
Paul's major theme here is unity or oneness. The faith in Christ now known by all removed the individual differences that separate. The heritage and promise made to the early community now is open to all.

Luke (9:18-24)
Prayer is often a sign of major moments in Luke's portrayal of Jesus. Here the question of identity is confronted. Jesus' personal sense of rejection may have urged the disciples to choose freely to follow in the final difficult times.

FOCUS

This juncture of Luke's gospel explores the identity of Jesus and the purpose of his mission. Asking similar questions of our Christian identity seems appropriate. Who Christians are in today's world, and what their message is, can be as obscure as in Jesus' time. This question of identity does not relate to styles of Christianity, such as, liberal or conservative, etc. But it relates to core values of our lifestyles, our attitudes and approaches.

Secondly, from the Old Testament, and from the rejection foretold by Jesus, comes the concern for compassion. Do we extend mercy and care freely? Are we able to choose freely to act in our communities? Are we constrained by the pressures of media, society, or group values? Does the manipulation of the larger society prevent compassion on the local level?

IDEA STARTERS

- *CCT Lectionary:* 1Kg 19-14; Ps 43; Gal 3:23-29; Lk 9:18-24.
- This second part of Ordinary Time after Pentecost has been called the "time of the church." Having recently completed the major seasons of the liturgical year, now is the time to reflect upon the cost of discipleship.
- Why do people view suffering as a punishment from God when Jesus says that we who have faith in him must bear our crosses?
- The Galatians reading calls us to reflect upon relationships. How do we treat people? Why do we treat people the way we do? God calls us to share a loving openness toward all people. How might this be related to the love shared by a father toward his children?
- For your consideration: Sprinkling Baptismal Water B; Opening Prayer; intercessions for the suffering, Christian unity, fathers, perseverance, end to prejudice; Reconciliation Eucharistic Prayer II; Memorial Acclamation A; Ordinary Solemn Blessing IV.

MUSIC

- Psalm 63
- *Glorious Praise* (Hilliard/Resource)
- *He Is The Lord* (Haas/Cooperative Ministries)
- *Lift High The Cross* (LBW)
- *Mighty Lord* (Jesuits/NALR)
- *One Bread, One Body* (Jesuits/NALR)
- *One Lord* (Haas/Cooperative Ministries)
- *Servants of the Lord* (Hummer/Resource)
- *Something Which Is Known* (Weston Priory)
- *Song Of Gathering* (Wise/GIA)
- *We Remember* (Haugen/PAA)
- *Your Love Is Finer Than Life* (Haugen/GIA)

SUNDAY PLANNING SHEET   Date _____

Parish focus _____

Environment & art _____

Ritual notes _____

Faith development (eg., in newsletter/classes) _____

Children's faith experience _____

Prelude _____

Hymn of gathering _____

Sprinkling/Penitential rite _____

Hymn of praise _____

Opening Prayer _____

First reading _____Responsory _____

Second reading _____Gospel acclamation _____

Gospel _____Profession of faith _____

General intercessions _____

At the preparation & presentation _____

Preface dialog _____Preface _____

Preface acclamation _____

Eucharistic prayer _____Memorial acclamation _____

Eucharistic amen _____

The Lord's prayer _____

Breaking of bread _____

The communion hymn _____

The post-communion hymn _____

Blessing _____At the dismissal _____

Memoranda:

THIRTEENTH SUNDAY OF THE YEAR

YEAR C

READINGS

1 Kings (19:16,19–21)
This story is the call of the prophet Elisha, who replaces Elijah and carries on his work. When summoning Elisha, Elijah allows him to finish his personal tasks. This is in contrast to Luke's portrayal of Jesus' call which demands instant commitment.

Galatians (5:1,13–18)
Freedom to Paul is the outcome of a life of faith in Jesus. This freedom is not merely a removal of the old law nor a time for unmeasured action. Now the harder demands of love guide the actions of the free person.

Luke (9:51–62)
Making a total commitment in Jesus implies for Luke the abandonment of all normal life. Our possessions, family, personal attitudes, etc., will be left behind to partake in Jesus' mission.

FOCUS

The tone of today's readings leads easily to questions about our commitments. Who calls us? To what do we make our commitments? What must we give up for the challenge of new opportunity? What safety or security must we confront before we can approach change?

Secondly, we must ask what is the measure of love? Isn't it easier to live by a law than decide where or what is the loving thing to do? What new requirements does the loving action demand?

IDEA STARTERS

- *CCT Lectionary:* 1Kg 19:15–21; Ps 44:1–8; Gal 5:1, 13–25; Lk 9:51–62.
- Today's readings ask us to look at the sin of half-heartedness. How committed are we to the Gospel of Christ?
- Am I open to what the Lord wants me to do, or am I creating obstacles along the way?
- What does Paul mean when he writes "you are not under the law"?
- The Sunday Eucharist during the summer should take into consideration that people are in relaxed moods, yet these Ordinary Sundays are still "little Easters." How do we reconcile the two?
- For your consideration: Opening Prayer; intercessions for summer safety, perseverance, single heartedness, farmers, Christian love; Ordinary Sundays Preface I (P29); Eucharistic Prayer III; Ordinary Solemn Blessing II.

MUSIC

- Psalm 16
- *Alleluia* (Horn/Resource)
- *Anthem* (Conry/NALR)
- *Before The Sun Burned Bright* (Jesuits/NALR)
- *Father We Sing Your Praises* (Zsigray/NALR)
- *I Danced In The Morning* (Carter/Galliard)
- *I Have Loved You* (Joncas/NALR)
- *Like A Sunflower* (Landry/NALR)
- *Show Me, Lord, the Way* (Keyes/Resource)
- *Speak, Lord* (Dameans/NALR)
- *You Are My Friends* (Reagan/NALR)

SUNDAY PLANNING SHEET

Date _____

Parish focus _____

Environment & art _____

Ritual notes _____

Faith development (eg., in newsletter/classes) _____

Children's faith experience _____

Prelude _____

Hymn of gathering _____

Sprinkling/Penitential rite _____

Hymn of praise _____

Opening Prayer _____

First reading _____ Responsory _____

Second reading _____ Gospel acclamation _____

Gospel _____ Profession of faith _____

General intercessions _____

At the preparation & presentation _____

Preface dialog _____ Preface _____

Preface acclamation _____

Eucharistic prayer _____ Memorial acclamation _____

Eucharistic amen _____

The Lord's prayer _____

Breaking of bread _____

The communion hymn _____

The post-communion hymn _____

Blessing _____ At the dismissal _____

Memoranda:

FOURTEENTH SUNDAY OF THE YEAR

YEAR C

READINGS
Isaiah (66:10-14)
In the concluding statements of the book of Isaiah, we read of the hope for rebuilding the city, Jerusalem. The renewed Jerusalem symbolizes hope for this nation, and for all of us, that the future will be restored to peace and prosperity.

Galatians (6:14-18)
The closing of Paul's letter is an attempt at reconciliation. Common faith in Jesus and the strength in Paul's mission eliminates their differences. It is no longer the Jewish law which distinguishes between people, but their lifestyles as Christians.

Luke (10:1-2,17-20)
This story chronicles the mission of the seventy disciples. They were instructed not to delay with even the customary hospitality or diet traditions. Those people who received these messengers received Jesus.

FOCUS
The personal internal complexities of the Christian lifestyle can be further muddied by the task of moving outward with the message of Jesus. No life in faith is complete unless it is being shared with the larger community.

One key to the task of mission is the role of Christian model. Like the renewed Jerusalem the Christian community can become a model of hope through their lives and works. How can we reconcile our internal messages of faith and our model to the world?

IDEA STARTERS
- *CCT Lectionary:* 1Kg 21:1-3, 17-21; Ps 5:1-8; Gal 6:7-18; Lk 10:1-12, 17-20.
- What responsibility do we Christians have today toward preaching the reign of God in our midst?
- The Gospel calls us to reflect upon how we are assisting in the missionary activity of the Church.
- For your consideration: Sprinkling Baptismal Water A; Alternative Opening Prayer; intercessions for justice and peace, joy for all peoples, safe travel, hope for the hopeless, missionaries, mothers and mothers-to-be, the sick and shut-in; Eucharistic Prayer IV; Memorial Acclamation C; Ordinary Solemn Blessing I.

MUSIC

- Psalm 66
- *Abba, Father* (Gilsdorf/Resource)
- *Come With Me Into The Fields* (Jesuits/NALR)
- *Gather Round* (Page/Resource)
- *Glory And Peace* (Jesuits/NALR)
- *Go Out To The World* (Gilsdorf/Resource)
- *Go Up To The Mountain* (Weston Priory)
- *New Life* (Landry/NALR)
- *O Healing River* (Traditional)
- *Peace* (Weston Priory)
- *Peace Is Flowing Like A River* (Traditional)
- *Praise Canticle* (Haas/Cooperative Ministries)
- *A Song Of Blessing* (Wise/GIA)
- *Spirit Of God* (Weston Priory)

SUNDAY PLANNING SHEET   Date _____

Parish focus _____

Environment & art _____

Ritual notes _____

Faith development (eg., in newsletter/classes) _____

Children's faith experience _____

Prelude _____

Hymn of gathering _____

Sprinkling/Penitential rite _____

Hymn of praise _____

Opening Prayer _____

First reading _____ Responsory _____

Second reading _____ Gospel acclamation ____

Gospel _____ Profession of faith _____

General intercessions _____

At the preparation & presentation _____

Preface dialog _____ Preface _____

Preface acclamation _____

Eucharistic prayer _____ Memorial acclamation ___

Eucharistic amen _____

The Lord's prayer _____

Breaking of bread _____

The communion hymn _____

The post-communion hymn _____

Blessing _____ At the dismissal _____

Memoranda:

FIFTEENTH SUNDAY OF THE YEAR

YEAR C

READINGS
Deuteronomy (30:10-14)
The author of Deuteronomy attributes this as the last passage by Moses. It becomes his request for a decision. Given the love of God, will the requirements of the covenant be carried out? Moses insists that this truth is not distant but close to each heart.

Colossians (1:15-20)
This may have been an early baptismal hymn for the church. It recounts the superiority of Christ in both the created universe and the church. Christ is both the first and the unity of all.

Luke (10:25-37)
That law is not a thing only to learn or manipulate is cleverly described by the lawyer's question. He understands the limits of the law and Jesus extends those boundaries for him. For Luke the practice of the law will also lead to those beyond the Jewish community.

FOCUS
On the obvious levels the question of who is our neighbor needs to be answered. The subject of our Christian mission must be freely examined and extended to all.

But Moses leads us to a second question: who reminds us of our obligations? Too easily we can wait for church leaders, national leaders, etc., to urge our involvement. Moses suggests that the deciding factor is within each of us. Personal courage is asked. What holds us back internally? externally? What binds us to inaction?

IDEA STARTERS
- *CCT Lectionary:* 2Kg 2:1, 6-14; Ps 139:1-2; Col 1:1-14; Lk 10:25-37.
- How welcome do visitors feel when they come to worship with your assembly? What kind of hospitality program has your parish developed toward vacationers and new families looking for a church home?
- What is compassion? How does God show forth his compassion today? How do we show Christian compassion to our neighbors?
- Have we imprinted God's commandments on our minds, lips and in our hearts?
- Why is stereotyping, discrimination and prejudice dangerous to any society — and out of the question for the Christian?
- A parish picnic sponsored by the parish youth group and Golden Age Club, the mens' and womens' societies, the charismatic and rosary prayer groups, etc. may further illustrate the mutual cooperation that Christians share "out of love" for one another.
- For your consideration: Alternative Opening Prayer (reword it!); intercessions for ethnic groups in the parish, end to prejudice and oppression, openness to God's law, responsible use of God's creation, summer travelers; Eucharistic Prayer II w/its preface; Ordinary Solemn Blessing II.

MUSIC

- Psalm 69
- *All Ye Servants* (Feiten/Resource)
- *The Cry Of The Poor* (Jesuits/NALR)
- *God And Man At Table* (Stamps)
- *Keep Me Safe* (Mondoy/Resource)
- *Lord, To Whom Shall We Go* (Joncas/NALR)
- *Our God Is Love* (Repp/K & R)
- *Sing Out His Goodness* (Dameans/NALR)
- *That There May Be Bread* (Weston Priory)
- *This Is Our Prayer* (Repp/K & R)

SUNDAY PLANNING SHEET   Date _____

Parish focus _____

Environment & art _____

Ritual notes _____

Faith development (eg., in newsletter/classes) _____

Children's faith experience _____

Prelude _____

Hymn of gathering _____

Sprinkling/Penitential rite _____

Hymn of praise _____

Opening Prayer _____

First reading _____ Responsory _____

Second reading _____ Gospel acclamation _____

Gospel _____ Profession of faith _____

General intercessions _____

At the preparation & presentation _____

Preface dialog _____ Preface _____

Preface acclamation _____

Eucharistic prayer _____ Memorial acclamation ____

Eucharistic amen _____

The Lord's prayer _____

Breaking of bread _____

The communion hymn _____

The post-communion hymn _____

Blessing _____ At the dismissal _____

Memoranda:

SIXTEENTH SUNDAY OF THE YEAR

YEAR C

READINGS

Genesis (18:1-10)
True and proper hospitality requires a total giving of self. This is the kind of hospitality that Christ looks for from us.

Colossians (1:24-28)
There is nothing lacking in the person of Christ. But the church, as his body, is as yet incomplete. It is this body which is built up through ministry.

Luke (10:38-42)
Busyness is seductive. It allows us to avoid the spiritual in our lives. Jesus calls us to simplicity and a right ordering of priorities.

FOCUS

Real hospitality, real listening to another is not something that comes easily to we who live such hectic lives. To listen is to experience a person in their essence. It requires concentration and care. This kind of listening is the essence of hospitality.

IDEA STARTERS

- *CCT Lectionary:* 2 Kg 4:8-17; Ps 139:13-18; Col 1:21-29; Lk 10:38-42.
- What organizations in the community provide hospitality to the needy; Catholic Worker, St. Vincent De Paul, Women's Shelters? Highlight one or more of these in the parish bulletin.
- Include an extended silence somewhere in the liturgy today. Stop the flow of words.
- Remove as much furniture as possible from the church for today's liturgy.

MUSIC

- Psalm 15
- *As a Family* (Page/Resource)
- *Chose Life* (Weston Priory)
- *One Bread, One Body* (Jesuits/NALR)
- *Here I Am* (Lisicky/Resource)
- *Earthen Vessels* (Jesuits/NALR)
- *Gather Round* (Page/Resource)

SUNDAY PLANNING SHEET

Date _____

Parish focus _____

Environment & art _____

Ritual notes _____

Faith development (eg., in newsletter/classes) _____

Children's faith experience _____

Prelude _____

Hymn of gathering _____

Sprinkling/Penitential rite _____

Hymn of praise _____

Opening Prayer _____

First reading _____ Responsory _____

Second reading _____ Gospel acclamation _____

Gospel _____ Profession of faith _____

General intercessions _____

At the preparation & presentation _____

Preface dialog _____ Preface _____

Preface acclamation _____

Eucharistic prayer _____ Memorial acclamation _____

Eucharistic amen _____

The Lord's prayer _____

Breaking of bread _____

The communion hymn _____

The post-communion hymn _____

Blessing _____ At the dismissal _____

Memoranda:

SEVENTEENTH SUNDAY OF THE YEAR

READINGS

Genesis (18:20-32)
The intimacy of God and Abraham allows Abraham to test the traditional belief that a few evil people can destroy the entire community. He does this by reversing the question and asking if a few good people can save the community. The story shows us a God who listens and shows the depth of justice.

Colossians (2:12-14)
The Church at Colossis is tested by the laws of the Jewish customs. Paul writes to put to rest the questions and requirements of the old law. Christ and the life of the church in him supersede all old requirements.

Luke (11:1-13)
The collection of sayings or prayers which we now repeat as the "Our Father" is recorded here. Persistence in our prayer is Luke's underlying theme. He believes we will win God's attentions as much by our constancy as by our plea.

FOCUS

Today's readings challenge our intimacy with God. Our lifestyle is a mirror of our spirituality. Everything we are about comes from our reflection of God. How can we encourage the many styles of prayer available for Christians? How can we quiet the busyness of our lives to allow reflection? What does intimacy with God include for the modern person?

Abraham reminds us of the role of the good person in the community. Who is the good person today? Can one person make any difference in our communities, work-places and schools? Is persistence the mere difference between the productive good person and others?

IDEA STARTER

- *CCT Lectionary:* 2 Kg 5:1-15ab; Ps 21:1-7; Col 2:6-15; Lk 11:1-13.
- Today our focus is on prayer, continuing our Sunday reflections on spirituality.
- What are prayers of petition? Are they effective?
- Provide a meditation on *The Lord's Prayer* (eg. as attributed to St. Francis of Assisi in Martin Luther's catechism). Use the ICET translation of the prayer.
- After all of Jesus' instruction about petitioning the Father, why does he conclude with the specific request for the Holy Spirit (cf. Luke 11:13)?
- Be careful that people not put their attention on God's punishment of the city in today's first reading, but rather guide their listening toward the prayer of Abraham.
- Highlight the special time of prayer with music (i.e., Intercessions and *The Lord's Prayer*).
- For further consideration: Alternative Opening Prayer; Intercessions for cities, perseverance, forgiveness, food for the hungry, safety to travelers; Ordinary Sundays Preface III (p31); Ordinary Solemn Blessing V.

MUSIC

- Psalm 138
- *Answer When I Call* (Jesuits/NALR)
- *Be With Me* (Haugen/GIA)
- *For You Are My God* (Jesuits/NALR)
- *In You I Take Refuge* (Hilliard/Resource)
- *In God Alone* (Andersen/Resource)
- *The Lord Is Near* (Dameans/NALR)
- *The Lord Is Near* (Jonas/NALR)
- *My Refuge* (Vessels/GIA)
- *Prayer Like Incense* (St. Meinrad Monks)
- *Song of the Exile* (Haugen/GIA)
- *Standing In The Need of Prayer* (ICEL)
- *You Are The Way* (ICEL)

SUNDAY PLANNING SHEET   Date _____

Parish focus _____

Environment & art _____

Ritual notes _____

Faith development (eg., in newsletter/classes) _____

Children's faith experience _____

Prelude _____

Hymn of gathering _____

Sprinkling/Penitential rite _____

Hymn of praise _____

Opening Prayer _____

First reading _____Responsory _____

Second reading _____Gospel acclamation _____

Gospel _____Profession of faith _____

General intercessions _____

At the preparation & presentation _____

Preface dialog _____Preface _____

Preface acclamation _____

Eucharistic prayer _____Memorial acclamation _____

Eucharistic amen _____

The Lord's prayer _____

Breaking of bread _____

The communion hymn _____

The post-communion hymn _____

Blessing _____At the dismissal _____

Memoranda:

EIGHTEENTH SUNDAY OF THE YEAR

YEAR C

READINGS

Ecclesiastes (1:2,2:21-23)

Vanity may be translated as breath or emptiness. This author saw our life experiences as fleeting things. Here are questions about the purpose of our lives. It will be Christians who answer with Christ's values.

Colossians (3:1-5,9-11)

Having turned to Jesus for a life of faith, Paul instructs the Church at Colossis to follow Christ's model. He is the model for their living and a primary example of hope for new life.

Luke (12:13-21)

With the parable of the rich fool, Christ demonstrates the continuing requirements of his call. This commitment cannot happen once and for all but must be a lifestyle of continuing Jesus' mission.

FOCUS

Where is the vanity or emptiness in our lives? Some would suggest material possessions, or our nuclear build-up, and for others it is personal attitudes. Understanding their emptiness is a test of our courage to explore internally. The risk to give up a false idol is far greater than the stress of status quo.

What do we unnecessarily store up? What items do we think will protect us? What attitudes of beliefs or behavior insulate us from life?

IDEA STARTERS

- *CCT Lectionary:* 2 Kg 13:14-20a; Ps 28; Col 3:1-11; Lk 12:13-21.
- Parish planning for the fall season usually begins in August. Look for volunteers to design Sunday forums about contemporary theological/human issues.
- How do people spend the day of rest, Sunday, as a day to grow rich in the sight of God?
- Simplicity is in order today. Focus upon the "basics": processional cross, the presider's chair, the Lectionary and ambo, the altar, the bread and wine, the acclamations, the gathering and communion hymns.
- A message to the workaholic, the stress-filled, and the depressed: "Set your hearts on what pertains to higher realms. Harden not your hearts.!"
- For your consideration: Alternative Opening Prayer; intercessions for employers and employees, those under stress or sorrow, judges, the wealthy, and harvesters; Ordinary Sundays Preface V (P33); Eucharistic Prayer III; Memorial Acclamation B; Ordinary Solemn Blessing IV.

MUSIC

- Psalm 95
- *All Our Joy* (Dameans/NALR)
- *Be A New Man* (Wise/GIA)
- *Come To Me* (Hummer/Resource)
- *Eye Has Not Seen* (Haugen/GIA)
- *The Father's Care* (Keyes/Resource)
- *God And Man At Table* (Stamps)
- *Hasten The Time Appointed* (ICEL)
- *I Have Loved You* (Joncas/NALR)
- *Only In God* (Jesuits/NALR)
- *Sing To God A Brand New Canticle* (Quinlan/NALR)
- *Song of Gathering* (Wise/GIA)
- *Spirit Psalm* (Keyes/Resource)

SUNDAY PLANNING SHEET

Date _____

Parish focus _____

Environment & art _____

Ritual notes _____

Faith development (eg., in newsletter/classes) _____

Children's faith experience _____

Prelude _____

Hymn of gathering _____

Sprinkling/Penitential rite _____

Hymn of praise _____

Opening Prayer _____

First reading _____ Responsory _____

Second reading _____ Gospel acclamation _____

Gospel _____ Profession of faith _____

General intercessions _____

At the preparation & presentation _____

Preface dialog _____ Preface _____

Preface acclamation _____

Eucharistic prayer _____ Memorial acclamation ____

Eucharistic amen _____

The Lord's prayer _____

Breaking of bread _____

The communion hymn _____

The post-communion hymn _____

Blessing _____ At the dismissal _____

Memoranda:

NINETEENTH SUNDAY OF THE YEAR

YEAR C

READINGS
Wisdom (18:6-9)
God's preference for Israel is reflected in choosing them over the Egyptians. The theme of faith in God's deliverance is repeated throughout the Old Testament. Here it is celebrated as the Passover.
Hebrew (11:1-2,8-19)
Old Testament heroes and heroines model for Paul the key aspects of faith. Christ continues their tradition of courage and for us becomes a new model for faithfulness.
Luke (12:32-48)
The journey to Jerusalem provides a training site for Christ and the apostles. Their conversations unfold like the story of our lives. All passages — school, grief, work — require faithfulness to the goal and watchfulness along the course.

FOCUS
What are all the synonyms for faithfulness? firmness? changelessness? resolve? commitment? steadiness?

The qualities of faithfulness in our time can be explored through the images, symbols, and words which describe contemporary faithfulness.

It also seems appropriate to explore how faithfulness changes. How do we remain attached to the ideals of our lives while allowing for the natural transitions and changes? Do we perceive reordering of values as loss of faith? Can our involvement in the community or church also change with these altered perceptions of ourselves and our faith?

IDEA STARTERS
- *CCT Lectionary:* Jer 18:1-11; Ps 14; Hb 11:1-3, 8-19; Lk 12:32-40.
- The promise and the journey: An appropriate meditation for vacationers, as we plan our travels with family or friends, let us reflect upon the heavenly Father's promise of great joy at the end of our earthly journey.
- How might this Sunday's Eucharist be a "taste" of God's promise, of life's journey, of the Kingdom of God in our midst?
- Do we expect "more of a person to whom more has been entrusted"? Do we really believe that God should have similar expectations?
- Some people in the world have a nihilistic attitude toward life. What words of hope can the Christian offer? Why does Jesus condemn hedonism?
- Prepare a values clarification exercise in your parish newsletter entitled, "Where your treasure lies, there will your heart be."
- For your consideration: Alternative Opening Prayer; Intercessions for those whom we do not love as we should, hope in the Lord, vacationers, people in foreign countries, newly married, maids and butlers; Eucharistic Prayer IV; Memorial Acclamation C; Ordinary Solemn Blessing III.

MUSIC

- Psalm 33
- *All The Ends of the Earth* (Foster/Resource)
- *Anthem* (Conry/NALR)
- *In Heavenly Love Abiding* (Dyer/Celebration)
- *Let Us Walk In The Light* (Haugen/GIA)
- *Love Divine, All Loves Excelling* (ICEL)
- *Mighty Lord* (Jesuits/NALR)
- *O Come, Divine Messiah* (ICEL)
- *Our Blessing Cup* (Joncas/NALR)
- *Remember Your Love* (Dameans/NALR)
- *To Be Your Bread* (Haas/Cooperative Ministries)
- *Wake, Awake! For Night Is Flying* (ICEL)

SUNDAY PLANNING SHEET   Date _____

Parish focus _____

Environment & art _____

Ritual notes _____

Faith development (eg., in newsletter/classes) _____

Children's faith experience _____

Prelude _____

Hymn of gathering _____

Sprinkling/Penitential rite _____

Hymn of praise _____

Opening Prayer _____

First reading _____Responsory _____

Second reading _____Gospel acclamation _____

Gospel _____Profession of faith _____

General intercessions _____

At the preparation & presentation _____

Preface dialog _____Preface _____

Preface acclamation _____

Eucharistic prayer _____Memorial acclamation _____

Eucharistic amen _____

The Lord's prayer _____

Breaking of bread _____

The communion hymn _____

The post-communion hymn _____

Blessing _____At the dismissal _____

Memoranda:

TWENTIETH SUNDAY OF THE YEAR

YEAR C

READINGS

Jeremiah (38:4-6,8-10)
Jeremiah here represents the height of rejection given unpopular causes or issues in the community. He is speaking to Jerusalem at the time just before its fall, repeating the call for renewal. He asks for changes in lifestyle that they are unwilling to make.

Hebrew (12:1-4)
Strength is required to remain faithful to the lifestyle modeled by the Old Testament heroes and heroines. This is not the strength to conquer but the strength to endure over the long haul. Christ exemplifies this for us so we may endure in our lifestyle.

Luke (2:49-53)
In continuing the apostolic training on the road to Jerusalem, Christ talked about the coming judgment. The symbols used here refer to the end of Christ's life, the final judgment and the role of the disciples.

FOCUS

Endurance has traditionally meant the singleminded pursuit of a goal despite any obstacle or adversity. The tone of the traditional meaning has been solemn and filled with images of work, sacrifice and suffering.

While endurance will always contain some of this tone, how can we re-image it in a more positive way? Endurance could be creatively pictured by the cycle of trees and plants...in animals that have been with us through the centuries...by the example of human love despite war, poverty, hatred.

What issues enliven our days so that drudgery doesn't become their tone? How do we create new excitement in our relationships, families, activities? How long has our individual parish endured? What changes have enriched it?

IDEA STARTERS

- *CCT Lectionary:* Jer 20:7-13; Ps 10:12-18; Hb 12:1-2, 12-17; Lk 12:49-56.
- The cross of Christ is placed upon the shoulder of his disciples in today's gospel. Living the spirit of God in the world is no easy task.
- How is your parish called to be a cloud of witnesses to the neighborhood, especially if your message may cause division?
- Why do some parishes themselves experience divisions among their own people?
- Have an ecumenical interparish cookout at one of the neighborhood parks. Close the evening of dinner and fun with an outdoor celebration of Evening Prayer.
- For your consideration: Sprinkling Baptismal Water A; Alternative Opening Prayer; intercessions for national leaders, individuals' rights, hope, peace in families, divided families; Reconciliation Eucharistic Prayer II; Memorial Acclamation A; Ordinary Solemn Blessing IV.

MUSIC

- Psalm 40
- *Before The Sun Burned Bright* (Jesuits/NALR)
- *Dance in the Darkness* (Landry/NALR)
- *Jesus Walked the Lonesome Valley* (ICEL)
- *Our Peace and Integrity* (Weston Priory)
- *Take Up Your Cross* (ICEL)
- *Turn Around* (Culbreth/Resource)
- *Show Us The Path Of Life* (Haugen/GIA)
- *Sing To God* (McGarry/Resource)

SUNDAY PLANNING SHEET   Date _____

Parish focus _____

Environment & art _____

Ritual notes _____

Faith development (eg., in newsletter/classes) _____

Children's faith experience _____

Prelude _____

Hymn of gathering _____

Sprinkling/Penitential rite _____

Hymn of praise _____

Opening Prayer _____

First reading _____Responsory _____

Second reading _____Gospel acclamation _____

Gospel _____Profession of faith _____

General intercessions _____

At the preparation & presentation _____

Preface dialog _____Preface _____

Preface acclamation _____

Eucharistic prayer _____Memorial acclamation _____

Eucharistic amen _____

The Lord's prayer _____

Breaking of bread _____

The communion hymn _____

The post-communion hymn _____

Blessing _____At the dismissal _____

Memoranda:

TWENTY-FIRST SUNDAY OF THE YEAR
YEAR C

READINGS
Isaiah (66:18-21)
Isaiah's vision of the endtime includes the acceptance of God's message by all nations. He dreams of gathering all peoples into the glorified city of Jerusalem.
Hebrews (12:5-7,11-13)
It is the virtue of discipline which is instilled by the model of the leader. Our internal courage then can lead us through times of stress. The result of our disciplined life is the peace and goodness of God.
Luke (13:22-20)
The focus on their closing time together is decidedly on the end of the "age" — both of Jerusalem and of Jesus. Like Jeremiah and other prophets, Jesus is ignored. Legalisms and traditional practices occupy the Hebrew leaders' time.

FOCUS
The theme of discipline is enjoying a new renaissance in our time. It emerges in the form of concern for personal health, fitness, diet, well-being, social survival.

This could be a good time to encourage and welcome the lessons of these new disciplines. How much better prepared are we for life because of them? How do they reflect a lifestyle that is more concerned for the larger social good?

New discipline may await us as we address the larger issues of our time; consumption of fragile resources; the peace movement; economic alterations. How can the Christian lifestyle contribute to the transformation?

IDEA STARTERS
- *CCT Lectionary:* Jer 28:1-9; Ps 84; Hb 12:18-29; Lk 13:22-30.
- How do you respond when someone asks, "Are you saved?"
- What is the "value" of our sharing in the Lord's Supper (cf. Luke 13:26-27)?
- Last week, Jesus spoke of family conflicts; today he speaks about privileges given to those considered lowly. What is Jesus' "social" message?
- How do we share the "glory of the Lord" with those we meet?
- The second reading looks at discipline. How may Christians use discipline effectively?
- For your consideration: Opening Prayer; intercessions for all nations, all faiths, misssionaries, parents, locksmiths, and those considered least by society; Ordinary Sundays Preface IV (P34); Eucharistic Prayer III; Memorial Acclamation D; Ordinary Solemn Blessing II.

MUSIC
- Psalm 117
- All Hail The Power of Jesus' Name (ICEL)
- Amazing Grace (ICEL)
- Anthem (Conry/NALR)
- Be Glad, Be Happy (Gilsdorf/Resource)
- Father, We Sing Your Praises (Zsigray/NALR)
- Gather Round (Page/Resource)
- He Is The Lord (Haas/Cooperative Ministries)
- Jesus Is Lord (Toolan/Resource)
- Mountains And Hills (Jesuits/NALR)
- You Are The Way (ICEL)

SUNDAY PLANNING SHEET

Date _____

Parish focus _____

Environment & art _____

Ritual notes _____

Faith development (eg., in newsletter/classes) _____

Children's faith experience _____

Prelude _____

Hymn of gathering _____

Sprinkling/Penitential rite _____

Hymn of praise _____

Opening Prayer _____

First reading _____ Responsory _____

Second reading _____ Gospel acclamation ____

Gospel _____ Profession of faith ____

General intercessions _____

At the preparation & presentation _____

Preface dialog _____ Preface _____

Preface acclamation _____

Eucharistic prayer _____ Memorial acclamation ___

Eucharistic amen _____

The Lord's prayer _____

Breaking of bread _____

The communion hymn _____

The post-communion hymn _____

Blessing _____ At the dismissal _____

Memoranda:

TWENTY-SECOND SUNDAY YEAR C OF THE YEAR

READINGS

Sirach (3:17-18,28-29)
It is the illusions around us that fill our life and keep us from the pursuit of wisdom in God. The emptiness of our actions can be replaced with an awareness of all that is God's and a profound humility in our awareness.

Hebrews (12:18-19,22-24)
Like the encounter in the desert of Mt. Sinai, Christ offers a similar relationship to the Hebrews. The friendship and love of his covenant make the encounter a pleasant one. It will not be feared as the desert once was.

Luke (14:1,7-14)
The parable again speaks to the arrogance of the leaders of the Jews. Their superiority over the poor and humble will be replaced by the model of Christ who is linked with the outcasts. Love is our measure, not power or influence.

FOCUS

Humility can be traced through two ideas. First is the awe of encounter with God. Transparency in our lives, issues, dreams reveals the Holy on the other side. We stand before the face of God continually and are amazed at that feat.

How do we lead the community to see the movement of God in its people? Where are the points of breakthrough where God is known? What is the tone of humility today? Could it be more thankfulness for meeting God in the maze of our lives than self-effacement?

Secondly, Paul tells us that the humble one is led to justice. The response. of such awareness of God is acting on the part of the lowly. How does our community respond? Can our very action toward others lead to further revelation of the Holy?

IDEA STARTERS

- *CCT Lectionary:* Ez 18:1-9, 25-29; Ps 15; Hb 13:1-8; Lk 14:1, 7-14.
- Jesus calls us to build up the self-esteem of others. We know that God loves us! How may we share his love with others?
- Where is the thin line between humility and pride? Can humility be taken too far?
- Relate today's parable to the life of Jesus, with God the Father as host.
- Have an "unexpected" summer's-end brunch after the liturgy today, prepared and hosted by the pastoral staff.
- For your consideration: Alternative Opening Prayer; intercessions for civil service personnel, leaders (of nation, as well as of clubs), the harvest, prisoners, family festal celebrations, ministers of hospitality (i.e.,greeters/ushers), beggars and the physically handicapped; Ordinary Sundays Preface I (P29); Eucharistic Prayer III; Memorial Acclamation D; Ordinary Solemn Blessing V.

MUSIC

- Psalm 68
- *Almighty God, Your Word Is Cast* (ICEL)
- *Canticle Of The Sun* (Haugen/GIA)
- *The Cry Of The Poor* (Jesuits/NALR)
- *Glorious Praise* (Hilliard/Resource)
- *Glory To God* (Hummer/Resource)
- *Jubilate, Servite* (Taize/GIA)
- *Magnificat*
- *Of The Father's Love Begotten* (ICEL)
- *Rejoice, The Lord Is King* (ICEL)

SUNDAY PLANNING SHEET   Date _____

Parish focus _____

Environment & art _____

Ritual notes _____

Faith development (eg., in newsletter/classes) _____

Children's faith experience _____

Prelude _____

Hymn of gathering _____

Sprinkling/Penitential rite _____

Hymn of praise _____

Opening Prayer _____

First reading _____Responsory _____

Second reading _____Gospel acclamation _____

Gospel _____Profession of faith _____

General intercessions _____

At the preparation & presentation _____

Preface dialog _____Preface _____

Preface acclamation _____

Eucharistic prayer _____Memorial acclamation _____

Eucharistic amen _____

The Lord's prayer _____

Breaking of bread _____

The communion hymn _____

The post-communion hymn _____

Blessing _____At the dismissal _____

Memoranda:

TWENTY-THIRD SUNDAY OF THE YEAR
YEAR C

READINGS
Wisdom (9:13-18)
Solomon prayed for wisdom and valued it above anything else. Wisdom came from God to be used for the welfare of the community.

Philemon (9:10,12-17)
The story of the slave and Paul reminds us of the reordering that Christianity brings to all societal patterns. These men are now considered brothers in Christ. They are guided by love rather than ownership.

Luke (14:25-33)
Commitment to a relationship with Christ exacts a heavy price from us. Ties to material surroundings or to human emotions may not sustain us. It is our willingness to be caught up in Christ's value of love which reassures us.

FOCUS
The pendulum is swinging and again the value of commitment is enjoying ascendancy. In personal relationships, work arenas, and community memberships, people are making a more concerted effort to bond together.

What are the contemporary signs of commitment in your neighborhood? How can we facilitate our community members' commitments? What sacrifices will be made for new bonds? What emotional biases or attitudes will yield to these commitments?

IDEA STARTERS
- *CCT Lectionary:* Ez 33:1-11; Ps 94:12-22; Ph 9:1-20; Lk 14:25-33.
- As we end the summer vacation season, our readings call us to reflect on our commitments: Is God at the top of my list; or must I reset my priorities?
- As we pray for God's blessings upon our labor this holiday weekend, paraphrase the words of Wisdom: May our concerns never weigh down our minds, O Lord.
- The processional cross may be a valuable symbol in light of today's Gospel. The leading ministers (representative of the entire community assembling) follow the cross "into worship," as well as out the doors of the building to "go out into the world rejoicing in the power of the Spirit — in us."
- For your consideration: Sprinkling Baptismal Water B; Alternative Opening Prayer; intercessions for families, carpenters and construction workers, monarchs, prisoners, purity of heart, end to oppression, students and teachers, all laborers, safety for travellers; Eucharistic Prayer IV; Memorial Acclamation D; Ordinary Solemn Blessing II.

MUSIC

- Psalm 90
- *Awake O Sleeper* (Dameans/NALR)
- *Breathe on Me, Breath of God* (ICEL)
- *Come Holy Spirit* (Repp/K&R)
- *Earthen Vessels* (Jesuits/NALR)
- *Gather Us In* (Haugen/GIA)
- *I Am the Light* (Repp/K&R)
- *I Long for You, O Lord* (Dameans/NALR)
- *Like A Sunflower* (Landry/NALR)
- *Lord, To Whom Shall We Go?* (NALR)
- *My God, Accept My Heart This Day* (ICEL)
- *Only A Shadow* (Landry/NALR)
- *Only In God* (Jesuits/NALR)
- *Speak, Lord* (Dameans/NALR)
- *Spirit, Be Our Spirit* (Weston Priory)
- *Take Heart* (Gilsdorf/Resource)
- *Tree of Life* (Toolan/Resource)
- *You Are My Witnesses* (Cry Hosanna #90/Fisherfolk)
- *Lord, Give Us Your Spirit* (Cry Hosanna #52/Fisherfolk)

SUNDAY PLANNING SHEET

Date _____

Parish focus _____

Environment & art _____

Ritual notes _____

Faith development (eg., in newsletter/classes) _____

Children's faith experience _____

Prelude _____

Hymn of gathering _____

Sprinkling/Penitential rite _____

Hymn of praise _____

Opening Prayer _____

First reading _____ Responsory _____

Second reading _____ Gospel acclamation _____

Gospel _____ Profession of faith _____

General intercessions _____

At the preparation & presentation _____

Preface dialog _____ Preface _____

Preface acclamation _____

Eucharistic prayer _____ Memorial acclamation _____

Eucharistic amen _____

The Lord's prayer _____

Breaking of bread _____

The communion hymn _____

The post-communion hymn _____

Blessing _____ At the dismissal _____

Memoranda:

TWENTY-FOURTH SUNDAY OF THE YEAR

YEAR C

READINGS

Exodus (32:7-13,14)
Moses, in a role forecasting Christ, intercedes for the Hebrew people. After they violate the covenant, he mediates their repentance and change of heart.

First Timothy (1:12-17)
Paul sets himself as an example for us of the mercy of God. God called Paul from the most grievous of offenses, persecution, to a key role in the church. Paul, Timothy and our communities are interlocked as key parts of God's design.

Luke (15:1-32)
Jesus' parables of the lost give us ample models for the concern, patience, and forgiveness of God. Even social conventions are surpassed in the expressions of loving forgiveness. Narcissism and misunderstanding are overcome by love.

FOCUS

Forgiveness and reconciliation have always brought to mind moods of penitence. We remember forgiveness from the viewpoint of going to confession and seeking ease of our transgressions.

Today's readings allow us to consider the opposing mood: that of easing the penalty or that of granting freedom. As persons capable of forgiveness, we can provide freedom.

Freedom does not always mean personal reconciliation, it can also point to social reconnection. What freedom can our community grant to others of different status? What reconciliation needs to take place between our church and others?

IDEA STARTERS

- *CCT Lectionary:* Hos 4:1-3, 5:15, 6:6; Ps 77:11-20; 1 Tim 1:12-17; Lk 15:1-10.
- Today's gospel presents three parables which follow a particular pattern. Note that the parable of the Prodigal Son was read this past Lent.
- Examine the Lucan pattern in light of the Communal Penance Liturgy: the parish examines its community — calling sinners back to God and fellowship; we experience reconciliation — God finding the lost/human embracing; we celebrate — forgiveness calls forth our greatest joy shared with others.
- Highlight the Penitential Rite during today's Eucharist. How might kneeling or another liturgical gesture be used? How might incense be used as a sign of reconciliation and as offering of prayers of repentance offered before the Lord?
- Reprint an act of contrition from the Rite of Penance (no. 90) in the parish newsletter.
- Ministers of hospitality may appropriately be commissioned at today's liturgy since they "welcome sinners" to the Lord's Supper.

- For your consideration: Penitential Rite A; Opening Prayer; intercessions for a true spirit of worship, faithfulness, mercy, patience, tax collectors, sinners; Reconciliation Eucharistic Prayer I; Memorial Acclamation B; Ordinary Solemn Blessing IV.
- During this time after Pentecost, the readings call us to be God's partners over creation — to "renew the face of the earth."
- The second reading lends itself to a teaching about·the purpose of intercessory prayer. Sing an adaption of the Eastern litany (often used in Evening Prayer) at today's Eucharist (cf. *Praise God in Song,* Chicago, GIA Publications).

MUSIC

- Psalm 51
- *Amazing Grace* (ICEL)
- *And the Father Will Dance* (Landry/NALR)
- *Ashes* (Conry/NALR)
- *Come, Let us to the Lord Our God* (ICEL)
- *Glory and Praise* (Jesuits/NALR)
- *Hosanna* (Medling/Resource)
- *I Have Loved You* (Joncas/NALR)
- *I Have Waited* (Gilsdorf/Resource)
- *Immortal, Invisible God Only Wise* (ICEL)
- *The Kingdom of God* (Deiss/NALR)
- *Like A Shepherd* (Jesuits/NALR)
- *Lord of Glory* (Jesuits/NALR)
- *Praise, My Soul, the King of Heaven* (ICEL)
- *Praise the Lord, My Soul* (Jesuits/NALR)
- *Remember Your Love* (Dameans/NALR)
- *Seek the Lord* (Jesuits/NALR)
- *Though the Mountains May Fall* (Jesuits/NALR)
- *Turn to Me* (Jesuits/NALR)
- *Yahweh, the Faithful One* (Jesuits/NALR)
- *Yes, I Shall Arise* (Deiss/WLP)
- *Fear Not, For I Have Redeemed You* (Fisherfolk/Resource)
- *I Have Decided to Follow Jesus* (Fisherfolk/Resource)

SUNDAY PLANNING SHEET   Date _____

Parish focus _____
Environment & art _____
Ritual notes _____
Faith development (eg., in newsletter/classes) _____
Children's faith experience _____
Prelude _____
Hymn of gathering _____
Sprinkling/Penitential rite _____
Hymn of praise _____
Opening Prayer _____
First reading _____Responsory _____
Second reading _____Gospel acclamation _____
Gospel _____Profession of faith _____
General intercessions _____
At the preparation & presentation _____
Preface dialog _____Preface _____
Preface acclamation _____
Eucharistic prayer _____Memorial acclamation _____
Eucharistic amen _____
The Lord's prayer _____
Breaking of bread _____
The communion hymn _____
The post-communion hymn _____
Blessing _____At the dismissal _____
Memoranda:

CYCLE C

TWENTY-FIFTH SUNDAY OF THE YEAR

YEAR C

READINGS
Amos (8:4-7)
Amos, one of the first prophets recorded in scripture, was a strong advocate
for social justice. Here the business practices of the time are contrasted with
God's demands of Justice for the poor.
First Timothy (2:1-8)
Paul's letter guided Timothy in the proper management of the community.
Worship is the theme of this paragraph where Paul emphasizes perseverance
in prayer.
Luke (16:1-13)
The parable is directed toward the religious leaders who have mismanaged
their role in the community. Those given to wise care of human affairs will
care appropriately for sacred ones. Again the tone is centered on social justice:
the care for those less fortunate in the shadow of the wealthy.

FOCUS
Leadership may be one of the key crises of our age. We worry about leadership
in government, industry, education. Our traditional image of a hero who is
above criticism has been shattered. In the end we are led by common people
struggling much like the rest of us.

This Sunday's readings speak of leadership in the Hebrew business community,
in the liturgical roles in Ephesus, and among the Pharisees. The injunctions
the social encyclicals after Vatican II. What insights can they offer to leadership
for all ages.

What roles of leadership does your parish take in the community? What values
are articulated by your actions and attitudes? For the individuals who lead
in your parish and in your neighborhood, what guides can be offered? Reread
thesocial encyclicals after Vatican II. What insights can they offer to leadership
in your community?

IDEA STARTERS
- *CCT Lectionary:* Hos 11:1-11; Ps 107:1-9; Tim 2:1-7; Lk 16:1-13.
- Amos and Luke speak about giving people what they are due. We owe God
  the first place in our lives. What do we owe our families, friends, parish,
  neighbors, coworkers, "others"?
- During this time after Pentecost,the readings call us to be God's partner
  over creation, to "renew the face of the earth."
- Quote from Vatican II documents and papal encyclicals about the church's
  social mission to the poor, the Christian's responsibility to honesty, the
  church's attitude toward employer, employee and unions.
- For your consideration: Alternative Opening Prayer; intercessions for those
  in authority, for piety and dignity, the poor, religious educators, managers,
  employers, employees, unions, for trust and faithfulness; Ordinary Sundays
  Preface V (P33); Eucharistic Prayer III; Memorial Acclamation C; Ordinary
  Solemn Blessing V.

- Are people in your community aware of the poverty within their own neighborhood, as well as the agencies available to provide help?

MUSIC

- Psalm 113
- *All That We Have* (Dameans/NALR)
- *Awaken, My Heart* (Deiss/NALR)
- *Come, My Children* (Dameans/NALR)
- *Come to Me* (Weston Priory)
- *Eye Has Not Seen* (Haugen/GIA)
- *Forgive, O Lord, Our Severing Ways* (ICEL)
- *God and Man at Table* (Stamps/NALR)
- *He is the Lord* (Haas/Cooperative Ministries)
- *How Can I Keep From Singing?* (Traditional)
- *I Am Lord* (Duesing/Resource)
- *Jesus Is Lord* (Toolan/Resource)
- *My Refuge* (Vessels/GIA)
- *Praise the Lord, My Soul* (Parker/GIA)
- *Sing to God A Brand New Canticle* (Quinlan/NALR)
- *A Song of Blessing* (Wise/GIA)
- *That There May Be Bread* (Weston Priory)
- *Trust in the Lord* (Jesuits/NALR)
- *Where Cross the Crowded Ways of Life* (ICEL)
- *When Two or More* (Repp/K&R)
- *You Are Near* (Jesuits/NALR)
- *Cry of the Poor* (Jesuits/NALR)
- *Come, Won't You Come* (Fisherfolk/Resource)
- *How Amiable* (Fisherfolk/Resource)

SUNDAY PLANNING SHEET

Date _____

Parish focus _____

Environment & art _____

Ritual notes _____

Faith development (eg., in newsletter/classes) _____

Children's faith experience _____

Prelude _____

Hymn of gathering _____

Sprinkling/Penitential rite _____

Hymn of praise _____

Opening Prayer _____

First reading _____ Responsory _____

Second reading _____ Gospel acclamation _____

Gospel _____ Profession of faith _____

General intercessions _____

At the preparation & presentation _____

Preface dialog _____ Preface _____

Preface acclamation _____

Eucharistic prayer _____ Memorial acclamation ____

Eucharistic amen _____

The Lord's prayer _____

Breaking of bread _____

The communion hymn _____

The post-communion hymn _____

Blessing _____ At the dismissal _____

Memoranda:

TWENTY-SIXTH SUNDAY OF THE YEAR

YEAR C

READINGS

Amos (6:1,4-7)
With foreign armies moving against Israel, Amos sought to bring the community back into favor with the Lord. The most wealthy opposed him the greatest. Their security proved a false one.

First Timothy (6:11-16)
Paul's life, as an imitation of Christ, is threaded through this letter as invitation to Timothy. Here perseverance to the ministerial work in the community concerns Paul. The advancement of faith in Christ should be the major role for Timothy and other Christians.

Luke (16:19-31)
This call to repentance was directed to the religious leaders of the community. Their lack of justice toward the poor among them caused further separation from God after death. The story reveals the Jewish symbolism of death and afterlife.

FOCUS

Gulfs, gaps, holes, chasms, canyons...the names vary but the experience of huge differences is the same for all of us. These remarkable differences come between people, between styles of management, conversational abilities, ways of seeing life. Deep inside there is the knowledge of an unbridgeable gap. We feel no good intention or effort will bridge the distance.

Within Hebrew prophetic tradition the gap between the wealthy and the poor seemed to be such an unbridgeable gap. The challenge was toward those more fortunate to become aware; to give of their excess; to shorten the gulf.

Where does our community unthinkingly enlarge the gap between people? How do we resist closing the space between differing attitudes or lifestyles? What values need to be cultivated to enlarge our care for those less fortunate?

IDEA STARTERS

- *CCT Lectionary:* Joel 2:23-30; Ps 107:1, 33-43; 1 Tim 6:6-19; Lk 16:19-31.
- Today's Gospel gives numerous opportunities to both the homilist and the adult education team: heaven and hell (a contemporary view); Bread for the World speaker (or similar organization); does God love the rich, too?; Has the resurrection changed our life?
- Are people in your community aware of the poverty within their own neighborhood, as well as neighborhood agencies working to help the poor?
- An ecumenical dialog about Redemption (heaven, limbo, purgatory, hell) may be an interesting forum, especially since we approach the end of the Ordinary Sundays and begin to hear stories about the "last days."
- This may be a good Sunday to renew parish interest in the St. Vincent de Paul Society (feast; Sept. 27) so that the concerns of the poor are unceasingly met by the community. Begin a first Sunday of the month program where people bring food and clothing for the needy to be distributed throughout the month.
- The Sunday Eucharist must not only be the place of consolation, but also

the place where we are reminded that God filled us with the Spirit to go out and be Christ for the world. Has our Sunday assembly "risen from the dead"?

- For your consideration: Alternative Opening Prayer; intercessions for the oppressed, the hungry, captives, the blind, orphans, the rich, for a gentle spirit, steadfastness, forgiveness; Eucharistic Prayer IV; Memorial Acclamation B; Solemn Blessing II.

MUSIC

- Psalm 146
- *Abba, Father!* (Gilsdorf/Resource)
- *Alleluia, People of God* (Deiss/NALR)
- *All the Rest of My Life* (Goglia/Resource)
- *Anthem* (Conry/NALR)
- *The Bread of Rejoicing* (Deiss/NALR)
- *Come to the Water* (Jesuits/NALR)
- *Dwelling Place* (Jesuits/NALR)
- *Eye Has Not Seen* (Haugen/GIA)
- *Faith of Our Fathers* (ICEL)
- *Fight the Good Fight* (ICEL)
- *Go Now In Peace* (Wise/GIA)
- *How Can I Keep From Singing?* (Traditional)
- *Immortal, Invisible God Only Wise* (ICEL)
- *In Him We Live* (Landry/NALR)
- *In Those Days* (Deiss/NALR)
- *Let Heaven Rejoice* (Jesuits/NALR)
- *Let Us Walk in the Light* (Haugen/Quiet Breeze)
- *Light of the World* (Kendzia/NALR)
- *Lord, To Whom Shall We Go?* (Conry/NALR)
- *Mountains and Hills* (Jesuits/NALR)
- *My Refuge* (Vessels/GIA)
- *On Eagle's Wings* (Joncas/NALR)
- *Service* (Dameans/NALR)
- *Sing A New Song* (Jesuits/NALR)
- *Sing Out His Goodness* (Dameans/NALR)
- *That There May Be Bread* (Weston Priory)
- *This Is A Holy Day* (Sylvester/NALR)
- *Abba, Father* (Fisherfolk/Resource)
- *Trust In The Lord* (Fisherfolk/Resource)

SUNDAY PLANNING SHEET   Date _____

Parish focus _____
Environment & art _____
Ritual notes _____
Faith development (eg., in newsletter/classes) _____
Children's faith experience _____
Prelude _____
Hymn of gathering _____
Sprinkling/Penitential rite _____
Hymn of praise _____
Opening Prayer _____
First reading _____Responsory _____
Second reading _____Gospel acclamation _____
Gospel _____Profession of faith _____
General intercessions _____
At the preparation & presentation _____
Preface dialog _____Preface _____
Preface acclamation _____
Eucharistic prayer _____Memorial acclamation _____
Eucharistic amen _____
The Lord's prayer _____
Breaking of bread _____
The communion hymn _____
The post-communion hymn _____
Blessing _____At the dismissal _____
Memoranda:

TWENTY-SEVENTH SUNDAY OF THE YEAR

YEAR C

READINGS
Habakkuk (1:2, 2:2-4)
This is a conversation between the prophet and God. The prophet doubts whether the Just will prevail when all seems to go the way of the unrighteous. God reassures him that justice will win out. The test of time reveals those members of the community faithful to justice.

Second Timothy (1:6-8, 13-14)
Timothy has been commissioned by the Spirit of God through the "laying on of hands" by Paul. Now he must persevere in his mission to the faithful. He has within himself all the strength needed if he would just call on it.

Luke (17:5-10)
While the religious leadership felt themselves deserving of special care from God and their community, Luke reminds us here that they were merely doing their duty. Following Jesus' message allows no reward but its own.

FOCUS
Conversation, human dialogue, implies free exchange of ideas and learning between people. Its very action offers hope that we may learn, alter an attitude, persuade or convince. Whatever the possible outcome, the act of dialogue needs to be honored and preserved. The process of free exchange of ideas and feeling is an art that can be cultivated and encouraged.

IDEA STARTERS
- *CCT Lectionary:* Amos 5:6-7, 10-15; Ps 101; 2 Tim 1:1-14; Lk 17:5-10.
- The message of Luke's excerpt may deal with a concept hard to accept: even though we live a good life (or close to it), God does not "owe" us anything, not even heaven! Being compared to a slave may hit some people between the eyes. We must remember, however, that we have not chosen God, God has chosen us.
- The second reading speaks of Timothy's ordination. As vocation week approaches it may be appropriate to recall the role of ministry in the church — ordained and lay, in worship and outreach: One Ministry, many ministers.
- The responsory appointed for this day is well known by Morning Praise participants as the invitatory psalm. This psalm may act as a springboard for a call to be more faithful to daily prayer, individually and communally, especially if the Hours are celebrated in your parish.
- For your consideration: Alternative Opening Prayer; intercessions for captives, the afflicted, unity, contrite hearts, the ordained, farmers, shepherds, maids, and butlers; Ordinary Sundays Preface VII (P35); Eucharistic Prayer II; Ordinary Time Solemn Blessing III.

MUSIC

- Psalm 95
- *All Our Joy* (Dameans/NALR)
- *Almighty God, Your Word is Cast* (ICEL)
- *Beginning Today* (Dameans/NALR)
- *Canticle of Mary*
- *Firmly I Believe and Trust* (ICEL)
- *Glorious In Majesty* (Cothran/GIA)
- *He Has Anointed Me* (Dameans/NALR)
- *The House Built on a Rock* (Deiss/NALR)
- *I Have Loved You* (Joncas/NALR)
- *Kyrie, Eleison*
  (Clark/Celebration Services)
- *Lay Your Hands* (Landry/NALR)
- *May We Praise Your* (Jesuits/NALR)
- *Mighty Lord* (Jesuits/NALR)
- *One Lord* (Haas/Cooperative Ministries)
- *Only A Shadow* (Landry/NALR)
- *Peace* (Weston Priory)
- *Praise Canticle*
  (Haas/Cooperative Ministries)
- *Spirit of God* (Weston Priory)
- *Take, Lord, Receive* (Jesuits/NALR)
- *You Will Draw Water* (Conry/NALR)
- *Psalm* (Fisherfolk/Resource)
- *Hosanna, Lord* (Fisherfolk/Resource)

SUNDAY PLANNING SHEET

Date _____

Parish focus _____

Environment & art _____

Ritual notes _____

Faith development (eg., in newsletter/classes) _____

Children's faith experience _____

Prelude _____

Hymn of gathering _____

Sprinkling/Penitential rite _____

Hymn of praise _____

Opening Prayer _____

First reading _____ Responsory _____

Second reading _____ Gospel acclamation _____

Gospel _____ Profession of faith _____

General intercessions _____

At the preparation & presentation _____

Preface dialog _____ Preface _____

Preface acclamation _____

Eucharistic prayer _____ Memorial acclamation _____

Eucharistic amen _____

The Lord's prayer _____

Breaking of bread _____

The communion hymn _____

The post-communion hymn _____

Blessing _____ At the dismissal _____

Memoranda:

TWENTY-EIGHTH SUNDAY YEAR C OF THE YEAR

READINGS
2 Kings (5:14-17)
Elisha, like his teacher Elijah, was renowned for his abilities to work miracles. Curing the leprosy of Naaman illustrates the power of God in the prophet and the reach of God's message beyond national borders. Naaman took home Israeli soil because God was best worshiped in his own land.

2 Timothy (2:8-13)
Calling on an early hymn used in baptismal ceremonies, Paul appeals to Timothy to maintain his courage in the faith. The difficulties of Paul's life are given as a model to maintain the work of the faith.

Luke (17:11-19)
In a story parallel to Elisha and Naaman, Jesus cures the ten of leprosy. Again it is the non-Jew who returns to affirm Jesus and his power. Luke strongly orients his Gospel to the Gentile believer in contrast to the unhearing Jews.

FOCUS
Miracles are rare these days. The sudden cure of a drastic illness is usually unseen. The alteration of the weather or a life situation rests not with magic powers but our abilities to see possibilities and make changes. In the absence of miracles, what remains is for us to seek out the special in the ordinary. To make obvious the implicit presence of the Holy is the task of today's prophet.

We read today of the curing of a dread disease in the biblical time, leprosy. The power of the prophets to work miracles often gave credence to the message. Reverence for the supernatural easily moved the people to action.

Where is the Holy found in our community? What implicit sacredness, specialness can be revealed by us? What skills of seeing, awareness, hearing, listening can be encouraged?

IDEA STARTERS
- *CCT Lectionary:* Mk 1:2, 2:1-10; Ps 26; 2 Tim 2:8-15; Lk 17:11-19.
- Today's readings focus upon the Gentile acceptance of Israel's God. Note also the approach of Mission Sunday (and Mission Animation Week).
- A focus today may concern the mantra or rosary of the Eastern Church, the "Jesus Prayer," found in today's Gospel. An elaboration of this style of prayer is found in the musical collection featuring hymns and acclamations used at Taize (available from GIA Publications).
- Use a "mantra" form of prayer in place of the Intercessions. Have all kneel and sing/recite a mantra for a couple of minutes (eg. "Jesus, hear our prayer").
- Paul's letter speaks about witnessing the resurrection: nothing can confine the Good News, not even prison chains! The Christian is called to "hold out 'til the end." How might your community be a witness to those blinded by the chains of their life?
- At first glance, the last line of our second reading (2 Tm 2:13) seems paradoxical, but upon careful reading, the statement is logical! Clarify how denial and faithfulness are related here.

- A communal celebration of Anointing the Sick may appropriately be celebrated with today's readings.
- For your consideration: Sprinkling Baptismal Water B; Opening Prayer; Intercessions for the Jewish people and other world religions, atheists, those unjustly imprisoned, the sick, the hopeless, for thankful spirits; Ordinary Sundays Preface VI (P34); Ordinary Solemn Blessing IV.

MUSIC

- Psalm 98
- *Amazing Grace* (ICEL)
- *And the Father Will Dance* (Landry/NALR)
- *City of God* (Jesuits/NALR)
- *Give Thanks to God the Father* (ICEL)
- *God Who Made the Earth* (ICEL)
- *Go Up To the Mountain* (Weston Priory)
- *How Beautiful* (Wise/GIA)
- *How Sweet the Name of Jesus Sounds* (ICEL)
- *I Danced in the Morning* (Carter/Galliard Ltd.)
- *In Him We Live* (Landry/NALR)
- *I Thank You, Lord* (ICEL)

- *I Will Sing, I Will Sing* (Dyer/Celebration Services)
- *Jesus, Remember Me* (Taize/GIA)
- *Lay Your Hands* (Landry/NALR)
- *Let Your Face Shine Upon Us* (Haugen/GIA)
- *O Healing River* (Joncas/GIA)
- *Song of Gathering* (Wise/GIA)
- *Son of David* (Jesuits/NALR)
- *We Are Many Parts* (Haugen/GIA)
- *Yahweh* (Weston Priory)
- *Teach Us To Love Your Word Lord* (Fisherfolk/Resource)
- *Come Follow Me, Now* (Fisherfolk/Resource)

SUNDAY PLANNING SHEET   Date _____

Parish focus _____

Environment & art _____

Ritual notes _____

Faith development (eg., in newsletter/classes) _____

Children's faith experience _____

Prelude _____

Hymn of gathering _____

Sprinkling/Penitential rite _____

Hymn of praise _____

Opening Prayer _____

First reading _____Responsory _____

Second reading _____Gospel acclamation _____

Gospel _____Profession of faith _____

General intercessions _____

At the preparation & presentation _____

Preface dialog _____Preface _____

Preface acclamation _____

Eucharistic prayer _____Memorial acclamation _____

Eucharistic amen _____

The Lord's prayer _____

Breaking of bread _____

The communion hymn _____

The post-communion hymn _____

Blessing _____At the dismissal _____

Memoranda:

TWENTY-NINTH SUNDAY OF THE YEAR

YEAR C

READINGS

Exodus (17:8-13)
Holy wars were not uncommon in the early Hebrew community. Moses, with unfailing determination, led the people through many of these wars. Moses and Joshua were steadfast in their communication of the will of God to the community.

2 Timothy (3:14-4:2)
Paul continues to urge strength upon Timothy in his mission to the community. The Old Testament books become models of this courage and strength for these leaders.

Luke (18:1-8)
Again the role of determination is illustrated. Jesus clearly states the point of his parable. If persistance is rewarded by the duty of the judge, then much more can be expected from the God who gives love so freely.

FOCUS

Not to lose heart, to persevere, to remain strong are major tasks of today. We read constantly about depression both economically and personally. The stresses of modern life deplete our internal resources. To lose heart is to lose hope; to lose the dreams which guide our quests.

Perseverance in justice threads through these readings. Here in war and before a judge, the one who remains strong wins out. Reliance on God's strength is a major factor for such a person.

We place before our communities weekly the values and ideals needed not to lose heart. We must articulate the reasons to hope in this generation. What are the causes for losing heart in your neighborhood? In the larger world community? What support is needed to persevere in altering these circumstances?

IDEA STARTERS

- *CCT Lectionary:* Hk 1:1-3, 2:1-4; Ps 119:137-144; 2 Tim 3:14-4:5; Lk 18:1-8. 18:1-8.
- A homily about "Praying the Scriptures" may call members of the assembly to take personal Bible reading more seriously.
- A group of parishioners may be interested in preparing for the Sunday Eucharist by breaking the bread of God's Word through prayer and sharing.
- Evaluate one of the symbols of the Liturgy: the Bible/Lectionary and the rituals that surround its use. What does the book look like? How is it held in procession? By the reader? Is it an effective translation for proclamation? Is meditation time a period of "dead" or "living" silence? Are the Responsory and Gospel Acclamation sung? Are candles and incense, as well as a "Gospel procession," ever used?
- Some communities have commissioned shut-ins to participate in a parish contemplative ministry. Called "pray-ers," these people pray at specific times throughout the day using Liturgy of the Hours and devotions. How might this program be adapted for your needs?

- For your consideration: Alternative Opening Prayer, intercessions for world peace, those in military service and leadership, evangelization, catechists, preachers, judges, layers, widows and widowers, justice; Ordinary Sundays Preface I (P29); Eucharistic Prayer III; Memorial Acclamation C; Ordinary Solemn Blessing III.

MUSIC

- Psalm 121
- *Alleluia, People of God* (Deiss/NALR)
- *Blessed Be Jesus At Your Word* (ICEL)
- *Before the Sun Burned Bright* (Jesuits/NALR)
- *Come My Children* (Dameans/NALR)
- *Give Thanks to God the Father* (ICEL)
- *Glorious In Majesty* (Cothran/GIA)
- *Go Up to the Mountain* (Weston Priory)
- *His Love Will Ever Be* (Fabing/NALR)
- *How Firm A Foundation* (ICEL)
- *I Lift Up My Soul* (Jesuits/NALR)
- *In Him We Live* (Landry/NALR)
- *In Your Love Remember Me* (Kendzia/NALR)
- *Lord, To Whom Shall We Go* (Joncas/NALR)
- *O God of Love, O King of Peace* (ICEL)
- *Praise the Lord, My Soul* (Parker/GIA)
- *Sing to the Lord a New Song* (Johnson/Resource)
- *You Shall Stand Fast* (Toolan/Resource)

SUNDAY PLANNING SHEET   Date _____

Parish focus _____

Environment & art _____

Ritual notes _____

Faith development (eg., in newsletter/classes) _____

Children's faith experience _____

Prelude _____

Hymn of gathering _____

Sprinkling/Penitential rite _____

Hymn of praise _____

Opening Prayer _____

First reading _____Responsory _____

Second reading _____Gospel acclamation _____

Gospel _____Profession of faith _____

General intercessions _____

At the preparation & presentation _____

Preface dialog _____Preface _____

Preface acclamation _____

Eucharistic prayer _____Memorial acclamation _____

Eucharistic amen _____

The Lord's prayer _____

Breaking of bread _____

The communion hymn _____

The post-communion hymn _____

Blessing _____At the dismissal _____

Memoranda:

THIRTIETH SUNDAY OF THE YEAR

YEAR C

READINGS

Sirach (15:12-14, 16-18)
It is the wise person who understands closeness to God. The humility of those who pray continually guarantees God's ear.

Second Timothy (4:6-8,16-18)
In speaking of his imminent death, Paul both forgives those about him and continues his model of faithfulness to the Gospel of Jesus. The wreath as a symbol of achievement and victory shows his belief that his mission was successfully completed.

Luke (18:9-14)
In one of the classic parables on humility, we are reminded of the faithful heart. While our outward behavior may fulfill the religious requirements, it is the inner activity of our heart which is the measure. Humility, wisdom, justice; these remain primary.

FOCUS

Integrity presents us with a high ideal. It speaks of honesty to oneself and to the community. It hints of wholeness in our internal and public behaviors.

The nearing end of Paul's life, the personal images of the publican and tax collector, and the wisdom of Sirach, point to integrity. These readings set a tone of humility and of self-honesty. They confront our faithfulness to inner values and goals of life.

How can we demonstrate personal integrity in our parishes? What support does the individual need to remain faithful to Christian ideals and lifestyles? How does a community maintain honesty in its values within the larger world?

IDEA STARTERS

- *CCT Lectionary:* Zeph 3:1-9; Ps 3; Tim 4:6-8, 16-18; Lk 18:9-14.
- "People who go to church are hypocrites!" and don't let anyone tell you otherwise. Every Christian must know his or her need for the Saviour.
- Sponsor a parish recognition day. In the bulletin and announcements acknowledge the contribution of every parishioner from the person in the last row to the president of the church council.
- Highlight the Penitential Rite in light of today's gospel, "Be merciful to me, a sinner." Note that these words may also be found in the Rite of Penance, "prayer of the penitent."
- As an alternative to the above suggestion, use the sprinkling of Baptismal Water. Through the homily and bulletin, teach about the one ministry shared by all the baptized. "All are one in Christ."
- Catechesis regarding the Rite of Peace always seems to be in order. May we never feel too proud to reach out, thus reminding a fellow believer of the Lord's unconditional love.
- Cathedral sign: "Help us form a worshiping community. Please sit toward the front" vs. Biblical literalist: "Don't sit in the back? But God wants me to!" How may these two viewpoints be reconciled?

- For your consideration: Sprinkling Baptismal Water/Penitential Rite (with special emphasis); Opening Prayer; intercessions for equality and justice for those whom we do not love as we should, and for spiritual virtue; Ordinary Sundays Preface VII (P 35); Eucharistic Prayer I; Memorial Acclamation D; Ordinary Solemn Blessing V.

MUSIC

- Psalm 34
- *Abba, Father* (Gilsdorf/Resource)
- *All My Days* (Jesuits/NALR)
- *Amazing Grace* (Traditional)
- *Ashes* (Conry/NALR)
- *Faith of Our Fathers* (Traditional)
- *Fight the Good Fight* (ICEL)
- *Here I Am Lord* (Jesuits/NALR)
- *Here Is My Life* (Wise/GIA)
- *I Heard the Voice of Jesus Say* (ICEL)
- *I Lift Up My Soul* (Jesuits/NALR)
- *Kyrie Eleison* (Clark/Celebration services)
- *Let Your Face Shine Upon Us* (Haugen/GIA)
- *Like a Sunflower* (Landry/NALR)
- *Magnificat*
- *May We Praise You* (Jesuits/NALR)
- *One Bread, One Body* (Jesuits/NALR)
- *Only This I Want* (Jesuits/NALR)
- *Renewal Song* (Andersen/Resource)
- *Shalom* (Reagan/NALR)
- *Sing Out His Goodness* (Dameans/NALR)
- *Standing In Need of Prayer* (ICEL)
- *You Are My Friends* (Reagan/NALR)

SUNDAY PLANNING SHEET   Date _____

Parish focus _____

Environment & art _____

Ritual notes _____

Faith development (eg., in newsletter/classes) _____

Children's faith experience _____

Prelude _____

Hymn of gathering _____

Sprinkling/Penitential rite _____

Hymn of praise _____

Opening Prayer _____

First reading _____Responsory _____

Second reading _____Gospel acclamation _____

Gospel _____Profession of faith _____

General intercessions _____

At the preparation & presentation _____

Preface dialog _____Preface _____

Preface acclamation _____

Eucharistic prayer _____Memorial acclamation _____

Eucharistic amen _____

The Lord's prayer _____

Breaking of bread _____

The communion hymn _____

The post-communion hymn _____

Blessing _____At the dismissal _____

Memoranda:

THIRTY-FIRST SUNDAY OF THE YEAR

YEAR C

READINGS
Wisdom (11:22-12:2)
The enormous power of God caused continual wonder in the Hebrew community. Even for Egypt the possibility for repentance still existed after the final plague. Israel is rescued from slavery by God's continuing care.
2 Thessalonians (1:11-2:2)
In an early Pauline letter we witness Paul's surprise and pleasure over the strength of the faith in this community. His words are meant to reassure them in the midst of confusion over a false report about the second coming of Christ.
Luke (19:1-10)
Zacchaeus has been celebrated in song, film and story. He is the example for Luke of the rejection by the Jews of the message of Christ and its subsequent acceptance by the Gentiles. Again Zacchaeus reminds us that all peoples are called to a covenant with God.

FOCUS
Internal to all of us is the hope of being special; of being selected from the anonymous crowds. The experiences of riches, exceptional talent, and status are rare among us. One only need look at fantasies of TV to see the quest of so many for uniqueness and honor.

Zacchaeus is everyone's favorite underdog. Selected from the fringe of Hebrew life and the fringe of the crowd, he is relocated briefly in the center of the world. Like Israel, plucked from the domination of Egypt, the story of Zacchaeus and every Hebrew is a story of being specially selected for God's attention.

Who are the quiet, behind-the-scenes people of your parish who could be highlighted this week? How do we communicate specialness and acceptance to each other in these days? How is our community special in the larger global context?

IDEA STARTERS
- *CCT Lectionary:* Hq 2:1-9; Ps 65:1-8; 2 Th 1:5-12; Lk 19:1-10.
- Avoid jokes about "stature."
- Jesus' eating with sinners is a common occurrence in Luke's gospel. "Happy are *we* who are called to this supper."
- When in your life must you climb away from earthly barriers so that you, too, may see the Lord?
- When our attitude is less than loving, recall the words of the Wisdom lesson, especially verse 24.
- A series of excerpts from 2 Thessalonians begins at today's Eucharist. Give biblical background in the bulletin. Also, note the eschatological emphasis of the readings during these last weeks of the Church Year.
- At this holy meal Jesus offers "the cup of my blood ... shed for you ... that your sins may be forgiven." In sharing the Bread and Cup let us remember that "God, the Father of mercies, through the death and resurrection of his Son, has reconciled the world to himself."

- For your consideration: Sprinkling Baptismal Water A, Alternative Opening Prayer; intercessions for stewardship of God's creation, Lutheran Unity, the Lutheran-Roman Catholic dialogue, perseverence in faith, safety for halloween ghosts and goblins; Reconciliation Eucharistic Prayer I; Memorial Acclamation C; Ordinary Solemn Blessing II.

MUSIC

- Psalm 145
- *City of God* (Jesuits/NALR)
- *Come to Me* (Hummer/Resource)
- *Dwelling Place* (Jesuits/NALR)
- *Father We Sing Your Praises* (Zsigray/NALR)
- *Gather Us In* (Haugen/GIA)
- *Glorious Praise* (Keyes/Resource)
- *God and Man at Table* (Stamps/Dawn Treader Music)
- *Hear Us, Almighty Lord* (ICEL)
- *Hymn of Initiation* (Westendorf/NALR)
- *Lord of Glory* (Jesuits/NALR)
- *Mountains and Hills* (Jesuits/NALR)
- *O Living Bread From Heaven* (ICEL)
- *One Lord* (Haas/Cooperative Ministries)
- *Our Blessing Cup* (Joncas/NALR)
- *Praise the Lord, My Soul* (Jesuits/NALR)
- *The Sun is Rising* (Weston Priory)
- *Though the Mountains May Fall* (Jesuits/NALR)
- *We Praise You* (Dameans/NALR)
- *We Remember* (Haugen/GIA)

SUNDAY PLANNING SHEET   Date _____

Parish focus _____

Environment & art _____

Ritual notes _____

Faith development (eg., in newsletter/classes) _____

Children's faith experience _____

Prelude _____

Hymn of gathering _____

Sprinkling/Penitential rite _____

Hymn of praise _____

Opening Prayer _____

First reading _____Responsory _____

Second reading _____Gospel acclamation _____

Gospel _____Profession of faith _____

General intercessions _____

At the preparation & presentation _____

Preface dialog _____Preface _____

Preface acclamation _____

Eucharistic prayer _____Memorial acclamation _____

Eucharistic amen _____

The Lord's prayer _____

Breaking of bread _____

The communion hymn _____

The post-communion hymn _____

Blessing _____At the dismissal _____

Memoranda:

THIRTY-SECOND   YEAR C
SUNDAY OF THE YEAR

READINGS
2 Maccabees (7:1-2,9-14)
Life after death and the theme of resurrection thread through this reading.
The martyrdoms point to loyalty to religious ideals.
Second Thessalonians (2:16-3:5)
Having reassured the community, Paul ends this letter with encouragement
for a faithful life. He is grateful for their model to the world and wishes them
the success achieved by constancy in Christian values.
Luke (20:27-38)
Following the long series of Gospels during their journey to Jerusalem, the
setting finally changes here. This is set within the daily teaching in the temple.
The testing with questions, like this one on the resurrection, comes from the
traditional religious leaders. Their ability to carry even the smallest point to
the absurd is undercut by Jesus.

FOCUS
Personal meaningful contribution to the larger reality of history haunts
everyone. We offer our children, our work, and our creative efforts as lasting
memory of our existence. We seek purpose in our daily living by our symbols
of eternity.

Concern for the end of time, Christ's return, and the afterlife fills these readings.
Mixed here is Paul's sense of the imminent return of Christ and Christ's tone
of continued existence due to God's care. Constant readiness mixes with
graceful acceptance.

A contemporary definition of salvation may be useful for today's liturgy. How
do we think about death given our relationship with modern medicine? What
is constant readiness for our Christian lifestyle?

IDEA STARTERS
- *CCT Lectionary:* Zech 7:1-10; Ps 9:11-20; 2 Th 2:13, 3:5j; Lk 20:27-38.
- The month of November has traditionally been a time to commemorate
  the lives of the faithful departed. Today's texts are in line with this venerable
  custom.
- Today's homily provides a time for reflection for meditation about death:
  of our loved ones and ourselves.
- Use excerpts from literature about the Christian understanding of death,
  for example: "O death, where is thy victory"; "Death be not proud";
  "Canticle of Brother Sun." You may also wish to include prayers from
  "Pastoral Care of the Sick and Dying" (USCC, Washington, DC).
- The hope and clear consciences of the family in today's first reading may
  be developed in relation to martyrs (past and present) who suffer willingly
  for the sake of God's Word.
- A Christian interpretation of Death and Dying by Elizabeth Kubler-Ross
  may make a worthwhile Sunday forum for high schoolers and adults.
- A listing of organizations to help the bereaved may be included in the
  bulletin.

- A book of names which includes members of the parish who have been born into eternal life during the previous year may be enshrined at the baptismal font, with the paschal candle lighted during this special month.
- For your consideration: Sprinkling Baptismal Water A; Alternative Opening Prayer; Gospel (long form); intercessions for consolation of the bereaved, hope in the resurrection of the body and the life-everlasting, for the dying, the hopeless, those suffering persecution for righteousness' sake, married couples and families, Lutheran-RC dialogue; Ordinary Sundays Preface VI (P 34); Eucharistic Prayer III (w/commemoration for the departed adapted); Memorial Acclamation B; solemn Blessing used at Funerals.

MUSIC

- Psalm 17
- *Canticle of Simeon*
- *Eye Has Not Seen* (Haugen/GIA)
- *For You Are My God* (Jesuits/NALR)
- *I Know That My Redeemer Lives* (ICEL)
- *In God Alone* (Andersen/Resource)
- *In Your Hands, O Lord* (Goglia/Resource)
- *Jerusalem, My Happy Home* (ICEL)
- *Journeys Ended, Journeys Begun* (Weston Priory)
- *Let Us Walk in the Light of the Lord* (Haugen/Quiet Breeze)
- *Lord, To Whom Shall We Go* (Joncas/NALR)
- *My Refuge* (Vessels/GIA)
- *Praised Be the Father* (Dameans/NALR)
- *Sing A New Song* (Jesuits/NALR)
- *This Alone* (Jesuits/NALR)
- *You Will Draw Water* (Conry/NALR)

SUNDAY PLANNING SHEET

Date _____

Parish focus _____

Environment & art _____

Ritual notes _____

Faith development (eg., in newsletter/classes) _____

Children's faith experience _____

Prelude _____

Hymn of gathering _____

Sprinkling/Penitential rite _____

Hymn of praise _____

Opening Prayer _____

First reading _____ Responsory _____

Second reading _____ Gospel acclamation _____

Gospel _____ Profession of faith _____

General intercessions _____

At the preparation & presentation _____

Preface dialog _____ Preface _____

Preface acclamation _____

Eucharistic prayer _____ Memorial acclamation ___

Eucharistic amen _____

The Lord's prayer _____

Breaking of bread _____

The communion hymn _____

The post-communion hymn _____

Blessing _____ At the dismissal _____

Memoranda:

THIRTY-THIRD SUNDAY OF THE YEAR

YEAR C

READINGS

Malachi (3:19-20)

Malachi speaks from a strong grasp of the covenant and its requirements on the community. He seeks faithfulness to its promise. These dialogues on the key questions of his time present a unique writing style and were addressed primarily to the priestly groups.

2 Thessalonians (3:7-12)

This community suffered from a confusion over a false report on the return of Christ. Many were living off others, having ceased to work themselves. Paul repeats his message of persistence to the work of the faith.

Luke (21:5-19)

This passage has companion ones in all the Gospels. It deals with the end of time and the second coming of Christ. Here the message of constant fidelity to Christian lifestyles comes through even clearer than usual. People prepared in everyday events will be amply able to meet the trials of the end line.

FOCUS

Famines, wars, and natural disasters move across our communities with surprising regularity. Whether these represent evil and whether these are permitted by God are questions for each generation. It is another way of dealing with God's concern for our fragile lives.

The scripture on the end of time points to these natural disasters as signs of Christ's return. The biblical writers would have these events remind us of the elusiveness of life. Trueness to the covenant and to the values of Christ require constant attention.

What are contemporary symbols of our fragility? Of the fragility of the earth? How do we engender care for our community and for the whole neighborhood? How do our present lifestyle choices bring about awareness of Christ alive?

IDEA STARTERS

- *CCT Lectionary:* Mal 4:1-6 (3:19-24 in huls); Ps 82; 2 Th 3:6-13; Lk 21:5-19.
- The readings today point toward a wonderfully majestic "day" when Christ, the Sun of Justice, will return. The use of incense preceding the processional cross and lights may effectively point toward this solemnity.
- In place of the Introductory Rites of the Eucharist, you may wish to use the solemn chant of "The Great Litany" (found in *Lutheran Book of Worship*, Fortress Press, Philadelphia, PA). Have the leading ministers (acolytes, choir, readers, clergy, etc.) slowly process through the assembly while singing the litany. Continue with the Opening Prayer of the Mass.
- "Christ will come again." What does the church believe about this?
- The Thessalonians reading speaks about work. A bulletin article may clarify Paul's call to work in light of his other call to charity.
- For your consideration: Opening Prayer; intercessions for instrumentalists,

laborers, peace, victims of natural disasters, and those unjustly persecuted; Reconciliation Eucharistic Prayer II; Memorial Acclamation B; Ordinary Solemn Blessing V.

MUSIC

- Psalm 98
- *All Flesh Is Grass* (Haugen/GIA)
- *All the Rest of My Life* (Goglia/Resource)
- *All That We Have* (Dameans/NALR)
- *All the Ends of the Earth* (Foster/Resource)
- *And the Father Will Dance* (Landry/NALR)
- *Be Glad, Be Happy* (Gilsdorf/Resource)
- *Behold the Mountain of the Lord* (ICEL)
- *Be Not Afraid* (Jesuits/NALR)
- *Blest Be the Lord* (Jesuits/NALR)
- *Come, You Thankful People, Come* (ICEL)
- *The Cry of the Poor* (Jesuits/NALR)
- *Eye Has Not Seen* (Haugen/GIA)
- *Go Now In Peace* (Wise/GIA)
- *How Can I Keep From Singing?* (Traditional)
- *I Believe in the Sun* (Landry/NALR)
- *I Danced In the Morning* (Carter/Galliard, Ltd.)
- *In the Day of the Lord* (Gutfreund/NALR)
- *In Your Love Remember Me* (Kendzia/NALR)
- *Journeys Ended, Journeys Begun* (Weston Priory)
- *Justice Shall Flourish* (Schoenbachler/Cooperative Ministries)
- *Let Heaven Rejoice* (Jesuits/NALR)
- *Love Divine, All Loves Excelling* (ICEL)
- *Magnificat*
- *My Refuge* (Vessels/GIA)
- *Patience, People* (Jesuits/NALR)
- *Redeemer Lord* (Jesuits/NALR)
- *Remember Your Love* (Dameans/NALR)
- *Save Us, O Lord* (Jesuits/NALR)
- *The Sun is Rising* (Weston Priory)
- *ubi Caritas* (Taize/GIA)
- *Watchman, How Goes the Night?* (Deiss/NALR)
- *Witnesses* (Weston Priory)
- *Yahweh* (Weston Priory)

SUNDAY PLANNING SHEET   Date _____

Parish focus _____
Environment & art _____
Ritual notes _____
Faith development (eg., in newsletter/classes) _____
Children's faith experience _____
Prelude _____
Hymn of gathering _____
Sprinkling/Penitential rite _____
Hymn of praise _____
Opening Prayer _____
First reading _____Responsory _____
Second reading _____Gospel acclamation _____
Gospel _____Profession of faith _____
General intercessions _____
At the preparation & presentation _____
Preface dialog _____Preface _____
Preface acclamation _____
Eucharistic prayer _____Memorial acclamation ___
Eucharistic amen _____
The Lord's prayer _____
Breaking of bread _____
The communion hymn _____
The post-communion hymn _____
Blessing _____At the dismissal _____
Memoranda:

CYCLE C

SOLEMNITY OF
CHRIST THE KING

YEAR C

(Thirty-fourth Or Last Sunday Of The Year)

READINGS
2 Samuel (5:1-3)
David is the symbol of all future hopes for the Hebrew people. He embodies the rule of a just kingdom. This is the account of taking power over the Northern tribes having already ruled the Southern tribes for some time. The year reign of David in Jerusalem begins in part here.
Colossians (1:11-20)
The community at Colossae was troubled by the teaching of false doctrines. This Pauline letter reaffirms Christ's message and his place as key revelation of the diety.
Luke (23:35-43)
Luke's message of repentance and faith is told here from the viewpoint of one person, the good thief. We usually see this message in the context of the larger community. Each person is ultimately challenged by the presence of Christ and must respond apart from position in the community

FOCUS
Our behavior constantly models for others our inner values. In the workplace, classroom, and at home our values affect every other person we meet. Young people are especially keen in understanding the connections between our inner life and our external behaviors.

Such whole people, holy people, are strong models in biblical tradition. David is the virtuous and just leader; Paul the strong messenger of faith. And the good thief models repentance even at the end of his time.

How does the modern Christian reveal interior values in daily life? How does our parish reveal Christian leadership in the larger community? Who are symbols or stories of strength in your neighborhood?

IDEA STARTERS
- *CCT Lectionary:* 2 Sm 5:1-5; Col 1:11-20; Jn 12:9-19.
- Today is the last Sunday of the liturgical year. We gather to: remember kings and kingdoms referred to in Salvation History; realize that we must remove the veils which prevent us from seeing God's Kingdom in our midst; and look forward to the day the Lord will return in glory.
- Today's liturgy should be "stately." Gold vestments, incense, full use of processions with cross, lights, Bible, banners, and ministers will mark the dignity to which we are called as a priestly and kingly people worshiping the Lord.
- An ecumenical Vespers liturgy and pot-luck supper may suitably mark the end of the liturgical year.
- Thanksgiving services (interfaith, ecumenical and parish) should be well publicized in today's bulletin.
- For your consideration: Sprinkling Baptismal Water B; "Glory to God" sung; Opening Prayer; intercessions for rulers of nations, communities

(re)building houses of worship, unity among all peoples, the stewardship of creation, soldiers, those imprisoned, those awaiting capital punishment, hope for the future; Christ the King Preface (P 51); Eucharistic Prayer III; Memorial Acclamation D; "Lord's Prayer" sung; Ordinary Solemn Blessing II.

MUSIC

- Psalm 122
- *Alpha and Omega* (Repp/K&R)
- *Anthem* (Conry/NALR)
- *Beatitudes* (Page/Resource)
- *Canticle of the Sun* (Haugen/GIA)
- *City of God* (Jesuits/NALR)
- *Earthen Vessels* (Jesuits/NALR)
- *Glorious Praise* (Keyes/Resource)
- *Glory and Praise* (Jesuits/NALR)
- *The Head That Once Was Crowned* (ICEL)
- *He is the Lord* (Haas/Cooperative Ministries)
- *In Him We Live* (Landry/NALR)
- *In Praise of His Name* (Jesuits/NALR)
- *In Those Days* (Deiss/NALR)
- *Jesus Is Life* (Landry/NALR)
- *Jesus, Remember Me* (Taize/GIA)
- *Jesus Shall Reign* (ICEL)
- *Lift Up Your Heads Ye Mighty Gates* (ICEL)
- *Like a Shepherd* (Jesuits/NALR)
- *Only This I Want* (Jesuits/NALR)
- *Praise Canticle* (Haas/Cooperative Ministries)
- *Sing Alleluia Sing* (Dameans/NALR)
- *Sing to God a Brand New Canticle* (Quinlan/NALR)
- *A Song for the Masses* (Schoenbachler/NALR)
- *Son of David* (Jesuits/NALR)
- *We Remember* (Haugen/GIA)

SUNDAY PLANNING SHEET   Date _____

Parish focus _____

Environment & art _____

Ritual notes _____

Faith development (eg., in newsletter/classes) _____

Children's faith experience _____

Prelude _____

Hymn of gathering _____

Sprinkling/Penitential rite _____

Hymn of praise _____

Opening Prayer _____

First reading _____ Responsory _____

Second reading _____ Gospel acclamation ____

Gospel _____ Profession of faith _____

General intercessions _____

At the preparation & presentation _____

Preface dialog _____ Preface _____

Preface acclamation _____

Eucharistic prayer _____ Memorial acclamation ___

Eucharistic amen _____

The Lord's prayer _____

Breaking of bread _____

The communion hymn _____

The post-communion hymn _____

Blessing _____ At the dismissal _____

Memoranda:

All Years

FEAST OF THE PRESENTATION OF THE LORD
February 2, Years A, B, C

READINGS
Malachi (2:22–40)
The prophet addresses the problem of priestly corruption after the return from exile. With only dim possibilities for real leadership, the prophet expresses hope that the Lord himself will rule.

Hebrews (2:14–18)
Jesus is superior over the angels precisely because of his humanity. By God becoming human, the gap between human beings and God is bridged. Jesus is the high priest because he is mediator.

Luke (2:22–40)
The holy family is obedient to the law requiring a mother's purification after childbirth (Lv 12:2-8) and the ransom of the first born (Ex 13:11-13, 22:28-29).

FOCUS
Jesus is recognized as the messiah and revealed through the proclamation of Simeon and Anna. The words of Simeon's canticle, "a revealing light to the Gentiles," associated this feast with light very early in the church's history. Candles were carried in procession representing Christ as the light of the all people. From this, the tradition of blessing candles on this day developed, hence the name, "Candlemas."

IDEA STARTERS
- In homilies and with decoration, make the connection between this feast and Christmas/Epiphany. In some calendars, this marks the official end of the Christmas season.
- Don't be afraid of the "Groundhog's Day" connection. This secular feast has elements of light (emphasis on shadow) and life (harbinger of spring) and is a transitional holiday between Christmas and Easter.
- Candle processions and candle blessings are in order. Distribute and bless candles for communion ministers to take to shut-ins.
- A good day to discuss importance of tradition.
- Small groups might use a candle ritual: lighting a candle and saying a blessing for a person next to them.
- Run a bulletin article about candle care or uses of candles in prayer.
- Invite families with new babies to a special evening blessing.
- Prayer of the faithful: for contemporary prophets, elderly, new parents.
- Preface of the Presentation of the Lord, Memorial Acclamation 6

MUSIC
- Psalm 24
- *Come, O Long-Awaited Savior* (Wesley/PMB)
- *Exult You Just Ones* (Jesuits/NALR)
- *Every Valley* (Jesuits/NALR)
- *God So Loved the World* (Antioch/K&R)
- *The Lights of the City* (Traditional)
- *Say the Word Again* (Repp/K&R)
- *Wonderful and Great* (Deiss/PMB)

CYCLE A, B, C

PLANNING SHEET

Date _____

Parish focus _____

Environment & art _____

Ritual notes _____

Faith development (eg., in newsletter/classes) _____

Children's faith experience _____

Prelude _____

Hymn of gathering _____

Sprinkling/Penitential rite _____

Hymn of praise _____

Opening Prayer _____

First reading _____ Responsory _____

Second reading _____ Gospel acclamation _____

Gospel _____ Profession of faith _____

General intercessions _____

At the preparation & presentation _____

Preface dialog _____ Preface _____

Preface acclamation _____

Eucharistic prayer _____ Memorial acclamation _____

Eucharistic amen _____

The Lord's prayer _____

Breaking of bread _____

The communion hymn _____

The post-communion hymn _____

Blessing _____ At the dismissal _____

Memoranda:

CYCLE A, B, C

SOLEMNITY OF ST. JOSEPH, HUSBAND OF MARY
March 19, Years A, B, C

READINGS
2 Samuel (7:4-5, 12-14, 16)
Nathan promises that David's lineage would be secure. After the exile, this promise came to be seen as a messianic hope that extends beyond earthly kingship.
Romans (4:13, 16-18, 22)
The proper response to the covenant is not keeping the law but faith.
Matthew (1:16, 18-21, 24)
Joseph's dilemma when faced with Mary's pregnancy is open to many interpretations: 1) He wanted to put her away quietly out of consideration for her 2) He was devoted to the Law and did not want to live with an adulteress or 3) He was humble and hesitated to identify with an act of the Holy Spirit.

FOCUS
Both David and Joseph surrendered their plan for the future and trusted in God.

IDEA STARTERS
- Alternate Gospel: Luke 2:41-51. This is Lent, How can the "feastday" theme and the seasonal spirit work synergistically instead of in opposition?
- This is the day for a St. Joseph's Table. Incorporate various breads to be used at the Table into the Preparation of the Gifts. Some of these festive breads might be distributed for the poor.
- St. Joseph's flower is the lily. A simple use of this flower, considering the season, may be more appropriate than elaborate decoration.

MUSIC
- Psalm 89
- *Happy Is the Man* (Schutte/NALR)
- *Forever I Will Sing* (Ellis Lynch/Raven)
- *Yahweh, the Holy One* (Gilsdorf/Resource)
- *Joseph, Patron Saint of Wonders* (Mischke/WLP)
- *Joseph and Mary* (Ehret/CF Peters)
- *Sweet Mary, Gentle Joseph* (Thum/Resource)

PLANNING SHEET

Date _____

Parish focus _____

Environment & art _____

Ritual notes _____

Faith development (eg., in newsletter/classes) _____

Children's faith experience _____

Prelude _____

Hymn of gathering _____

Sprinkling/Penitential rite _____

Hymn of praise _____

Opening Prayer _____

First reading _____Responsory _____

Second reading _____Gospel acclamation _____

Gospel _____Profession of faith _____

General intercessions _____

At the preparation & presentation _____

Preface dialog _____Preface _____

Preface acclamation _____

Eucharistic prayer _____Memorial acclamation _____

Eucharistic amen _____

The Lord's prayer _____

Breaking of bread _____

The communion hymn _____

The post-communion hymn _____

Blessing _____At the dismissal _____

Memoranda:

SOLEMNITY OF THE ANNUNCIATION OF THE LORD
March 25, Years A, B, C

READINGS
Isaiah (7:10-14)
King Ahaz, a descendant of David, capped his infidelity to the Lord with a refusal to ask for a sign for God. Isaiah refers to Immanuel (God-with-us) who is probably Ahaz' son, Hezekiah, who sought to return the nation to the ways of the Lord. Messianic hopes were built by remembering these good kings.
Hebrews (10:4-10)
Sacrifice is an attitude of heart, not merely giving up a material thing. The one complete sacrifice is obedience, of which Jesus Christ is the perfect model.
Luke (1:26-38)
The angel uses messianic titles ("He will have great dignity" and will be "the son of the most high God") from Jewish traditions to announce the forthcoming son and promises that he will bring unity to God's people by extending David's throne (Judah) to the house of Jacob (Israel).

FOCUS
How will this new messiah and "good king" bring people to the ways of the Lord and unify all peoples?

IDEA STARTERS
- Remember that this is a solemnity of the Lord, not of Mary.
- Prayers of the faithful: for oppressed peoples, victims of civil wars, fragmented families, divided churches, expectant families.
- In Lent, keep it simple.
- Good time for healing and reconciliation services.
- See Step 2 of Alcoholics Anonymous 12 steps (it stresses hope for restoration to sanity).
- Invite expectant couples to special evening liturgy or blessing within Sunday eucharist.

MUSIC
- Psalm 40
- *I Have Waited* (Gilsdorf/Resource)
- *Here I Am, O Lord* (Lynch/Raven)
- *Here I Am, O Lord* (Proulx/Gelineau/GIA)
- *Happy Are They* (Farney/Resource)
- *And Gabriel* (Schola/Resource)
- *Glory of Jerusalem* (Keyes/Resource)
- *Hail Mary* (Goglia/Resource)

PLANNING SHEET

Date _____

Parish focus _____

Environment & art _____

Ritual notes _____

Faith development (eg., in newsletter/classes) _____

Children's faith experience _____

Prelude _____

Hymn of gathering _____

Sprinkling/Penitential rite _____

Hymn of praise _____

Opening Prayer _____

First reading _____Responsory _____

Second reading _____Gospel acclamation _____

Gospel _____Profession of faith _____

General intercessions _____

At the preparation & presentation _____

Preface dialog _____Preface _____

Preface acclamation _____

Eucharistic prayer _____Memorial acclamation _____

Eucharistic amen _____

The Lord's prayer _____

Breaking of bread _____

The communion hymn _____

The post-communion hymn _____

Blessing _____At the dismissal _____

Memoranda:

SOLEMNITY OF THE BIRTH OF JOHN THE BAPTIST
June 24, Years A, B, C

READINGS
Isaiah (49:1-6)
The Servant Song speaks of the effectiveness of God's word to accomplish his will.
Acts (13:22-26)
This excerpt from Paul's missionary sermon looks to John's role as a messenger who calls attention to the fullness of the message and then diminishes himself before it.
Luke (1:57-66)
The story of John's birth evokes similar stories about Isaac, Samson, and Samuel. He may have been a relative, but the story is obviously symbolic, meant to show God's deeper works of salvation.

FOCUS
Preparing the way of the Lord calls for a combination of boldness and humility.

IDEA STARTERS
- *Alternate readings from vigil:* Jer 1:4-10, 1 Pet 1:8-12, Lk 1:5-17.
- How does the natural season (summer solstice) with its symbols of blood and fire fit into the liturgical season and this particular feast?
- Prayer of the faithful: for servants, ministers, the pope (servant of the servants of God), evangelists, lectors, politicians, domestics.
- Be sure to sing the Canticles of Zechariah during the liturgy.
- Take Luke 1:76 personally.

MUSIC
- Psalms 71 and 139
- *John the Baptist* (Gilsdorf/Resource)
- *The Lord, He Comes* (Keyes/Resource)
- *Lord, Come Quickly* (Keyes/Resource)
- *With Words of Praise* (Deiss/WLP)
- *Draw Me to You* (Marchionda/WLP)
- *Stilled and Quiet Is My Soul* (Toolan/GIA)
- *The Lord Is My Light* (Hallock/GIA)

PLANNING SHEET

Date _____

Parish focus _____

Environment & art _____

Ritual notes _____

Faith development (eg., in newsletter/classes) _____

Children's faith experience _____

Prelude _____

Hymn of gathering _____

Sprinkling/Penitential rite _____

Hymn of praise _____

Opening Prayer _____

First reading _____ Responsory _____

Second reading _____ Gospel acclamation _____

Gospel _____ Profession of faith _____

General intercessions _____

At the preparation & presentation _____

Preface dialog _____ Preface _____

Preface acclamation _____

Eucharistic prayer _____ Memorial acclamation _____

Eucharistic amen _____

The Lord's prayer _____

Breaking of bread _____

The communion hymn _____

The post-communion hymn _____

Blessing _____ At the dismissal _____

Memoranda:

SOLEMNITY OF STS. PETER AND PAUL
June 29, Years A, B, C

READINGS
Acts (12:1-11)
The liberation of Peter echoes many events from Jewish history: the deliverance of Joseph, the three young men, Passover. His person becomes a sign of God's deliverance of his people.
2 Timothy (4:6-8, 17-18)
Paul writes from prison at the end of his life and proclaims death the greatest deliverance of all.
Matthew 16:13-19
Peter proclaims Jesus the messiah, the son of the living God, and receives the "keys to the kingdom."

FOCUS
Avoid locking into the Gospel as a proof text for the primacy of the Pope. Instead, focus on the power of the church, each of us as members, to welcome or close the doors to anyone we encounter. The church as the body of Christ becomes the instrument of deliverance for individuals.

IDEA STARTERS
- *Alternate readings from the vigil:* Acts 3:1-10, Gal 1:11-20, Jn 21:15-19.
- Prayers of the faithful: for the pope, for evangelists, for communications workers, for bishops, for lawyers, for the fishing industry, for Jewish-Christian dialogue.
- Symbols: Rock, key, chain.
- Bulletin article: "Theology of Parish Church"
- Kickoff summer outreach efforts: Send invitation letters to non-parishioners; organize a "bring-a-guest" picnic; welcome summer visitors especially; move after-mass refreshments outside, weather permitting.

MUSIC
- Psalm 34 or 19
- *Peter, Do You Love Me?* (Randall/Resource)
- *Lord, To Whom Shall We Go?* (Joncas/NALR)
- *The Ballad of Paul* (Gilsdorf/Resource)
- *Jesus the Lord* (Keyes/Resource)
- *New Life* (Landry/NALR)
- *In Honor of the Holy Cross* (Dicie/Resource)
- *I Will Bless the Lord* (Hytrek/WLP)
- *Taste and See* (Haugen/PAA)
- *The Cry of the Poor* (Foley/NALR)
- *The Law of the Lord* (Gelineau/GIA)

PLANNING SHEET

Date _____

Parish focus _____

Environment & art _____

Ritual notes _____

Faith development (eg., in newsletter/classes) _____

Children's faith experience _____

Prelude _____

Hymn of gathering _____

Sprinkling/Penitential rite _____

Hymn of praise _____

Opening Prayer _____

First reading _____ Responsory _____

Second reading _____ Gospel acclamation _____

Gospel _____ Profession of faith _____

General intercessions _____

At the preparation & presentation _____

Preface dialog _____ Preface _____

Preface acclamation _____

Eucharistic prayer _____ Memorial acclamation _____

Eucharistic amen _____

The Lord's prayer _____

Breaking of bread _____

The communion hymn _____

The post-communion hymn _____

Blessing _____ At the dismissal _____

Memoranda:

FEAST OF THE TRANSFIGURATION
August 6, Years A, B, C

READINGS
Daniel (7:9-10, 13-14)
Daniel dreams apocalyptically of a "son of man" (human being) appearing and reestablishing the kingdom.
2 Peter (1:16-19)
The author appeals to the apostolic witness of the tranfiguration to show that Jesus already possessed the glory to be revealed in his second coming.
A. Matthew (17:1-9)B. Mark (9:2-10)C. Luke (9:28-36)
The gospel readings for this feast is the same as that of the Second Sunday of Lent in the same year. Refer to that commentary.

FOCUS
Today is the anniversary of the first atomic bomb used by one nation against another (U.S. against Japan on Hiroshima, 1945). How does this event connect with the apocolyptic imagery of the first and third readings — and with the whole gospel message?

IDEA STARTERS
- *Prayers of the faithful:* For victims of nuclear explosions, for victims of radiation, for scientists, for world leaders.
- Use white or bright vestments and paraments in a celebration commemorating Hiroshima in light of transfiguration.
- Contact other churches for possible ecumenical celebration around transfiguration and peace themes.
- Sponsor a retreat day in the country.

MUSIC
- Psalm 97
- *Come, Let Us Worship* (Alstott/OCP)
- *The Lord Is King* (Keyes/Resource)
- *Rejoice, the Lord Is King* (Schoenbachler/NALR)
- *A Light Will Shine* (Kreutz/WLP)
- *Praise the Lord* (Dougherty/Resource)

PLANNING SHEET

Date _____

Parish focus _____

Environment & art _____

Ritual notes _____

Faith development (eg., in newsletter/classes) _____

Children's faith experience _____

Prelude _____

Hymn of gathering _____

Sprinkling/Penitential rite _____

Hymn of praise _____

Opening Prayer _____

First reading _____ Responsory _____

Second reading _____ Gospel acclamation _____

Gospel _____ Profession of faith _____

General intercessions _____

At the preparation & presentation _____

Preface dialog _____ Preface _____

Preface acclamation _____

Eucharistic prayer _____ Memorial acclamation _____

Eucharistic amen _____

The Lord's prayer _____

Breaking of bread _____

The communion hymn _____

The post-communion hymn _____

Blessing _____ At the dismissal _____

Memoranda:

SOLEMNITY OF THE ASSUMPTION
August 15, Years A, B, C

READINGS
Revelation (11:19, 12:1-6, 10)
The woman of this reading refers to the people of Israel from whom Christ came and to the new people of God suffering persecution.
1 Corinthians (15:20-26)
Paul speaks of Jesus Christ as the first born of the dead to new life.
Luke (1:39-56)
Mary visits her cousin Elizabeth in the hill country of Jerusalem — a passage which echoes the entry of the ark into Jerusalem (see first reading for vigil of this feast — 1 Ch 15-3-4, 15, 16, 16:1-2). Even the infant's leaping in the womb recalls the singers and dancers before the ark. Mary's hymn is a victory song in which she speaks for all who can claim a share in God's saving power — the poor and the weak, the powerless, and the oppressed.

FOCUS
The readings emphasizes the cosmic dimensions of Mary's role in God's plan of salvation. Explore this feast as a link between body and soul, heaven and earth, royalty and poverty, Israel and the church, men and women, God and humanity.

IDEA STARTERS
- Consider this the first feast of the harvest with Mary the first human being "harvested" to the kingdom. Consider moving the celebration outdoors.
- For preparation of gifts, bring harvest fruits and vegetables forward. Use them afterwards in a parish picnic.
- Celebrate the redemption of our bodies — in dance, in word, in visual art.
- Celebrate ecumenically. For Lutherans, Episcopalians and others, this is *the* Marian feast.

MUSIC
- Psalm 132
- *Praises* (Keyes/Resource)
- *Glory of Jerusalem* (Keyes/Resource)
- *The Cry of the Poor* (Foley/NALR)
- *O Lord, Remember David* (Gelineau/GIA)
- *Pour Out Thy Spirit* (Montgomery/Concordia)
- *Blessed Is She* (Mullins/Resource)
- *My Soul Is Joyful* (Andersen/Resource)

PLANNING SHEET

Date _____

Parish focus _____

Environment & art _____

Ritual notes _____

Faith development (eg., in newsletter/classes) _____

Children's faith experience _____

Prelude _____

Hymn of gathering _____

Sprinkling/Penitential rite _____

Hymn of praise _____

Opening Prayer _____

First reading _____ Responsory _____

Second reading _____ Gospel acclamation _____

Gospel _____ Profession of faith _____

General intercessions _____

At the preparation & presentation _____

Preface dialog _____ Preface _____

Preface acclamation _____

Eucharistic prayer _____ Memorial acclamation _____

Eucharistic amen _____

The Lord's prayer _____

Breaking of bread _____

The communion hymn _____

The post-communion hymn _____

Blessing _____ At the dismissal _____

Memoranda:

FEAST OF THE TRIUMPH OF THE CROSS
September 14, Years A, B, C

READINGS
Numbers (21:4-9)
Faith and repentance on the part of the people is the important thing in this story — along with their willingness to confront what held the most terror for them.
Philippians (2:6-11)
The humility of God the Son and the glorification of the Son of Man are inseparable and balanced elements in the meaning of Jesus.
John 3:13-17
This passage looks backward to fiery serpent mentioned in the first reading and forward to the crucifixion. In the crucifixion, the Son of Man is "lifted up" to be recognized as the suffering servant of Isaiah.

FOCUS
The cross — and the fiery serpent — are mysterious symbols where death becomes life and the humble become exalted.

IDEA STARTERS
- Decorate the processional cross with bells and streamers.
- Exalt the cross, literally, lifting it up for all processions: entrance, presentation of gifts, dismissal.
- For children's liturgy: Use everyday symbols — stop light, etc. — asking children what it says. Finally, present a cross and ask them what it says.
- The symbol in the first reading has become the cadaceus, symbol of the medical profession. Bulletin Article: "Nurses and Doctors as Ministers." Include medical professionals in Prayer of the Faithful. Use Red Cross or cadaceus as visual symbols.

MUSIC
- Psalm 78:1-2
- *All Hail the Power of Jesus' Name* (Perronet/PMB)
- *Behold the Wood* (Jesuits/NALR)
- *Christ Is Alive* (Wren/PMB)
- *On Eagle's Wings* (Joncas/NALR)

PLANNING SHEET

Date _____

Parish focus _____

Environment & art _____

Ritual notes _____

Faith development (eg., in newsletter/classes) _____

Children's faith experience _____

Prelude _____

Hymn of gathering _____

Sprinkling/Penitential rite _____

Hymn of praise _____

Opening Prayer _____

First reading _____ Responsory _____

Second reading _____ Gospel acclamation _____

Gospel _____ Profession of faith _____

General intercessions _____

At the preparation & presentation _____

Preface dialog _____ Preface _____

Preface acclamation _____

Eucharistic prayer _____ Memorial acclamation ____

Eucharistic amen _____

The Lord's prayer _____

Breaking of bread _____

The communion hymn _____

The post-communion hymn _____

Blessing _____ At the dismissal _____

Memoranda:

SOLEMNITY OF ALL SAINTS
November 1, Years A, B, C

READINGS
Revelation (7:2-4, 9-14)
Christians are heirs in faith to God's promise to Israel. The 144,000 is a symbolic number — a large but not faceless multitude. The mark on the forehead refers to God's protection — and the seal of Baptism and Confirmation. The refers to the persecutions of Nero — and the trials all Christians must face.

1 John (3:1-3)
Being one with God is incompatible with sin and hatred, but this relationship is in a state of growth.

Matthew (5:1-12)
The kingdom belongs to the poor, the weak, the compassionate, and the peace-makers. But do not mistake these characteristics for passivity and timidity.

FOCUS
All Saints recognizes the diversity in the lives of those who grasped the kingdom through fidelity to the Spirit of the beatitudes.

IDEA STARTERS
- Children's liturgy: Have them dress up as favorite saints and talk about who they are.
- Use litany of saints in place of introductory prayers.
- Process to statues and icons in the church, lighting a votive candle before each one.

MUSIC
- Psalm 24
- *Be Glad, Be Happy* (Gilsdorf/Resource)
- *I Have Loved You* (Joncas/NALR)
- *Open Wide the Gates* (Gilligan/ACP)
- *The Whole Earth Is the Lord's* (Held/Augsburg)
- *Yahweh, Who Can Enter?* (Gilsdorf/Resource)
- *Prepare the Royal Highway* (Franzen/Augsburg
- *Heavens Pour Down Your Waters* (DeVinck/Norbet/Weston)

PLANNING SHEET

Date _____

Parish focus _____

Environment & art _____

Ritual notes _____

Faith development (eg., in newsletter/classes) _____

Children's faith experience _____

Prelude _____

Hymn of gathering _____

Sprinkling/Penitential rite _____

Hymn of praise _____

Opening Prayer _____

First reading _____Responsory _____

Second reading _____Gospel acclamation _____

Gospel _____Profession of faith _____

General intercessions _____

At the preparation & presentation _____

Preface dialog _____Preface _____

Preface acclamation _____

Eucharistic prayer _____Memorial acclamation _____

Eucharistic amen _____

The Lord's prayer _____

Breaking of bread _____

The communion hymn _____

The post-communion hymn _____

Blessing _____At the dismissal _____

Memoranda:

ALL SOULS DAY
November 2, Years A, B, C

READINGS
Isaiah (25:6-9); Lamentations (3:17-26); Job (19:1, 23-27); Wisdom (3:1-9); (4:7-14); Daniel (12:1-3); or 2 Maccabees (12:43:46)
Each reading shows some stage of the development of Jewish thought on the afterlife.
Acts (10:34-43), 1 Thessalonians (4:13-18); Philemon 3:20-21); 1 Corinthians (15:20-24, 25-28); (15:51-57); 2 Corinthians (5:1, 6-10); Romans (5:5-11); (5:17-21); (6:3-9); (8:14-23); (8:31-35, 37-39); (14:7-12); 2 Tim (2:8-13); 1 Jn (3:1-2); (3:14-16); Rev (14:13); (20:11-21:1); (21:1-7)
The eighteen readings show the development of Christian understanding of death and resurrection.
Mt (5:1-12); (11:25-30); (25:1-13); (12:35-40); (25:31-46); Mk (15:33-39); (16:1-6); Lk (7:11-17); (11:17-27); (23:33, 39-43); (23:44-49); (24:1-6); (24:13-35); Jn (6:37-40); (6:51-58); (11:17-27); (11:32-45); (12:23-28); (14:1-6); (17:24-26)
The available gospel readings variously concern Jesus' own death and resurrection, hints of the resurrection to come, and the qualities that lead to eternal life.

FOCUS
We are still one with all those who have gone before.

IDEA STARTERS
- When All Souls Day falls on Sunday, see if the Sunday reading will work.
- Note the proximity of this commemoration to All Saints.
  How are they similar? How do they differ?
- Especially if this feast falls on Sunday, connect it to the week's following feast of the Dedication of the Basilica at St. John Lateran. Both feasts focus on the gathering of the people — one over time and one over space.
- Symbols: paschal candle, funeral pall, Book of Life.
- Personal experience: Imagine your own death. What would your obituary say? What would your funeral be like? Possibly use a liturgical guide to plan your own funeral.
- Start a bereavement ministry on this day.
- Hold a special service for those who have lost a loved one in the past year.

MUSIC
- Psalm 17
- *Fear Not* (Raffa/Ekklesia)
- *Hymn of the Lord's Supper* (Ivancic/GIA)
- *I Know That My Redeemer Lives* (Hughes/PMB)
- *The Cry of the Poor* (Foley/NALR)

- *Hear, O Lord* (Callahan/ACP)
- *Be Happy, Be Glad* (Gilsdorf/Resource)
- *Come, Holy Spirit* (Culbreth/Resource)
- *Come to Me* (Hummer/Resource)
- *We Are Called* (Patterson/Resource)
- *We Are One* (Lawrence/Resource)

PLANNING SHEET

Date _____

Parish focus _____

Environment & art _____

Ritual notes _____

Faith development (eg., in newsletter/classes) _____

Children's faith experience _____

Prelude _____

Hymn of gathering _____

Sprinkling/Penitential rite _____

Hymn of praise _____

Opening Prayer _____

First reading _____ Responsory _____

Second reading _____ Gospel acclamation ____

Gospel _____ Profession of faith _____

General intercessions _____

At the preparation & presentation _____

Preface dialog _____ Preface _____

Preface acclamation _____

Eucharistic prayer _____ Memorial acclamation ___

Eucharistic amen _____

The Lord's prayer _____

Breaking of bread _____

The communion hymn _____

The post-communion hymn _____

Blessing _____ At the dismissal _____

Memoranda:

FEAST OF THE DEDICATION OF THE BASILICA OF ST. JOHN LATERAN
November 9, Years A, B, C

READINGS
Gn (28:11–18); 1 Chr (5:6–10, 13–6:2); Ez (43:1–2, 4–7); Mac (4:52–59); 1 Kgs (8:22–23, 27–30); Is (56:1, 6–7)
The six selections relate to God's dwelling with people.
1 Cor (3:9–13, 16–17); 1 Pet (2:4–9); Eph (2:19–22); Heb (12:18–19, 22–24)
These four passages affirm that God's people themselves, not any particular building, are God's favorite dwelling.
Jn (2:13–22); (4:19–24); Lk (19:1–10); Mt (5:23–24)
The four choices affirm the value of the temple, but that worship is not dependent on the temple or any particular place, that the church building is the home not of God but of the people, and that all who gather must be reconciled to each other before worship.

FOCUS
How is the church building symbolic of the church people?

IDEA STARTERS
- This is a day to celebrate your worship space as an expression of the community.
- Use this feast to celebrate any part of your building or renovation process.
- Review the architectural history of the building in the church bulletin.
- Prayer of the Faithful: for architects, liturgical consultants, artists, contractors, construction workers, janitors, altar guild members — any players in the design and construction and maintenance of your worship space.
- Appeal for participation in your art and environment committee.
- Conduct a tour of the church building.

MUSIC
- Psalm 84
- *All the Days of My Life* (Goglia/Resource)
- *Earthen Vessels* (Jesuits/NALR)
- *Gather Us In* (Haugen/GIA)
- *How Lovely* (Proulx/GIA)
- *How Lovely* (Toolan/GIA)
- *How Lovely Is Your Dwelling* (DeBruyn/OCP)
- *The Sparrow Finds a Home* (Foley/NALR)
- *Your Dwelling Place* (Farney/Resource)
- *Shout Joyfully to God* (Brubeck/St. Francis)

PLANNING SHEET

Date _____

Parish focus _____

Environment & art _____

Ritual notes _____

Faith development (eg., in newsletter/classes) _____

Children's faith experience _____

Prelude _____

Hymn of gathering _____

Sprinkling/Penitential rite _____

Hymn of praise _____

Opening Prayer _____

First reading _____ Responsory _____

Second reading _____ Gospel acclamation _____

Gospel _____ Profession of faith _____

General intercessions _____

At the preparation & presentation _____

Preface dialog _____ Preface _____

Preface acclamation _____

Eucharistic prayer _____ Memorial acclamation _____

Eucharistic amen _____

The Lord's prayer _____

Breaking of bread _____

The communion hymn _____

The post-communion hymn _____

Blessing _____ At the dismissal _____

Memoranda:

CYCLE A, B, C

SOLEMNITY OF THE IMMACULATE CONCEPTION
December 8, Years A, B, C

READINGS
Genesis (3:9-15, 20)
The three curses uttered by God — to the serpent, to the woman, to the man — speak more of the consequences of sin than of punishment for it. The refusal to face sin and seek reconciliation results in alienation from the rest of the created order — from nature, from fellow humans, from God. But we are left with hope.
Ephesians (1:3-6, 11-12)
God's will does not limit salvation to a single "chosen people."
Luke (1:26-38)
The angel's greeting echoes Zephaniah 3:14-16, in which the prophet is speaking to Jerusalem. Mary is to be the New Jerusalem, bearing the Lord within her. Mary, a Galilean, is the symbol of God's taking a new and hitherto rejected people.

FOCUS
God redeems the lowly, the rejected, the outcast — and chooses them for his very own.

IDEA STARTERS
- This is the national feastday of the United States? How is this fitting? How does it make you uncomfortable?
- Explore the image of the Statue of Liberty as an icon of Mary. How do the words at the base of the statue call to mind the spirit of the Gospel, especially the Magnificat?
- This feast celebrates the beginning of a new creation and fittingly comes at the beginning of the church year.

MUSIC
- Psalm 98
- *Hail Mary* (Goglia/Resource)
- *Song of Mary* (Aridas/Resource)
- *Messenger Song* (Gilsdorf/Resource)
- *All Creatures of Our God* (Francis of Assisi/Augsburg)
- *Mountains and Hills* (Schutte/NALR)
- *All the Ends of Earth* (Haas/Haugen/GIA)
- *Shout Out for Joy* (Peloquin/GIA)
- *Sing a New Song* (Schutte/NALR)
- *The Lord Has Revealed* (Della Picca/WLP)

PLANNING SHEET

Date _____

Parish focus _____

Environment & art _____

Ritual notes _____

Faith development (eg., in newsletter/classes) _____

Children's faith experience _____

Prelude _____

Hymn of gathering _____

Sprinkling/Penitential rite _____

Hymn of praise _____

Opening Prayer _____

First reading _____ Responsory _____

Second reading _____ Gospel acclamation _____

Gospel _____ Profession of faith _____

General intercessions _____

At the preparation & presentation _____

Preface dialog _____ Preface _____

Preface acclamation _____

Eucharistic prayer _____ Memorial acclamation _____

Eucharistic amen _____

The Lord's prayer _____

Breaking of bread _____

The communion hymn _____

The post-communion hymn _____

Blessing _____ At the dismissal _____

Memoranda:

MUSIC PUBLISHERS

Cooperative Ministries:
P.O. Box 4463
Washington, D.C. 20017

FEL: FEL Publications
1925 So. Pontius Ave.
Los Angeles, CA 90025

GIA: GIA Publications Inc.
7404 So. Mason Ave.
Chicago, IL 60638

ICEL: ICEL Publications
1234 Massachusetts Ave. NW
Washington, DC 20025

K&R: K&R Music, Inc.
P.O. Box 616
Trumansburg, NY 14886

NALR: No. American Liturgy Resources
2110 West Peoria Ave.
Phoenix, AZ 85029

PAA: Pastoral Arts Associates
Old Hickory, TN 37138

PMB: People's Mass Book from
World Library Publications, Inc.
3759 Willow Rd.
Schiller Park, IL 60176

Raven: Raven Music
4107 Woodland Park No.
Seattle, WA 98103

Resource: Resource Publications Inc.
160 E. Virginia St. #290
San Jose, CA 95112

Weston Priory: Weston Priory Productions
Weston, VT 05161

WLP: World Library Publications, Inc.
3759 Willow Rd.
Schiller Park, IL 60176

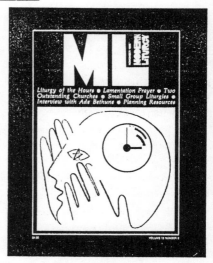